THE DIRECTOR'S CIRCLE BOOK FOR 2002

The Johns Hopkins University Press gratefully acknowledges members
of the 2002 Director's Circle for supporting the publication of works
such as *Venice Triumphant*.

Alfred and Muriel Berkeley · John J. Boland · Alberta and Jim Gamble
Charles and Elizabeth Hughes · Douglas R. Price · Anders Richter
R. Champlin and Debbie Sheridan · Angela von der Lippe
Robert L. Warren and Family

VENETIAE CONDITA
CIVITAS ANNO
ADMIRABILIS A·SALVTE
POST·EVERSAM HOMINIBVS
AB·ATTILA RESTITVTA
HVNNORREGE CCCCLIIII
AQVILEIAM

VENICE *Triumphant*

The Horizons of a Myth

Elisabeth Crouzet-Pavan

Translated by Lydia G. Cochrane

THE JOHNS HOPKINS UNIVERSITY PRESS

BALTIMORE AND LONDON

This translation was brought to publication with the generous
assistance of the French Ministry of Culture.

Originally published as *Venise triomphante: Les horizons d'un mythe,*
© 1999 Éditions Albin Michel S.A.

The Johns Hopkins University Press
2715 North Charles Street
Baltimore, Maryland 21218-4363
www.press.jhu.edu

Library of Congress Cataloging-in-Publication Data
Crouzet-Pavan, Elisabeth.
[Venise triomphante. English]
Venice triumphant : the horizons of a myth /
Elisabeth Crouzet-Pavan ; translated by Lydia G. Cochrane.
     p.   cm.
Includes bibliographical references and index.
ISBN 0-8018-6958-7
1. Venice (Italy)—History. I. Title.
DG676 .C8813 2002
945'.31—dc21   2001006617

A catalog record for this book is available from the British Library.

FRONTISPIECE: Ignazio Danti (1536–1586), *Panoramic View of
Venice.* (Scala / Art Resource, NY)

CONTENTS

MAPS

INTRODUCTION

Yet another book about Venice? The city seems to inspire an endless succession of works evoking its waters, stones, colors, and odors; time and death; the real and the fictive; art and life; the Renaissance and Carnival. So incessantly has Venice been written about, commented on, sensed, narrated, and imagined that such a flood of words perhaps invites silence.

That silence might seem all the more necessary, even urgent, in the light of an equally full historiographic tradition. Although the list of studies that Venice has inspired is long, it is somewhat unvaried since for a long time historians approached their subject with only a few questions in mind. First there was the history of the Republic itself and the astonishing longevity of a regime that for a time seemed to provide a model and elicit reflection. Next there was the question of trade, the Venetian commercial empire, and Venetian power in the Mediterranean, topics that have offered ample opportunity for analysis and investigation, especially in recent years, when economic history has been dominant. Many histories have made use of these themes to relate interconnected narratives: political histories moving from one war, or one doge, to the next; histories of a commercial expansion punctuated by brilliant successes up to the arrival of a decline that was as brutal as it was sudden.

More recently, however, new interests have recast Venetian history following scenarios other than movements of sacks of pepper or votes of one council or another. Other texts have been written, but, somewhat curiously, they have been confined to the narrow world, not even of specialists of Italy, but of the still more restricted circle, rendered increasingly exclusive as more and more works appeared, of the professionals of Venetian history, subscribers to *News on the Rialto,* who frequent the Archivio di Stato or the Biblioteca Marciana. A widening gap has grown up among histories of Venice between a history cast in the mold of a still active, still available vulgate and a new history marked by the perspectives and the acquisitions of studies that have, as the result of a highly positive heuristic necessity, shattered the historical object into increasingly scholarly and increasingly focused fragments.

The present book joins the mass of available titles regarding Venice. Although it attempts to give an account of recent historiographic advances, it also lays claim to a certain specificity: it is only an essay, a sketch. The choice was either to "tell everything" about Venice—and here the way has already been marked out by the multiple volumes of the monumental *Storia di Venezia*, with its tens of thousands of pages and its collective authorship—or else to select, cut out, pare down, and write a profoundly subjective history of Venice, one of many possible histories, one among all the histories that have already been written or will be written one day, which is the modest aim of the pages that follow. They are an attempt—an honest one, I hope—to discuss what has been published, discovered, and subjected to criticism in recent years and to give each writer his or her due. The historical narrative that follows makes no claim to being exhaustive: it includes deliberate lacunae, omissions, and silences, and it reflects my own interests, reading, research, and even opinions.

Like many of the goods produced in Venetian workshops in the fifteenth and sixteenth centuries, this book has required patient, conscientious craftsmanship, but it is also personal. Any historian of Venice will necessarily think that he or she would have written it differently. All that I have tried to do, and all that I hope to have done, given that I have not written exclusively for historians of Venice, is to produce a book that historians can view without excessive irritation.

My analysis of the various modes for approaching Venice's past follows several axes. Even when history focuses on a strikingly singular human environment, it is never totally self-contained; it becomes meaningful only from the perspective of other contemporary situations. I have attempted to use comparison to bring a breath of fresh air to the topic of Venice, which a certain historiographic tradition, still alive today, treats as uniquely, irreducibly different. Venice is not Florence, Milan, or Genoa, but its history gains by the use of comparison with the great political, economic, and social constructs represented by the cities of medieval and Renaissance Italy. Explanations of Venice are often to be found elsewhere.

On the other hand, I have deliberately broken with the traditional narration of events, which chops the Venetian adventure into chronological segments that often are justified only by stereotypes or arbitrary choice. Although I have chosen a thematic approach over one that divides history into predetermined phases, my choice does not exclude the essential elements of duration and the events that punctuate duration. This means that the history of Venice that I propose might at first seem fragmented, and its framework fragile. This was to some extent intentional: I have chosen to treat the slow-moving past of Venice in the Middle Ages and the Renaissance by deconstructing or destabilizing the usual linear logic, received ideas, and familiar facile judgments.

My problem has not been to replace a strict periodization with a compartmentalization, rigid or fluid, of the various elements of the creation of Venice. Rather, it has been to construct another principle of unity than that of passing time and the rhythm of events in either the short or the long term. It has been to start with an evaluation of dynamic and connected strands that operated for the most part spatially in order to seek a logical unity in the history of Venice. This requires a return to the point of origin of the process of irradiation underlying the development of the power of the Serenissima. My objective is to explain Venice on the basis of the places where it became Venice.

In order to do this, I have had to invert the order in which historiographic categories usually function. I have given primacy to space, or, more accurately, to the interplay among the dovetailing spaces that seem to have produced Venetian history. This does not, of course, mean that I have ignored time as determinant in the processes by which Venetians differentially invested in spaces close to hand, nearby, or far away. My point of departure was a simple realization that can be backed up by a study of semantic frequency: when we look carefully at the words the Venetians themselves used to inscribe or write the living history of their city, we see that time—their time—was marked out in terms of space and spatial implications. An awareness of history was primarily a grasp of a toponymy that evolved, expanded, or retracted, that disappeared and reappeared: Zara, Modon, Tana, Negroponte, Constantinople, Alexandria, Candia, but also Vicenza, Bergamo, Bruges, and Nuremberg, and of course Torcello, Chioggia, and Malamocco.

I also attempt to show that none of Venice's various spheres of action—the city, the lagoon, the Adriatic, the distant waters of the Mediterranean and even the Black Sea, the Terraferma, the house, the Rialto or Piazza San Marco—can claim to have developed autonomously or even parallel or in succession to the others. In Venice everything is connected; everything fits together following a principle of superimposed planes, and history can only be a matter of convergences. In these spaces that become temporal vectors the history of Venice is one history. That is why economic "factors," social "realities," "cultural" phenomena, and "political" expressions are not put into a hierarchy here but are always associated or intertwined, if not fused.

I do not postulate that Venice was propelled by one motive force more than another. Even the movement to gain power that is so characteristic of the Venetians' relation to space and, simultaneously, to the production of a representation of time proves that a narrowly causal interpretation would be overly reductive and would constitute a form of anachronism in the face of the complexity of the representational universe and the acts of Venetians of times past. In the final analysis, I have not opted for an "objective" approach to history. The history of Venice is one, and it can be decrypted within the realm of the symbolic.

The symbolic, precisely, is always present in this book. It appears, more or less explicitly, in the necessities and contingencies, the discourses and justifications, and the postures and speech of men in both acts of power and daily activities. The imaginary of the Venetians, continually recomposed and reactivated, bore within it the myth of a spatial realization and, by extension, of a duration that needed to be staged, dramatized, and visualized within the very space of Venetian life. Hence the notions of dovetailing and convergence that guide this book. Every space, from the most distant to the closest to hand, that was the target of the Venetian adventure refers back to the same symbolic experience. That experience had a center, but above all it was made of signs that became more or less perceptible as the city came into view. As we shall see, the city of Venice provides the code for reading Venetian history because the city was constructed, piece by piece, as a space that produced time and hence fabricated and envisioned the imaginary of a transcended duration.

It is hardly surprising that a book about the history of a city-state of multiple spaces, and about the organization of its image, should recall the famous map that graces the walls of the Galleria delle Carte Geografiche in the Vatican. Words, maps, and representations have long functioned to project an image and a meaning of Venice in which the city, a harmonious structure of stones, wood, and brick, an assemblage of filled and empty space, a daring and successful artifact, reigns over the lagoon. The various islands gravitate toward and fall into order around a center that is more symbolic than geographical, more imaginary than the reality that the map attempts to depict with the greatest realism. In the distance we can see a shore, a countryside with a few fields and trees marking the frontiers of a different world, one that Venice the Dominant gradually subjected. Opening up in the foreground is another broad space defined by the tenuous barrier of littoral islands that hold back the sea that nourishes both the lagoon and the city. That aquatic space quite naturally amplifies the first circle of Venetian waters. It permits the city to escape finitude, it brings life and depth; it seems to call out to the city, signifying its history.

This is how fifteenth-century travelers saw Venice, and it is a view reflected in maps and views of Venice as they continued to be reproduced throughout the modern age. As is often true of Venice, the real cannot be dissociated from its dramatic presentation. And as is also often true of Venice, that dramatic presentation made such an impression on its historian-spectators that they were incapable of criticism or reaction. In this figuration the city, a triumph of human industry, dominates the elements, ruling over an orderly, pacified nature. The suggestion is clear: the Venetian community had subjugated the waters of the lagoon just as it had built up its wealth and power and established its mastery in the maritime domain before turning to the conquest of the mainland.

In my search for the waters of Venice and for the relations the Venetians maintained with their milieu, I begin by examining this image: Venice is "seated in the sea," surrounded by a space that is presented as positive, something like a protective cocoon that bolsters it and guarantees it life. I first sketch the establishment and the building of the city. Then, in the name of an interest in "discourse" as much as an interest in "realities," I show how, within the fabric of Venetian awareness, a tangible relationship with the milieu existed, despite all that the apologetic literature might have us think. The image of Venice suggests, without explicitly saying so, that space had a history, that space *was* history.

Next, while remaining in the analytical mode, I consider how the waters of the lagoon opened out onto other spaces that were soon tamed and appropriated. The shelter of the lagoon made maritime adventure possible. If Venetians quite naturally turned their backs to the land, they received the sea as their portion, or at least they chose to believe that to be true as they set off on ventures that took them far from their native islands. When they were not navigating the waters of the lagoon or sailing the high seas, they traveled up the rivers that emptied into the lagoon basin, soon broadening the scope of their commerce. Chapter 2 traces the commercial expansion of Venice and then examines the causes and the bases of Venetian power.

In chapter 3 our gaze shifts to Italian horizons and to the land, which the Venetians long claimed to be unaware of. I intend to show that the frontier between the mainland and the world of the lagoons was less closed than traditional representations would have us believe. Here I insist on a point that carries us back in time and suggests a correction of what has conventionally been presented as a rupture. The history of the relations between Venice and the Continent cannot be limited to the flow of goods through the city: that history begins, often surreptitiously and informally, well before the conquest of the *stato di terra*, which transformed Venice into one of the principal land powers of Italy in the fifteenth and sixteenth centuries. Venetians did not choose to interest themselves in the mainland because maritime adventures had become more difficult: their experience of the spaces beyond the lagoon had already been inscribed in the long span of time.

Chapter 4 proceeds from the same sort of spatial logic to concentrate on how the various domains and spheres of Venetian activity combined. First, I examine how the merchandise that flowed into Venice from land and sea converged on the quays of the port, in dockside warehouses and store-houses, and in the market—that is, on both the water and the land of Venice—only to be sent off again, by both land and sea, according to a strict calendar and carefully regulated exchanges. I describe the daily life of an economic power in the port and the market, the very places where the city most proudly presented itself as an import-export capital. I also attempt to show that Venice was not only and not always a capital in the economy of exchanges of the Middle Ages and the Renaissance. In this connection I seek out an industrial Venice and the worlds of labor that industry implies.

In chapter 5, I begin within the city and at its center to examine the rules and customs of politics and comment on the grammar of Venetian institutions, from the earliest doges to the commune, and then move on to the Signoria. This implies dismantling the mechanisms of a system that operated in a complex manner and with an undeniable flexibility despite oft-repeated affirmations of its long duration and its "constancy." I also consider the nobility—the "first in the land"—wherever they were to be found in Venetian space: on the galleys of the Republic, in command of Venetian outposts and possessions in Candia, Crete, or Padua, supervising the unloading of cargo in Monemvasia, or serving at the head of a squadron in the Adriatic.

In the final chapter I attempt to breathe new life into the human scene in Venice, the men and women who inhabited the houses, courtyards, and alleys of the city whose building and organization we have witnessed. Whereas in earlier chapters Venetians are shown going about their economic or political business in Venice's far-flung empire or on the Venetian Terraferma, here they are described in their normal context, within their ordinary networks and their customary relations with their environment, and in conjunction with all the manifestations that make up the "culture" of a given group in the serene (or troubled) organization of daily life. Finally, I take a look at the islands painted on the wall of the Vatican Map Gallery, ending up in Piazza San Marco to seek in its monuments, its decor, and its passing crowd a possible meaning of the history of Venice.

I EXTEND warm thanks to my friends Claudia Salmini, Piero Lucchi, Stefano Stipitivich, Jean-Claude Maire Vigueur, and Laurent Feller for their help, both direct and indirect. My friendship and my thanks also go, in these first days of January, to Gérard Rippe, with whom I worked side by side for days on end in the Venetian archives. My thanks also, for their patience, to the graduate students on whom I tried out certain chapters. Many thanks to Denis, who held up admirably under the burden of reading and rereading this text. This book is written for Guillemette, to make up for the way the "incomparable" Morosini disappointed us in Athens.

CHRONOLOGY

1177	Peace of Venice ends hostilities with Holy Roman Emperor Frederick Barbarossa
1189	Byzantine emperor restores Venetian privileges in Constantinople
1204	Fall and sack of Constantinople
1205–7	Venice occupies Negroponte and Crete
1207–20	Institution of Quarantia (Council of Forty)
1222–25	Establishment of Fondaco dei Tedeschi (German Merchants' Warehouse)
1224	Institution of offices for tutelage of canals and the public domain
1234–35	War with Padua
1242	Compilation of Venetian laws under Doge Giacomo Tiepolo
1256–58	Venice and Genoa clash in rivalry over Acre
1260	Spread of flagellant enthusiasm from Perugia into Venice
1261	Byzantine emperor Michael VIII Paleologus recaptures Constantinople
1268	Lorenzo Tiepolo first doge elected under new procedures
1291	Great Council bans glass furnaces in Venice
1294–99	Second war with Genoa
1297	*Serrata* (Closing) of the Great Council
1307–50	Silk workers from Lucca arrive in Venice
1308	War with Ferrara
1310	Bajamonte Tiepolo-Marco Querini conspiracy leads to establishment of the Council of Ten
1317	Venice establishes trade with western Mediterranean and North Sea
1322	Pope places interdict on Venetian trade with Egypt
1324	Project to protect the lagoon and divert the Brenta River
1324–25	Enlargement of the Arsenal
1336–39	Venice, Padua, and Florence ally in war against Verona

1339–40	Construction of the Zecca (Venice's Mint)
1348–49	Plague epidemic
1351–55	Third War with Genoa
1355	Execution of Doge Marin Falier
1355	Establishment of Council of Ten as a permanent body
1362	Petrarch leaves his manuscripts to Venice
1378–81	War of Chioggia (Fourth War with Genoa), ending with the Peace of Turin
1381	Inclusion of thirty-one new families in Great Council
1386–1402	Extension of Venetian control over a number of its former possessions in Greece, including Corfu, Lepanto, Argos, and Athens
1394	Installation of clocks and bell in tower in Rialto
1396	Venice regains control of Scutari along Dalmatian coast
1404–5	Venice gains control of Vicenza, then Verona
1410	Institution of Auditori Nuovi to supervise administration of Terraferma
1412	Establishment of shipping lane to Provence and Catalonia
1420	Venice conquers Friuli
1420	Creation of Savi di Terra Ferma
1421	Tomaso Mocenigo protests Venetian expansion onto the terraferma
1421–40	Bartolomeo and Giovanni Bon build Cà d'Oro
1425–28	War with Milan
1430	Turks wrest Thessalonica from Venetian control
1430–40	First wave of Greek immigrants arrive from the East
1431–33	War with Milan
1436–41	War with Milan
1439	Turks conquer Serbia
1444	Turks defeat Christians and Venetian fleet at Varna
1446	Venice signs truce with Sultan Murad II

1446	War with Milan
1446	School at San Marco opens
1450	Bishop of Castello is elevated to Patriarch of Venice
1452–54	War with Milan, ending with the Peace of Lodi
1453	Turks conquer Constantinople, bringing a formal end to the Byzantine Empire
1455	Alvise Cà Da Mosto makes first voyage reaching Cape Verde
1457	Doge Francesco Foscari deposed
1469	Cardinal Bessarion's bequest of his manuscript collection to Venice establishes the Marciana Library
1469	Printing begins in Venice
1470	Turks conquer Negroponte
1476	Venice institutes policies to preserve forestry resources
1478	Limitation of ducal chancellery post to original citizens only
1481–84	War with Ferrara, ending with the Peace of Bagnolo
1481–89	Construction of Santa Maria dei Miracoli
1488	Publication of Sabellico's *De Venetis magistratibus*
1489	Caterina Corner cedes Cyprus to Venice
1489	Founding of Scuola Grande di San Rocco
1496	Venice grants "nation" status to Greek community allowing it to found a confraternity
1498–99	Bank failures in Venice
1501	Inquisition in Venice instituted at death of Doge Agostino Barbarigo
1509	Venice defeated by League of Cambrai at Battle of Agnadello
1511	Construction begins on the Procuratie Vecchie
1515	Appointment of Andrea Navagero as Venice's official historian
1516	Establishment of Venetian ghetto
1517	Turks conquer Egypt and Syria
1522	Turks conquer Rhodes

VENICE *Triumphant*

ONE

A City Born in the Water

Venice was born in the water, Venice was born of the water. Today as yesterday, it triumphs over the water. At least this is the destiny that Venetian history assigned to the city.

In the last centuries of the Middle Ages those who arrived in Venice for the first time saw a dense concentration of houses and palaces, shops and churches rising over a watery horizon. The French ambassador Philippe de Commynes was astonished at the "si grand maisonnement" that he found in the midst of the lagoons.[1] Visitors to that city set "in the water" thought Venice the most profoundly urban of all the cities they knew. All foreigners' narratives from the fifteenth century stress the same striking paradox. Here houses, courtyards, and streets replaced grass and trees, revealing the urban landscape of a city made up exclusively of stones and people. Venice was admired for its imposing monuments but also for its more ordinary constructions. A place of plenitude, it seemed to hold all beauties and all wealth. One visitor wrote, "It seems to me all of jasper, chalcedony, and alabaster." This was how the glory of Venice was perceived. The city had been built on an ungrateful, even hostile site, but wonderstruck visitors declared it a miracle of stone rising above the water.

When they turned to the history of their city, Venetians wrote exactly the same thing. From the earliest medieval chronicles to the official histories of the modern age, all texts exalt the singularity of a city situated at the heart of the lagoons. No theme is more frequently repeated, developed, and embroidered on in local discourse. Senators spoke of themselves as "we who have built such a great city in the middle of salt marshes," and the community at large concurred. Venetians reiterated the notion that their city was unique and its organization admirable. This can easily be seen in many famous paintings that functioned as a genuine reflection of the texts and written discourses, putting the history of the city into images.[2] We need only look at

Gentile Bellini's *Miracle of the True Cross at the Bridge of San Lorenzo* or his *Procession of the Relic of the True Cross in Piazza San Marco.* These and other compositions show the people of Venice and the places in which they lived with a profusion of details, depicting a city as more than a simple framework or an obligatory backdrop. Chimneys and roofs, bridges and boats, porticos and loggias played just as important a role in the full intensity of Venetian life as did the many human actors, both the stars and the walk-ons, who performed on the same stage. Water, domesticated by human toil, enhanced the monumental decor and the theatricality of the urban scene, creating the conditions for the very special magic of Venice.

Venetians and foreigners agreed: the first challenge facing Venice was to subdue the surrounding waters. The Venetian adventure began in the unhealthy marshlands that ringed the northern gulf of the Adriatic.

Our first task will be to see why Venice arose in such a spot. But it is not enough to recall the origins of Venice before it was Venice. All too often, even though a host of recent works have revised the old views, histories of the medieval and postmedieval city are content to present two scenes. First they devote a few brief paragraphs to life among the lagoons in the early centuries, when those brackish waters began to be colonized. Then they depict the Venice Triumphant of the late Middle Ages and the modern age, as if the city, immutable and marvelous, had emerged from the water in its full beauty and order.[3] The history of that densely settled city, however, was like that of a living organism: Venice grew thanks to a long and arduous process of organization involving many construction projects. It also seems to me that we cannot recreate the life of that urban community—the life of the people who inhabited it and the places they altered and organized—unless we also revive the greater territory of the entire lagoon basin. The very survival of the nascent city depended on that greater space and that natural environment: Venetians did not separate the city they had built and organized from the waters that surrounded it.

This notion provides the theme and the cadence for this first chapter, which treats the ways in which those stretches of water and mud were transformed to produce Venice. What I hope to describe is the complex and difficult dynamics of the construction of a monumental order in the water.

Our story begins between land and sea, in vast lagoons of brackish water.

IN THE SHELTER OF THE LAGOONS

Although they were attentive to paradoxes and marvels, our fifteenth-century visitors were unaware of one of the strangest facts about Venice. The fictions of official history were sufficiently potent to hide an astonishing truth: that center with a population of some 100,000 inhabitants, that dominant commercial metropolis, that powerful city-state, was a new city.[4]

Traces of human occupation throughout the area go far back in time, but because they are difficult to interpret and related studies are few, the history of the origins of Venice is still a matter of controversy. We can at least simplify the debates and polemics by reviewing some of the hypotheses and some of the facts.

Before Venice

It was long thought, following the Venetian histories, that during the barbarian invasions population groups from the mainland sought refuge in the lagoons and continued to live there.[5] A return in recent years to the question of the origins of Venice has offered an original defense of the thesis of Roman colonization of the lagoon basin and ongoing inhabitation of the area between late antiquity and the early Middle Ages.[6] This argument, which rests on a systematic morphological analysis of the territory of the lagoons, states that the lagoons were created in their current form only during the eleventh and twelfth centuries.[7] The Roman system of land division known as *centuriatio* was presumably applied in large parts of the lagoon basin, which in this interpretation is confirmation of both radical changes in the morphology of Venetia and its incontestable Romanization. It is true that a large number of Roman objects and other materials were found in the northern lagoon, in particular on Torcello. They inspired a good deal of early commentary and interrogations, and a few authors have gone so far as to posit the existence of a stable Roman presence in the area.[8]

If these theories about the evolution of the lagoon remain hypotheses—at times they have been vigorously contested—archaeological discoveries in the 1960s brought confirmation of the thesis of a Roman colonization, albeit temporary, of the northern lagoon. Systematic excavations helped to define

Roman implantation north of the basin at least. In the first centuries of the Common Era there was a prosperous mainland town at Altino; some sort of settlement, probably a stable one, existed at Torcello some five kilometers away across the water. The marshy ground of the island was reinforced with materials brought, in all likelihood, from the mainland. Traces remain of works dating from the late first century c.e. that created a central plaza and marked its perimeter, but the natural calamities of the fifth and sixth centuries brought colonization to an almost complete halt. Alluvial deposits from the Piave and Sile Rivers increased, covering the island, which was already sinking.[9] The mainlanders had troubles of their own, and the inhabitants of Altino could not afford costly operations to rescue the site at Torcello.

The bitterness of the debates regarding the origins of Venice might seem excessive viewed in the light of historical importance. The explanation of the polemic lies in the simple but bothersome fact that the thesis of even a limited Roman colonization of the lagoon runs counter to one of the dogmas of local historical discourse, which insists that an absolutely unique history began in the lagoon basin with Venice, and only with Venice. The fact remains—and this is what matters for our purposes—that the early occupation of lagoon lands was both modest and circumscribed, and settlement remained limited until the late sixth century and the Lombard invasion.[10] When the settlement at Torcello was abandoned, only a few fishermen, sailors, and salt gatherers continued to live in the lagoon area, which remained a dependency of the mainland and its successive regimes of political domination (first Ostrogoth, then Byzantine). This dependency was not only political and administrative but also economic, given that beginning in the imperial age the exploitation of salt had been a government monopoly. Dependency was also religious because the dioceses of the towns of the Adriatic shore, under the metropolitan of Aquileia, had jurisdiction over the lagoon.

Cassiodorus's famous letter to the "tribunes of the maritime population," dated 537–38, gives the earliest known description of the site and its inhabitants.[11] The letter describes an uncertain landscape of brackish waters, silt, and reeds peopled by men in boats who were just as aquatic as the birds they hunted. These lagoon dwellers were engaged in fishing, transport, and exploitation of the salt flats. With evident curiosity, Cassiodorus describes in detail the rudimentary water economy that was already in place.[12] Everything in this picture, embellished by the rhetoric of the author, speaks of an uncertain existence and of laborious but successful beginnings. These men were poor, but they were free, and concord and harmony reigned in a society in which an existence shared with water established a basic equality: "Poverty therefore may associate itself with wealth on equal terms. One kind of food refreshes all; the same sort of dwelling shelters all; no one can envy his neighbour's home; and living in this moderate style they escape that vice [of envy] to which all the rest of the world is liable." Even though human settlement on these immense "liquid plains" was precarious and the threat of inundation was constant, the first Venetians had already learned how to cope with the difficulties of their environment. Their houses were fragile; currents constantly eroded lands that were also subject to flooding; a high tide could carry off anything not fortified or raised above ground level. Still, the inhabitants of these islands consolidated the ground, protecting it with mats woven of flexible reeds. Little by little, land gained over water.

The lagoons were thus first durably populated in migrations that followed invasions. In the late sixth century, however, human settlement changed form. The Lombard invasion marks a break. Led by their chief, Alboin, the Lombards left Pannonia and moved south into Friuli: by 569 they had reached the walls of Cividale. Their conquest advanced rapidly, especially on the flatlands, and they soon overran the territory between the Tagliamento and Isonzo Rivers. Verona and Vicenza fell. Most of the bigger towns, however—Oderzo, Padua, Cremona—were strong enough to resist and were not taken during the first phase of the Lombard advance. Soon the Lombards had invaded all of northern Italy, even though Pavia, their future capital, did not surrender until 572. Wherever the Lombards approached the lagoon between Aquileia and Concordia, peasants and townspeople alike abandoned the mainland and sought refuge on the islands of the lagoon and the littoral. The Byzantines, who concentrated their forces to defend Ravenna and who had traditionally counted on their fleet to fend off successive waves of barbarians, may have encouraged this flight to the lagoon.

The first groups of refugees probably considered their installation provisory. Earlier threats had led other groups to migrate, always more or less temporarily, to the shelter of the lagoons. In the early fifth century the Visigoths under Alaric set off a first move; another occurred in 453–54, when Attila's Huns swept through the area. But as soon as the storm had passed, the refugees tended to return to their mainland towns.[13] Lingering insecurity must have ruled out a similar return at the end of the sixth century, and Venetia found itself at the center of renewed Lombard military activities in the early seventh century. Monselice and Padua were conquered, which set indigenous population groups in movement, probably in the direction of Ravenna but also toward the basin of the lagoons.

Beginning in the final decades of the sixth century the lagoon thus saw a new type of settlement that totally changed the nature of the widely scattered earlier communities. The exodus to the islands was not only massive but definitive. By that time the Lombards had reached the shores of the mainland between the Adige and the Brenta, and their permanent establishment there prevented the fugitives' return. Life amid the marshlands took on new dimensions.

Within the "Liquid Plains": A Lagoon Venice

Small settlements grew up, and according to the tradition set by the earliest chronicles, each one sheltered the population of one mainland town. Grado and Caorle were supposedly settled by refugees from Friuli and the lands between Aquileia and Concordia. People from Oderzo went to Cittanova and Jesolo.[14] The inhabitants of Altino are thought to have gone to Torcello; those of Treviso, to Rialto and Malamocco. People from Padua fled to Chioggia and perhaps also to Malamocco.

An important event in this history is the taking of Oderzo by the Lombards, occasioning a migration to the lagoon basin. Led by their bishop, the people of Oderzo took refuge on the island of Eraclea-Cittanova, where they set up offices of the Byzantine administration, which meant that the *magister militum* (master of the soldiers) resided there. That high functionary was responsible only to the exarch of Ravenna, the representative of the Roman emperor in this part of Italy, which had remained Byzantine.[15] Eraclea-Cittanova was thus the first political center in the lagoons. The lagoon communities at Torcello, Caorle, Jesolo, and Malamocco were under the civil authority of a tribune recruited from among the indigenous aristocracy who served under the *magister militum*. Although local history presents such tribunes as the natural leaders of these first societies, they were really district officials. The communities worshiped under their own priests because the bishops had accompanied their flocks as they fled. Nonetheless, the religious organization of the lagoon area was still far from stable. The bishop of Altino, for example, managed to maintain his title, though most scholars agree that he now resided in Torcello. The diocese of Oderzo, on the other hand, seems to have disappeared with the death of its last titular bishop, in the late seventh century.[16] The smaller islands had no independent status in this administrative and ecclesiastical structure and were subject to the island center closest to hand.

Reconstructions of Venetian history tended to transform or conceal these basic facts. The oldest existing history, the chronicle of John the Deacon, set the tone for narratives of the origins of Venice for centuries to come by endowing the men of the lagoons with a primitive liberty. John's chronicle says nothing about ties with Byzantium or the subjection of the Venice basin to the Eastern Roman Empire; John chose instead to depict free men fleeing subjection who settled in the lagoon area to preserve their liberty. Once we abandon this imaginary of an ontological liberty, it is clear that emancipation was a long process and that even when it had been launched, Venetians struggled to avoid the grasp of the Byzantine Empire and then of the Carolingian Empire.[17]

The Venice of the lagoon and of the islands and the littoral barrier was thus organized first under the authority of a "master of the soldiers" and then, beginning in the eighth century, under that of a doge. Communities had been established within the confines of the amphibious world of the lagoon all the way from Grado to Cavarzere.[18] Marshes and mud flats offered shelter and protection from rampant danger on the mainland, but on a daily basis the environment was ungrateful, even repellant, its resources were meager, and life there was genuinely difficult. It was out of necessity that these communities soon launched improvements. Here too, however, we need to guard against the legend of origins. According to John the Deacon, the newborn Venice was immediately endowed with order, beauty, and urbanity. As soon as the refugees had settled, they founded fortified centers and towns on the various islands. The landscape presented in John's chronicle is already a city in which churches and houses of an admirable decorum seemed to have emerged spontaneously. In reality, however, the Venetians struggled with their boggy terrain for many centuries, and their existence

The Duchy of the Venetians

long depended on their ability to cling to discontinuous fragments of mud and ground.

A Slow Colonization of Brackish Waters

Anyone intent on doing justice to the history of those centuries enveloped in a nearly complete documentary darkness should imagine a long series of labors patiently repeated. In order to survive, the inhabitants of the lagoon had to consolidate the shorelines, drain the land, and construct buildings, at first with precarious materials, later with bricks and stones transported from the mainland. Soon, however (quite soon, considering the obstacles to be surmounted and the rudimentary nature of the technology available), tens of churches were built, and with them small settlements that have left little or no trace today, swallowed up by advancing marshlands in a changing environment. An inscription discovered at Torcello in the late nineteenth century bears witness to this building activity and this movement of people.[19] It establishes that the cathedral, dedicated to the Virgin, the Mother of God, was founded on that small island in the northern lagoon in 639, only three-quarters of a century after the migration from the mainland.[20]

The architecture of that church demonstrates how rapidly these brackish waters were populated and how, little by little, the newcomers established their hold over land that they wrested from the marshlands and the reeds. The original church was a classical structure whose Eastern influence was apparent only in its decoration,[21] which probably included mosaics.[22] There is evidence of fairly considerable work from the late seventh century, when the church was enlarged and marble decorations better suited to its new dignity were added. Some architectural traces of this first monument, along with some stylistic elements useful for establishing chronology, still exist. In contrast, historians have available only legends, dates, or anecdotes of marvels connected with the many other religious establishments that graced the lagoon area at the time, meager indications that weave only an uncertain history. What all such traditional accounts describe, with or without supporting documentation, is a good many active human communities that had settled in the area as early as the seventh century and were ready to colonize all the dry land standing above the water. The lagoons were already more than a mere shelter: they had been exploited and improved; they were dotted with edifices and crosses; and they were thickly populated.[23] Moreover, the list of the churches that were founded grew rapidly, proof of an increasingly dense human presence.[24]

In 810 an event that was to have far-reaching consequences interrupted this slow growth. The seat of the duchy, which in the eighth century had been transferred from Eraclea-Cittanova to Malamocco, on the littoral islands, passed in turn to a group of small islands somewhat farther from the sea, at Rialto-Venice. The island confederation had a new capital, and a new history—the history of the building of Venice—was launched. Men and forces were concentrated on the Rialto archipelago, which slowly and gradually emptied the other islets as it established its power over the basin of the lagoons.

THE INVENTION OF A CITY

This was the beginning of a long history, the history of the creation of a city where once there had been only damp and fragile ground and unhealthy mud flats.[25] Time in Venice was first displayed in space, the space of a city that took shape, grew, and beautified itself amid the marshes.

Centuries of Creative Energy

Aside from a few rocky outcrops, for example, Dorsoduro, and the few more substantial islands on which communities initially formed and constructed their houses and their churches, there was no such thing as solid ground in or around Venice. This is a first and strikingly singular feature of the Venetian experience. The urban fabric of Venice was developed— without benefit of an existing ancient site, with no organizing central nucleus, and no tradition of town planning—from a limited number of pivotal growth points, the few plots of dry land. Little by little, as the city moved out to conquer its space and each small island was drained, organized, and divided into lots, that urban fabric tightened. The relationship between land and water was thus constantly changing, and their shifting limits defined the urban corpus. This brings us to a second feature that made Venice unique among new cities at the time. Everywhere else the medieval city threw up walls that it then maintained, supervised, and enlarged, often several times.

The construction of the successive rings of city walls punctuated moments of intense urbanization. In the lagoon, only water surrounded the built-up areas. Venice's only physical defenses were built at its points of contact with the outside world: a tower at Mestre (before Venice embarked on territorial expansion on the mainland, creating its Terraferma) and small bastions at San Nicolò del Lido to defend the sea side of the principal passageway through the littoral islands. Venice was a city whose walls were salt water.

The first step in urban expansion was thus to create solid ground on which to build. This involved a series of advances and conquests over the lagoon and the interior salt ponds in wave after wave of drainage operations, land-reclamation projects, and efforts to consolidate what soil there was with palisades and dirt.[26] Those first initiatives, which increased as the population of the islands grew, were followed by others. Over the centuries they became a formidable enterprise that multiplied inhabitable spaces and created new islands where once there had been water. Nor was the network of canals in Venice a permanent feature, except for the central axis of the Grand Canal, which set the general form of the city, and the broad waterway of the Giudecca. Unlike in other cities that had a river as an important part of their landscape, in Venice canals were continually being drained and filled in, while new ones were being dug in newly reclaimed zones. The system as a whole was constantly being remodeled. To this day the toponymy of Venice offers names like *rio terrà* or *rio nuovo*, constant reminders of waterways of the past. Similarly, the few straight streets that stand out from the tangle of narrow alleyways often follow the courses of drained canals otherwise lost to memory. Elsewhere in Venice, urban expansion pushed back vegetation as it absorbed fields and gardens, but it bears repeating that here, too, it was water and mud that were being colonized.[27]

These brief remarks cannot possibly do justice to all the many construction projects, great and small, that were carried on through the centuries, interrupted only by outbreaks of epidemics and periods of demographic and economic recession.[28] In its early phases, expansion was the work of the major property owners, some of whom were laymen, but more typically the entrepreneurs were ecclesiastics or religious institutions embarked on land-reclamation projects on the scale of an entire quarter.

The religious orders long played a determinant role in the creation of the city. The Benedictines were particularly active in the Dorsoduro area. In the early thirteenth century they launched a vast operation of land reclamation around the monastery of San Gregorio, between the Grand Canal and the Canal of the Giudecca. By the end of the century the entire perimeter of the area had been divided into lots. Houses were built of brick with tile roofs. New means of land communication were created to reinforce the old aquatic network, which was also reorganized. The establishment of the mendicant orders had vast consequences for urban development in the city. When the Franciscans built their first church in the area of San Tomà, in the southern part of the city, it gave encouragement to a phase of development that had already begun, thanks to the efforts of the noble Badoer family and the people in the parish to reclaim the vast stretches of marshland and water that hindered building. To the north, the Dominicans broke open a genuine frontier with the church of Santi Giovanni e Paolo, and other orders—Carmelites, Friars of the Sack, and Augustinians—launched pioneering campaigns in other outlying areas. On the fluid and continually redefined margins of the city, religious institutions long played an important role.[29]

A turning point occurred during the last decades of the thirteenth century, however, when the political authorities began to control and even organize urban expansion as a collective enterprise.[30] Public power reasserted its rights over the waters and the marshes. In exchange for a "water rent," it granted rights to basins and ponds, marshlands and putrid dumps, and, in general, all the surface areas that formed enclaves, fragmenting the urban fabric and slowing development. The commune even took direct command of certain major land-reclamation projects, the most spectacular of which was that of the Giudecca Nuova, an island created in the early fourteenth century between the island of San Giorgio Maggiore and the Giudecca itself. More often, the communal government charged its magistrates with supervision of ongoing reclamation projects that were being pursued on a daily basis in the various parishes, where small property holders and neighbors within a *contrada* took on the task of reclaiming marshes and draining interior basins to gain ground at the edge of the lagoon. Urbanization increased thanks to minor but repeated efforts to dry the soil and effect timid but persistent gains of dry ground over water.

Expansion continued throughout the thirteenth century, but the pace was particularly brisk up to the early 1340s.[31] In spite of the large numbers of victims of epidemics, the first demographic declines, in 1307 and in 1320, did not yet affect the rising population curve. Pressure continued, and building activity must have been intense. Day after day, at the edges of Venice, at the foot of hundreds of gardens on the Giudecca, at Santa Croce, or at Cannaregio, Venetians planted pilings and set planks into place to shore up a few square meters of spongy soil. Householders dumped their rubbish there, along with a bit of soil or mud, slowly nibbling outward to gain ground. Flotillas of boats loaded with dirt and refuse circulated among the various quarters of the city. Mud from canal dredging, gravel from construction sites, sweepings from the market or the streets—everything contributed to filling in one more pond or reclaiming one more parcel of land. Communal construction projects peaked about 1343, slowing even before the shock of the Black Death. Urban expansion did not pick up again until about 1385, and although land reclamation continued on a variety of fronts, plague years continued to mirror low points in construction, and expansion never matched either the intensity or the formidable vitality typical of the early fourteenth century.

During those same fruitful early decades of the fourteenth century other transformations conducted or encouraged by the government or delegated to its many magistracies shaped the urban fabric of Venice.[32] Alleyways were pierced or enlarged, and a few main axes—the first paved streets—were laid out, opening up city neighborhoods and facilitating foot traffic from the secondary network of passageways that ran through parishes or groups of parishes.[33] Quays were improved, consolidated, or reconstructed when the water had eroded them. Bridges were constructed and reconstructed, at first in wood, then, during the fifteenth century, in stone. All these improvements enlarged established main routes through the various quarters of the city, adding to the early network of canals a second network of land communications during the final centuries of the Middle Ages and bringing about a genuine revolution that totally changed circulation in Venice.[34] The two systems of communication, by water and by land, began to serve different functions, with pedestrians using the *calli* (unless a waterway without a bridge obliged them to use a gondola *traghetto*) and merchandise and heavy ships circulating on the canals from the port to the market, from the Arsenal to the basin of San Marco, or from one warehouse to another.

The construction, at the heart of the lagoons, of one of the biggest urban complexes in the medieval West demanded, as we have seen, continuous work, cumulative efforts, and imaginative techniques. The milieu multiplied the difficulties, and the list was long of operations required in this particularly ill-adapted site full of obstacles. Nonetheless, Venetians learned to live surrounded by water, proving that relations of force are not the only active elements in history and that imagination plays a role as well. Two examples will serve to illustrate this.

Imagination as Actor

Techniques of land reclamation and construction differed from one work site to another. If drying out a marsh was relatively easy, extending dry land into the water was a longer, more arduous operation. Once a permit for a plot had been granted, the first step was to close it off, building a stout palisade of planks and pilings reinforced with stones or cofferwork when the polder reached out into the lagoon and the current was strong. Once the area was tightly closed off, water and mud could be pumped or dug out and the soft, spongy terrain could be consolidated. Large-scale operations required digging a channel to let the water drain out. Even all this did not solve every problem. The ground remained fragile and slippery in spite of these efforts and could not support heavy constructions. That meant that sizable buildings had to be constructed on pilings, the spacing and disposition of which varied with the configuration of the terrain and the weight of the projected construction. The usual technique for compacting the subsoil was to insert a large number of short, tightly packed pilings, but these reached no deeper than the surface layers. Long, more thinly spaced pilings could reach the harder underlayers and support a solid foundation. The best-constructed buildings used both techniques. Once this substructure had been put into place, something resembling a wooden raft made of horizontal crossed beams was assembled on top of the pilings. The foundations of the building were constructed on that raft, with the lower parts of the building itself resting on top of those foundations.[35] Present-day projects that attempt to replace these pilings using the latest technological systems prove to be both extremely lengthy and costly.

The history of Venice's water supply is further proof of the difficult conditions of daily life in the city. All cities in the *ancien régime* suffered from an insufficient supply of drinking water, but in Venice scarcity could become dramatic because water was omnipresent but not drinkable. One fifteenth-century French traveler put this paradox best: "In a city in which the inhabitants are in water up to their mouths, they often go thirsty." How was the community to solve this important problem?[36]

First, water drawn from the lagoon and the canals served many domestic uses. Postmortem inventories of even the most modest households list large numbers of pails, which were emptied and rinsed, the ones used to carry the brackish canal water kept separate from those intended for fresh water.[37] Still, even serving such needs would have been impossible if the *rii* of Venice had been extremely polluted. The government was obliged to impose controls, and in the early fourteenth century the Great Council prohibited the washing of all cloth and dyed woolens in the canals, adding that water used for dyeing could not be flushed into the canals. Henceforth dirty water of that sort was to go into the lagoon. Thanks to resistance on the part of the dyers, infractions were many, and the law did not reflect common practice. A century later, however, most of the dye works that used blood or indigo had shifted to the periphery of the city, as had all activities "that let off bad odors and smells," such as meat butchering. Blood, carcasses, and spoiled meat were carried to the lagoon. The canals of *el corpo de Venexia* began to be protected in the name of a nascent ecological awareness.[38]

Much more stringent measures were necessary to guarantee a supply of drinking water, however. In the early centuries of settlement in the lagoon basin the populations depended on natural wells on the offshore littoral that were dug into sand deposits and protected by a thick underground stratum of clay. There is no evidence that the islands and the *lidi* had artificial cisterns. These became necessary, however, with the increase in population density that occurred when settlement was concentrated on the Rialto archipelago. Artificial wells became widespread in the growing city. They were constructed in a way so characteristic of the site that they are known as "Venetian wells." The cavity of the cistern was dug to a depth of some three to four meters below the level of the highest tide, and its bottom and sides were coated with clay. A brick conduit called a *canna* was placed on a stone slab at the center of the cavity. The mortar that held the bricks together, a mixture of sand and clay, also served as a filter.[39] The rest of the cavity was filled with sand brought from the littoral islands. A cover with a raised edge topped the cistern, while conduits for rainwater were attached to openings (two or four, depending on the size of the well). Each of these openings was capped with a stone, also pierced with holes. The rainwater passed through the sand, which purified it, filtering it into the *canna*. From there the water rose to a distribution point above the edge of the well, which soon came to be decorated and sculpted, as can be seen in the few remaining examples from the ninth century.[40]

A construction of that sort was obviously costly.[41] Thus, the first wells, which were of course private, were in the courtyards of aristocratic houses, where they were used by an entire community of dependants, servants, family members, and tenants. The aristocratic house of the time formed a vast block in which a sizable group of people lived, lodged, and worked. This dwelling and the family that owned it controlled not only a series of small adjoining houses but also an impressive infrastructure of annexes and dependencies. Texts list wells in much the same way that they enumerate *calli*, bridges, quays, wharves, warehouses, and boat hangars. Over time the vast family properties were broken up, so that it was up to the sellers, the new owners, or the heirs to regulate access to the well. Houses were put up for sale with a right to use the cistern and with the "servitudes" indispensable for rights of passage through tiny streets and courtyards that remained private.[42]

During the final centuries of the Middle Ages, wells became more and more numerous. By then all houses of a certain size had such a commodity. Humbler households shared a well, and in parts of the city that were undergoing rapid urbanization, where Venetian proprietors had built groups of small houses to be offered for rent, one or two cisterns were provided for each small street. According to the notarial documents, Venetians had a complex system of collective usages, "servitudes," and neighborly relations shaped by access to water. Well water had to be shared, but often there was also shared responsibility for constructing, maintaining, and repairing the *gorne*, the gutters that carried rainwater to the well. In patrician houses these *gorne* might be made of stone, even marble, or of lead lined with wood. Elsewhere, they long continued to be made of wood, which meant that they had to be replaced when the wood rotted. Written agreements and permissions describe many ingenious installations: the *gorne* might extend over the small streets; they might start from several houses and lead to one conduit that reached the well. All these pipelines made for an astonishing landscape.[43]

A network of public wells paralleled these private and semiprivate arrangements. Every *campo,* a small open place or square, usually next to the parish church, had a well to serve the poorest Venetians. The fourteenth century brought a dramatic change of scale in the system of communal wells, however.[44] A decision was made in the 1320s to create fifty additional wells, primarily in the recently urbanized areas at the edge of the city. At the same time a campaign was launched to repair the existing cisterns. This campaign continued until the Black Death struck, when, not surprisingly, improving the city's system of wells was put off. In the fifteenth century new, larger cisterns were installed; the old ones were repaired, and their upper walls were raised to keep salt water from invading them and spoiling their contents in periods of *acqua alta.*

In spite of all these efforts, Venice never had an adequate water supply, especially during dry spells. Flotillas of boats had to be dispatched to the mouths of nearby rivers—first to the Bottenigo, then to the Brenta—to fetch fresh water. The fresh water was then sold by the bucket or poured into the cisterns. The public authorities made efforts to take bolder action to assure fresh water from this parallel source of supply, and a number of projects were suggested during the fourteenth and fifteenth centuries to channel river water and even to construct an aqueduct. The high cost of such initiatives precluded their execution, which meant that every summer the Signoria was obliged to purchase boatloads of fresh water to satisfy the needs of the poor of Venice—the *povera zente*—and distribute it to public wells that had gone dry. In Venice more than in any other city, good government and fulfillment of the principles of the common good were measured by the abundance of water, which meant that the authorities strenuously avoided crises related to the water supply. Thanks to a series of stopgap measures, and in the face of enormous difficulties, the community continued to exist in the midst of salt waters.

Jacopo de Barbari's *Perspective View of Venice,* executed in 1500, shows all of these improvements.[45] It depicts a densely settled city configured roughly as Venice is today. At the edges of the settled areas the city's contours are at times fluid, and we can see empty spaces and plots of cultivated marshland.

Hangars stand next to workshops and areas for stocking raw materials. Away from the city's margins, however, the city is densely settled, houses crowd together, and neighborhoods are compact. All the structuring elements of a complex urban fabric are present. Above all, we see the city in the very particular shape that became obligatory in later centuries since this map was a primary reference that influenced and even imposed its form on later representations. Jacopo de Barbari depicts the whole circuit of the waters, including the land areas that circled the lagoon all around Rialto and made up the lagoon world, but the city of Venice, by its sheer size and its central position, incontestably dominates the view and is the true focus of the viewer's gaze and attention. Various small islands are shown, but they are modest satellites of the imposing ensemble that is Venice.

What are we to deduce from this? The forces of the lagoons had converged to create Rialto. The wealth of Venetians operating in all the economic marketplaces of the world had permitted construction in wood, brick, limestone, and marble. Spoils and trophies taken from an East wide open to merchant enterprise had been brought back to decorate and enrich Venice. Centuries of work had gone into the production of a prodigious artifact. The creation of Venice was nearly complete in 1500.

The result was visible. Its artisans were many. The fact remains that although credit must be given to a collective actor for the construction of Venice—that is, to all those who were responsible for overseeing the innumerable works projects—individual efforts also dotted the course of that long history. The creation of Venice must be seen as a long-term, continuing dynamic, but that does not mean we cannot discern moments of acceleration in that process.

Public and Private, or, How Venice was Built

One of those moments of accelerated growth occurred during the latter half of the thirteenth century, when public authority began to play a more determinant role.

The Era of Public Enterprise

At first, as I have pointed out, the commune took increasing responsibility for tutelage of the waters, the marshes, and all land-reclamation projects.

One result, as demonstrated by serial study of permissions to carry out such projects, was a higher level of coordination on several fronts. Another result was the imposition of new norms of urbanization and construction in those terrains, a more rectilinear platting (because the reclaimed lots tended to be regular in form), and the organization of a dual system of communication on both land and water (the virgin territories tended to have a more land-based structure). Gradually, however, the prescriptions laid down by the central authorities also covered collective infrastructures, the morphology of buildings, and the equipment of houses with wells, *gorne*, and gutters.[46] Undeniably, there were times when public supervision was weak or nonexistent. There were many unauthorized reclamation projects, and in spite of all that the magistrates could do, there were usurpations of the communal water supply that encouraged speculation and led to the enrichment of a few.[47] All of this is attested, but the infringements were insufficient to deflect growth or negate the principles of order and rationality that the commune attempted to apply to that growth.

Governmental support encouraged or accelerated other changes as well. Public space expanded remarkably during those same decades. The decisions handed down in the waves of suits that came before the magistrates show how and on what basis the heart of the city was opened up.[48] Wherever private spaces, recently reclaimed ponds, small streets, or bridges were in dispute, the public powers decided in their own favor, thus diminishing the holdings of the aristocratic lineages. In these new spaces open to common use, to the "general commodity," the officials of the commune attempted to impose respect of the many police regulations dictated by the city councils. As we have seen, the city of Venice numbered at least 100,000 inhabitants in the early fourteenth century. The size of the population and the proliferation of its activities made it necessary to maintain public spaces and manage resources, which meant setting rules regarding security and hygiene, attempting to control the rise to power of the crafts and trades, and passing measures regarding public order. Within these public spaces, however, urban order applied not only to streets and waterways, regular garbage retrieval, or a preference for creating lines of buildings and for regularity. Building projects also reflected a desire for beautification. Within certain privileged spaces—Piazza San Marco and the market of the Rialto were the first of these—the commune launched early experiments in urban aesthetics.

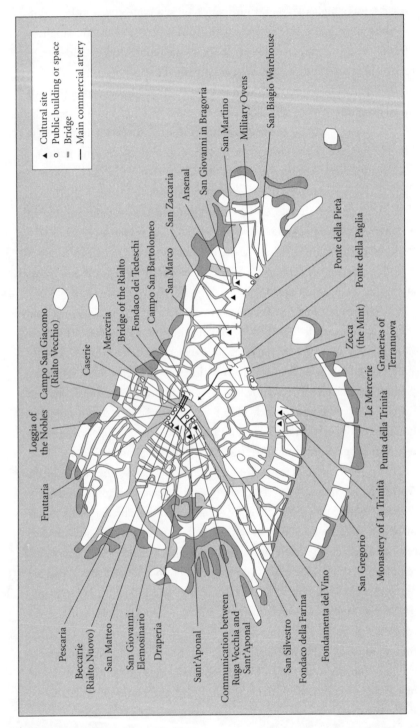

Public Buildings and Facilities

Those two prime sites, chosen for their economic and political importance, served in many ways as test cases for the entire process of managing public space.[49] In later years the communal authorities, increasingly echoed in official discourse, worked to extend that policy and those principles of order and beauty to all of the public domain.

A variety of urban magistracies staffed by a sizable corps of public officials were charged with applying the commune's directives and decisions in the various quarters of the city. The officials of the Piovego were responsible for oversight of the waters and for the public domain; the Signori di Notte supervised works projects regarding streets and bridges and provided fire protection; *capisestiere* took care of water distribution and street cleaning in their sections of the city. All of these magistracies had jurisdiction regarding public order; above all, they had a common aim of imposing a new control over space.[50]

We need to guard against the mirage of Venetian insularity and not exaggerate Venice's accomplishments in this realm. Towns and cities throughout Italy of the communes acted in a broad variety of ways to further urban development. Tutelage of the city arose everywhere. It was expressed in prestigious enterprises, monumental programs, and the realization of great collective works—palaces and squares, fortifications and fountains—but it was also expressed on a more daily basis by improvements in the system of streets or in regulations regarding public health. Officials were delegated and considerable sums allocated as communal councils in Perugia, Siena, or Orvieto passed decrees and decisions, devoting a considerable portion of their deliberations to public works. These were public times, then, and the effect on the urban setting was considerable.[51] A glance at the overall chronology shows a conjunction of various elements, among them an increase in both population and wealth that continued without interruption at least until the end of the thirteenth century. I might add that the political situation in Italy was in many ways unique and that the powerful free towns with communal regimes, especially the recently established popular regimes, were determined to leave their mark on space.

Nonetheless, Venice was different in two important ways. The first regards chronology: urban management in Venice was both precocious and strikingly continuous. That precocity was evident as early as the twelfth century by a first set of facts. In the late eleventh century, when its remaining members were elderly and there were no direct descendants, the Orio family, aristocratic owners of the first commercial installations on the Rialto island, solemnly deeded the family lands and the buildings on them to the city.[52] The act drawn up to sanction this gift calls this space a "market." In the decades that followed, the role of the Rialto and its powers of attraction became firmly established when the offices of the economic magistracies and the structures indispensable for financial exchanges moved there.[53]

Piazza San Marco also underwent extensive changes. The Ducal Palace was built in the 820s, when Agnello Participazio became doge. Built on the *brolo* (garden) and fruit orchard of the friary of San Zaccaria, it faced the lagoon basin. The basilica of San Marco was constructed behind the palace, away from the water. For many years these two monuments conditioned the history of the central city. Narrative sources make a point of describing the successive reconstructions of both the palace and the basilica under various doges—Pietro I Orseolo (976–78), Domenico Contarini (1043–71), and Sebastiano Ziani (1172–78). They also note new buildings and landmarks that established an order of importance in space: the Ospizio Orseolo, the Campanile (a construction that served as a lighthouse as much as it did as a bell tower and was always a symbolic high point on the landscape),[54] and the buildings of the Procuratie, the offices of the prestigious magistrates who served as administrators of the basilica and the island of San Marco. By the mid-twelfth century a vast public space had already been created thanks to projects to fill in the basin (which, according to tradition, had formerly reached the base of the tower) and the small canals that interrupted the line of the quay at the edge of the basin.[55] Changes made under Sebastiano Ziani enlarged that space, which was still judged to be insufficient, and modified the morphology of the square. The Rio Batario, a small waterway that barred extension of the space to the west, was filled in; the church of San Geminiano, which had stood "in the middle of the square," was demolished and rebuilt at the end of the square.[56] Every year, on the Sunday after Easter, the doge led a procession to implore divine pardon for these sacrilegious changes. When the church of San Teodoro, an ecclesiastical building north of the original basilica, was demolished in 1071 to permit the enlargement of San Marco, this move, along with the relocation of San Geminiano to the edge of the square, simplified the religious landscape of the square, focusing attention on the glorification of St. Mark the Evangelist.

The last obstacle to the development of the Piazza was eliminated when the Rio Batario was filled in. Other works were undertaken involving the Ducal Palace, which lost its fortress look, and the Procuratie. This made it possible to erect two tall columns brought back from Constantinople at the edge of the basin, where they created an idealized meeting place between land and water.[57] Doge Ziani, whose wealth was proverbial, was probably interested in assuring his own prestige and that of his house when he ordered and financed these projects.[58] In any event, the enlarged and embellished open space of Piazza San Marco, probably inspired by the open spaces of Constantinople, was exceptional for a Western city of the late twelfth century.[59]

Also in the late twelfth century, the Arsenal, the public shipyard, was founded on the eastern edge of the city.[60] It soon became increasingly active. Moreover, its founding had a lasting influence on the urban landscape of Venice. Once the conquest of the marshy eastern edges of the Castello quarter had been launched, such projects were pursued resolutely. With the new century, public power made its way deeper and deeper into the urban fabric of Venice as communal initiatives intensified. It has been shown that in the name of "common utility" those initiatives radically changed the morphology of the city and its customs.

Continuity is always cited as one of the outstandingly original features of Venice. Here as elsewhere, the demographic and economic hard times of the latter fourteenth century interrupted public construction and suspended regulatory efforts. When the city returned to urban improvement, all the old dispositions were reactivated. The first thing the authorities did was to make sure that the old laws were observed; then new texts were promulgated to complete and refine the first prescriptive apparatus. At the same time, land-reclamation projects began anew, and the campaign to conquer additional terrain picked up again exactly where it had left off six or seven decades earlier. The only difference was that in the late fifteenth century the state, which previously had provided funds as a silent partner, increased its own control, taking a direct role in managing the two large projects at the city's edge, reclamation of the marshy ground and the creation of building lots in the areas of Sant'Andrea della Zirada and Sant'Antonio.[61] A similar continuity can be seen in the improvement and upkeep of streets and waterways and in the management of public space. Work began anew on bridges and wharves, in the port area, in the market, and at the Arsenal, reaching a steady pace and a broad distribution during the latter half of the fifteenth century.

That rapid pace slowed toward the end of the fifteenth century, but some large-scale projects signaled a new surge in urban renewal[62] that ushered in sweeping achievements during the long dogeships of Leonardo Loredan (1501–21) and Andrea Gritti (1523–38).[63] Many of these projects involved the central areas of San Marco and the Rialto.

A new structure, the Clock Tower, designed by Mauro Coducci, was built where the major pedestrian axis of the Mercerie opened into Piazza San Marco. It took nearly four years to build the tower. A row of houses had to be demolished to clear the necessary space, and when the tower had been built, its decoration required time, the work of many artisans, and large amounts of money. The archives tell us just how much was paid to the carpenters, the painters, the gilders, and the other workers. As public texts proudly state, the tower, with its angels, giants, and stars, not to mention the Virgin and Child and the winged lion, was intended to be the most beautiful in Italy.[64] The old public clock in the market of the Rialto continued to strike the hours and define the working day, but the Clock Tower in Piazza San Marco expressed the magnificence of Venice, offering a continuous show staged for both Venetians and visitors. Next, Coducci constructed the Procuratie Vecchie, a building continued by Bartolomeo Bon and Guglieno Bergamasco. As for the Rialto, the market underwent sweeping renovation after a fire in 1514 that the texts describe as particularly catastrophic. Work to complete the Procuratie in San Marco began in 1511; the restructuring of the Fabbriche Vecchie, the market building at the Rialto, began after the fire, with designs by Scarpagnino. Both projects continued for some time.[65] The decades between 1495 and 1525 were marked by many urban-renewal projects and architectural improvements.

Work continued unabated. Jacopo Sansovino respected the traditional duality, working in both major city centers, where he created some of the major monuments of sixteenth-century Venice.[66] Sansovino's projects at San Marco included the Loggetta (1537–40), the Libreria Vecchia (completed after his death), and, at the edge of the basin, the Mint (or Zecca, 1536). At the Rialto he built the Fabbriche Nuove.[67] Another series of beautification projects was launched at the end of the sixteenth century with the Procuratie

Nuove of Vicente Scamozzi and Baldassare Longhena, the prisons of San Marco, and the Rialto bridge, supervised by Antonio da Ponte.

In the early sixteenth century urban renewal was the order of the day. Projects and work sites were many, and new modes of architectural expression were introduced in the lagoon. Still, as was always the case in Venice, continuity and fidelity to tradition mitigated the effects of *novitas*. Magnificent decor was emphasized, a clearer hierarchy of importance was imposed on the city's central spaces, and the spaces themselves were more clearly defined, but the basic urban structure of Venice and the balance between the city's two centers remained unchanged.

Continuity is incontestable, but how are we to explain it? The nature of the Venetian political regime counts for much here. Myth, against which we always need to be on guard, tended to disguise history and hide tensions, rivalries, and crises under a revised, perfectly smooth narrative. One fact remains, however: the great ruptures that troubled the history of the other Italian cities and defined the periods of their history were unknown in Venice. The political organism changed, but it evolved smoothly and empirically, without destroying anything, as power was transferred from one council to another in a series of gentle shifts that all worked to reinforce the structure of the state. Elsewhere, successive forms of power found it necessary to mark the city with their presence, modeling the territory, influencing the city's aesthetic, and working, at least in a few central places, to create a symbolic geography that would legitimate and sacralize the power structure. Political interventionism was not exclusive to Venice, of course, but elsewhere it usually occurred in the form of rupture. Thus, in many Italian cities we can follow the shift, employing varying solutions with equally varied success, from communal urbanism to princely urbanism. Later it was up to the prince to promote large-scale public works. Anyone interested in the history of Italy cannot help but be struck by the abundance of studies devoted to princely construction projects, in particular their own palaces in Urbino, Mantua, and Ferrara but also those in Pienza, Sabbioneta, or Vigevano. The list is long, and it includes palace-cities, real and ideal cities, utopias, and aborted projects.[68] The number and the richness of these initiatives explain the diversity of the studies devoted to them, which sometimes emphasize the aesthetic and ideological side of the projects and at other times take a more functional approach to investigate their political dimension and the process of constructing the princely state. What such studies have in common, however, is a desire to describe the forms that power took as they analyze the way space was shaped or the style and the architecture of monuments. Space is, in fact, the language of domination, a language that justifies politics as the power to distribute an urban order as a projection of the social order to be created.

We find none of these successive mutations in Venice because by the late thirteenth century the nature of the political regime had become crystallized. Admittedly, the composition of the first circle of governing families changed with the passing centuries, as did the balance among the councils. But until Venice lost its independence its institutions were not radically modified. Places and the memory of place continued to symbolize a Republic that thought of itself as "constant." No political organism could ever claim to exert a decisive influence on art or urbanism in Venice. It was always the task of the principal governing assembly, first the Great Council, then the Senate, to execute the architectural projects that the majority had selected. Finally, an ideology of government further reinforced Venice's concern for continuity. Duration, seen as a desideratum, and an explicit respect for previous modes of governance explain the Venetian attachment to tradition and to the culture of the city's origins. Conservation, restoration, and refashioning were long the rule. The Byzantine portion of the Ducal Palace did not disappear until a fire gutted it in the fifteenth century. The fire of 1514 at the Rialto swept away the buildings that had been erected there. Even fire did not authorize elimination of what had gone before. There were several rival plans for the reconstruction of the market at the Rialto, but a persuasive reason for accepting Scarpagnino's project was that he respected the history and the nature "of the place." Venetians deliberately chose to maintain their ties with the architectural past and rebuilt in coherence with it. It is thus understandable that Palladio's project was rejected and the portion of the Ducal Palace damaged by a fire in 1577 was rebuilt in a Gothic style that blended with the facade, with its large Gothic bays, and with the highly ornate and very sculptural Porta della Carta (1438–43).[69]

Because Venetian power as it was constituted in the Middle Ages or the beginning of the modern age derived its primary legitimacy from the city's duration and conservation the power structure showed great respect for the sedimentation of history contained in every individual space. As a result, necessary reforms and adjustments always had to take into consideration what existed and what remained. In Venice the transformations of the Middle Ages were not an isolated episode; even less were they forgotten or combated. They were a heritage to be assumed, a continuity to be preserved. This is the first of Venice's unique features.

There was a second one, however. I have noted that rather than accepting the postulate of Venice's irreducible difference, we need to adopt a comparatist point of view. That approach enables us to establish that overall Venice's urban policy resembled the policies of other cities of Italy in the age of the communes. Public works in Venice were utterly unique, however, where the city's ongoing efforts to improve its site and preserve a balance in the lagoon were concerned. Many Italian cities of the communal age had a genuine policy of hydraulics: a growing urban population needed to be supplied with drinking water.[70] Often both land and people required protection against costly floods. The many uses of water also implied a need to make considerable changes in the hydrographic network, especially on the plains of the Po Valley. Some cities used canals as a complex system of defenses, but in later times their function became more strictly economic. In the case of Venice, however, problems related to the city's site required much more sweeping action. It was not enough to control the water supply and enable consumers to share it. In a lagoon environment in constant evolution, Venetians confronted singularly active and always hostile natural forces. Mastery of those forces was a necessity: life in the lagoons was only possible at the price of constant labors and incessant maintenance operations.

Hence my hypothesis is that the public authorities in Venice were undoubtedly more interventionist than their counterparts elsewhere. Once again, the ways in which memory reconstructs the facts have worked to present the creation of Venice as a historical occurrence accomplished by a founding and uncontested pact between a community and its leaders. According to the chronicles, political initiative played a determinant role from the very beginning. The doges (Agnello and Orso Partecipazio and Piero Tribuno) are viewed as having launched the peopling of the area, guiding and advising the population, from the time the community moved to the Rialto islands. A first magistracy charged with "amplifying the land, reclaiming the lagoons, containing the exuberance of the marshlands that formed the insalubrious setting of this site" is supposed to have been instituted under the first Partecipazio doge. Hence the political power was seen as having control over the land, the water, and the genesis of the city from the beginning of Venetian history.[71] It should not be necessary to point out that these official versions of the history of Venice are deceptive simplifications. The first traces of public action came later.

It does seem to me, however, that the public authorities in Venice intervened with more firmness and consistency than elsewhere. It may indeed be true that the history of the Venetian state encouraged not only the success but also the tenacity and longevity of an interventionist policy, but first there was the environment of the lagoon, along with the constraints and the challenges that it imposed on development and on the ordinary life of a populous and an active urban area. If the city was to respond to those challenges, and if the survival of the community was to be assured, collective discipline had to be imposed, intervention had to be continuous, and Venetians had to reflect on their milieu and their space. This, then, is the second particularity of Venice. It enables us to pierce some of the mystery and understand how the Venetians managed to construct such a city.

These successes, much like a documentation that tends to emphasize the role of the state, must not lead us to yield to the common temptation of viewing urbanism as the product of public action alone.

And Private Initiative?

The communal government played a determinant role in urban transformation, but must we conclude that changes were the result of its will alone? We cannot deny the violence inherent in the grandiose public-works projects of the thirteenth and fourteenth centuries.[72] Expropriations and sweeping abrogations of ancient rights were required in order to open up passageways and knock down walls. A framework of coercion made of prohibitions and regulations shaped both the habitat and circulation within it. The archives reveal major property owners who were reticent or hostile and staunchly defended their holdings and their rights. Some of the wealthiest of these were engaged in developing real-estate strategies of their own, for example, in the profitable enterprise of creating building lots in the newly urbanized outlying quarters of the city. It is impossible to grasp the amplitude and the rapidity of the changes that occurred if we fail to take into account one often misunderstood fact: urban policy responded to social demand. How could anyone not understand the need for convenient communications or new means for bringing drinking water to a rapidly expanding city? How could anyone not see the urgent need to organize collective spaces and infrastructures in the port area or the market, at a time, after the Fourth Crusade, when the city was engaged in an accelerating commercial expansion? Many examples could be cited of improvements that were launched to meet new daily needs.

Support for such policies went much further, however, and in many cases organic changes in the form and structure of the city arose from a collaboration, not a rivalry, between the public and private spheres. Leaving aside the somewhat banal example of the creation of new lots, the history of urban expansion and of the settlement of new quarters provides obvious illustrations of this collaboration. Public works were often launched in response to demands by private citizens or to petitions from groups of neighbors who argued both their own "common utility" and "the honor of the city."[73] Above all, the history of the habitat, considered in the light of the dynamic of restorations or improvements, shows that private proprietors subscribed to the urban model suggested by the public prescriptions.[74] An analysis of building permits enables us to isolate periods in which there were waves of requests for modification of existing buildings, as opposed to more routine maintenance projects. Many of these concern requests to reconstruct walls in order to bring them into alignment with neighboring buildings. Such requests were always favorably received, even when the rectification called for a slight encroachment on public space. Moreover, the relative frequency of such projects confirms a generalized interest in rectilinear plotting that reflects the norms imposed by the commune in areas of recent land reclamation. Many other sorts of projects—installing rain gutters, doors, stairways, chimneys, or windows and their decorative surrounds—also required preliminary approval. Such requests came in waves, and once again permission was forthcoming. These and similar initiatives in the early decades of the fourteenth century present a picture of an active renewal of the housing stock of Venice. Thanks to the concerted efforts of the public authorities and private individuals, the criteria of a new urban organization that redefined aesthetics were realized not just in a few work sites in the center but throughout the city.

With the economic upturn of the fifteenth century, the archives reflect a feverish increase in construction that proves that the rhythm of work in the public and the private sectors was not necessarily discordant. Once again, building permits reflect renewed activity. Moreover, we can see in the brisk pace of the permissions granted, primarily to aristocratic proprietors, a desire to translate equal wealth into monumental terms and to show equal status and prestige through a harmony in adjacent structures.

This landscape merits a closer look. In the fourteenth and fifteenth centuries a number of wealthy Venetian lineages chose the Gothic style when they remodeled the family palace—or, more accurately, the *cà*, given that the texts of the time reserve the terms *palatium* and *palazzo* for the Ducal Palace, the residence of the doge and the seat of government.[75] Prominent among these was the family house of the Contarini family, the famous Cà d'Oro, built on the Grand Canal in the parish of Santa Sofia between 1421 and 1440 by the Bon brothers, who gave it a carefully calculated asymmetrical sculpted facade. Even today a visitor traveling by boat along the Grand Canal, the principal waterway of Venice, is impressed by the number of palatial residences that were built at that time.[76] Some two hundred palaces that remain standing essentially unchanged, with their original decor and structure, bear witness to both that building boom and the long triumph of the Gothic style as it was adapted to the Venetians' preference for color, chromatic variation, busy decoration, and fresco.[77] Architectural conservatism preserved those forms up to the final decades of the fifteenth century, with only such variations as a smaller courtyard, the elimination of the loggia, or an internal staircase connecting the floors to replace the earlier external one.[78] Although these houses had a secondary entrance opening onto the network of *calli*, their principal entrance was on the canal: they breathed over the water, and their ground floors contained storage areas opening onto the canals, where merchandise floated past. Venetian palaces of this period display little interest in perspective: none are isolated blocks, independent of neighboring constructions. All were constructed on the traditional L plan, which tightly connected them with the city's dual communications network, or else in the newer C shape, which linked them with the urban fabric.[79] Venice had no houses like the Palazzo Strozzi in Florence, audaciously detached from nearby buildings, using its imposing mass to dominate an entire city block. Venetian palaces formed a line of buildings more or less identical in shape and size. Their Gothic windows, often grouped in threes, give a rhythm to facades that overlook entire reaches of the Grand Canal, thus creating a certain harmony in spite of the differences in their ornamentation.

It is difficult to dissociate the evolution of urban morphology and decor in Venice from the aspirations and the culture of the major Venetian families. The houses of noble families long reflected the notion that a certain *mediocritas* was seemly.[80] What was true of the political society of Venice was equally true of its architecture: no patrician *cà* should too visibly outclass the others. The guidance of the state was firmly in the hands of a circle of families who organized the division of power and wealth among themselves but who also were quick to shatter any thought of establishing personal power. Hence the architectural order of the city faithfully translated the complex relations that connected families, society, and the state. That order long continued to have its partisans. In the early sixteenth century, Doge Leonardo Loredan criticized the monumental quality of certain aristocratic dwellings that were undergoing renovation or reconstruction, but, paradoxically, he followed the newer trends when it came to remodeling his own palace.[81] One of his successors, Andrea Gritti, also condemned what he considered to be the ostentation of Cà Foscari and Cà Loredan, both on the Grand Canal.

In fact, however, both the old style and the old ideology were contested.[82] Mauro Coducci had opened the breach to outside influences in the late fifteenth century.[83] Jacopo Sansovino followed Coducci, and the strong, well-balanced architectural works constructed while he was *proto de supra* (superintendent of public works) put his mark on the city and its central areas. Styles in domestic architecture changed as well. The Corner family was the first to build a palace in the new style, and although it does not follow the floor plan typical of the Renaissance palace, its dimensions broke with the old harmony. The structure of family houses also changed when the space that had been given over to commercial functions in the old Venetian *casa-fondaco* was eliminated, allowing the first-floor water entrance and the vestibule, the *androne,* to become truly monumental. By the time the Dolfin and Grimani families built new palaces, Venetian particularism had ceded to the Renaissance, somewhat late and in a style acclimatized to the lagoon.

Even before noble Venetian families accepted a change of style and began to build in new ways, notable changes in both style and equipment took place in the dwellings of more ordinary people throughout the fifteenth century. Emulation undoubtedly played a role in such changes, as homeowners eagerly copied their neighbors, hastening to imitate their remodeling projects. Competition had invaded the realm of appearances, resulting in richer, more beautiful, and more ornate dwellings. Honor, no longer a value reserved to the few, now found expression in buildings endowed with certain obligatory ornaments or conveniences. As a consequence, the urban structure of Venice was completed in the fifteenth century by thousands of construction projects that usually escape notice because they were circumscribed, left no trace in archival documents, and created no stir. They established a degree of freedom in the morphology of the housing unit.

The theatrical aspects of Venice did not have to wait for the noble architecture of Pietro Lombardo, Scarpagnino, or Sansovino. Urban construction in the sixteenth century worked quite deliberately to create a theatrical setting in the central areas of the city, but even before that time a creative logic was at work in the governing bodies and in the minds of individuals to further the physical and ideological emergence of a city destined to be beautiful. The public authorities expressed an interest in urban aesthetics by proclaiming the necessity of the *pulcher* and the *ornatus* in their projects. That interest in aesthetics did not cause them to go so far as to get rid of the tangle of booths and stands that crowded the Piazzetta in the late fifteenth century, and at the Rialto it encountered resistance from old habits and from a disorderly system of retail sales and secondhand commerce. Furthermore, for some time the central authorities concentrated on the center of the city, abandoning its margins to industry and to the poor and their shacks. Still, as early as the fourteenth century Piazza San Marco was generally thought of as a stage where the entire city was on display.[84] Private citizens were gradually drawn into a dynamic of building projects that allowed them, each according to his means, to manifest wealth and status and to participate in the celebration of appearances that the city as a whole was organizing on a grand scale. The urban spectacle gained in order and beauty, perfecting its play of appearance through vast numbers of operations on the scale of a street, a canal, or a block of houses.

Any attempt to reduce the history of the relations between the public and the private in Venice to this largely harmonious interaction would, of course, do an injustice to the real political and social scene. Similarly, we must not minimize the effect of all the aspects of the morphology of building in Venice that evolved autonomously, escaping public control despite all the government's efforts. Moreover, the history of the house in Venice was also strongly influenced by complex patrimonial strategies that differed according to the type of wealth the family possessed and to geographical location.[85] Finally, although the timing of developments in the public and the private sectors was not discordant, neither was it strictly parallel. These are all factors that should be kept in mind because they affected all urban structures.

These consideration, important as they are, do not alter the conclusion that I would like to propose. What was set into motion was a culture of the city, of its forms, and of its customs. Moreover, that culture seems to have been widely shared in Venice, all the more so because in Venice as elsewhere the beauty of sacred buildings was intended to celebrate more than the glory of God.

"So Many Stately Churches in the Sea"

Beauty could also be mobilized in support of the jealously guarded honor of the commune and the collectivity; it served as a weapon in an inter-city war of vanities.[86] A good many churches were built in an appeal, characteristic of Italian cities, to "civic religion."[87] Such constructions were not only grandiloquent symbols on the part of the urban community that had raised them of its intent to renew the epiphany of its original pact with God; like other architectural achievements and political successes, but on a different scale, they were also intended to reflect the power and prestige of the city and the need of its governing class for affirmation and recognition.

I shall not evoke the splendor of San Marco and its various reconstructions through the centuries. It should suffice to think of the tens of churches that formed the nuclei of the earliest island communities, some acting as bridgeheads or relay stations for urban expansion, others standing detached on the edges of the city, protecting and sacralizing those outlying areas. All of those churches were gradually rebuilt, embellished, and decorated. Their architectural history is well known. Some of them—Santa Eufemia, San Polo, Santa Sofia, and San Nicolò dei Mendicoli—were built on the basilica plan. Others, fewer in number, have a layout in the form of a Greek cross, a

Churches and Scuole

Santa Maria Gloriosa dei Frari
San Rocco
Santa Croce
Sant'Andrea della Zirada
Santa Maria Maggiore
Santa Marta
San Nicolò dei Mendicoli
Santa Maria dei Carmini
Santa Eufemia della Giudecca
Santa Maria della Carità
Church of the Redentore
San Marco
San Zaccaria
San Domenico
Sant'Antonio
Santa Elena
Santa Anna
San Pietro di Castello
San Francesco della Vigna
Santi Giovanni e Paolo
San Giovanni Grisostomo
Santa Maria dei Crociferi
Santa Caterina dei Sacchi
Santa Maria della Misericordia
San Giovanni Evangelista
San Gregorio

model that was repeated, in fidelity to a certain style and ambiance, in some Renaissance constructions, among them San Giovanni Grisostomo, Coducci's last building project. Roman stylistic elements and borrowings from Arabian art were grafted onto these Byzantine and exarchal traditions;[88] after 1300, Gothic influences began to dominate, for example, at Santi Giovanni e Paolo and Santa Maria Gloriosa dei Frari. Earlier elements are still visible in the structure of the church of San Zaccaria in spite of Coducci's contributions to its rebuilding, proving once again that in Venice stylistic renewal was infinitely respectful of the past, even in a church considered to be an outstanding example of the religious architecture of the Renaissance. Every change in urban aesthetics corresponded, unsurprisingly, to a wave of church construction and reconstruction. Two examples from the period in which a neo-Byzantine style prevailed are San Michele in Isola near Murano and Santa Maria dei Miracoli (1481–89). For a later date, one might cite Palladio's church of San Giorgio Maggiore or the Church of the Redentore.

Harmony was thus the rule, and it worked to the benefit of the city and its image. I do not deny the existence of conflict in the history of the construction and management of the urban organism. There were many clashes, and they went beyond a simple, mechanical confrontation between the general interest and particular interests. Organizing a city is a process that secretes exclusions, encounters resistance, and elicits cultures and practices of opposition. The Venetian model was no exception to the rule. Stevedores and dockhands recently arrived from the Padua countryside or the mountains of Friuli, workers in the lumberyards on the edge of the city, or oarsmen living in cramped quarters in miserable huts near the port obviously did not have the same vision or the same experience of the city as the Foscaris or the Grimanis, who ran their businesses authoritatively from the city center.

Still, it seems that a "theater of the imaginary" functioned, almost necessarily, more intensely in the lagoon than elsewhere and that it created essential solidarities among the actor-spectators of that theater. The struggle to settle and survive at the heart of the lagoons was constantly renewed. The awareness of living in a unique city may have been produced by the dominant culture, but it was broadly shared. I draw a hypothesis from this: in Venice, *la terra* was more than an abstraction. For a Venetian led by trade to

Constantinople, Alexandria, or Bruges, it was not just a community of men and houses, a recollection of a landscape, a history, and an identity, viewed with a tinge of nostalgia. Above all, and for all Venetians, *la terra* was primarily the unstable soil that human labor had solidified through enormous effort. It was the bricks hoisted and laid in the many work sites; it was the marble, porphyry, and serpentine facings and ornamentation made possible by wealth from commerce. In its deepest sense, *la terra* was a refuge that everyone—the rich and powerful and the rest—knew was precarious.[89]

A WORLD OF PERILS: ANGUISH AND REACTION

The lagoon was always a fragile environment, and that fragility has never been conjured away, neither yesterday nor today. Worse, during the fifteenth century, in the decades of Venice's greatest triumph, when the image of the city's power radiated everywhere, that fragility seemed to increase.

Then as now, the existence and the very survival of Venice depended on something bigger than mastery of the environment of the city proper. The destiny of the urban complex was inseparable from that of the lagoon basin, a fragile milieu in constant evolution. If we are to understand the history of that evolution, we first need to consider some of the basic facts of lagoon geography.

Toward a History of the Environment

The Venetian basin is the largest ensemble of lagoons on the northern Adriatic coast.[90] A remnant of the vast complex that once lay between the Po and the Izonzo, these large stretches of salt or brackish water are protected and nearly completely separated from the sea by a chain of sandy littoral islands, the *lidi*. Their waters are renewed, however, by the flow of tides that penetrate the barrier islands through shifting passageways that Venetians called *porti*, where the waters of the lagoon and the sea meet. At a relatively late date these channels were reduced to three: the southernmost at Chioggia and, closer to Venice, the Porto di Malamocco and the Porto del Lido. A few areas of low-lying land emerge above this flat aquatic landscape of unrelieved horizontality. These are the *barene*, wetlands covered with a unique vegetation that rise only a few centimeters above the water and are flooded by the highest tides. There are also small islands and miniature archipelagos, probably formed by alluvial deposits from the rivers emptying into the lagoon basin, that have gradually been consolidated and enlarged by human labor.

This entire ecosystem has been, and remains, subject to ceaseless transformation due to the combined action of the sea, the rivers, and human intervention. The Venetian lagoon of today is profoundly different from its counterpart of the final centuries of the Middle Ages.

One seemingly surprising fact should be stressed: this milieu, far from being some sort of intangible given or even a system that changes extraordinarily slowly, is in constant motion and is being transformed by antagonistic forces not easily mastered by human efforts. For one thing, the sea level varies; for another, throughout this zone the ground is sinking under the weight of fluvial deposits. At certain times, when the phenomenon of subsidence combines with a temporary rise in sea level, the result is the familiar threat that water will cover the emergent portions of land. The tides at the northern end of the Adriatic are higher than anywhere else in the Mediterranean. This means that the tidewaters that penetrate the openings in the littoral islands and flow along the channels in the lagoon to the canals of the city set the pace of life in Venice. The tides renew and purify the waters of the lagoon, thus guaranteeing the survival of the lagoon basin.

When unusually high tides are joined with heavy rain and strong winds, in particular the famous sirocco, a southeast wind that blows water into the lagoon, the result is the *acqua alta,* the flood tide that temporarily invades the low-lying portions of the city. This exceptionally high tide can also cover low-lying islands in the lagoon, undermine the shore, wash away protective walls, and submerge parts of the littoral islands, which are already subjected to daily attack from swells, waves, and marine erosion.

At one moment in the early twelfth century the *lido* of Malamocco was partially flooded; in the mid-thirteenth century the littoral barrier of Sant'Erasmo was breached. If the city's littoral defenses were to break down completely, the sea would flood in and sweep away everything in its path. The lagoon and Venice would both disappear. There was another danger, however: river-borne alluvium filling in the lagoon with silt would also condemn the lagoon to an irreversible decline. Another threat was that the *lidi,* which were constantly being reinforced by alongshore currents dropping their burden of sand, might form a solid barrier. If the *porti* should be sanded in, the lagoon basin behind them would be isolated from the sea, and it too would soon fill in.

This fragile equilibrium clearly demonstrates how high the stakes were for life amid the lagoons. Without public works to safeguard that balance, the site of Venice would have been condemned.

Workers in the Lagoon

The people of the lagoon soon sought to act upon the various elements of their complex milieu. Their labors began early and were constantly kept up, or nearly so. The history of the consolidation of the littoral islands, a process that continued uninterrupted up to the completion of the levees and walls of the *murazzi* in 1782, clearly demonstrates that from the fourteenth to the eighteenth century political powers in Venice continually sponsored public-works projects, spending considerable sums of money. Hundreds of pages in the archives of the Salt Office, the magistracy responsible for the maintenance of those outer defenses, chronicle an almost uninterrupted and widely varied series of works projects during the fifteenth century alone. A storm opens a breach in the littoral barrier and it is quickly closed; elsewhere, construction, restoration, and consolidation are needed. Embankments are built as buffers and later raised. On the sea side, stones are laid along the channel bottom to take the direct assault of the waves. In a never-ending ballet cargo ships bring stone blocks from the Dalmatian coast to reinforce the breakwaters. Elsewhere double and triple ranks of pilings form palisades that stabilize the shoreline. Contracts granted one after the other in the later fifteenth century give a detailed account of the entrepreneurs and crews of specialized workers who were commissioned, always at public expense, to construct these stone defenses.[91]

For some time, Venice's only solution to the problem of alluvial deposits in the lagoon, because it did not control the upper courses of the rivers, was to build dikes. A first overall plan to defend the lagoon was drawn up in 1324 after a number of studies and provisory arrangements. It called for diverting all the water in the Brenta River to an outlet far from the Rialto basin, which would thus be isolated and protected (according to the plan) by a series of dikes.[92] The aim of this project was to prevent currents of fresh water from entering the lagoon, hence to keep the lagoon—the port in particular—from silting up. Later, Venice's conquest of its Terraferma gave Venetian engineers access to the mainland shores of the lagoons and enabled them to devise more radical projects for diverting the rivers. During the second half of the fifteenth century, whether to change the course of the Brenta was a matter of constant debate as deposits of river mud became an increasing threat, especially at Punta Santa Marta. A number of projects were launched, and a more radical diversion of the Brenta was eventually carried out, thus shifting the menace of sedimentation to the south of the lagoon, a move that aroused new fears and elicited other questions.

Genuine changes took place during those decades of the fifteenth century. The lagoon environment had always been described as a positive space, something like a protective cocoon that guaranteed life. For centuries the history of a Venice in the course of construction displayed a dynamism attested by events as well as by repetitious discourses. Until the fourteenth century the vocabulary of public acts had been that of a young, active, all-conquering city. Despite technological difficulties, a few inevitable failures, and the heavy financial burden of public works, the texts reflect optimism. During the fifteenth century, however, that optimism seems to have faltered. From the time of the settlement of Rialto, conquest of the land had been the dominant note; now water began to be seen as a menace. Vocabulary evolves, and Venice is described as threatened by water and by the milieu out of which it had emerged. From then on, the history of Venice becomes that of a place of life, providentially constructed by human labor but subject to aggression from a death force in an ongoing, daily struggle. The mechanisms of a rhetoric of the city in danger were put into place one by one.

The first treatise on the lagoon, written in the latter half of the fifteenth century, is a clear indication of increased thought being given to questions of hydrology and a more acute sensitivity to problems related to the city's site.[93] The author of this treatise was part of the elite that had taken over the new bureaucracy of the Venetian state. Marco Corner had for a time been charged with oversight of the city's wood supplies, and in that connection he had made a systematic inspection tour of the north end of the lagoon basin and of the rivers used to transport wood to Venice. Later he was twice elected to the Water Commission, where his responsibilities included the large project, just begun, to divert the Brenta.[94] One can sense his growing competence from his communications and reports. This nobleman became a specialist in hydrography and then wrote a history of the lagoon in which he proposed an entire series of works projects, arguing their urgent need because of the serious threat of river deposits.

It might be objected that this text was largely propaganda for a systematic program to divert rivers,[95] but an examination of the public acts of the time reveals a picture just as somber as the one that Corner paints. He writes deploring the encroachments of sand in the passageways through the littoral islands and the irremediable advance of marshlands and the "dead" lagoon. Councils and the pertinent magistracies debated the same dangers, and public texts portray a rising tide of perils.

The situation of the port illustrates the seriousness of the problem. The outlet to the sea closest to Venice, the Porto del Lido at San Nicolò, had always operated under difficult natural conditions. In the fourteenth century, several works projects (with contradictory aims) had attempted to deepen the passageway and increase the flow of water.[96] During the latter half of the fifteenth century, however, works projects succeeded one another without pause. The engineers hoped that by narrowing the channel at Malamocco through the use of submerged wooden caissons and rafts, they could increase the rate of water circulation through the Porto di San Nicolò. Their efforts were in vain. The usual palliatives (e.g., unloading part of the cargo onto smaller barges) no longer sufficed, and larger ships were diverted to the Porto di Malamocco, farther south.

Silting continued apace; the channels were getting shallower. The living lagoon was shrinking to the profit of a "dead" lagoon no longer subject to tides. In 1505 Piero Sambo, an engineer, attempted to measure the frightening progression of the phenomenon in the time since his father had directed a lagoon project.[97] Where the water had previously stood fourteen feet deep, there was now only three feet of water; where the salt water had stood three, four, five, or six feet deep, there were meadows, fields, and pasture lands.[98] The urban canal system was threatened as well. The canals lacked water, and fetid air and noxious miasmas rose from their silted channels. Decay lay in wait. Text after text describes the danger and states that it was increasing. Marshlands and canebrakes besieged the city, nibbling away at the lagoon and moving toward the built-up areas. Even within the city itself grass grew in the *rii,* and Venice faced the threat of being stranded high and dry. The same expressions recur dozens of times as all the texts speak of mud, silt, garbage, filth, and "corruption." The senators declared that not only the canals but the city itself was in danger. Dredging operations were carried out regularly.[99] These were still done by hand, or rather by the shovelful, once the waterway had been dammed off and drained. The Grand Canal required the use of machines, as demonstrated by requests for "privileges" (an early form of patents) for their manufacture that have been conserved. Behind the cascade of works projects and the recourse to technological innovation lay the inexorable fact that silting was accelerating.

A final series of events corroborates Corner's treatise, confirming his description of the northern lagoon and its morphological transformation. An abundant documentation enables us to follow, almost step by step, the changes that occurred in the landscape of the lagoon basin, in particular the terrible degradation around Torcello. Until the fourteenth century the mud flats that marked the edge of the mainland had advanced in only limited fashion, but when the Dese River changed course to flow directly into the lagoon, it had devastating consequences.[100] Sedimentation increased as more fresh water poured into the lagoon, bringing not only silt but also a rise in halophilic plants. The population of the northern end of the lagoon gradually declined, thanks to the deleterious effects of the invading marshlands and the increase in fresh water, where the anopheles mosquito flourished, bringing on a genuine wave of deaths. The archipelago of Costanziaca was the first area to be affected: its population was wiped out in the early fifteenth century. Next came the islands of Ammiana, where mud invaded the pasture lands and orchards, the bell towers collapsed, and little remained save a landscape of ruins surrounded by marshes and a few lingering stands of bushes. Last came the islets of Torcello, which had already been ravaged by a longstanding demographic decline and structural economic difficulties.[101]

The ecosystem was thus profoundly and widely degraded. In the face of these perils, Venice, the triumphant community that for centuries had pursued the conquest of its space and worked to create an urban order, admitted its anxiety. Behind the image of the admirable city seated amid its friendly and protecting waters lurked fears and problems. The equilibrium of its watery environment had to be preserved, but council and magistrates repeatedly declared that such an enterprise, although necessary, faced multiple obstacles. How are we to interpret this discrepancy?

Can we speak of the failure and deficiencies of public action and of technological hesitation? Or does this defeat show humanity's inability to dominate its milieu and, in the last analysis, its submission to the vicissitudes of nature? In the latter view, despite concerted efforts and enormous numbers of works projects, the most powerful city-state in the West met with a clear limit to its entrepreneurial capacities and its success in managing the ecosystem.

Three factors of unequal importance influenced the long history of these efforts. The first of these was obviously the hydrographic problem. As we have seen, until Venice extended its dominion over portions of the mainland, Venetians were reduced to a passive role: their lagoon received alluvial deposits from rivers that they could not control, but they also reaped the benefit of operations carried out by their neighbors.[102] Technological limitations hindered improvements to the site as well. Work on the Brenta in 1452 was carried out with extremely humble means. The Venetians' stubborn efforts to shore up their outer defenses on the barrier islands show that despite repairs made at regular intervals, the city was condemned to incessant projects to rebuild breakwaters that were soon destroyed by the sea, only to be rebuilt with an equal regularity by human labor.

Knowledge of the milieu and its multiple problems progressed only slowly. We have to wait for the fifteenth century to see the beginnings of an attempt to understand the operations of nature. At that time Venetians turned more readily to the experience and the specialized knowledge of ship pilots, fishermen, and older men.[103] Some nobles who were called to serve on a commission charged with supervision of the dikes, ports, and canals or who were responsible for coordinating inquiries and reports began to take an interest in the problems of the lagoon. A pool of information was created. Reports, descriptions, and drawings began to be kept; archives were founded for the collection of the older provisions regarding hydrography and the lagoon. In the final third of the fifteenth century, when the election of the *savi* who served on the Water Commission became better regulated, that body could count on the support of permanent employees and technical personnel. The new commission even engaged and paid its own engineers.[104]

By the early sixteenth century the situation had changed considerably.

Henceforth the Venetian Signoria was capable of effective action. It had a pool of competent engineers, and it could call on the services of a group of entrepreneurs who specialized in hydraulics. A practical culture had gradually been formed. Debate continued to rage, however, and contradictory solutions to Venice's problems continued to be proposed. Above all, many projects proved useless or were poorly executed, and entire stretches of the basin were lost, victims of silt deposits and shallow water.

It is true that considerable obstacles awaited all human action. Indeed, how to achieve an ecological equilibrium in the lagoons remains uncertain to this day. Then as now, the requirements for the conservation of a fragile milieu were often in conflict with the demands and needs of a thickly populated, industrious city, a situation reflected in environmental legislation that vacillated between laxity and severity.

Such environmental problems were real; incontestably, they worsened in the fifteenth century. There are a number of reasons for the degradation of the lagoon. First, the lagoon environment follows its own timetable, and we can grasp its evolution only very imperfectly. Second, human intervention, although often inefficacious, was never neutral: if at times it was counterproductive, at other times it was disastrous. Finally, men took a heavy toll on their site, as convergent data in times of demographic upturn demonstrate. There was bitter competition for agricultural land on the shores of the mainland, overexploitation of the available resources disturbed the equilibrium of the lagoon, and Venetians became increasingly aware of pollution and unsanitary conditions in the city itself. Beyond doubt, however, the authorities exploited the ideological possibilities of these problems and anxieties, especially in the early fifteenth century.

A rhetoric of perils served a variety of ends. First, it legitimated increased governmental involvement in the management of resources and the maintenance of the ecosystem. It justified a radical reform of the administrative apparatus in which a long list of new offices replaced the old, medieval magistracies, by then in decline. It aimed at tightening solidarities among members of the lagoon community at a time when ties seemed to be slackening as urban expansion passed its peak. Finally, and principally, it conferred on Venetian politics the high charge of guaranteeing the conservation and continuity of the city. What was the principal message of discourse on the perils facing Venice? That it was up to the state to see to it that the city triumphed over adversity and emerged victorious from its face-to-face combat with time.

Thus, there was a certain ambivalence in the imaginary of Venice. On the one hand, the city's site in the middle of the water gave rise to an ideological operation displaying the image of a city constantly menaced, even attacked, by hostile waters. On the other hand, the narrative sources always presented the water surrounding Venice as protective, some commentators going so far as to prepare the way for an aphorism that became universal in later centuries, when the brackish waters of the lagoon were called the "saintly walls of the homeland."

It seems that throughout the history of Venice, there were phases in which the dynamism of the community was channeled and utilized in the name of an explicit "common good." It also seems that we must allow that political power used such means to resolve a good many tensions and conflicts to its own benefit. Anyone who has an interest in the history of building in Venice soon discovers at least two phases of this sort. First, there was the time of the land, a time of urban expansion and triumphant land reclamation. Then, beginning in the fifteenth century, there came what I shall call the time of the water, when greater attention was paid to the preservation of the site. The state tightened its grip as urban-renewal projects proliferated and were increasingly presented as urgent and necessary. Obviously, one can distinguish other phases centered on different goals or objects. The program of *renovatio urbis* launched under Doge Andrea Gritti—a "renewal" that concerned the urban setting just as much as it did institutions or representations—animated a central moment in the fashioning of Venetian identity.

This all took place during the "time of the water." The interpretation given by the community was that the overall precariousness of the site, combined with the difficulties of the fifteenth century, helped to make the city's existence even more miraculous. According to this interpretation, Venetian history reflected, on its own scale, the history of the relationship between man and the environment. It was an exemplary demonstration of how long it took, and how difficult it was, for humans to dominate the elements of nature. It also demonstrated, however, that since Venice existed in spite of all obstacles, the city had won the combat.

What conclusions can we draw? It is incontestable that attempts at hydraulic engineering were weak and included a number of mishaps. Resolve often slackened and gave way to declared impotence, or else the authorities opted for circumscribed and contradictory remedies that proved useless or positively harmful. On many occasions the city simply failed to act. Moreover, its choices were often political rather than technological. The central lagoon, that is, the waters around Venice, often received preferential protection. Council meetings were often rent by a bitter opposition between partisans of agricultural exploitation of the Terraferma and champions of the greater lagoon. How could the demands for a sweeping reclamation of the marshlands at the edge of the lagoon be reconciled with concern for a fragile aquatic equilibrium? Not until the first half of the sixteenth century were there any clear signs of a nascent water policy, and it was only in the seventeenth century that the first "macrohydrographic" operations were launched, eventually putting an end to the menace of the rivers and giving the lagoon basin its current configuration.[105]

The fact remains that many works projects were carried out during the period that interests us here. It is also true that the various parts of a complex system—the rivers, the chain of offshore islands, the *porti*, the marshlands, and the urban complex—slowly came to be seen as a unit. This chronicle of works projects, ordinary and exceptional, describes the slow emergence of a city and of an urban order. It also shows how, as the group asserted its mastery over an unstable environment, a political and social organization came to be built, at least in part in response to the challenge of the waters. Venetian society was not merely a social object; it was also an interdependent part of a universe of moving waters, invasive mud, winds, sand, and marsh grass. Its task was thus to perceive, early on, the relations that its historical duration might possibly maintain with its ecosystem and then to take charge of that order, albeit awkwardly and with setbacks but also with some genuine intuitions. In the broader history of the environment, Venice was perhaps a pioneer in a common search for an equilibrium between human life and the environment's time scale.

TWO
A City Wed to the Sea

After the waters of the lagoon and the history of their uneasy mastery, we come to other waters, some of them nearby, whose regular rhythms carried life and merchandise to Venice with every incoming tide that surged through the passages in the littoral islands, and others far away, colonized by Venetian seamen and merchants. Thus I shall speak of the maritime spaces on which the fortune and the force of Venice were built, of convoys of ships, of the port and its wharves, and of cargoes arriving from the Mediterranean and the East. Before we turn to what was long the most familiar chapter in Venetian history, I want to recall a few images.

VENICE AND THE EMPIRE OF THE WAVES

For everyone, today as yesterday, those images proclaim that Venetian power was constructed on the sea. One such image is the personification of "Venetia" in the famous fresco of Jacopo Tintoretto on the ceiling of the Senate Chamber in the Ducal Palace, where Venice is shown as a queen receiving bountiful gifts from tritons and nereids, her subjects.

The Sea as Its Portion

Pictorial cycles hang at the heart of the Ducal Palace, in the very halls where the affairs of the Republic were decided. In 1587 two illustrious patricians gave a report of a mission. With the help of a famous historian, they had pored through chronicles and histories; they had read Pietro Giustiniani, Bernardo Giustiniani, Marc'Antonio Sabellico, and Girolamo Bardi, and they had drawn up a list of Venice's greatest naval battles. When they had made their choice, the Signoria was quick to give its approval; historical research had served a political purpose. All these famous combats, painted by Veronese, Tintoretto, and Francesco Bassano, decorated halls in the Ducal Palace, including the Hall of the Great Council: "And may the third painting show the naval battle that the doge Domenico Michiel waged in the year 1123 against the calif of Egypt"; "And may the fourth painting show how the same doge Michiel took Tyre in 1124." Ten years earlier a fire had gutted the palace, and in 1587, when the remodeling had been completed, it was time to arrange for appropriate decorations by commissioning a cycle of paintings.[1] The iconographic program, realized in the years following the Battle of Lepanto, depicted the long series of (mostly marine) victories, beginning with the earliest days of Venice, that made up Venetian history.[2]

The 1587 commissions quite explicitly focused on Venetian military successes and the construction of Venice's maritime power. The triumphs of the Republic and its fearless troops colonized the walls and the ceilings of the seat of government. Images much older than these still lived, though only in memory, and the Venetian penchant for illustrating the glorious history of the city in the halls of government had begun long before. What do the earlier projects tell us? Although less martial, or less immediately so, the earlier decorative cycles also celebrated Venice's supremacy on the seas. As early as 1365 the Hall of the Great Council was decorated with paintings depicting the Venetian version of the conflict between Pope Alexander III and Emperor Frederick Barbarossa, a conflict that ended in 1177 with the Peace of Venice and the triumph of papal authority. That episode quickly took on prime importance in local legend.[3] The pope was supposed to have conferred on the doge the symbols of power known as the *trionfi*—the sword, the ring, and the dais—as a gesture of thanks to the Venetians for their aid, an aid that they had not in fact given him.[4]

These representations proclaimed to both the Venetians who frequented the Ducal Palace and important visitors that Venice's domination over the seas was legitimate because it was founded on papal privileges.[5] It is thus hardly surprising that the decorations were carefully preserved through the centuries, then reproduced. In the early fifteenth century a painter was appointed to supervise their care, a sort of official conservator.[6] In later restoration campaigns the most prominent artists in the history of Venetian painting redid some scenes that had deteriorated beyond repair.[7] This maintenance program continued its uninterrupted struggle against the damaging effects of humidity during the sixteenth century. Titian, Veronese, Pordonone, and Tintoretto participated in this effort, which means that styles and manners changed. The decoration of the halls of government continued, however, thanks to a succession of talented artists who worked in the service of Venice's self-celebration. In 1587 a new decorative cycle was devoted to the truce of 1177 and to the epic of the Fourth Crusade.[8] The past was thus remodeled by means of both historical writings and a profusion of paintings that were taken as historical documentation and historical proof, illustrating Venice's *dominium* over the sea again and again.

Another image was the famous celebration on the lagoon for the Feast of the Ascension. It is immediately clear that this ritual as we know it from the literary descriptions and the paintings was connected to the Venetians' dominion over the sea and the mythical donation of Alexander III. There are attestations of a ritual celebrated on Ascension Day well before 1177 since the Sensa originally commemorated Doge Pietro II Orseolo's victorious expedition to Dalmatia in 1000, the first step in the transformation of the Adriatic Sea into a Venetian gulf. Every year, the doge's ceremonial galley made its way through the littoral barrier at San Nicolò to render homage to the sea, whose waters the patriarch then blessed.[9] This was the ancient rite. During the thirteenth century, after the conquests of the Fourth Crusade, the rite of wedding the sea was grafted onto it. The doge threw into the sea a gold ring like the one Pope Alexander III was supposed to have given the doge, and by that gesture he wedded the sea and renewed Venetian privileges: "We espouse thee, O Sea, as a sign of true and perpetual domination." The thirteenth-century chronicles give the two rituals, the blessing and the marriage, equal importance; later, the doge's wedding to the Adriatic became the central ritual.

According to the accounts they gave of it, foreign visitors were astonished by the Sensa, and although awe-struck, they were occasionally subject to a sense of irritation and prone to sarcasm. Some saw the ritual as the most prideful act of a prideful Republic. Pilgrims on their way to or from Jerusalem were disturbed by its sexual and magical overtones.[10] In a period of growing Turkish threat in the Mediterranean, there were times when the claims of the Venetian Republic seemed unfounded, inflated, or simply pitiful. That mattered little to the Venetians. Behind the Bucintoro, the sumptuous ceremonial galley that bore the doge's throne, came boats and gondolas, decorated with tapestries, fine stuffs, flowers, and branches, carrying nobles, citizens, and crowds of lagoon dwellers. The craft were so numerous that they nearly carpeted the water. Their stately procession made the tour of Venetian space as it made its way from the lagoon to the sea and then back to Piazza San Marco. Various analyses have been made of this marriage to the sea. Some give it an explicitly political interpretation; others insist on the ceremony as an act of augury and on the rite of possession as a mystical marriage.[11] First and foremost, however, as the foreigners clearly saw, the city took to the water to confirm and symbolize its own power and to prolong that power in an alliance as indissoluble as Christian marriage that expressed and authenticated its unique vocation. The ritual was an inherent part of the mystique of a Venice divinely emerged from the waters and whose commerce and opulence, like the space on which it was built, had been wrested from the grasp of those waters. The sea, dominated by the city at its creation, had also been tamed by commercial enterprises. Every year—until the late eighteenth century, when trade had dried up and Venetia was pictured on the walls of villas of the Terraferma surrounded by bundles of harvested wheat—the act of the *spozalizio* reminded Venetians and everyone else that Venice had won its glory at sea.

All of these images, words, signs, and symbols depict the city on the lagoon as queen of the sea; they all show Venice happily installed on the billows, buoyed up by the Adriatic in a protective embrace. Facile and oft-repeated plays on words—Venice as a new Venus, like the goddess born naked and beautiful amid the waves—continued up to the fall of the Republic. As Alberto Tenenti has shown, there were other depictions of Venice's relationship to the sea.[12] Mariners' songs were not the only expressions of fear of the storm's fury, devastating winds, and shipwrecks or of the chance and uncertainty that lurked in the sea's vast expanse. Nature and its elements were just as unstable as Fortune: the weather could change without warning; when black night fell danger increased; winters were harsh. Distances were immense and delays frequent. Moreover, Venice had many enemies over the long history of the Venetian Republic. A varied corpus of materials—letters, treatises on maritime affairs, poems, opera libretti, and theatrical backdrops—reflect these mixed sentiments. Fears may even have increased as Venice's maritime enterprises declined.[13] They had perhaps existed, sometimes stifled, sometimes avowed, from the time of Venice's origins.

The dangers that faced the community that settled amid the waters explain the dual images of death that haunted the Venetians. Documents from the fifteenth century reflect the fear that the lagoon basin would die, filled in by alluvial river deposits, or that the city would perish by slow asphyxiation, without water, without boats, as the encroaching marshes closed in. Death might choose another way to strike, however. Every time an exceptional flood tide opened a breach in the littoral islands that protected the city from the sea, part of the shoreline was destroyed and low-lying land was submerged, thus threatening the community with death by drowning. The risk of sinking into the sea inspired one of the central scenes in lagoon mythology. On 15 February 1340 a flood tide brought such high water that Venice seemed threatened with annihilation. St. Mark, St. George, and St. Nicholas appeared, then moved over the rebellious waters in a boat from Piazza San Marco to the island of San Giorgio Maggiore, then from the monastery on that island to San Nicolò del Lido. The city was in grave danger of going under. St. Mark is reported to have said as much twice: "See," he said to the captain of the boat, "how high the water has risen in the houses, and how many boats have sunk"; and again, "Do you see, this city is going to the bottom and will perish by the waters." At this point in the legend the saints and their boatman see a galley in the open Adriatic bearing countless armed devils, but the saint makes the sign of the cross and the demons are swallowed up by the sea. The storm abates. Thanks to the intervention of its patron saint, Venice recovers a pacified domain in which the elements have been tamed.[14]

These complex and ambivalent relationships did not hinder the early development of a dominant idea, purveyed in images, texts, and rituals, all of which added elucidations, reflections, echoes, or commentaries of their own: the sea belonged to the Venetians, to the seamen who claimed that they were at home—*a casa*—wherever they went in the eastern Mediterranean.[15]

Venice, a maritime city, developed a much more acute sense of thalassocracy than was typical of maritime cities. Hence when local histories report that Venice enjoyed a maritime hegemony from its very beginnings, they are simply expressing what the community sincerely believed. The broad reaches of the sea were part of the bargain when Venice was granted the asylum of the lagoon. Marc'Antonio Sabellico states that the new city grew thanks to maritime ventures. Even before the Lombard invasion, it had defeated brigands and ended pillage from the sea, and its name shone brightly.[16] Paolo Morosini relates a succession of naval victories against the Narentines, the Dalmatians, and the Goths.[17] In 529 the Venetians defeated the Slavs. In 552 a first controversy arose with Padua, which objected that it no longer had access to the sea because Venice kept firm control of the mouths of the rivers and the portal to the sea at Malamocco.[18] One early-nineteenth-century historian expressed the opinion that the lagoons, situated as they were at the frontiers of Italy and the nearby Alps, within reach of all the lands beyond the mountains and the Danube basin, were predestined for commerce. According to him, these estuaries had always been populated by sailors and merchants because they had always been foreordained for such activities. At the turn of the sixth century Venetians were already notable traders. Commerce had declined, he wrote, but with the coming of a powerful sovereign both commerce and navigation would rise and flourish once more.[19] This author raised geographic determinism to the level of implacable necessity, granting it the role that earlier historians had attributed to the will of God, but whoever or whatever determined history, Venice had a unique destiny. In short, whether texts such as these were written in the sixteenth century or the nineteenth century, they reinforced a myth that seemed for a time to be confirmed by Venetian power: the city of the lagoons had been given command over the waves.[20]

It was probably in the tenth century, the time of Venice's first successful expansion into the Adriatic, that the theme of the city's legitimate sovereignty over the seas began to circulate,[21] completing the more general providential theme. According to the legend of origins, the lagoons were a propitious shelter that God had reserved for the realization of Venice, the site of his privileged pact with the infant community. Logically, the sea was the rightful portion of these "men born of and nourished by water."

Similarly, the cult of St. Mark the Evangelist, the patron saint of the city, did more than simply serve the purposes of the political and symbolic emancipation of the rising power of Venice; it also supported the enterprises of the Venetian fleet and the image of a growing naval power.[22] A brief summary of this copious dossier follows.

The Saint, the City, and the Sea

The problem of the *translatio* of the relics of St. Mark (828) has given rise to an extraordinarily abundant literature. During the past century all aspects of this major moment in Venetian history have been examined. Interpretations of both the duchy's placing itself under a new patron saint and the broader meaning of that event differ, but all explanations link the translation of the saint's body to a complex political context. In one view the adoption of St. Mark as patron saint was intended to counter Carolingian influence but instead encouraged the struggle between the patriarch of Aquileia and the patriarch of Grado.[23] The fabrication, in the late sixth or early seventh century, of the hagiographic episode of St. Mark preaching at Aquileia had been founded on a similar quarrel over jurisdiction. In another interpretation, the cult of St. Mark had a more general explanation: the desire of the older subject cities of the Eastern Roman Empire to find a basis for their independence from Byzantium.[24] By placing itself under the protection of the saint who had evangelized the lagoons, Venice exchanged its first, Greek patron saint—St. Theodore—for a Latin saint and for the saint who, in fact, had always been preferred amid the lagoons for patriotic reasons. Analyses of the *translatio* itself vary even more, according to whether they deny or accept the reality of the event. Giustiniano Partecipazio, who was doge in 829, supposedly provided in his testament for the construction of a church (the future basilica of San Marco) to shelter the holy remains and serve as a chapel for the Ducal Palace. Writers who contested the historical accuracy of the translation of St. Mark's relics to Venice claimed that this was legend, and the passage, an interpolation.[25] These debates of course produced a good many studies of the text narrating the *translatio*, its various manuscripts, and the circulation of those manuscripts.[26]

Whether or not the relics of St. Mark were actually transported to the capital city of the lagoons, we can ascertain certain things. The oldest manuscripts conserved in Venice concerning the act of the *translatio* date from no earlier than 1050. The mosaics in the basilica of San Marco that show the

event in full detail date from the end of the eleventh century or the beginning of the twelfth century. There are some indications of an earlier account.[27] By the ninth century it was common knowledge throughout Christendom that the holy body of St. Mark was kept and honored at Venice.[28] A
century later the chronicle of John the Deacon made the story an integral
part of Venetian history. For Venetians and outsiders alike, the process of the
mystical identification of the city with its patron saint had thus already been
put into place.[29]

Venice thus placed itself under the protection of a patron saint and
privileged intercessor who permitted it to proclaim its originality and the
growing strength of the world of the lagoon in the face of Aquileia and the
mainland but also to state its will for independence from Byzantium.[30] This
occurred in the early ninth century, a few years after the ducal seat had been
transferred to Rialto, at a time when the new capital city of the lagoon was
growing rapidly.

An aspect of this story that is more specific to our interests, however,
requires a closer look at the circumstances of the transfer of the saint's relics.
We are told that ten Venetian ships entered the port of Alexandria in 828.
After the Fatimid conquest of Egypt, trade with Christians was officially
prohibited. The Eastern Roman emperor, Leo V the Armenian, forbade all
relations with the Muslim world, and Doge Giustiniano Partecipazio confirmed the interdict. Thus, the presence of Venetians in the port of Alexandria was, as the text insists, involuntary. Wind had driven their ships to
this harbor. It soon appeared, however, that this accident had been a mani-
festation of God's will. What in fact had happened? Two of the Venetian
merchants had taken advantage of this forced stopover to worship the relics
of St. Mark, who had met his martyrdom in that city. They repeated their
pious visits. By an entire series of arguments they persuaded the Greek
priests who guarded the reliquary to give them the saint's body. The Greek
priests' church might be transformed into a mosque, in which case the relics,
thus threatened with profanation, would be safer in Venice. They reminded
the Greek priests that before coming to Alexandria, St. Mark had evangelized in Aquileia and in Venetia, so that the lagoon had a legitimate claim
to hold and to honor the holy relics.

The priests finally agreed, and the Venetians left with the relics. The
Egyptian guards did not even blink as the merchants embarked with their

holy cargo carefully hidden under a shipment of pork. The trip back to Venice was punctuated by miracles, as were the triumphant and fervent welcoming ceremonies that the doge and the city had prepared for the precious and saintly body.[31] What can we deduce from this tale? On a positivist level, it highlights the early vigor of Venetian commerce in the eastern Mediterranean in the ninth century.[32] On the symbolic level, it tells us how Venetian maritime enterprises found a privileged protector. As the ships made their way to Venice with their precious cargo, they were saved from shipwreck by the personal intervention of the saint. In the decades that followed, the holy relic was seen as committed to the protection of a city that was still far from being a major power and had many enemies in the Adriatic.

At the end of the tenth century the situation gradually changed and Venice went on the offensive. Venetian forces won their first victories, and the name of the Evangelist was connected with them. On 26 May 1000, Doge Pietro Orseolo II departed at the head of the fleet for a successful expedition in Istria and Dalmatia, receiving from the hands of the patriarch the *vexillum*, a banner that was to float over these victories.[33] The sources do not describe it, but everything indicates that it portrayed St. Mark. Under the aegis of its patron saint, the city moved on to other ventures, and from that moment on, the name, the figure, and the colors of Mark accompanied its expansion.

The less well known episode of the "war of the relics" of St. Nicholas confirms the importance of the cult of saints who specialized in the protection of maritime adventures in the creation of the Venetian self-image. Sailors from Bari managed to gain possession of some relics of St. Nicholas and returned to their city with them. Their account of that *translatio* insists on Barese rivalry with the Venetians. At the time of the First Crusade, the Venetians responded and canceled out the affront. They organized the transfer of relics from Myra, the seat of the bishopric of the historical Nicholas, in a move aimed at discrediting the Barese relics. The chronicle that recounts the event cites multiple proofs of the authenticity of the relics conserved in Venice over the ones in Bari.[34] Above all, it gives a limpid account of the benefits of the maritime city's dual patronage: Venice the Fortunate, the hagiographer tells us, was doubly so because its splendor reposed on the two pillars of the lion (St. Mark), who made it victorious in combat, and the intrepid sailor (St. Nicholas), who feared no tempest at sea.

Relics—all its relics—played a special role in the history of Venice. Although the sailors of this active port carried out many such translations, there were moments when "holy thefts" increased for patently propagandistic reasons. These varied, at one time legitimating certain political enterprises that supported the city's claims to an overseas empire, at another time presenting Venice as the sole and ultimate rampart of Christianity. Translations played another role as well: by the possession of so many saintly relics and by their presence in the dense network of churches in the city, Venice protected and sanctified, perhaps supersanctified, its communal space. The chronicler Marino Sanudo put it best. Speaking of this formidable patrimony, he attributed the serene preservation of Venice to its relics: "And they are very numerous, and it is they who maintain our city that has no walls."[35] The patron saint of Venice and his chief aid, St. Nicholas, also had the more specific task of protecting the maritime space that had gradually been added to the waters and lands of the lagoon.

It seems quite justifiable to emphasize the abundance of representations of Venice at the head of a chapter devoted to the classical topic of political and economic history. Representations did more than simply influence the way the history of Venice was perceived and written. Because they had been deeply internalized by the community, they had an effect on the conduct of Venetian enterprises and were even among their motivations.[36] Thus I found it impossible to reduce the study of the commercial power of Venice to an account of how that power was constructed, or to a simple description of Venice's supremacy, when it had become what Immanuel Wallerstein and Fernand Braudel have described (perhaps with some exaggeration) as a "world economy."

Studies of the causes of the commercial success of Venice reflect two complementary historiographical tendencies. The more recent of these posits that "there is really no satisfactory explanation for this primordial and soon absolute preponderance of commerce" in Venice. It goes on, quite logically, to insist on the skill of the economic operators in Venice, their mastery of certain techniques, a clever manipulation of capital, and a constant collaboration between seamen and merchants, in short, on "the Venetian creative spirit."[37] The second tendency follows a more traditional line to trace the effects of the formation of a merchant spirit, an entity that is difficult to circumscribe but becomes, by implication, the defining trait in the Venetian character.[38] Here we can recognize the image of the merchant, skilled but intent on gain, and a city that is rich and beautiful but also wily and focused on its interests, a city clever enough to exploit its limited natural resources to become a dominant power. I do not deny the importance of the various parameters that have long been invoked to account for the Venetian paradox. Venice did indeed display the "internal logic of a maritime vocation."[39] A landless city that at the outset had nothing to offer but its salt, Venice turned toward the sea: maritime expansion was the condition of its provisioning and of its survival. An Eastern land isolated in the West, Venice also managed to put to profit its role as an intermediary. For a time Amalfi also exploited its situation at the borders of several worlds and its connections to the Byzantine world. Still, the determinants of the Venetian adventure cannot have been specifically economic. The "luck" of that community was also that it believed in its "luck." I can justify this apparently rhetorical statement: The insupportable arrogance of the Venetians, decried by both Greeks and Latins throughout the Mediterranean, cannot be explained by their wealth alone. Very early on, Venetians were persuaded that wealth was their due and that the sea belonged to them.

This is why I have chosen to preface a discussion of the size of that wealth, the activities of Venetian ships and galleys, and the movement of capital and merchandise with an account of what is sometimes considered at best an a posteriori legitimation or a superstructure: the imaginary of the call of the sea. The time has come for facts, however, and for the history of the dynamism that enabled Venice to construct a "maritime republic." I shall therefore reconstitute the chronicle of Venetian enterprises as they moved out toward progressively more distant seas.

ACCOUNTS OF AN ADVENTURE

From the early centuries of Venice's history we have only a few references to guide our way, and that meager corpus of documents will be our first concern.

Genesis

First (and again) there is Cassiodorus. The population of the lagoon in Byzantine times did more than fish and process sea salt. The shortest route between Ravenna and Aquileia was across the lagoon basin.[40] Moreover, the "welcoming havens" of the lagoon offered a safer way to travel than land routes in those centuries of invasions and troubles. Boats carrying merchandise from Istria to Ravenna plied the waters of the lagoons. Lagoon traffic was even the subject of Cassiodorus's letter: as praetorian prefect, he wanted to contact the "tribunes of the maritime population" to negotiate the passage of merchandise (wine, oil, and wheat), activities that the "numerous ships" of the Venetians were engaged in as they sailed up and down the coast or penetrated the interior by channels that "opened to you through the most charming river scenery."

Then came the Lombard invasions, and there is no information until the eighth century, when sources once more attest to the presence of Venetians on the Adige, the Sile, and even the Po. They looked to broader horizons as well. Here we can turn to a famous text, always cited and often scrutinized, the testament of Doge Giustiniano Partecipazio (829).[41] Like the will of Orso Partecipazio at a somewhat later date, Giustiniano's will proves the existence of trade by its list of the goods that made up his sizable fortune: spices, ornamental objects, money in coin, and investments "in navigation by sea."[42] The importance of this document should not be overestimated, however: as Gino Luzzatto has stressed, it comes from a member of one of the wealthiest and most powerful families in the lagoon area. Still, it merits a place in the slim bundle of information we are assembling.

The Venice of the lagoons thus seems to have profited from being a part of the Byzantine Empire. When the two ports of Ravenna and Comacchio, on the Po delta, passed under Lombard domination, Venice was the only means of access to the plains of the Po for Byzantine products, as demonstrated by the next stage in this obligatory documentary journey, a treatise written between 948 and 952 by Constantine Porphyrogenitus, the Eastern Roman emperor. All references to Venice in this work ring true.[43] The topographical description is fairly accurate. The broad lines of the history of the lagoons are retraced, but it is the passage concerning Torcello that has elicited the most commentary. The text correctly situates the island between the small neighboring islands of Ammiana and Murano and calls it an *emporion mega*. Even though this text is our only mention of the commercial functions of Torcello, it seems trustworthy. Without exaggerating the volume of Venetian commercial activities before the eleventh century, and while recalling the long predominance of Eastern seamen in shipping merchandise to the West, we nonetheless note that Venetian ships are attested in the eastern Mediterranean as early as the ninth century. We can presume that the *emporium* of Torcello played an important role both as a commercial outlet for the Byzantine Empire and as a supply center. A large portion of the Byzantine export goods destined for the West (luxury silk cloth, spices, precious metals) went through that site in the northern lagoon, and slaves, salt, and wood were shipped from there toward Byzantium and the Muslim Levant.

Trade soon increased, in part thanks to the lagoon people's accelerated penetration of the mainland along the great river arteries of northern Italy. It was during this period that Venice launched its campaigns against the city of Comacchio, the Lombards' main commercial base since the early eighth century, which competed with the Venetians for control of commercial activity on the Adige and the Po.

Although the functions of Torcello in these early exchanges between East and West are attested, it is difficult to date them precisely. On the one hand, Emperor Constantine Porphyrogenitus wrote his treatise on the basis of earlier documents, which means that it contains out-of-date information. On the other hand, the importance of Rialto, predictable by convergent signs, was reinforced when the ducal seat was transferred there. The settlement at Rialto grew throughout the ninth century. It is thus probable that Constantine's reference to market activity at Torcello should be moved back to an earlier date. The new capital of the lagoons seems to have taken over from the former *emporium* rather early on. Venice's only fortifications were built under the government of Doge Piero Tribuno (888–912), in the time of the Hungarian incursions. A chain was stretched over the water between the churches of San Gregorio and Santa Maria Zobenigo to bar entry into the Grand Canal. A wall was also constructed from the mouth of the Rio di Castello to Santa Maria Zobenigo. These defenses protected the principal waterway and its banks, along which urbanization was progressing: they fulfilled the first priority of safeguarding the central region of San Marco, the site of the basilica and the Doge's Palace. On the embankment at Castello the authorities were probably trying to protect the port, which was active at an early date.

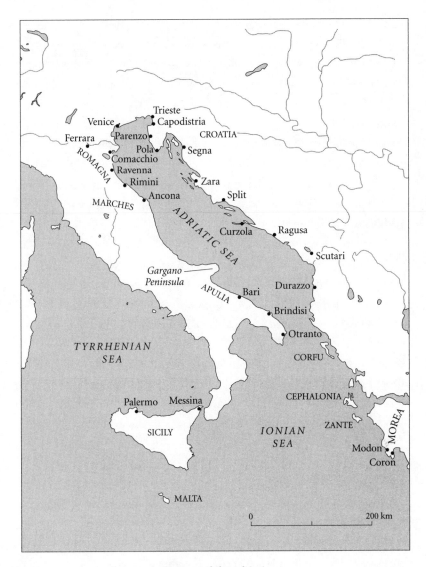

Venice and the Adriatic

The chronicle of Venice's earliest enterprises continues, showing increased connections with the Eastern Empire (the first extant agreement between Venice and Constantinople is dated 993) and trade with the Muslim world. The better part of Venice's maritime activity still took place within the Adriatic, however, north of an imaginary line between Pola and Ravenna. It was precisely to guarantee the safety of this trade that the Venetians, under the leadership of the Candiano doges, put increasing pressure on other cities of the Adriatic. Comacchio was defeated definitively.[44] Capodistria was taken, and an economic blockade was set up against the other cities of Istria. At the end of the tenth century the lagoon dwellers had firm control of their positions in the northern gulf. The same was not true of the middle Adriatic.[45] The Venetians launched police expeditions against Slav piracy on the Narenta River from bases on the nearby islands of the Dalmatian coast (Curzola, Lagosta), but they also maintained commercial relations with those same Slav merchant-pirates, who supplied them with slaves, a highly profitable commodity.

Venetian enterprise continued to broaden. The Venetians still traveled the rivers of northern Italy in their traditional role of forwarding agents, but their more strictly maritime activities developed as well. Under the government of Doge Pietro II Orseolo Venice's expansion in the Adriatic increased considerably: in 1000, on his victorious return from an expedition from Zara to the large islands of the Quarnero inlet, Curzola and Lagosta, the doge added "duke of Dalmatia" to his title. Those Dalmatian cities, however, never recognized Venice as holding more than a distant (and often disputed) lordship over them. The history of Zara, a city taken, lost, and retaken before it rebelled and was again repeatedly besieged, illustrates these difficult relations. Political and military vicissitudes aside, the fact remains that by that time the Venetian fleet firmly controlled the middle Adriatic. Moreover, Venetians were increasingly eager to intervene in the southern waters of the Adriatic because it was their task to assure the western defense of the Byzantine Empire. The irruption in Italy of the Normans, who soon "established themselves as redoubtable competitors,"[46] shifted the balance of power in the Adriatic. Not only did the Venetian expedition in 1002 break the Muslim siege of Bari but the Venetians also defeated the Normans at Durazzo in 1081. This Venetian naval victory did not prevent Robert Guiscard from taking the city, the Adriatic terminus of the Byzantine Via Egnatia, which was the land route across the Greek peninsula to Thessalonica and Constantinople. The aid of the Venetian fleet was well rewarded: henceforth the *basileus* treated Venice as an ally rather than a subject city, according to the famous chrysobull of 1082.

The 993 agreement had already stipulated that Venice would receive customs privileges in return for a promise of future aid, but in 1082 Emperor Alexius I Comnenus made even greater concessions. First, "in its tenure, the present chrysobull" listed several "liberalities," concessions that, although far from negligible, were nonetheless in the domain of honor. Next came economic concessions, which were considerable. The Venetians, whose colony in Constantinople was situated around the church of St. Akindinos, were granted sizable improvements in its infrastructure that included a bake oven, storage facilities, and three anchorage sites on the Golden Horn. At Durazzo, where a good number of Venetians had already settled, they were granted the right to have a quarter of their own. In numerous places and ports throughout the imperial territories the Venetians were granted the right to trade freely, with no impediment and no customs duties. Venetian interests enjoyed favored status in northern Syria, in Cilicia, in Pamphylia, all along the west coast of Asia Minor, in Thessalonica, in Attica, in Nauplia, in Corinth, in the south of the Peloponnese, and on Corfu. The only areas not covered by this privilege were the Black Sea ports and the islands of the eastern Mediterranean (Crete and Cyprus).

What is there to add about a text that has received so much comment? Let me simply note that it confirms what a number of other documents have begun to clarify. For one thing, broad-ranging Venetian business already involved complex commercial associations. For another, the Byzantine world was clearly predominant in these exchanges, though Tripoli and Alexandria continued to be habitual ports of call in Muslim territory. Moreover, a long list of Greek ports from Euboea to Modon and from the Gulf of Volos to Coron occupied a privileged place in this trade with the East. After a century of continuous maritime expansion, Venice had accumulated a long list of advantages. At Constantinople and in the Eastern Roman Empire Venetian merchants enjoyed such duty-free advantages that their foreign competition—merchants from Amalfi, for example—found themselves relegated to a secondary position. The Venetian fleet sailed the Adriatic as its master. A treaty with Imola in those same years shows that Romagna and Emilia worked to supply Venice with agricultural products, and Doge Ordelaffo Falier added the title of *dux Croatiae* to his title of *dux Venetiae et Dalmatiae*. Then came the First Crusade.

The Crusades

The old cliché of the "rupture of the Crusades" is apt to be played down today. Nonetheless, what so many other books have stated needs to be repeated: the First Crusade was a turning point. As is known, the Venetians at first temporized, and they only joined the movement to prevent the Genoese and the Pisans from being the only ones to make spectacular profits from Latin expansion. It is also well known that expansion was not, or not at first, particularly favorable to the interests of Venice. True, the city won the right to establish a merchant colony at Haifa, but the Genoese had acquired a dominant position in Syria and the Pisans had infiltrated the commercial game, suddenly reshuffling the cards. Everywhere in the eastern Mediterranean, and even in Byzantine areas, the Venetians saw their former preponderance challenged. First, the chrysobull of 1111 granted to the Pisans deprived the Venetians of their quasi monopoly; next, in 1118 the new emperor, John II Comnenus, refused to confirm the privileges that had been accorded to Venice in 1082. During the same period, the Hungarians descended into Dalmatia, principally to the coastal cities of Split, Traù, and Zara. If we add tension with Venice's neighbors Ravenna, Padua, and Treviso, we have a full picture of the difficulties that Venice faced.

Venice soon mounted a counteroffensive: two successive expeditions were sent to Dalmatia, the second of which, in 1125, enabled the Venetians to reconquer, this time more durably, the positions they had lost. Moreover, an imposing fleet under the command of Doge Domenico Michiel swept through the Mediterranean (1122–24). The Egyptian fleet was defeated at Ascalon in 1123; Tyre fell in 1124. For their part in the Crusade the Venetians received the right to have a Venetian quarter in Acre. At Tyre, as stipulated in preliminary negotiations with Baldwin II, the king of Jerusalem, they entered into possession of one-third of the city. Throughout these operations, however, Byzantine possessions had suffered: Rhodes was occupied, and the islands of the Ionian Sea were sacked, once on the Crusaders' way to the Holy Land and again on their return. Domenico Michiel's ships returned to Venice loaded with spoils taken as much in Romania as in Palestine. Venetian pressure had increased in the Ionian and the Aegean. The *basileus,* John II Comnenus, ceded; in 1126 he felt constrained to reestablish the privilege of

1082. The first chrysobull had rewarded a demonstrated loyalty to the Empire of the East; the renewal was made under threat.

Once peace was concluded, business picked up with renewed vigor. By sea or by the overland routes that joined the Adriatic to the Aegean, Venetian merchants reached Romania, and their activities at Constantinople, Durazzo, Corinth, Thebes, or Thessalonica increased enormously.

From then on Venetian expansion accelerated. In the middle decades of the twelfth century Venice enjoyed absolute control over the Adriatic to the north of an imaginary line drawn from Ancona to Ragusa. Fano, on the Italian shore, made an act of submission in 1141. Venice's hold on Dalmatia tightened; the revolt of Istria was put down. Despite resistance from Ancona, the Adriatic tended to become the "Venetian Gulf" that the geographer al-Idrīsī depicted. Next, the merchants of the Rialto made a notable breakthrough to the south. During the campaign of 1147–49 the Venetian fleet, which had come to lend aid to the Byzantine forces, battled the Normans to reconquer Corfu. That long series of combats ended in the latter half of the century. Intensive commercial traffic ensued. Venetian ships took on cargoes of wheat in Apulia and later in Calabria and in Sicily (Palermo and Messina in particular), but they also shipped the cotton that was so necessary to Lombard industry.

Eventually long-distance exchanges involved regular sailing dates and organized convoys of ships that ventured beyond the Strait of Otranto. Trade with the Latin possessions in the East increased during the second third of the twelfth century, but it never equaled the volume of Venetian trade with Fatimid Egypt. Above all, it was often unbalanced. Venetian ships unloaded voluminous cargoes of arms, metals, wood, and horses at Saint-Jean d'Acre, but the cargo that they took on there was costly but light in weight: glass, sugar from around Tyre, silk and linen stuffs. This meant that a part of the fleet had to set sail for Alexandria or Constantinople if it wanted to return to Rialto with a full hold.[47]

In Egypt and in Constantinople the Venetian merchants enjoyed smooth relations and fat profits. More than is generally thought, Egypt of the Fatimids attracted businessmen and investments, and the Venetians had a choice place in the markets of Alexandria and Damietta. They sold the strategic raw materials, including slaves, indispensable for naval construction and ship fitting; they bought highly prized local products (alum, linen, soon cotton) and goods from the East that converged on the Egyptian market by land and, increasingly, by sea (spices, silks). In Romania trade soared. The two newly opened marketplaces of Cyprus and Crete were totally free. The Venetian colony in Constantinople grew, and thanks to their customs advantages, the Venetians consolidated their own positions over those of their competitors from the Tyrrhenian Sea.[48] Venetian commerce was not restricted to the few principal routes from the north Adriatic through the Mediterranean, nor was it limited to the usual East-West exchange of oil and silks for woolen cloth, metals, arms, and wood. It thrived because of Venice's profitable activities as an intermediary: Venetians operated as liaisons between Constantinople and Acre or Alexandria; they were present in force in all Greek markets,[49] transporting foodstuffs from Greece to Constantinople, which was not only the Byzantine capital but an enormous center of consumption. Throughout Romania the Venetians were increasingly numerous, increasingly wealthy, and increasingly indispensable. After controlling foreign trade, they controlled internal commerce.

Then the crisis exploded. The Greek chroniclers make it clear that their countrymen felt a growing hostility in the face of this invasion by people whom they considered rapacious, ignorant, and arrogant barbarians. Soon their resentment became avowed and was backed up by arguments. Relations worsened between the Greek populations and all the Latin merchants, whom the Greeks judged to be aggressive and greedy and whom they accused of bringing the Empire to ruin and of sowing trouble and corruption.[50] Although there were still some Venetians in Constantinople who remained attached to the Empire and who had intermarried with the population of the city, outside of that restricted milieu mistrust grew. Moreover, the intense, sometimes ferocious competition between Venetians, Genoese, and Pisans heightened the tension in the capital city. Manuel Comnenus's stance weakened, thus bringing on a first series of violent incidents and reprisals. The disaster of 1171 followed. The Venetian quarter was put to sack. Throughout the Empire, Venetian merchants were arrested and their wealth confiscated. Many, however, managed to flee either to Syria or back to Venice. In one well-known scene, the merchant Romano Mairano, who had traded throughout the Mediterranean since the 1150s, took some of the Venetians of Constantinople on board his immense three-masted ship. They escaped pursuit by the Greek fleet, but only barely, and Mairano, like many others, returned to Venice with his fortune decimated.

Next, a fleet of Venetian ships swept through the Aegean, carrying out acts of retaliation and pillage. Embassies were exchanged. It was not until 1183–84, however, that Venetians could again be seen in Constantinople. (There were none in the city in 1182, when the Latin quarters were sacked for a second time.) It was only in 1189 that Venetian privileges were reinstated. Sequestered goods were returned, sizable damages were paid, and Venetians who resided in Constantinople were even invited to form their own military contingent. Venice seemed to have regained her place and her role in the defense of the Empire. The impression was illusory. Access to the Black Sea was firmly denied to the Venetians, and the Pisans and the Genoese were granted favors. From one year to the next, depending on the circumstances, the Venetian positions were weakened or consolidated. Because the 1171 affair revealed just how precarious the Venetian situation was, it was one of the principal motivations for the Fourth Crusade.

In the final years of the twelfth century the maritime power of Venice was dealt many blows. In the Adriatic the Pisans, the Normans, and the Hungarians weakened Venetian hegemony. Dalmatia was in rebellion, Ancona restive. Aggressive piracy threatened trade in the Aegean.[51] In Frankish Syria, after the victories of Saladin, only a few coastal cities were still in Christian hands. The prosperity of commerce with Egypt was the only bright spot in this more than dreary picture. There are several reasons for the upsurge in Egyptian trade. For one, the main spice route now ended at the Nile delta. Traders came to Alexandria more than to the other markets to replenish their supplies of spices, pepper in particular. Moreover, after 1171 the Venetians concentrated their activities in Egypt. The number of Venetian convoys grew, and Mairano was not the only merchant to rebuild a small fortune thanks to trade with Acre, with the Maghreb, and especially with Egypt.

This, then, is the story of Venetian expansion in its first two centuries. At first Venice, potentially mistress of the Adriatic because it was able to make its loyalty and its aid to Byzantium pay, established its position as an intermediary. Later, successfully launched on its road to wealth and growth, it traded and waged war much like an imperialist power. A new phase in Venetian history began with the Fourth Crusade and extended to the time of the Peace of Turin.[52]

I shall not review the full circumstances of the Fourth Crusade. As is known, the Crusaders set off for Egypt but ended up besieging Zara at the behest of the Venetians. In 1203 the expeditionary force then took Constantinople in support of the son of the legitimate but dethroned *basileus* and in the hope of reestablishing the unity of Christendom. In 1204 the Crusaders took the city again, to their profit. I will simply remark, following other writers, that contemporaries perhaps exaggerated the Venetians' role in this expedition. Venice gained such great advantages from the division of Romania, and the glory of its doge, one of the leaders of the Crusade, was so striking, that some saw the hand of the Venetians in the deviation of the Crusade. It must be admitted that this was enough to cement the Venetians' reputation for craftiness, calculation, and pride. The black legend thus found in this episode arguments so choice, seemingly so solid, and so widespread that it survived for centuries.[53] Such interpretations point to Doge Enrico Dandolo as responsible;[54] as the sinner, the guilty party, the man by whose will Constantinople—"so rich a city," with "high walls and strong towers . . . rich palaces and mighty churches," "the city which above all others was sovereign"[55]—was taken. Other observers suggested that the Venetians, perhaps better reined in by their leaders, were more moderate in their pillage than the Frankish crusaders despite the relics and trophies that filled Venetian ships and made their way back to Rialto to enrich an already considerable store of relics and reinforce the city's echoes of Byzantium.

In the final analysis, this quarrel is important only for the historical concepts that animated it. What matters is that the Venetians always countered accusations and condemnations and justified their role by inscribing it within a Christian legitimacy and arguing that the Greek Empire had fallen into the hands of heretics.[56] The taking of Constantinople, they insisted, had been foretold in prophecy. What crops up once more is the motif, common in Venetian history (and merely implicit only to those who refuse to see it), that the expansion of Venice played a central role in working out the will of Providence.

It also matters that the Venetians obtained a good deal more out of their role in the Fourth Crusade than the gilded quadriga taken from the Hippodrome in Byzantium, which still stands over the portal of the basilica of San

Marco, or even the finest pieces from the treasury of the Monastery of the Pantocrater, which decorate its golden altar screen. Enrico Dandolo had refused election as ruler of the Latin Empire organized on the remains of the Byzantine Empire, but he became *dominator quarte et dimidia partis totius imperii Romaniae*. The prize awarded to Venice in May 1204 for its part in the conquest was one-fourth of Romania, which the victors split among themselves: Venice received coastal holdings and islands in the Ionian Sea, the greater part of the Peloponnese, the Cyclades and some of the Sporades, trading stations on Euboea, Gallipoli and Rodosto on the Dardanelles, and three-eighths of Constantinople itself, including the Church of St. Sophia. Venice bought the *dimidia partis* and added it to this considerable group of possessions in August 1204. In exchange for a great many silver marks, Venice obtained Crete from Boniface, margrave of Montferrat, and that island, a natural stopping place on the great routes of the eastern Mediterranean, was a fortunate completion of a system of ports of call, marketplaces, Venetian quarters, and strategic fortifications scattered across the Mediterranean from Corfu to the Dardanelles. Other guarantees and concessions added even more to this fabulous booty, weakening the positions of Venice's rival cities. It was decreed that the territory of the Latin Empire could be closed to any citizen of a commune at war with Venice. Finally, the Veneians gained access to the Black Sea, where commerce had long been closed to them.[57]

The brilliance of this triumph does not mean that the conquest of Venetian Romania was easy. In fact, the commune soon abandoned the mainland territories and concentrated on places that would provide the support indispensable to its commerce: Durazzo and Corfu, both of which it soon lost; Coron; Modon, the "eyes of the Republic," in the Peloponnese between the Ionian and the Aegean; Negroponte, the pivotal point for commerce in Lower Romania (1205–7); and of course Crete. The Venetians fought hard for Crete, which became a genuine Venetian colony. Several waves of soldier-colonists left the six *sestieri* of Venice for Crete after 1211; they were given fiefs, as well as the task of defending that much-coveted land against the Greeks and the Genoese and of putting down revolts on the part of the indigenous population (1212, 1217–19, etc.). Military colonization was not enough, however, and the better part of the Latin population of Crete was the result "of an individual, spontaneous, and non-military immigration."[58]

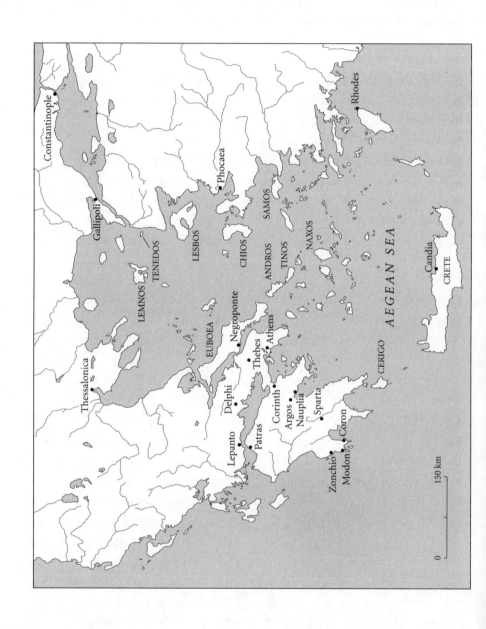

Constantinople

Gallipoli

Thessalonica

LEMNOS

TENEDOS

LESBOS

Phocaea

SAMOS

CHIOS

ANDROS

TINOS

NAXOS

Rhodes

AEGEAN SEA

Candia

CRETE

EUBOEA

Negroponte

Athens

Thebes

Delphi

Lepanto

Patras

Corinth

Argos

Nauplia

Sparta

Zonchio

Modon

Coron

CERIGO

0   150 km

The other territories were held by the Venetian feudatories who had conquered them. Although certain of these were subject to the authority of the Latin emperor, they all maintained their loyalty to the doge and the commune. A few names of individuals dot this military chronicle, mitigating the more common and overly simplistic image of the Venetian as a wily merchant. The most famous of these territorial lords is doubtless Marco Sanudo, who made himself master of Naxos and at least a dozen islands in the Cyclades, where he founded the very solid Duchy of Naxos. Another example is the Barozzi family, on Santorini. Henceforth the Venetian aristocracy included a colonial nobility rich in fiefs, titles, men, and fortresses.[59] Some of these colonists kept up their ties with the homeland on the lagoon, making voyages back and forth, and their names crop up in the city archives. Others did not, however, and "colonial" branches of some of the great aristocratic lineages became distinct from the main trunk. These distant relatives probably did not abandon their connections with Venetians at home who "bore the same name," connections that occasionally crop up in accounts of trade and careers in the eastern Mediterranean. More often, however, these families reappeared at the Rialto only much later, when the Latin Empire was unraveling and they returned to reclaim their right to sit on the Great Council.

The early years of Venetian Romania bear witness to the danger that an autonomous empire might be established in the eastern Mediterranean. One tradition that is pure legend is nonetheless interesting: it states that there was some talk of making Constantinople the capital of Venice, thus showing that even after its victory over Byzantium, Venice could not rid itself of a fascination with a city that it had so ardently imitated. In any event, for some years tension was acute between the home city and its oversees holdings. Venetians of Venice and Venetians of the East did not give the same level of importance to defense of the fragile Latin Empire. Above all, the Venetian colony of Constantinople, under the authority of its leader, the *podestà* Marino Zeno, yielded to the mirage of emancipation from the mother city, attempting to found a second Venice in the East. Gradually, however, the crisis passed, and unity was reestablished, thanks to a new *podestà* and future doge, Giacomo Tiepolo.

For the next half-century the Venetians succeeded in besting their commercial rivals. No group in the Latin Empire was strong enough to contest their supremacy. The Pisans were reduced to allying themselves with the Venetians; at first the Genoese lent a hand to their compatriot, Enrico Pescatore, the count of Malta, in his ventures in Crete, but they later obtained ratification of their former privileges. How could anyone compete with Venetian merchants, who enjoyed a total exemption from customs fees? Trade was sluggish at Constantinople, however. During the lull of the early thirteenth century, growth was nothing like what it had been in the more turbulent twelfth century. The capital of the Latin Empire saw its function as a great marketplace decline somewhat because of competition from new markets in Lesser Armenia and Cyprus. In the rest of Romania, however, business was good; in the Dardanelles, for example, the Venetians' key positions enabled them to control grain exports from Thrace.

Outside the marketplaces and trading stations that they held firmly, Venetian commercial establishments multiplied, and the area of Venetian influence spread as shipping convoys and a flood of travelers, sailors, and merchants from the lagoons came and went, temporarily swelling the ranks of the expatriates settled abroad. The overall picture of the Venetians' merchant ubiquity runs thus: Venetians were active in the Black Sea, where commercial exchanges intensified thanks to the constitution of the Tartar khanate of the Golden Horde in southern Russia.[60] They had a foothold at Sudak, on the east coast of the Crimean Peninsula, from which they exported grain, furs, and slaves. An agreement with the sultanate of Rum facilitated trade with the Asia Minor coast. We also find them in markets in Egypt, still their preferred source for goods from the Orient. They ruled as masters in Acre and Tyre. In the Adriatic their monopoly was undisputed. Finally, they ventured more bravely into the western Mediterranean. Although a Venetian presence cannot be attested in Spain at this date and they did not manage to bring the Genoese and the Pisans to their knees, they nonetheless intensified their relations with Tunis, Bejaï, and Ceuta.[61]

This was the first peak in Venetian influence, but it faltered in only a few years. The prosperity of Venice was untouched, but Venetian preponderance was a thing of the past. The division of Romania had signaled the beginning of the formidable rise to power of Venice's rival city, Genoa, brutally challenging the balance of power and setting off a struggle for hegemony between the two merchant cities.

Combats

The trouble began at Acre. There the Genoese and the Venetians found themselves face to face, active, solidly established, and in open competition. After many skirmishes, hostility between the two colonies began in 1256–58: the Genoese quarter was sacked, and fighting broke out.[62] At first the Venetians won the sea battles, but the Genoese soon took their revenge. The Greeks, whose resistance had never ceased and who had on several occasions raided the Latin Empire from their capital, Nicaea, and launched attempts to reconquer their empire, took advantage of this crisis. Emperor Michael VIII Palaeologus allied himself to the Genoese in the Pact of Nymphaion, in March 1261, and in July he retook Constantinople. The restoration of Greek control of the Empire brought severe losses to the Venetians: their quarter in Constantinople was destroyed, the Black Sea was closed to their trade, and their influence was compromised in the northern Aegean. Naval battles continued with the Genoese, who proved themselves redoubtable adversaries in engagements off Monemvasia, the Peloponnese, and Trapani (1261–70). The islands and ports of the Venetian possessions were well defended, however; they resisted, and fairly soon the Greeks temporized. The Venetians regained a foothold at Constantinople and Thessalonica thanks to a series of chrysobulls in 1265, 1285, and 1302. Hostilities with the Genoese ceased for twenty years. The result of this long period of turbulence was a division of spheres of influence in the East. Both commercial "nations" were represented at Constantinople, where a thriving Genoese quarter was established at Pera (1267). Elsewhere each power had zones of special privileges, although neither was really satisfied with the status quo. The Genoese had the Black Sea, expanded possibilities in Pontus, and, from Pera, access to the Crimean Peninsula and the rivers of southern Russia. They also enjoyed preeminence in Syria and Palestine, and they controlled production in the alum mines of Asia Minor from their base in Phocaea. The Venetians still had preeminence in the Aegean and at Alexandria.

The fall of the Latin settlements in the Holy Land (1291) upset this fragile equilibrium. Competition between the two maritime cities grew in both the Black Sea and the Aegean. Since neither could prevail through commerce, they reopened hostilities. War between Venice and Genoa continued for almost a century. Fighting was not constant, but there were hard-fought battles, raids on coastal areas, acts of piracy, and cargo seizures. It was a war of fleets and their captains, of ship patrons and merchants, and it disturbed the history of the Mediterranean for decades, all the more so when the great powers of the age—the Angevins, the Aragonese, the Hungarians, the Byzantines, and even the Turks—took one side or the other.

The second war with Genoa broke out in 1294 and ended in 1299. Stunning Genoese naval victories (at Lajazzo in 1294, Curzola in 1298) responded to the Venetian successes of the first conflict, showing just how much the situation at sea had changed. During the last decades of the thirteenth century the naval and economic expansion of Genoa was well begun. In the West, once the Genoese were rid of the Pisans, whom they defeated at the Battle of Meloria (1284), they enjoyed a true supremacy. In the East, they attempted to do the same against the Venetians, but with less success. Peace in 1299 left both powers present, and the inability of either one to achieve dominance explains why war broke out again twice during the fourteenth century.

The story takes a new turn after 1317, when the Venetians, who were lagging behind the Genoese in trade, set up regular maritime routes between the Mediterranean and the North Sea (Flanders and England). Henceforth Venetian ships could carry goods from the East far into the West, taking on cargoes of metals, wool, and textiles for the return voyage. Growing Venetian colonies sprang up in London and Bruges. In the Black Sea and the Aegean, history seemed to repeat itself as Venetian interests clashed again with those of the Genoese, now based on Chios (1346). The interdict placed on commerce with Egypt and with "the lands subjected to the sultan," effective after 1322, sharpened competition even further. Thus, until about 1345 the marketplaces on the Black Sea played a greater role in the spice trade, whereas trade in other products (e.g., cotton) shifted to Lajazzo, in Lesser Armenia, and Cyprus.[63] History seemed to repeat itself again in the Venetian-Byzantine rapprochement after 1324. Although anxious to preserve its commercial interests in the Golden Horn, the Venetian commune had for decades been seriously considering various projects (those of the Angevins and the Valois) to restore the Latin Empire. It abandoned that policy in favor of a return to Venice's role of protecting the Byzantine Empire and supplying military and naval support but also, and especially, financial aid. The Venetian war fleet was in fact finding it difficult to man its ships in the decades of demographic depression that followed the Black Death. Many of the more typical conscripts, healthy Venetians between the ages of twenty and sixty, chose instead to buy their way out by paying for a substitute.[64] The human resources of the lagoons proved insufficient, in particular to provide oarsmen for the galleys, who now had to be recruited in Dalmatia or in the Greek colonies.

These difficulties were painfully apparent in the third conflict between Venice and Genoa (1351–55), a war that involved all seafaring peoples. Pisa was no longer a major contender, so Venice allied itself with Catalonia, Genoa's enemy in the western Mediterranean. Several squadrons were armed, and they fought with varying success. Both sides had victories and defeats—at Castro, the Bosporus, Alghero—and their respective alliances gave the conflict an international dimension. The Genoese under Paganino Doria triumphed in a final combat, the Battle of Porto Lungo, but losses were heavy on both sides and the fleets clashed with a violence that contemporaries found extraordinary. Trade was disturbed in both the Adriatic and the Aegean, and all parties carried out raids, devastation, and pillage. The Peace of 1355 settled nothing.

The decades that followed were no more propitious for Venice. Even before the third Genoese war, Venetian interests in Dalmatia and Istria had been weakened by a coalition of Venetian enemies, old and new. Rebellion broke out in Zara at regular intervals. Venice lost Dalmatia after a war with Hungary (1358), and the doge was reduced to being merely *dux Veneciarum et cetera,* losing the title of *dux Dalmatie,* which had been his since Pietro II Orseolo had added it to the doge's title. When it lost Dalmatia, Venice lost ports for its ships, bases of operations against pirates, and a reserve of naval manpower. A serious revolt was put down in Crete only at the high cost, paid by the public treasury, of sending a contingent of mercenaries. Competition with Genoa remained bitter. Enemy merchants confronted one another in the Black Sea, especially at Trebizond, a port on the northern coast of Anatolia and a starting point for routes to Persia, and at Tana in Crimea, a major slave market. The two powers also clashed on Cyprus, where the Genoese, after several incidents, took Famagusta in 1374. A fourth war with

Genoa soon broke out. When the Venetians occupied the island of Tenedos, fortifying their position there and thus controlling the Dardanelles, the Genoese were quick to respond, and hostilities began anew in 1378.

Venice stood alone against Genoa and its allies, the king of Hungary, the duke of Austria, and Francesco da Carrara, lord of Padua. The Venetian fleet, under the command of Vettore Pisani, was brutally defeated off Pola. Venice was no longer capable of holding its own gulf. Soon the lagoons were besieged. Grado and Caorle were taken. On the mainland, Paduan forces organized a blockade; at sea, the Genoese ships fired on the littoral islands. Chioggia fell on 16 August 1379. Until the fall of the Republic, the memory of this extreme peril burned brightly in memory, in particular because of the way the Venetians reacted to it. The wealthiest families contributed to the war effort by subscribing to forced loans, and the financial sacrifice of thirty "popular" families was recognized by an invitation to sit on the Great Council, hence to join the ranks of the nobility and the governing class. Manpower levies were ordered throughout the duchy. Guard posts were manned at the *porti,* which were blocked; on the *palate,* palisades controlling the river mouths; and on the highest towers. New ships emerged from the Arsenal, which requisitioned all available ship construction workers. These emergency forces, finally joined by the squadron commanded by Carlo Zeno that had been patrolling the Mediterranean since the spring of 1379, inflicted serious damage on the Genoese ships and broke the Genoese blockade of the lagoon basin. The Genoese, besieged in turn at Chioggia, capitulated on 21 June 1380. Fighting continued for a year, however, ending officially with the Peace of Turin on 8 August 1381. The danger had been repelled; Venetian control of the Adriatic had been restored. But Venice was obliged to accept harsh conditions: renunciation of its claim to Dalmatia, recognition of Genoese rights in Cyprus, and the neutralization of the island of Tenedos.[65]

The Republic was thus severely weakened both in its resources and in its ability to recuperate. Several episodes of plague had reduced its population. War had exhausted its financial resources. Its naval power was wavering. The sources reflect many problems in these terrible years: the crisis left a mark both on the city and in the texts. In spite of all, Venetian historiography has always interpreted this apparent defeat as an actual victory. The watershed year of 1380 did in fact mark the beginning of a new momentum for Venice.

Venice soon returned to a triumphant advance. It reconstructed its primacy in only a few decades, and for several decades more that primacy
seemed solid. It would be a mistake to impute that obvious success solely to
Venetian capacities for recuperation. These existed, were genuine, and will
be analyzed, but the 1380s also marked another turning point, the shrinking
of Genoese power.

It is not as if that Ligurian city had ceased to be a wealthy merchant and
colonial power. Quite to the contrary. Rather, in a tendency that increased
throughout the fifteenth century, the world of Genoese trade shifted its
center of gravity toward the West. Genoese influence was still strong in the
Black Sea, but Kaffa and the other trading stations that had served as windows to the north after the closing of the "Mongol route" played a diminishing role in supplying wood, grains, and furs. Slaves were the only export
commodity that remained firm. The spice trade in Pontus had dwindled
since the late fourteenth century, declining even before the devastations of
Tamerlane. Alexandria and Beirut now controlled that market. The Venetians still predominated in Syria, Egypt, and even Cyprus.[66] The Genoese
still held Chios, the most important Western possession in the East. A colony
governed by the very solid commercial and colonial society of the Maona,
Chios was the place where ships took on cargoes of mastic, alum, silk, and
cotton from the Turkish world. More globally, however, trade with the East
seems to have shrunk when traffic with the western Mediterranean and the
North Sea increased. This change in the balance of trade occurred much
earlier than the loss of the colonial settlements that were taken by the Turks
between 1453 and 1475 (the exception was the island of Chios, which remained in Genoese hands until 1566). Above all, the Genoese spirit of enterprise found new opportunities in North Africa and the Iberian Peninsula.[67]
In short, because the commercial role of the Black Sea lessened, competition
between Venice and Genoa declined.[68] Venice seemed to have triumphed in
the East and to have reconquered the dominance that Genoa had attempted
to wrest from it. After four wars, the Venetian monopoly was reinstated.

Historians of Venice usually explain the "superiority" of Venice by the
excellence of its institutions. They greet every Venetian military reversal,

which means every Genoese success, with the comment that the Genoese community, prey to internal discord, was never able to take advantage of its victories. Venetians contrasted the "constancy" of their own institutions, the intransigent will of their governing class, and the "civic spirit" of the Venetian population to Genoese internal strife and frequent changes of regime and leadership. Venice could boast a centralized empire, a sizable but efficient administration, and a rational economic exploitation, whereas the Genoese empire lacked unity and the home city exerted only a weak political control over its possessions, which were instead governed by the resident citizens or by families, noble or popular *alberghi* such as those of the Embriaco, the Cattaneo, the Zaccaria, and the Giustiniani.

To my mind such interpretations unduly favor Venice. The Venetians often vacillated in their pursuit of their interests. One prime example is Vettore Pisani, commander in chief at Zara. When that battle turned into a Venetian rout, Pisani was imprisoned and threatened with death; at the darkest hour of the War of Chioggia he was released from prison in response to public pressure. Nor does the Venetians' administration of their empire merit as much praise as it has received. It may be going too far to evoke, as Freddy Thiriet has done, an *évanouissement du dynamisme* of the Genoese during the years in which their clearly capitalistic enterprise, which operated on the scale of the known world, was increasingly shifting to the Atlantic. Rather, luck smiled on Venice when Genoa passed through a series of foreign dominations in the late fourteenth century. Hostilities ended because neither antagonist had been defeated decisively and because Venice and Genoa set up an implicit division of spheres of influence, even though fifteenth-century Venetians turned increasingly toward their interests in the West and, as in the past, Venice continued to fear the audacious ventures of Genoese citizens in the Levant. The example of Chios, perched in the eastern Mediterranean only a few cable lengths from the Turkish coast, was there to recall Genoese capacities for initiative and the infinite resourcefulness of individual Genoese citizens.[69] It is also true that there was a structural specificity to Venetian dynamism. For a long time it was the merchants of the Rialto who assumed the direction of public affairs. The same men and the same families held political power and economic power, with the result that there were continual connections and a genuine permeability between the two spheres. Tensions or interfamily antagonisms might at times disturb that collective direction. In Venice as in many other Italian cities the common good was not distinct from the good of the commune. In Venice more than elsewhere, however, the common good was often confused with what was good for the merchants.

It follows that once the war was over, Venetian galleys set sail again for Romania, Beirut, Alexandria, and Flanders. Step by step, Venice built a new primacy. To make up for the loss of Dalmatia, in 1386 the commune acquired Corfu, which Venice had briefly occupied after 1204. It was thus mistress of an island that controlled navigation entering or leaving the Adriatic. Imposing fortifications were built on the island, which Venice retained until the fall of the Republic. This first success opened a series of other takeovers. No one in the Balkans seemed strong enough to stand up to the Turks except the Venetians, whose fleet controlled the sea. First the Bulgars and then the Serbs were swept away. In 1396 the Ottoman Turks inflicted a crushing defeat on the French and Hungarian Crusaders at Nicopolis. In Romania, where the Byzantine Empire survived only in the limited area around Constantinople, cities and princes rushed to place themselves under Venetian protection. Venice's empire was swelled by ports, cities, and islands either bought by Venice or taken under Venetian *dominium* at the request of the locality itself. In Albania the Venetians gained Durazzo (1392) and Scutari (1396); in Morea, Nauplia (1388), Lepanto (1393), Argos (1394), and Patras (1408). For a time the Venetian *dominium di mare* also included Athens (1395–1402), and Venetian influence expanded to Negroponte and the Aegean (the islands of Tinos and Mykonos).

Thus the metropolis on the lagoons had a far-flung chain of trading posts, colonies, and fortifications that stretched from the Adriatic to the Aegean and as far as Thessalonica (1423). In 1409 Venice even regained a foothold in Dalmatia; in only a few years it forced the region into submission and settled in as the dominant power, this time until 1797.[70] Venetian watchtowers and castles dotted the shores. When, beginning in 1416, the Turks challenged this domination of the seas, a Venetian fleet under the command of Piero Loredan responded decisively. The dogeship of Tomaso Mocenigo ushered in a period of equilibrium and prosperity, enabling the doge to cite prodigious figures in praise of the wealth of the city and boast of fabulous revenues that flowed into the cash boxes of both the merchants and the state. Ten million ducats were invested in commerce each year.

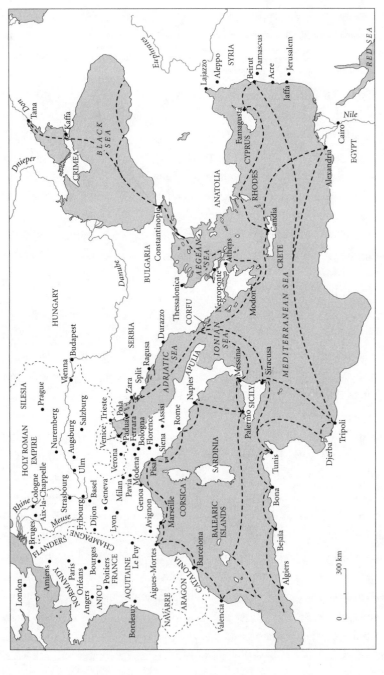

Venetian Commerce

Revenue from trade amounted to 4 million ducats. Three thousand boats, three hundred round ships, and forty-five galleys sailed under the banner of St. Mark. The course of events may also have given an extra nudge to Venetian wealth and power: in 1402 the Mongols under Tamerlane inflicted a harsh defeat on the Turkish army, thus weakening a power whose expansion had until then seemed unstoppable.

In short, the first decades of the fifteenth century present the image of Venice at the apex of its power. Venice had undergone a long series of encounters, both in the recent past and in more distant times, and the Venetian forces had been defeated on several occasions. With the War of Chioggia Venetian power came close to going under. Soon, however, Venice was again dominant, and again its reconstructed power surpassed all expectations. In the East an immense economic area seemed reserved to Venetian enterprise, thanks to the uncontested supremacy of the Venetian fleet. Expeditions on the Italian peninsula soon opened the way to territorial expansion. In the West the export trade was growing apace. A shipping line was organized in 1412 to serve the ports of Provence and Languedoc. Continuing on to Barcelona and Tortosa, it delivered goods from the Levant to the fairs of Languedoc and stimulated trade in Catalonia. Some years later a line was created to the Barbary Coast that served the ports of North Africa, selling spices and textiles and taking on cargoes of gold, skins, and slaves before sailing on to the Muslim kingdom of Granada. In a final initiative that illustrates the vast extent of Venetian commerce, another line created in 1462 operated between Tunis and the ports of the Levant, linking the two basins of the Mediterranean.[71]

The history of the city-state of Venice seems to have strictly conformed to its chroniclers' most flattering interpretations. Historians of the lagoon typically deny any hint of decline. Venice, they repeat, always resists the blows it receives, no matter how hard they are, and triumphs. Thus the city has lasted and will last, free, wealthy, and triumphant, because it has reached a privileged state of development. As a civic body in full flower, it cannot descend to decrepitude. The city has excluded itself from time; it has been immobilized in its splendor. For a brief moment in the years from 1420 to 1430 the reflection and the reflected seemed to coincide. It was a time of plenitude.

One might remark, however, that far from following the organic, continuous development that historical revision confers on it, the course of Venetian naval and commercial power was somewhat more tormented. The 1082 chrysobull and the territorial division of the former Byzantine Empire in 1204 were not the final word. On several occasions Venetian supremacy was bitterly disputed, in particular by Genoa, its chief rival. One result is a historiographic oddity: the many histories of Venice propose quite different dates for the height of Venice's glory. Some opt for the fourteenth century, despite repeated wars and a context of generalized crisis. Others prefer the decades of brilliant reconstruction in the early fifteenth century.[72] Although Venetians tended to read their own history according to a pattern of biological development—a life cycle very similar to the cycles that some economists apply to the history of nations as one after another exerts economic primacy—the growth curve for Venice was a good deal less smooth and regular than the models seem to suggest.[73]

In reality, the plenitude of the first third of the fifteenth century was no sooner established than it began to be attacked. Early in the century various treaties with the Turks had been signed guaranteeing the Venetians unhindered exercise of trade and sanctioning a continuation of the current balance of power. The Republic paid tribute for some of its possessions in the Balkans; the Turks left the Venetians mastery of the sea and of the Dardanelles. With the War of Thessalonica that equilibrium began to be shaken: In 1430 the Turks overcame a long resistance and conquered Thessalonica. The invasion of Epirus followed, after which the Ottomans marched on to become masters of Serbia in 1439. In 1444 they defeated the Christian forces, backed by the Venetian fleet, at Varna, on the Black Sea. Two years later a truce was signed between Venice and Sultan Murad II. The Venetians, who liked to call themselves "the rampart of Christendom against the Turks," chose to negotiate with the Turks in exchange for assurance that they could continue to pursue trade freely.

During those same years hostilities in Lombardy required men, money, and constant attention. It would be artificial, however, to set up an opposition between the two realms of Venetian intervention and influence, as if the Italian peninsula had replaced the Mediterranean. Senate deliberations prove that a balance was maintained between these two preoccupations. The *dominium di mare* was defended, and its defense put a heavy burden on public finances. Merchant convoys departed regularly for Syria, Constantinople, and the Black Sea. The simple fact is that for the sake of their commerce, the Venetians adapted to a new deal in the Mediterranean, a deal they no longer had the power to change.

The Downward Path

What happened next is a familiar tale. The collapse of Constantinople had been predictable for years, but when the city fell to the Turks in 1453 the Signoria made no move to come to its aid. Only the merchants of the Venetian colony in Constantinople participated in what was a hopeless defense. Some months later, however—and the black legend finds nourishment here—Venice drew up a treaty with Mehmed II, sultan of the Ottoman Empire. In exchange for payment of a 2 percent tax levied on all transactions, the Venetians were granted freedom to trade in the Empire and permission to reconstitute a Venetian quarter in Constantinople governed by a Venetian consul, or *bailo*.

It was not until 1463 that the situation changed. The Crusade called by Pope Pius II and assembled with great difficulty came to naught. In the lagoon the party that favored negotiation and compromise was in the minority: sixteen years of war followed. After early successes in the Peloponnese, Venice suffered a string of defeats: Negroponte fell in 1470, and the Christian trading posts in Crimea were taken by the Turks, who also redoubled their raids in Friuli and Dalmatia. Forced to conclude a truce in 1479, Venice gave up its claim to Negroponte, to various Aegean islands, and to Scutari. The size of the losses makes us tend to forget that Venice also registered a few gains (Cervia, Monemvasia). Those few gains demonstrate that the city-state of Venice was determined to resist in a desperate defense of its empire. One last major diplomatic success was still to come: Caterina Corner, the Venetian widow of the last king of Cyprus, made a gift of that island to the Venetian Republic in 1489. But the situation in the Mediterranean worsened in the following decades. The Venetians' empire was crumbling. After the Battle of Zonchio in 1499, the Turks conquered most of the Venetian fortresses in Greece: the trading stations at Modon and Coron were lost, as were Navarino, Lepanto, and the Albanian base of Durazzo. During that same war, however, the Venetian fleet managed to acquire the Ionian islands of Cephalonia and Ithaca, to replace the lost bases and provide stopping places for ships on their way to the Levant, where, despite everything, commerce was enjoying a half-century of prosperity.[74] These were last throes, however.

The Turks, reputed to be land creatures, rapidly gained a new preponderance in Mediterranean waters. After the conquests of Egypt and Syria (1517) came those of Rhodes (1522) and Algeria (1529). In Venice, the Signoria prevaricated, witnessing the eclipse of Venice without reacting.

The weakness of Venice's reserve fleet was obvious in the fall of Negroponte, which was taken in 1470 by a Turkish squadron so formidable that its ships made "a forest on the sea, when described incredible but when seen stupefying," according to the commander of one Venetian galley. Beginning in 1473 the heightened activity at the Arsenal was aimed at introducing greater efficiency into the construction of naval ships, combat galleys in particular. The results of the arms race that was launched are easily measured. The fleets that the Republic sent into battle during the campaign of Preveza (1538) and at Lepanto (1571) numbered four to five times more ships than had fought during the first decades of the fifteenth century.[75] In tonnage and in firepower the Venetian navy had made spectacular progress, but these efforts were not enough. Although all foreign visitors to the Arsenal in the early sixteenth century exclaimed that "the Arsenal of the Venetians is the most marvelous thing in the world," the Turkish naval yards were about to challenge that supremacy. War on the sea had changed scale, and soon only the Spanish fleet could compete with the Ottomans. The Venetians, Marino Sanudo Torsello stated, "may well have been from time immemorial raised in the water," but henceforth they sailed more restricted seas. Their losses in the succession of wars with the Ottoman Turks were considerable.

Narrations of the Venetian adventure usually end on this crepuscular note, even though fragments of the Venetian empire still held out and even though the Venetians continued to fight with the Turks, come what may, until the eighteenth century. The decline of Venetian trade in the Mediterranean coincided with another shock: Venice lost the battle for the pepper trade.[76] For a time historians took at face value the somber prognostications of Girolamo Priuli, a chronicler who commented in his *Diarii* on the discovery of the Cape route by the Portuguese and the resulting collapse in the price of spices and thought that it had dealt a mortal blow to Venetian trade.[77] There is an understandable attraction to parsing out history in neat sequences and seeing primacy shift when one European economic entity suddenly replaces another. The facts, however, work against systematic periodization. It is true that during the early years of the sixteenth century the Portuguese sought to monopolize commerce with the Indies, even using armed force, and to supply France and the Holy Roman Empire through Antwerp. This brought bad times to the markets of both the Levant and the Rialto. By the 1520s, however, the worst of the crisis had passed. Venice was once again well supplied, thanks to shortcuts in the buying cycle that reduced costs, and had resumed its function as a distributor, in particular to German lands. Antwerp, the rival marketplace, had failed to establish a monopoly in spices.

The spice trade even experienced a revival during the second third of the sixteenth century, and the volume of spices reaching Egypt via the Red Sea equaled that of the 1490s.[78] It was the war with Cyprus that weakened the Venetian positions. The Atlantic did not suddenly deprive the Mediterranean of life: commerce in agricultural products, grains in particular, remained active. Both the traditional export trade in spices and trade in silk and cotton with the Levant and, above all, with Alexandria and Aleppo remained quite profitable. Times had changed, however, as the economic center of gravity of Europe gradually shifted north: during those same years trade on the northern and Atlantic coasts of the Continent increased considerably. No longer did the better part of long-distance trade pass through the Mediterranean, so the merchants' headquarters were now installed on other shores. Moreover, French ships, English ships, then Dutch ships slowly began to penetrate the Mediterranean. Venice itself was enjoying a genuine prosperity far superior to that of the preceding century, but that prosperity was no longer based on maritime trade alone. Venice, for so long at the center of activity in Europe, now found itself in a semiperipheral position.

These are the facts, and in general they conform to European economic history. For centuries this was how the preponderance of Venetian trade was established on the high seas and how it was expressed in practical terms by the incessant movement of Venetian ships. It is not enough, however, simply to state that preponderance, nor to say that for centuries it gave meaning to the life of Venetian society. What stimulated the construction of that prosperity? How are we to explain, if not the primacy of Venice, at least its successive peaks of dominance and its fabulous wealth? What are the principal determinants of that history of Mediterranean expansion?

I have already drawn up a brief inventory of Venice's resources and advantages. The lagoon had little to offer but its salt and its situation as a bit of the world isolated between land and sea, at the frontier between the East and the West. Those resources and those advantages may well seem insufficient to explain the destiny of the lagoon communities, but they were exploited early on. I shall not rehearse them again. What we need to insist on is that Venice also knew how to make the best use of its naval power.

Warfare and Naval Power

The military services that Venice rendered to the Byzantine Empire marked the first stages of the city's commercial expansion, as we have seen. It was that military strength, which soon became a supremacy, that transformed the Adriatic into the Gulf of Venice. The nascent maritime power pursued a resolutely aggressive policy based on an inextricable mix of military and commercial interests. Rival cities were destroyed; for some time swift raids of pillage and devastation took the place of military operations; Venice's commercial penetration in Romania was resolutely predatory. That model of development, which the rival cities of Pisa and Genoa also espoused, explains the violence of the encounters between the various Italian communities in Byzantium and in the Levant and, later, the deadly combat that flared up when those cities' will to hegemonic domination brought them face to face in one zone of influence. Warfare is thus an essential part of the history of Venice, a maritime city that has too often been presented as prudent and wary. Is there anything surprising about this, though? In a city that until the fifteenth century presented itself as created by the will of God, that divine election granted to the community was also realized in war, the accumulation of wealth, and a stranglehold on circuits of exchange.

To judge by its enterprises in the name of the Byzantine Empire or its successes in Dalmatia, Venice quickly gave itself the means for its expansion. What public records reiterate ad infinitum was that the fleet was, and remained, the primary basis of its power. What was the composition of that fleet, for example, in the years following the conquest of Romania or somewhat later, when the commune began to maintain a permanent naval and military force, the famous Gulf Squadron, commanded by the grandest names of the urban aristocracy and charged with "neutralizing" any ship that penetrated into Adriatic waters?[79] The Venetian fleet was made up of two types of ships. The first was round ships with lateen sails, used for trade, heavy cargo, and bulky freight. When constructed with one deck they were called *tarette;* with two or more decks, made for long voyages, they merited the name *navi.* These might weigh as much as five hundred tons, like the famous *Roccaforte,* but their average tonnage was more like two hundred tons. The second type was longships propelled by oars. Lower on the water, more maneuverable, and faster, these were used for warfare. During these same years Venetian shipyards turned out biremes, swift galleys with two decks of oarsmen that protected merchant shipping. This division of functions is a simplification, however. Despite their smaller cargo capacity, galleys were also used to transport more costly merchandise; large round ships, or *navi,* massive vessels with castles high over the water that rode the sea well, proved resistant in combat and were on occasion requisitioned for warfare. In all cases, the same men, recruited in the parishes of Venice and the communities of the lagoon, provided the ships' crews of sailors and oarsmen.

About 1300 the effects of a naval revolution began to be felt in Venice as elsewhere.[80] The first trireme galleys were built; when their cargo capacity was augmented, the merchant galley was born.[81] The development of that type of ship led to the formation of the Venetian system of merchant shipping. An improved version of the "great galley" reached its maximum size toward the end of the fifteenth century. This was a two- or three-masted craft that retained the rapidity of the longship but was used to transport merchandise and even such passengers as pilgrims on their way to Jerusalem.[82] The great galley required a crew of two hundred men, who manned the oars in case of danger or in case the ship was becalmed.[83] In times of war or skirmishes with pirates or Turks those same crew members, armed, helped defend the galley, whose high sides made it difficult to board.[84] The war fleet was composed of light galleys. In times of peace these same fast ships with one lateen sail, commanded by the *capitano generale,* patrolled the Adriatic and all waters that served Venetian trade; on occasion they also escorted convoys of great galleys and fought in naval engagements, reinforced by reserve ships.[85] Technical innovations improved the round ships as well, although the *cocha* (cog, or carrack) came somewhat later. A large cargo ship with a square sail and a stern rudder, the *cocha* had a brief but successful career toward the end of the fourteenth century. The new *nave*, which "borrowed its many masts—three, four, or five—from Mediterranean tradition and its square sail and its rudder from the cog," replaced the latter during the fifteenth century.[86] Round ships, cogs, and nefs built by private shipyards supplied the better part of the merchantmen.

Finally, the latter third of the fifteenth century brought changes connected with such technological advances as the development of artillery but also with sweeping changes in both trade and warfare in the Mediterranean. For one thing, the regular shipping companies organized by the state were facing hard times, and because the round ships could transport goods more cheaply, they gradually replaced the galleys. For another, the menace of the Turkish fleet had become more acute, and the Arsenal specialized in the production of combat great galleys with impressive firepower, later producing the super-sized galleys made famous by the Battle of Lepanto. At that time the vast public shipyard deployed its full potential in the service of the navy and became the "logistical center of the *stato di mar.*"[87] For the defense of Venice's empire an entire naval culture was mobilized and modernized, and equipment was improved. Between 1525 and 1546 Vettor Fausto, a humanist and a professor of Greek literature, was active at the Arsenal, where he did exceptional work that renewed naval architecture and demonstrated that at least in the realm of ship construction techniques no nation outstripped Venice.[88] Even if the Genoese, both in 1280 and in 1450, were capable of sending bigger merchant ships out to sea, ships and shipbuilding accounted for a large part of Venice's success. Another source of exceptional prosperity was Venice's colonial empire.

Empire

Once the division of the Byzantine world had been accomplished, commerce and wealth changed scale. This does not means that the domination of those Eastern lands was always easy. Their administration was complicated in Crete by rebellions followed by chronic insecurity, elsewhere by difficult relations with the local populations, and everywhere by wars to defend those coveted territories. Venice the "Dominant" attached a price to its overseas possessions—"its eyes" and "its arms"—that was both economic and symbolic, and that price did not waver even after the constitution of the *stato di terra*. In fact, when the Byzantine Empire was coming unraveled Venice wept over every Turkish advance. The fall of Negroponte was truly traumatic. All contemporary texts, public and private, deplore the unhappy times, the mounting perils, and the anguish gripping Christian hearts. Marino Sanudo, for example, describes the atmosphere in Venice in September 1499, when news of the defeat of the Venetian fleet reached the city. Losses in men and ships were great, and Antonio Grimani, the captain general of the fleet, had shown proof of negligence.[89] Murmurs circulated in the city, and fear soon turned to anger. Walls and shops were covered with injurious inscriptions. Bands of children ran through the streets shouting doggerel curses: "Antonio Grimani, ruin of the Christians, rebel to the Venetians, may you and your sons be eaten by dogs!"[90] In the sixteenth century, although revenues from the *dominium* were diminishing, the Republic was still exhausting its resources in defense of its territories in the East. Thanks to an enormous military and financial effort and skilled political maneuvering, it even managed to postpone some inevitable defeats: Candia capitulated only in 1669.

The garland of Venetian bases and trading concessions that stretched across the Mediterranean had furnished indispensable relay stations for large-scale commerce. Those ports and those outposts marked the sea route to Constantinople and commanded the sea lanes that led to Syria and Egypt. First the Adriatic ports of call (Pola, Zara, and Ragusa, then Corfu after Ragusa won its independence and became a competitor), and then other Venetian positions at the southern end of the Adriatic operated as turntables for shipping. All ships stopped at Coron, and even more certainly at Modon, to take on water and stores. These posts were supplied from Crete, Negroponte, and the islands of the Aegean by ship traffic that traveled the network of routes running throughout the colonial world. Major shipping lanes fanned out from those same ports. For merchant convoys headed for Alexandria, Cyprus, or Beirut, Crete was a usual stopover on the way out and sometimes on the return voyage as well, hence Crete was an important junction point in the Venetian navigational system. Galleys of the Venetian navy in Romania touched base at Negroponte before reaching Constantinople or continuing on to Trebizond and Tana, but private merchantmen on their way to Thessalonica stopped there as well, as did all ships that traded in Lower Romania.[91]

Agricultural products and raw materials also arrived from all parts of Venice's empire. Such supplies were indispensable, and their importance increased even more in the fifteenth century, although Venice had always needed to buy massive amounts of produce, grains in particular, in Italy (Apulia, the Marches, Romagna) and in the East (Thrace, the Black Sea). Istria, Dalmatia, and the Venetian possessions in Albania had a part in this system as well: wine, salt, pelts, wood, and construction materials (Istrian stone) departed regularly for the lagoons. Romania had greater resources, however. Crete, once again, played the role of "nucleus and strength of the Empire." The markets of Candia and Canea transhipped products from Cyprus, Syria, and Egypt, but they also served as veritable warehouses for grains and wine (enormous numbers of barrels of which were loaded onto Venetian ships after the grape harvest), wax, oil, honey, and cheeses.[92] It has been calculated that a third of the grain in Venice warehouses came from Crete. The island was held under a working monopoly, given that Venice fixed the quantity and the price of the grain to be delivered to it after each harvest.[93] The same Mediterranean products—wheat and wine—were loaded at Negroponte by the many unarmed ships that anchored there, which then stocked up on malvasia wine at their ports of call on the Peloponnese. Wine destined for home consumption but also for reshipment to England and Flanders was an essential product in marine commerce, but cargoes of fruit (oranges, lemons, and raisins from Zante, Corfu, and the Peloponnese) were also unloaded in Venice and transhipped to the urban centers of continental Europe, as were oil from Corfu, salt, sugar, and cotton, though Venice's commercial empire produced far too little cotton to satisfy the demand. Sugar was traded in even greater quantities after Venice took over Cyprus and its riches.[94]

It should be added that the colonial world furnished human resources as well. Subjects were expected to do their part in the defense of the *dominium*— to man the watch or form contingents—according to systems of recruitment that varied over time (feudal levies at Cyprus and Corfu, peasant militias in the sixteenth century on Crete and at Zante, Cephalonia, Cerigo, and Zara). In the latter half of the fifteenth century, Greeks and Albanians were also recruited to serve in light cavalry, or stradiot, units to man observation posts and defend the coasts.[95] Finally, given that the fleet needed oarsmen, Venice's overseas empire had to provide what the metropolis could not. The demands of the Venetian Senate increased further during the fifteenth century. Volunteers were scarce, and able-bodied men fled to the mountains; the colonies were not eager to furnish oarsmen, which meant that the shortage of crews to man the Republic's ships became increasingly acute.

One fact remains. The city that had so long been without land drew its strength from those distant lands scattered throughout the Mediterranean. The advance of the Turks and the constitution of the Venetian territorial state did not cause trading activity to slacken its pace or the commercial network to weaken, as the correspondence of Venetian merchants throughout Romania demonstrates. Cyprus and especially Candia continued to bring in substantial profits. As Benjamin Arbel has remarked, until Venice lost Cyprus in 1571 the Venetian trade empire functioned "for the profit and the honor of the Republic," but first and foremost for its profit. The enormous sums that Venice offered the Turks in order to recuperate some of the possessions it had lost (250,000 ducats for Negroponte; an annual payment of 100,000 ducats for Cyprus) clearly attest to the economic worth of those possessions and of the colonial nature of their exploitation.[96]

Commercial and Financial Methods

What are we to make of Venetian "capitalism" today, of the commercial and financial techniques that Venice employed, of its enterprises, and of the associations that backed those ventures? The Venetians, as many have justly remarked, were not great innovators. Where did a large body of notaries specialized in maritime affairs develop? In Genoa. Who can boast of having organized the first great financial companies? The cities of Tuscany. In spite of all the merits of Alvise Cà Da Mosto's voyages of exploration, who did the most to develop new maritime routes? The Genoese. There seem to be many proofs of a Venetian lack of inventiveness, even conservatism. The first examples of double-entry bookkeeping are attested at the Rialto a century later than in Genoa. The Venetians also borrowed the use of marine insurance and letters of exchange.[97] Venetians showed little interest in the commerce of money: it was foreign merchant-bankers, Florentines in particular, who operated at the Rialto.[98] It is true that the Venetian Mint, the Zecca, produced a stable silver coin, the grosso, but the city only began to strike gold coins (ducats) three decades after Genoa and Florence. There are indications that Venetians long resisted other innovations as well: in the sixteenth century the endorsement and payment of letters of exchange was current practice in Antwerp but still forbidden at the Rialto.

The commercial rise of Venice was thus based on simple financial techniques. Lending, both simple and *ad negotiandum*, appeared early, and in the twelfth century it became an indispensable tool even though borrowing money was expensive. Commercial companies existed in Venice; for the most part they were used for acquiring shares in boat leases, where risk was reduced by dividing the global investment into twenty-four shares, or *carati*. In this system a certain number of investors shared both profits and losses proportional to their investments. The preferred sort of association for raising capital, however, long remained the classic *commenda*, in Venice called a *colleganza*, which was a limited-liability contract that might be unilateral or, more often, bilateral and ended at the completion of a voyage, which might last for some time.[99] Every merchant who entered into a contract of this sort worked with several moneylenders, however, and every financier invested in several merchant ventures, hence someone who borrowed money might also be an investor. A first result was that arrangements for credit and short-term associations were highly supple, and in the early centuries of commercial expansion the system for financing such ventures penetrated deeply into Venetian society because it required sizable accumulations of capital. Another result was a sizable number of contracts and provisory societies, which split up the risks and the tasks but ended up mobilizing considerable funds and permitting an equally considerable activity. A third result, judging by the very large divisions of profits attested in the notarial documents, was rapid enrichment. By the end of the Middle Ages, however, practices had changed. The *colleganza* tended to disappear, and the merchants, after an apprenticeship abroad, no longer left Rialto, Constantinople, or Candia, managing their affairs from there through their correspondents and mandatories in the various commercial marketplaces. This is what has been called the "sedentarization" of the merchant.[100]

Scholars have of course attempted to find explanations for this relative conservatism. The easy wealth of Venice is often suggested.[101] One might expand this notion to remark that Venetian culture, whether merchant, political, or artistic, was apt to show a preference for consistency, for respect of traditions, loyalty to origins, and an attachment to the past. Even well into the fifteenth century the supple and traditional family association of the *fraterna* proved able to fund the enterprises of the big economic operators and to facilitate the constitution of enormous fortunes.[102] Moreover, even though techniques for the exchange and transfer of capital were imported from other cities, Venetians mastered them completely and adapted them to business practices in Venice. The exchange activities of the Rialto and the bookkeeping and financial practices that were used there were admired by foreign visitors in the later Middle Ages. Even if Venetian capitalism avoided innovation, and in retrospect its methods might seem to have worked against economic evolution, they were effective. Venetians operated by practical inventiveness.

A variety of highly effective instruments served merchant activity in Venice. The first of these was monetary. In the mid-fourteenth century the ducat replaced the silver grosso as the basic coinage for commerce and finance, and until the fall of the Republic the ducat remained almost stable in weight (3.5 grams) and value (24 *carati*). By the fifteenth century the Venetian ducat had become common coinage on the markets of the East and had replaced the gold florin on the international monetary market. The deposit banks of the Rialto could perform other banking operations as well.[103] The principal function of these banks was not to furnish credit, even though overdrafts were authorized, permitting some leeway, but rather to facilitate payments by simple transfers from one account to another. The economy of exchange in the fifteenth century depended on the smooth operation of such banks because all sizable payments went through them. When such establishments failed, as they often did, panic swept through the marketplace because the bankers used the funds on deposit with them in commercial operations, at times exposing their clients to great risks. Among the many shadows looming over Venetian history at the end of the fifteenth century we would have to include the series of bank failures of the years 1498–99. They explain why traders rushed to withdraw their money and why the state felt constrained to intervene to guarantee funds. It is true that such deposit banks managed the public debt and that the Signoria often had recourse to them for substantial advances.[104] That severe crisis did not prevent the system from being perpetuated, and the first public bank was created only when the last private bank had disappeared, in 1587, many decades after the rise of public banks in Genoa and Barcelona.

It was thanks to inside information that the chronicler Marino Sanudo, who had close connections in the inner circles of power, managed to withdraw the five hundred ducats his family had on deposit with the Garzoni bank when it, like the other banks, was threatened with failure at the end of the fifteenth century. This precipitous rescue was the reward for a very Venetian nose for news. Another of the instruments available to Venetian businessmen was the city's formidable information network. This seems only logical. An economic center, the capital of both a state and an empire, and a dominant city, Venice resonated with news brought by its convoys of ships or received from its connections in Romania, on the Italian peninsula, or in Germany. Prices, commercial shipbuilding, and market variations were closely dependent on this information network. One historian has seen "news and speculations" as the key to activity on the market of the Rialto at the beginning of the modern age.[105] A second political and administrative news network was superimposed on this first network of merchants, voyagers, and business associations. The public archives of the Republic contain a vast amount of direct evidence of this network for the management of information: letters, couriers, reports, dispatches, narratives, and summaries, written and oral, from all the *baili*, consuls, *podestà*, ambassadors, *rettori*, and persons named or sent off by the councils with some special mandate for a specific mission. The same men held political and economic power in Venice, which means that the two networks mingled. Information collected by Venetian correspondents on all the economic marketplaces of the Venetian nebula was exaggerated, confirmed, or corrected by the information from political agents, and the two sources directly influenced the conduct of business on the Rialto.

These mechanisms are a perfect illustration of the particular characteristics of the Venetian marketplace. In Venice collaboration between the political and economic spheres was so strong that they blended into one. Here we reach the heart of the mechanisms that propelled Venice; we touch its profound originality. The state, in the course of its creation, created an interventionist and monopolistic system.

State Intervention and Monopoly

The principal manifestations of that system are familiar. At first unique to Venice, they were later imitated, for example, by the Florentines, who, after the conquest of Pisa, armed merchant galleys on the Venetian model. We can summarize this thick and complex dossier with one simple observation: all merchant activity at the Rialto was fashioned and conditioned by strict rules. Through the centuries the principles of commercial centralization were imposed and made increasingly clear. The guarantee of abundant customs receipts laid the foundation for Venice's functions as an intermediary and for the wealth of the state. How can we summarize this long process?

In a first stage, rival cities that threatened to capture a share of the trade transiting between East and West were defeated or led by war or maritime treaties to accept Venetian domination. Next, Venetian law triumphed in the north Adriatic, where all trade, including ships that were headed up the rivers of northern Italy, had to pass through the port of Venice. In the mid-thirteenth century the joint action of its fleet and its river patrols gave Venice control over all commercial movements north of an imaginary line drawn from Ancona to Zara. And the forward march continued. With time, the system was perfected and stabilized. Germans who came to the Rialto to deliver their iron or their fustian were prohibited from engaging in long-distance trade; those who did risked having their merchandise seized. Export by sea was exclusively reserved to Venetians, who of course used Venetian ships. There were other prohibitions: except in the case of special concessions, cities subject to the maritime law of the Republic could not engage in import or export activities without passing through Venice.[106] Venetians too were obliged to pass through their home port and to use Venetian ships to carry merchandise they had bought in Constantinople, Alexandria, or Aigues-Mortes even if their final destination was Sicily or England. The same rules applied to the Venetian overseas territories: all merchandise produced in the Venetian colonies or merchandise that had transited through them had to travel to Rialto before continuing on its way. Rare exceptions aside, merchandise sent within the *stato di mar* went through the port of Venice as well. In all cases, ships of the Venetian merchant fleet provided transport.[107]

A genuine economic policy was thus put into place, and Venice gradually positioned itself at the center of commerce. By the final centuries of the Middle Ages the city had become, for a large part of international business, a necessary transfer point for unloading and reloading cargo and an obligatory warehouse facility. Merchandise of all sorts converged there, and everyone—Italians and others—came there to buy. The various economic offices of the Venetian state encountered few difficulties in levying their profitable taxes and duties on all these exchanges.

The history of salt provides a fine illustration of the mechanisms of this monopoly. Very early on, Venice, the capital of its duchy, was not content to sell only what its own salt works produced, and it determined to capture a monopoly on the sale of salt. In order to increase fiscal receipts and to finance the purchase of the grain supplies it needed, Venice reserved to itself exclusive rights to provide salt to the river towns of the middle and lower Po Valley. War was incessant in this first phase, in which Venice either attacked rival centers of salt production or imposed its conditions on neighboring cities by force. Next, the Venetians opted to supply more far-flung Mediterranean lands with salt, engaging in long-distance trade. In order to do so, they discouraged Adriatic salt production in order to guarantee the market for their own imports. From Ibiza in the West and Cyprus in the East, sailors and merchants brought back salt, which had the further advantage of serving as inexpensive ballast for the ships. All this cargo, stocked in the immense warehouses at the Punta della Dogana, was resold at monopoly prices within the Venetian states, and at prices that were negotiated but still high, thanks to a lack of competition, in Lombardy, Emilia, the Marches, and Romagna. In a final phase, during the latter half of the fifteenth century the saltworks of the Adriatic (Piran and Cervia), which were controlled by the Signoria, accounted for an increased share of the salt supply, and the Venetian monopoly held firm until the War of the League of Cambrai and the catastrophe of Agnadello (1509).[108] It has been calculated that at the time of its greatest extent the Venetian salt market handled something like 33,000 tons of salt.[109] Considerable receipts were drawn from this commerce, which financed the city's building projects or went into the war chest.

The commune's system for controlling the shipping lines was another part of the economic organization of Venice.[110] The Senate organized the first convoy to set off for Romania and the Black Sea in the beginning of the fourteenth century, a time of growing competition.[111] Other state-backed shipping lines were soon put into place, and until the early sixteenth century, despite certain difficulties, these *mude* continued to guarantee a network of regular commercial relations.[112] During the final centuries of the Middle Ages the Venetian merchant marine was thus divided into two sectors. Ships engaged in private trade and unarmed ships (cogs and round ships) specialized in the transport of heavy and bulky cargoes: grains, salt, wine, alum, cotton, and also slaves. They sailed when and where they wanted during the season, and they handled the bulk of transport. The galleys of the state sector sailed in convoys, according to itineraries and at times decided by the Senate. They had an exclusive right to transport the more costly cargoes, such as spices (pepper, cinnamon, ginger, nutmeg) and silk, which had been stocked on the wharves of Alexandria or Beirut awaiting their arrival.

This transport system functioned within the context of a dual monopoly aimed at making exchanges more efficient and lowering costs: the ships carried only citizens of the Republic, and Venice controlled the cargo. The itineraries, the size, and the schedules of the merchant convoys were established every year by decision of the public authorities based on political and economic circumstances. The ships were well defended, in particular by poor nobles who served as "bowmen" (so called even after the introduction of firearms),[113] and sailing in convoy provided both security and increased regularity, which led to more competitive rates, thanks in particular to lower insurance costs.

Every year the commune held an auction *(incanto)* of the ships that made up the various *mude,* ships that had been constructed at the Arsenal and remained public property. Before announcing the auction at the Rialto the city government determined the number of convoys, the number of galleys in them (two, four, five, or more), and the various clauses of the *incanto,* including a possible subsidy to be paid to the investors in hard times. Noble shipfitters who had been awarded a ship, individually or in association—and only nobles were authorized to bid—then received payments from other merchants for the merchandise to be shipped. From the beginning of the fourteenth century two shipping lanes followed the two principal axes of medieval commerce, with convoys leaving for Constantinople and the Black Sea or for Flanders and England. Next, convoys were formed to go to the Levant, the principal source of Venetian wealth, with stops in Egypt and Beirut. In more episodic fashion, convoys also set off for Cyprus and Lesser

Armenia. The *mude* that sailed west and a convoy route to North Africa called *al trafego* completed the Venetian trade network. At the beginning of the fifteenth century a fleet of some twenty great galleys sufficed; a half-century later Venice's seapower had increased considerably, with forty-five merchant galleys serving the system at its height.

All means were thus put to the service of commercial dominion and supremacy on the maritime routes. The Venetian state mobilized its resources: those of its Arsenal to build galleys; those of diplomacy and the information network to establish the routes,[114] the number, and the rate of turnover of the ships; and those of its treasury when it took on transport costs or granted subsidies. In both war and commerce, mobilization was total and structured by the state.

Marino Sanudo claimed that Venetians had always been merchants and would always continue to be merchants.[115] Thanks to the regular voyages of the Venetian galleys, wealth from both East and West—*Levante* and *Ponente*—met in Venice and filled the hangars and the warehouses of the Rialto. This is how the history of Venice unfurled, following its natural and immutable course, and the prosperity of the entire community was guaranteed by the prosperity of the group of merchants and shipbuilders who dominated Venice and the sea.

At the very end of the fifteenth century, Sanudo, one of the most famous Venetians, found that nothing, not even the staggering blows dealt by the Turks or the conquest of a territorial state that anchored the basin of the lagoons more and more firmly to Italy and to continental Europe, had changed the admirable order of a city constructed "per le mercadantie fatte col navigar in diverse parte del mondo."

THREE

The Lion and the Land

That Venetians were destined to frequent the sea is an axiom that runs throughout the uninterrupted narrative of the history of Venice. When they betrayed what had been their vocation and their mission, renouncing the wise policies of their fathers to pursue interests on land, the course of their history wavered. Tomaso Mocenigo's declaration in 1421 that commerce would make the fortune of Venice is the finest illustration of that certitude.[1]

A HISTORICAL PREFACE: SITUATING A LION

In Mocenigo's harangue a doge warns the city's various councils and its governing elite of the dangers of war and of the adventure that Venice has launched in Lombardy. He inventories the many components of Venetian wealth, born of and nourished by trade. He cites the many partners who helped to make Venice a commercial center; he enumerates the cargoes of pepper, sugar, and cinnamon, cotton cloth, wool, and silk. He reminds his hearers of the thousands of ducats pouring into the city week after week. Above all, he states again and again, arguing against the "young" procurator of San Marco and future doge, Francesco Foscari, that Venetians must continue to live in peace. This was how they were to maintain themselves, because they alone sailed the rivers and the seas, furnished everyone with needed commodities, and were approved and loved by all.

Historians have used Mocenigo's famous discourse as a source for analyzing the economic power of Venice. They have also sought in it clear traces of the political conflicts that rent the city assemblies, and they have extracted from it the arguments of one of the most famous spokesmen for what is usually called "the party of the sea." Such interpretations usually put little emphasis on Mocenigo's genuinely providentialist conception of Venetian history. He expresses it clearly, however: God inspired men to seek the refuge of the lagoons. God permitted them to remain there safely while Atilla ravaged the West. At that time the community made a pact with God: the Venetians were a chosen people. But, Mocenigo warned, if the Senate ceded to Francesco Foscari and followed the mirage of war with Milan, the Venetians' election was in great danger of being lost. By continuing to live at peace and remaining loyal to commerce, Venice would remain within the election of God, immutable in its power and prosperity. Mocenigo's reiterated arguments carefully concealed the fact that on the Mediterranean the Republic was far from being a peaceful power. All the terms he used to evoke peace, commerce, and wealth were deliberately connected, repeated, juxtaposed, and used as near synonyms in order to establish the prime verity of Venetian history: mastery of trade was God's gift to the Venetians. Even when Italy was at war and France, Spain, Burgundy, Russia, or Persia faced troubled times, the world's gold continued to arrive at the marketplace in Venice.

Chroniclers and historians had not waited for Doge Mocenigo's discourse to view commercial expansion as the first principle of the city's existence, but his discourse (and another that he gave not long before his death) have traditionally been taken as marking a turning point, even though a portion of the Venetian Terraferma had been conquered some twenty years earlier.[2] When Francesco Foscari succeeded Mocenigo as doge, Venice did indeed become deeply involved in Italian affairs, winning an enlargement of its territorial state but also setting up its decadence and its future ruin. At least this is what Venice's enemies said of the Italian wars and the reverses suffered by Venice the "Dominant" on the mainland. In his *Legende des Venitiens* Jean Lemaire de Belges describes two lions depicted in a pavement mosaic in San Marco. The first was "fat and sturdy and seemed to swim with his whole body over the waves, except for his front paws, which were on firm ground"; the second "had his entire body stretched out on the land and only his hind feet in the water, but he was extraordinarily thin and emaciated." A prophecy of Joachim of Fiore provided the explanation of this "portraiture." It was based on a simple opposition: the lion was fat and Venice would be wealthy as long as the Venetians sailed the seas; the lion would be thin, war would be inevitable, and the city would be ruined when the Venetians took it into their heads to conquer the mainland.[3]

Soon there were Venetians who said as much. The idea that territorial expansion was a fatal mistake runs throughout the *Diarii* of Girolamo Priuli. When Venice's domination of its mainland holdings collapsed in June 1509, Priuli drew up a list of the sins for which God was severely punishing Venice by its defeat. The sin of pride headed the list, but Priuli attributed overweening pride to all the rulers of the Italian mainland.[4] Ultramontane troops were close to Venice, and fear reigned in the city. As Priuli describes preparations for its defense, what does he write about? Stocking foodstuffs, of course, and troop movements, as well as bastions the Venetians erected at the river mouths and at the passageways through the littoral islands. The community's first line of defense, however, was its waters, which were abundant and deep and which, the experts on lagoon hydraulics assured the city, the enemy could not cross. Priuli's hope was that external disorders would die on the *ripe salse* (salty shores) of the lagoon. The city did what it had always done to survive: it closed itself up within its *aque maritime et salse.*[5] War had validated the ancient borders of the basin of the lagoon. The Venetians intended to resist at Santa Marta, at Lizzafusina, and at Chioggia.

Priuli's hopes were not disappointed. Venice remained impregnable, thus reinforcing one of the most solidly entrenched assertions of local historical discourse. The lagoons had provided a refuge from the time people first settled on the islands and the chain of offshore beaches. The waters of the lagoon, secure as thick walls, had always offered a protection that kept the city inviolate. But for those who know the texts, the *ripe salse* that our memorialist praises so highly evoke more than this first stereotype. Beginning with John the Deacon's first history of the city, all chroniclers agreed that within the shelter of the lagoons the expanding community realized a unique destiny. The isolation that Venetians so often vaunted was thus more than uniquely geographical: everything that was specific to Venice in fact resulted from that isolation. When populations from mainland towns took to the lagoon to escape the Lombard invasion, taking with them their holy relics and the treasures from their churches, an absolutely singular history began. The islanders cut all ties with their former home cities, which the chronicles tell us the new conquerors soon razed. The new lagoon society was born sovereign; it owed no allegiance to the powers that fought for dominance of the Italian peninsula.[6] This detour into Venetian legend is basic to our purposes. What does it tell us?

The lagoons founded the independence and the future power of Venice.

When the first populations settled among those waters, they were free of all jurisdictions because that site had been promised to them, assigned to them by God. Water enabled them to found a new city and invent a new history. The first mission of the water was to keep the inhabitants of the lagoon apart from the vicissitudes of Continental affairs. The corollary was the notion that Venetians were by nature unmindful of the land. When they were not navigating the waters of the lagoon or the open sea, they forged up the rivers that emptied into the lagoon basin, thus broadening the horizons of their original commerce.[7] Only the king of Italy, Pepin, was supposed to have attempted to reduce the liberty and the singularity of Venice by invading a space that escaped his power. According to local tradition, his expedition turned into a disaster because the waters played their protective role to perfection. The doge put the women and children, the magistrates, and the priests on the safest islands at the heart of the lagoon. The Franks arrived by sea, and they soon devastated the settlement at Malamocco, on the littoral islands. Encouraged by that first victory, they moved into the lagoon basin, but their big ships were soon helpless, defeated by the marshes, low tides, and the tangle of channels. The invaders were massacred.[8] This was the last time that the lagoons were violated. Many centuries later, in 1379, the Genoese successfully besieged Chioggia but failed to enter the lagoons.

In this focused view Venetian history turned its back to the land, as if its coherence and its deepest meaning depended on maritime involvement. For the Venetians (and for their historians, both past and more recent), Cassiodorus had already said it all. There were no scythes in the lagoons, no tools to cultivate the land, but only boats and cylinders used for the earliest operations to exploit the salt flats. The Venetians had no plows; they were mariners. Some centuries later their precarious reed huts had been transformed into a stone city. When that happened, Venetians were rich: they remained unacquainted with plows, and they were still mariners.

Such representations explain why the history of Venice was written as it was until not too long ago. I shall cite only one example, that of the ample and in many ways extremely interesting work of Pompeo Molmenti.[9] According to Molmenti, there is no ambiguity. Venice's golden age ended with its conquests on the Italian mainland, though the power of the Signoria seemed the most solid in those same decades. The final blow to the Venetian monopoly came when the Portuguese opened a new trade route for shipping pepper. Venice was thrown into decline.[10] For Molmenti, the territorial state was a useless, even harmful appendage; in any case, it was of little interest to the historian because it was foreign to the ontological realities of the Republic, which were political and economic. Historians' awareness of what Venice's *dominium di terra* represented was long superficial because it was considered of secondary importance. The historians analyzed long-distance trade and merchant convoys; carefully scrutinized the history of Venice's far-flung empire; and evaluated the results of the Turkish advance and the great voyages of discovery, which they judged to have been catastrophic for Venice. Aside from the military events that punctuated the conquest and then the reconquest of mainland territories, they ignored the Venetian *stato di terra*.

In the past three or four decades historians' perspectives have changed radically. A vast critical enquiry has been opened. Launched by two pioneering studies,[11] it continues to be fed by a number of monographs and by differing examples and viewpoints. One new theme is a broad-ranging interest in the political and social character of the regional state in Italy. Scholars became interested in Venice and the Veneto as one geopolitical area among others. Their aim was to determine the "modernity" of the system of government that the Venetian Republic set up in its provincial holdings, hence to test how well the bureaucracy of the *Dominante* functioned. They also attempted to measure the process of creating an aristocracy in local societies and the long-term effects of conquest on the mechanisms of political and social transformation. The set of topics treated in analyses of regional states continued to be enriched and diversified after those pioneering studies.[12] The history of systems of powers, central and local, was investigated, in particular with regard to Vicenza, the first city to place itself voluntarily under Venetian domination.[13] Another study focused on the relations between the center and the periphery to elaborate a different model of political and social organization in Brescia, at the edge of the sphere of Venetian domination.[14] Other scholars have examined the system of relations structuring Venice's mainland state by means of a long-term survey of the central topic of taxation.[15] Comparison with Milan or the Grand Duchy of Tuscany is no longer necessary; the Venetian Terraferma is now a field unto itself and is in fact one of the most active sectors of historical analysis today. The history profession has finally grasped the fact that Venetian domination depended on two structural realities, two spaces over which the Republic and its governing class established their sovereignty and from which they gained their wealth. Just as the Venetian Senate, the city's principal assembly, had separate registers for land and sea in the fifteenth century, so historians now discriminate between the two directions of Venetian expansion—toward the Continent and overseas—as they reconstruct how Venetians moved out from the city itself and the lagoon basin.

If these areas of investigation have been established, however, they have not yet been connected with one another, which poses a problem. A simple fact explains why a division between them has persisted.[16] A fascination with distant horizons makes us forget that the city on the lagoon was closely dependent on its hinterland. Even when that hinterland is not forgotten, the relations Venice maintained with the mainland are often seen as little more than the indispensable complement to its maritime vocation. Until the fourteenth century, the texts repeat, the shores of the lagoon marked a frontier between two worlds, two histories, and two cultures. Until the fourteenth century Venice did not even possess the village of Mestre, which was part of the district of Treviso. Venice was "a great ship moored off the Italian mainland."[17] This view of Venice existing in splendid isolation requires a sudden and radical change in Venetian policy taking place at the end of the Middle Ages. Without ever possessing a *contado* and, unlike the principal cities of Italy of the communes, without going through a difficult and bellicose subjection of a first, nearby area of domination, the maritime city is supposed to have done a sudden political about-face in order to undertake the conquest of vast dominions on the Terraferma, thus becoming a major Continental power.

Interpretations of this sort neglect three important facts. First, the lands and the waters of the lagoon formed a sort of aquatic *contado* within the limits of the Duchy of Venice, serving the capital city as a manpower pool and a reservoir of resources. Next, the frontier between the mainland and the world of the lagoons was never so tightly closed that it created two separate histories: men, merchandise, and capital circulated. Finally, even before the period of its conquests on the mainland Venice played a role in Italian affairs.

This is the reasoning that underlies my own analysis and determines its pace. Venetian commerce cannot be conceived of without the networks that connected the port to the lands to the west, to rural Lombardy, and to the valleys of the Alps. Still, the history of the relations between Venice and Italian and Continental lands cannot be restricted to the flow of merchandise in transit, the movement of boats on the rivers, or the caravans of pack animals that made their way over the Alpine passes.

TERRESTRIAL HORIZONS

Venice and the Duchy: An Aquatic Contado

First, the lagoon basin. What is the lagoon? Anyone who has read Cassiodorus or the medieval descriptions of the site will answer, without hesitation, that it is water and marshes. It was from that water and those marshlands that the Venetians drew their first wealth: fish and, above all, salt, which they soon sold in northern Italy.[18] According to local documentation, exploitation of the salt flats preceded the existence of Venice, since the saltworks began to be known somewhat before the year 1000,[19] and references increase up to the twelfth century. The salt-producing marshlands finally emerged from the shadows. Salt trade does not seem to have thrived in the period of the construction of Venetian power: the saltworks were in crisis. We have no information on the causes of their decline, which were perhaps ecological. Several *fondamenti* were even abandoned. Later restoration projects signaled revived activity, and by the eleventh century the lagoon was again exporting salt. The better part of the lagoon salt was produced in the northern basin, where some place names—Sette Soleri, for example—are fossilized reminders of those earlier activities. Later, during the final decades of the eleventh century, the major saltworks were located in the southern parts of the duchy.

At that point salt production was concentrated around Chioggia, which in the twelfth century became one of the most active centers for the exportation of salt in the Mediterranean. Venetian salt was distributed via the Adige and the Po Rivers.[20] Jean-Claude Hocquet tells us that "in 1200, at its height, the production [of salt] from Chioggia arrived in all the lands to the south and east of the curving line of the crest of the Alps, and it crossed the passes of the Apennines to Tuscany."[21] Thus, at one time, when the great Benedictine monasteries and the Venetian lineages of the Gradenigo or the Ziani controlled these properties, Chioggia was genuinely prosperous. That prosperity did not last, however; in the thirteenth century a decline that was already under way accelerated. Its causes were several: heavy Venetian taxation, competition from new centers of salt production,[22] and the economic policies of the capital city. We have seen that the port of Venice imported massive amounts of salt, thus giving the Venetians a supply monopoly.[23] By the end of the Middle Ages salt production in the lagoon was only residual. In Chioggia fewer than 10 percent of the *fondamenti* that had been exploited at the height of salt production were still active. Most of the saltworks at the southern end of the lagoons had given way to the much more profitable pursuit of fishing. Three centuries earlier the same thing had happened in the waters of the northern end of the basin.

This brief summary of the history of the salt marshes throws light on the early resources of the duchy, but it also confirms another fact: the landscape of the lagoon evolved. The environment provided the first populations of the lagoon with an ample supply of fish and game, but the rising tide of refugees after the Lombard invasion made it necessary to exploit those resources more intensely. Following the Byzantine tradition, the open waters and salt ponds within the borders of the duchy were appropriated by regalian right. Vast stretches of water, tidal flats *(barena)*, and somewhat higher ground *(tumba)* were ceded at an early date to the various communities and religious establishments if these did not simply usurp them. Great aquatic domains were created, and many of them were soon developed,[24] as a quick tour of the archives of the monasteries of the lagoon and the city, with their wealth of eleventh- and twelfth-century donations, cessions, and rental agreements for fishing zones, will demonstrate. These many contracts reflect immense monastic properties, whose quitrents are given in terms of fish and birds. The holdings of the aristocratic lineages were probably not far behind those of the religious institutions, but more sporadic evidence conceals their profits better.

During the final third of the thirteenth century the judges of the Piovego, who supervised the public domain, launched a vast campaign to verify titles to property. That sweeping judiciary action was aimed at returning to communal ownership lands and waters that had been usurped by private persons. The register of the decisions rendered by these judges (the extant records begin in 1282) reveals the scope of the infrastructure that was put into place at that date to regulate fishing.[25] Venice was one of the most populous cities of the West, and the lagoon worked to feed its immense market.[26]

Even iconographic evidence at a later date fails to communicate what fishing was like in the lagoon basin. Thousands of texts speak of an intense activity. Weirs made of reeds and marsh grass lashed to pilings kept fish confined within in the *valli* of the lagoons. This technique made use of a well-known natural phenomenon. At the end of the winter, in February and March, certain species of fish left the sea to seek the shallow waters of the lagoon, which warmed more quickly than the sea. They remained there until the end of autumn, when they returned to the sea in search of waters that cooled at a slower rate. The reproductive cycles of other species dictated their return to the sea. From July to Christmas the *valli* were closed off, thus controlling the migration of the fish and facilitating an abundant catch. In the thirteenth century the councils concluded that the intensive use of weirs in the *valli* was impeding water circulation and accelerating silting in certain lagoon bottoms. A number of measures were passed, but the need to feed the population proved stronger than a desire to preserve the environment. Investment in lagoon fishing continued to the point that by the fifteenth century signs of overexploitation were perceptible. Venetian capital controlled the better part of this sector of activity, which employed a sizable labor force concentrated in certain parishes of the city and on the islands of the lagoon.[27]

The wealth of the Venetian *contado* and the activities pursued there— fishing for eels, shrimp, and mullet and hunting water fowl—belong within this general scheme. Still, this accurate but familiar picture of a prevalent water-based economy has all too often led to neglect of other sources of wealth and other activities. The lagoon communities attempted to practice agriculture on lands recently reclaimed from the water, small islets soon consolidated by human industry, and the littoral islands. This primarily took the form of kitchen gardens, which are mentioned in even the earliest chronicles that speak of the colonization of the lagoon.[28] As Venice became more densely populated and more urban, gardens and vineyards withdrew to the center of the basin, but the documentation shows that vegetable plots and chicken coops existed at the edges of the duchy as well. At the mouth of the Brenta, near Chioggia, a genuine "countryside" appeared. Beginning in the eleventh century, land-clearance and land-reclamation projects turned an amphibious landscape of reeds, salt ponds, and *barene* in a delta that for centuries had marked the frontier between Venice and the Kingdom of Italy into a landscape of carefully cultivated plots conquered from water, mud, and brush and protected by dikes.[29]

Garden plots separated by drainage ditches provided another typical lagoon landscape. Even at the end of the Middle Ages the north lagoon resembled a countryside interspersed with water. Grapes grew at Torcello and Mazzorbo, although the fragile vines were regularly threatened with inundation and produced a wine of mediocre quality, probably with an odd, salty bouquet. Vegetable plots and orchards must have been numerous, to judge from the way gardens invaded the built-up areas and trees grew amid the ruins as the population of the islands dwindled and people abandoned their lands for Venice. The history of human occupation worked backwards. Eventually the meadows of the islands and the barrier beaches were cut for fodder, and animals were put out to pasture on them; a few fields were still sown, and the few remaining wood plots were intensively exploited.

When all these small notations are put together, they make up a surprising picture of an agricultural lagoon where all available space was coveted in spite of ongoing depopulation. The natural milieu was profoundly different from that of the northern lagoon today. Animals wandered from one island to another, crossing the channels; untended, they penetrated into the fishing preserves of the *valli* and into the hunting zones, where they devastated the canebrakes and reed beds. Herds could even reach the shores of the lagoon without boat transport, following paths that today's archaeologists have traced. Do we need better proof that the water was shallow or that the milieu that stretched between the shore and the lagoon was a watery mix of salt ponds and lands subject to flooding? Later, that entire landscape disappeared in land-reclamation projects that drew a firmer border between the land and the world of the lagoon.[30] And do we need better proof of the permeability of the lagoon basin? Not only fish, game, and agricultural products but also men moved incessantly from the lagoon to the land and from the land back to the lagoon. The islands at the northern end of the lagoon belonged to Venice and were part of the duchy, but since they lay only a few oar strokes away from Altino, they were anchored to the mainland as well. That proximity explains why immigrants from areas around Treviso or

Padua settled at Torcello or Burano. It was just as easy for the islanders to get to the shores of the lagoon as it was for their animals; they rented fields or meadows there; they worked there. On that frontier not only the land but also the water and the marshes were part of the complex morphology of the lagoon, where the two worlds of land and lagoon communicated and mingled.

Salt and fish were not all that the lagoons furnished. From the islands and the *lidi* craft piled high with fruits and vegetables—melons, cabbages, beets and other roots, greens, onions, and plums—made their way to the capital city; from the chicken coops of Mazzorbo and Ammiana came eggs and fowl; San Felice and Sant'Erasmo sent animals to be butchered. Garden produce went, for the most part, to the great city market of Rialto; hens, cows, and pigs served to feed the island communities even though there were also circuits of exchange with Venice and the mainland. I might remark that during the early phase of their domination of the duchy Venetians did not scorn capital investments or profits drawn from a modest amphibious agriculture. Who, in fact, owned those muddy thickets, those meadows attacked by the tides, those vines planted in the shelter of dikes and low walls? The names that return again and again in notarial acts give eloquent proof that from as early as such matters can be documented, which means the tenth century, the leading families of Venice showed a marked interest in lagoon land that had to be wrenched from the water.

The fact remains, however, that this "aquatic *contado*," this Terraferma before the fact within the lagoon, offered only limited possibilities. Venetians added to it a second, less marshy space that Sante Bortolami has aptly called the "invisible *contado*."

Venice and the Mainland: "An Invisible Contado"

As we have seen, the wills of two members of the Partecipazio family are of great importance to the history of maritime commerce, but the extensive landholdings of that family of doges have received less attention. The Partecipazios concentrated within their hands sizable properties situated both inside and outside the duchy, for example, near Treviso. A century later there was a clear pattern of Venetians moving in the direction of the mainland, infiltrating the coastal plain in a broad arc from Grado to Cavarzere. They generally did not penetrate more than twenty or thirty kilometers from the shores of the lagoon, although there are signs of holdings in country areas along the rivers, including the Po.

It seems that for decades capital from Venice was systematically, patiently, and widely invested. Massive purchases seem to have been rare. The various economic operators, in particular the monasteries, waited for property to become available in a few privileged zones, where they then accumulated lands, houses, and vineyards. By the twelfth century ecclesiastical institutions and to a lesser degree a few "great" families had managed to concentrate sizable estates near Treviso, from Mestre to Mirano, and around Altino, Campalto, and Tessera. The same was true of certain regions around Padua, such as the Saccisica and the Riviera of the Brenta.[31] The list of property owners contains few surprises: we find the Venetian monasteries of San Giorgio Maggiore and San Zaccaria, monasteries from the lagoon areas such as San Cipriano in Murano and San Giovanni Evangelista in Torcello, and the Michiel and Contarini families. A map of all these Venetian holdings would show a few feelers reaching out as far as Istria and Romagna. Such isolated bits of evidence of the wealth of a few should not obscure the larger fact that although Venetians quite naturally left their lagoons to take to the sea, they also penetrated into the nearby districts of the March of Treviso. There they found agricultural products to feed a rapidly growing city, and they gained control over the grain needed throughout the lagoon.

The holdings of one institution or of one family might thus include fishing grounds, open water, canebrakes, fields, and woods. A marshy, muddy patch did not constitute a frontier. To the contrary, both in their composition and in the forms of their exploitation, these holdings reflected the reality of the relations between the lagoons and the mainland.

This phenomenon, already discernible before the thirteenth century, thus illuminates even more clearly the modus operandi of the aristocratic houses governing the Venetian commune. I do not think that the change can be attributed simply to the nature of the documentation. Let me give two examples. The first of these, that of the Badoer family, is well known. In 1288 a vast patrimony of lands, waters, vineyards, meadows, mills, and houses on the left bank of the Brenta between Mestre and Padua was divided among Marco Badoer's sons.[32] The Badoer family held a second group of properties in the territory of Treviso, along the Musestre, and still others in the *contado* of Ferrara. It was around Padua, however, that the family possessions were the most valuable and the most longstanding. The family *castrum*, probably built by Marco's father, was at Borbiago. My second example is that of the Querini and the Tiepolo. In the thirteenth century the circle of the governing families of Venice was somewhat enlarged, and first the very wealthy Querini family, then the Tiepolos, joined the elite. These new aristocrats hastened to imitate the strategies worked out by the older aristocratic clans. In 1255 Marco Querini purchased from the canons of the cathedral of Adria a piece of land called Le Papozze, the transmission of which we can follow in a series of Querini family wills. The Tiepolos invested instead in the district of Treviso, where their property at Marocco henceforth identified one branch of their segmented lineage.[33] Finally, less famous newly rich *popolari*, the Bellegno and the Viaro, for example, also made substantial investments in land.

Thus Venetian capital penetrated increasingly into rural areas of the March of Treviso. Beginning in the latter half of the thirteenth century, matrimonial alliances reflect reinforced ties between the governing families of Venice and the most famous lineages of the mainland. At the same time, however, the social base of the landowner group broadened. The generation after the pioneers who participated in the prosperous times of the *gran guadagno* and made the family fortune often put some of the profits into land around Padua or Treviso. Their first priority was to reinvest those profits in commerce, however. They also continued to finance Venice's advancing urbanization, participating in the fever for land reclamation and construction that characterized the thirteenth century. Putting these few facts together, we get a clear picture of the financial repercussions of the expansion that occurred during that century. If income from land enabled some Venetians to accumulate capital (as was equally true elsewhere), the sea enabled many of Venice's nouveaux riches to gain access to land.[34]

There are many explanations for the increasing presence of people from the lagoon area on the mainland, among them a desire for a sure supply of agricultural products and, for families recently enriched, a search for social prestige. The older lineages, who had for some time concluded prestigious alliances outside the duchy, had less need of this added luster. There is no doubt, however, that the investments themselves brought attractive earnings.

The trend toward mainland investment further intensified during the second half of the thirteenth century. The final defeat of Ezzelino da Romano in 1259 gave free rein to Venetian interests, to the point that the political authorities soon reacted. In just a few years the commune passed a series of laws aimed at Venetians who yielded to the acquisition fever. The first of these laws forbade certain purchases; a second made ownership of such properties incompatible with holding some public offices. Still others show that the councils were attempting (in vain) to avoid undue pressure and eliminate partisan votes. At one point, for example, it was decreed that when debate in the Great Council involved the mainland, all members who owned land or held fiefs in the areas concerned were to leave the hall.[35] In 1290 similar legislation concerning the March of Treviso and the *contado* of Ferrara was broadened to include not only direct proprietors but also all council members whose relatives or allies held property in those two regions. During the fourteenth century practical difficulties in enforcing these measures tended to limit their impact, and they eventually applied only to the proprietors themselves. There is a simple explanation for this greater laxity: as mainland investment grew, the Great Council found it impossible to bar so many nobles from its sessions, so it relaxed its requirements. Legislation may also have become less urgent.

How are we to understand these events? Recent studies have corrected the picture of what had long been seen as a continuous evolution throughout the thirteenth century.[36] Some have detected in wills and other texts produced during the final third of the century reflections of a crisis of conscience among Venetians.[37] In the religious sphere, that crisis seems to have been translated as an emotional spasm, traces of which can be seen on both the individual and collective levels, that viewed the Evil One as responsible for Venice's troubles. Its effects can also be seen on the economic level, however. Some Venetians seem to have preferred the more secure revenues from real estate and land ownership to the uncertain profits and risks of long-distance trade. At any rate, this is Giorgio Cracco's interpretation. Be that as it may, the many laws voted within a limited timespan mark the existence of dissent within the governing group and also demonstrate the victory, at least on the legislative level, of those who supported trade.

There is another element that we should not lose sight of. What the texts call the "interest" of the commune of Venice was of course often identical to the interests of a few powerful persons. Marco Zeno's properties around

Padua, for example, were one of the causes of the conflict between Venice and Padua in 1234–35. Among the groups urging greater intervention on the mainland, the major landowners brought enough pressure to bear to determine policy on several occasions in the thirteenth century. We can see from the way it fluctuated, however, that such a policy was in no way linear. Moreover, the fact that its aims were at times imputable to a group of powerful men makes the policy no less real.

The history of the connections between Venice and Italy does not end with an account of the empirical relations between the city and the mainland. Myth or no myth, Venice, the city built in the middle of the lagoons, had no predetermined destiny. Its ties with the *Regnum Italiae* were created in various phases. A study of those relations is indispensable, for it will enable us to place Venice in the context of a broader history.

Italian Tribulations

Even in the very early centuries of Venice's history the lagoons never constituted a closed, isolated political universe. Situated between empires,[38] by sheer necessity they maintained relations with both East and West. The history of Venice in the lagoons is usually cast as an opposition between Francophiles and Grecophiles. One such episode ended in 805 with the probable establishment of the duchy's allegiance to the emperor of the East. Byzantium soon won back Dalmatia, Venetia, and the "maritime provinces." The Grecophile faction triumphed that time, bringing to power Agnello Partecipazio, who organized the transfer of the seat of the duchy to the Rialto archipelago. The series of treaties organizing the Venetians' relations with Carolingian lands dates from the decades that followed. The attraction of the Empire of the East had not been eliminated definitively, however, even in the face of growing Venetian power.

The affair of the Candiano doges illustrates the complexity of this long history, which was also marked by interminable struggles with the patriarchates of Aquilaea and Grado. The Candiano family had vast landholdings on the mainland and enjoyed close relations with the kings of Italy, beginning in the mid-tenth century with Otto the Great, who was also the king of Germany.[39] The doge, Pietro IV Candiano, married a German woman, Waldrada, and an entire deputation from the *Regnum Italiae* transformed the ducal court. As Roberto Cessi depicts the situation, the nascent Venice was about to lose its soul.[40] Throughout the reign of the fourth Pietro Candiano the pull of the Continent increased, and in 976 a violent riot put an end to his tenure as doge. He was killed, along with his young son, and their bodies were dragged to Rialto and deposited at the butchers' hall, while a fire devastated the center of Venice. The original Ducal Palace went up in flames, as did the basilica of San Marco and the church of San Teodoro. Three hundred houses disappeared with these holy monuments. From San Marco to Santa Maria Zobenigo, the city was in flames. Pietro Orseolo was chosen to succeed the assassinated doge, and although he was saintly enough to merit canonization at a later date, peace did not last long. The intrigues of the Candiano party, still supported by the German emperors, began anew. Three years later Vitale Candiano became doge, but it was under his successor, Tribuno Memmo, an ally of the Candianos and heir to some of their fortune and their clientele, that the imperial menace became pressing. The duchy was attacked; territories on its frontiers at Chioggia and Cavarzere were occupied. (I am following the dramatic account of these events by the chronicler John the Deacon.) The death of Emperor Otto II in 982 saved the independence of Venice. His son Otto III, who reigned at the end of the century, at the time of the triumphant dogeship of Pietro II Orseolo (991– 1009), renounced the traditional tribute that Venice had paid to the Empire and accorded Venetian merchants unimpeded access to Pavia via the Po and the Adige.

Thus ended a dramatic and bloody phase of lagoon history, and after Doge Orseolo's expedition to Dalmatia, Venice could turn to its ultimate aim of maritime expansion. Still, and I insist on this point, the city's ties to the mainland periodically mitigated the attraction of distant horizons and the eastern Mediterranean. Moreover, such returns toward the mainland and toward Italy were more than simple reactions to tensions, crises, and setbacks to Venetian sea power. What, then, should we think of them?

First, an obvious point needs to be stressed. Any attempt to reconstruct the history of the relations between Venice and Italy must involve the history of Venetian trade. In order to fulfil its function of commercial middleman, Venice had to make sure that its merchandise could circulate throughout a wide network of overland and river routes. Any change in the political and military balance of powers in the March of Treviso or in northern Italy in general threatened that redistribution system. The hostilities between Frederick Barbarossa and the Italian communes, for example, seriously perturbed commercial exchanges with the Holy Roman Empire, and only the Peace of Venice in 1177 allowed the situation to return to normal. We have seen how that truce was exploited in order to legitimate Venetian hegemony over the Adriatic and bolster the sovereignty of the doge.[41] Still, a well-attested fact indicates that Continental commerce was not forgotten: the emperor extended throughout the Empire the customs privileges that the kings of Italy had accorded to Venice.[42]

It is important not to separate what was intrinsically mixed in Venetian policy. Economic preoccupations, it bears repeating, were at the heart of diplomatic events and wars. It is within this framework that the hostilities of the first half of the thirteenth century between Venice and Emperor Frederick II and his allies must be understood. Venice threw its full weight against the da Romanos and their attempt to dominate the March of Treviso. As early as the second decade of the century the rise to power of Ezzelino II prompted a reaction in Venice.[43] Later Venice, Padua, the Lombard League, and Rome formed a united front against the da Romanos in an alliance that included some of the great houses of the region, the Camposampiero and Sambonifacio families in particular. Until 1237, with the exception of the low point of the war between Venice and Padua in 1234–35, the Venetians attempted to oppose the constitution of a hegemonic seignory in the March of Treviso. That policy intensified until the victorious attack against Ezzelino da Romano and his forces, in which both the ancient families and more recent additions to the Venetian aristocracy participated.

Opposition to Frederick II enabled the Venetians to regain their hold over the Po delta. They joined the coalition grouped around Gregory IX against Ferrara, held by Salinguerra, and they helped to take the city.[44] Their reward was an extremely advantageous commercial treaty giving them control over Ferrarese trade. Henceforth all merchandise on its way to Ferrara from overseas had to go through Venice. For a while a squadron of Venetian ships patrolled the mouths of the Po to enforce respect of these clauses, and in 1258 the Venetians reinforced their control by building the fort of Marcamò, which gave them control of the Po di Primaro, the branch of the Po that had the most traffic.[45] The original wooden fortifications were rebuilt in stone in 1270. This time the Venetians had bested all the competition, the merchants of Ravenna, Ferrara, and Ancona. They held the Po, and they had the power to ban access to it. They used that absolute economic weapon during the last third of the thirteenth century by closing the Adriatic to the Lombards, as the chronicler Salimbene da Parma noted with irritation.[46]

This is the context of the disastrous episode of the War of Ferrara. In 1308 the Venetians took advantage of a crisis of succession in Ferrara and the civic unrest that followed to take Castello Tebaldo, a fortress at the gates of Ferrara that controlled the bridge over the Po. Clement V organized a sharp reprimand, placing Venice under interdict, and eventually even called for a crusade against Venice. All the cities that were rivals or traditional enemies of Venice—Adria, Ravenna, Cervia, and Padua—responded to his call. The Venetian troops were defeated, Venice lost Fort Marcamò, and normal transit was interrupted. Venice conceded defeat and recognized the territorial rights of the Holy See, and Ferrara passed to the Papal States.[47] The Venetian ambassadors insisted that the Venetian commune had not been motivated by territorial ambition or any desire for domination but had only wanted to protect the full and entire exercise of its rights over the waterway of the Po. On that point Venice did not yield.[48]

The agreement with Verona, concluded rapidly and in great secrecy, was in fact intended to compensate Venice for the disastrous effects of its sorry defeat. In exchange for a promise to reduce the price of salt and renounce Venice's right to levy customs duties, in 1310 the Venetians were permitted to dig a canal between the Adige and the Po that would allow river traffic to bypass Ferrara. The project was carried out, but a treaty with the pope soon made the new waterway obsolete.[49] The swiftness of the Venetian reaction confirms the vital importance to Venice of relations with its hinterland and of its control of the waterways.

The successive events in this brief narrative are in themselves convincing. They show a tenacious pursuit of an economic policy, but they also show that Venice's intervention in Italy, and particularly in the Venetian Terraferma, was complex over the long term and that it had broader implications than a simple response to a need, imperious as that need was, for free transit. Studies tell us that the large landholders intervened decisively on several occasions. Moreover, networks and alliances were constituted that from one phase to another brought Venetians into the broader political arena. Venice single-mindedly pursued the objective of maintaining a balance of forces among the various communes, at least in its own hinterland. Beginning in the fourteenth century Venice intervened diplomatically or militarily on an increasing number of occasions. One such occasion was Venice's participation in league with Padua and Florence in the Scaliger War, a campaign in 1336–39 against the expansionist policies of the della Scala lords of Verona. Another example is the repeated conflicts between Venice and the Carrara dynasty in Padua. Venice had a discernible Continental policy that cannot be totally explained by the tribulations of a community torn between a land party and a sea party, though those factions did exist. In short, the lagoon lived breathing the salt sea air, but it and its inhabitants lived on and off the nearby land as well.

Recent studies support this view.[50] It has been shown that contrary to the thesis of the splendid isolation of the lagoons, Venetians occupied the post of *podestà* in Padua, Bologna, and Todi. Thus, such officials were part of an itinerant political personnel long thought to have been exclusively Lombard, Emilian, or Tuscan. They were chosen to serve as magistrates at a time when that characteristically Italian system of government was spreading among the communal cities. The phenomenon of Venetian participation in this system, which for a long time was treated anecdotally, turns out to have been more widespread than previously thought. Although at first Venetians may have been called to serve as *podestà* in towns of the Venetian Terraferma and the Marches that fell within the privileged zones of influence of their city of origin, they also served in the rest of communal Italy. What are we to deduce from this? In the first place, this system put into place a finely tuned chronology of relations with various other cities of Italy. Next, we can learn much from biographies of these men and their careers. In the early thirteenth century the Terraferma offered the Venetian noble an extraordinary opportunity to enlarge his field of action on both the political and the economic level. The system gave the great houses new ways to conserve or augment their power, wealth, and honor: when they discovered the office of *podestà*, they incorporated it into their career choices, and some of the most prestigious among them soon served in posts much more distant from home than Padua or Vicenza, for example, at Fermo, Mantua, or Florence. It is clear, however, that the wealthy landowners of the Terraferma did not renounce their interests in the Mediterranean and the Venetian colonial domain. Individual careers alternated between the mainland and the empire, with many men pursuing a career in first one area and then the other according to their stage in life or the political situation.[51] Men and families made use of the sea and the land, drawing profits from both.

To conclude, Venice's ventures on the Italian mainland underwent periods of acceleration, some of which we have seen. Moments of more clearly defined and more radical changes were yet to come, but they came gradually, first in the period of the Venetian conquest of the Terraferma, when Venice became one of the great territorial powers in Italy, and then later, when the life of the Republic and its elites no longer followed the rhythms of the shipping convoys of the *mude*, following instead those of the harvests and of summer retreats to the country. As I have tried to show, the narrow islands besieged by the sea were always connected to the land, and the primary lines of communication between those *sedes marinae* and the Continent were the waterways.[52]

NARRATIVES OF COMMERCIAL DYNAMICS

The earliest sources show Venetian merchants moving toward the hinterland and beyond, plying the river network of the Po, the Adige, and their tributaries. In the ninth century their presence is attested as far inland as Pavia.

On the Adige and the Po

From the time of the first treaty between Emperor Lothair and the doge of Venice, Piero Tradonico, organized trade relations had existed with the *Regnum*. The rivers were open to the Venetians, who were promised freedom to trade "without difficulties or violence." The *ripaticum* and other fees were levied "in the ports and on the rivers" following "the ancient custom." These pacts were confirmed by the successive sovereigns of the Kingdom of Italy, and they were eventually rendered even more favorable to the "men of Venice" by a reduction of taxes granted by Berengar I in 888. A silver coin struck at Rialto at the time shows proof of active exchanges with Italy. Arabic and Byzantine gold coins circulated in the Mediterranean, which means that this new coin was used exclusively for Continental trade, where silver was the rule. The obverse of this silver coin, which resembled the Carolingian denier, bore the name of the emperor of the West, perhaps less in recognition of any sort of sovereignty than to make the coin minted in Venice conform more strictly to the characteristics of Carolingian coinage.[53] The reverse, however, bore the distinguishing mark of Venice, a symbol that grew in importance as time went by.[54]

By the final decades of the ninth century the Venetians were sufficiently powerful to attack their competitors, moving simultaneously to consolidate their positions in the Mediterranean and toward the Continent.

This outward movement had its high and low points. One temporary reversal was a commercial blockade of the lagoon area by Otto II that ended with his death soon thereafter. Brief as it was, the episode shows how strongly Venice depended on its hinterland for provisions and even for survival. During the decades of the laborious and turbulent construction of its power, Venice experienced more successes than setbacks, however. Pacts with the Empire were renewed. The Venetians installed river trading stations on the Piave and Livenza Rivers, and the foothold they gained at Treviso gave them control of the Sile River and an important intersection of overland routes. Some texts of the early eleventh century furnish further details about the shadowy figure of the Venetian merchant. An imperial placit authorized Venetians to sell their silks at Pavia, capital of the *Regnum,* and at Ferrara, at the time the site of the biggest fair in northern Italy. The *Honorantiae civitatis Papiae,* a well-known text of Lombard law, describes the Venetian merchants. They and their counterparts from Amalfi provided costly products from the East to the court and the wealthy, and they returned to the duchy with the agricultural products indispensable to it, notably wheat bought from the monasteries of Lombardy. Venetian riverboats still plied the inland waterways, distributing fish and salt in the valleys of the Adige, the Brenta, the Piave, and the Tagliamento.

We can extract a few essential points from this thicket of events. Under the reign of Conrad II the turbulent revolts and uprisings that shook the *Regnum Italiae* seemed to slow, if not actually halt, the Venetians' traditional commercial activities. Trade picked up again during the second half of the eleventh century,[55] but soon commercial expansion was seriously shaken. Commerce on the lagoon was born and had developed on both land and sea, but after the First Crusade everything changed. Maritime trade rose steeply. Individuals and families found new financial and social opportunities, and increased trade was a source of generous profits, social promotion, and renewal. Some fortunes were consolidated; others were built. The era of the *gran guadagno* had arrived, bringing with it an excitement that carried mariners and merchants, filled with pride and confidence, to Romania and Egypt. Land was still indispensable, however: the community depended on it to feed its population and to provide the raw materials needed to fit its ships and swell its exports. Control of the river routes was more imperative than ever because the better part of the merchandise that passed through Rialto on its way to Italy or to the Empire used those waterways. Venetians gradually ended their own participation in river trade, however, and the boatmen who plied the Po and the Adige came increasingly from the nearby cities of the mainland.

Venice protected its interests in a number of ways. The 1107 treaty with Verona offers an excellent illustration of Venetian policy. It established a political alliance between the two cities, but it also included commercial clauses. The Veronese promised to guarantee free circulation on the Adige between their city and the border of the duchy. The customs duties to be paid were carefully stipulated, and a juridical framework was instituted to handle eventual commercial litigation.[56] A long series of treaties, interrupted by occasional outbreaks of hostilities, punctuated the twelfth century. There were repeated pacts with Verona in which the Adige played a central role; a treaty with Ferrara in 1191 guaranteed open navigation on the Po; there was an accord with Treviso, a treaty with Friuli, and more.[57] These texts describe, examine, and display mastery of every segment of the system of waterways that linked the urban centers of northern Italy to the Adriatic. To the north there was the Sile, which at the time emptied directly into the lagoon, thus connecting Venice to the district of Treviso and to the point of convergence of overland routes to Germany. Next came the Brenta, the water route to Padua, rendered navigable by major works projects. Improvements made in 1141 led to a conflict between Venice and Padua;[58] other projects were launched in 1186 and 1209. The Adige required constant surveillance: boats could travel upriver as far as Trent, where merchandise was transhipped to Bolzano and on to the Tyrol.[59] Finally, the Po and its many tributaries provided the principal routes to northern Italy. The Venetians fought constantly, first with Comacchio, then with Ferrara, to retain mastery of the delta.[60]

At the risk of seeming to ignore strict chronology, we can state that treaties followed one another in an unending litany (which I shall not recite) up to the Venetian conquest of the Terraferma. Some of these, for example, the treaties that concluded the various episodes of the wars with Ferrara, have already been mentioned. The risk is a calculated one, however. The history of Venetian commerce shows strong ups and downs. We are told that in the twelfth century the sea opened wider to Venetian sailors and merchants. That may well be so. In that case the land served to complete the Venetian monopoly, that is, the obligation common to all to provision their ships in Venice, hence to pay Venetian customs. The Venetians not only assiduously pursued this goal, they realized it. One after the other the treaties just cited served the dual objectives of giving the Venetians control of the mouth of all the rivers between Istria and the Po delta and granting special protections to Venetian merchants. Still, as we have seen, although those objectives were of primordial importance, they did not totally exhaust the goals of Venice's Continental policy.

Slowly, then, as Venetians took to the sea in greater and greater numbers, they no longer traveled up the rivers. Here we can do no better than to turn to Martino da Canale.

"The Germans and the Bavarians, the French and the Lombards . . ."

Martino da Canale offers an explicit summary of the situation in Venice at the election of Doge Marino Morosini in 1249: "And the Venetians went on the seas and they bought merchandise . . . and from all places they brought it to Venice. And there came there directly to buy it the Germans and the Bavarians, the French and the Lombards, the Tuscans and the Hungarians, and all the peoples who lived from commerce, and they carried that merchandise to their own countries." In only a few sentences Canale describes the activity of the Rialto as a market and the changes that had occurred in the city's land commerce. The Venetian monopoly was in place, and the Venetians left it to others to transport merchandise. Now Venetians seldom crossed the Alps on business; their presence at the fairs in Champagne was sporadic; they seem to have been totally absent in the Empire. At best, their presence is noted in regions as far off as Lombardy.[61] This is by no means surprising. Henceforth Italian, German, and even French merchants came to Rialto and departed again from Rialto.

There is a record of some Germans established in Venice in the early thirteenth century. One of these was Bernardus Teotonicus, a man from a ministerial family in the Munich area who traded in precious metals and operated as a banker. On the surface he held impressive credentials: he had connections with the patriarch of Aquileia; he had negotiated the financing of the Third Crusade for Emperor Frederick Barbarossa; he had lent money to a number of German princes. His personal wealth, according to the will he drew up in 1213, was immense. How did he make his fortune? The money market of Venice required large quantities of precious metals because financing the Levant trade was a costly operation. The silver mines of Bohemia and the gold mines of Hungary supplied its needs, and Bernardus, operating at the Rialto, seems to have been a very active middleman.[62]

Commercial relations between Venice and German lands benefited from a long and stable tradition. The Germanic area, like the northern Italian plain, was a natural outlet for Venetian trade. Unlike Milan, which had no access to its German hinterland until the thirteenth century, when the route over the Alps via the St. Gotthard Pass was opened, Venice had use of the Brenner Pass, a longstanding and heavily used route. According to Philippe Braunstein's count, the German emperors descended into Italy via the Brenner Pass no fewer than thirty-seven times, and during the latter half of the thirteenth century the Brenner route was further improved. In reality, however, there were two routes across the Alps. The "German" route, to the west, put Venice in connection with the Germanic world through the upper Piave, the Val Pusteria, and the Brenner Pass; this was the way to Augsburg, to Ulm, and eventually to Flanders. The second, more eastern route went through Tarvisio to Salzburg, then on toward Prague or Nuremberg. These relatively easy communications were backed up by a number of lesser passes over the Alps in Friuli, Cadore, and the Trentino.[63]

The Venetian commune was well aware of the importance of the Germanic merchants, and it was equally aware that there were clandestine transactions between Germans and Venetians on the Terraferma that eluded taxation. Between 1222 and 1225 the city moved to put a stop to this loss of revenue by opening the famous Fondaco dei Tedeschi. This establishment, built for the convenience of the German merchants at a bend in the Grand Canal, on the north bank at the Rialto, was at once a warehouse and a residence.[64] As is known, Venice was reproducing the model of the *funduk,* the housing for foreign merchants in Muslim lands. The Venetians had an installation of the sort at Alexandria, which they administered themselves, a concession the Germans never obtained on the Grand Canal. After a transitional phase the new seat of Germanic commerce in Venice passed under the direct control of the commune and its officials, the Vicedomini of the Fondaco. A new system for controlling trade had thus been instituted. Modena already had a house at the Rialto, and soon Lucca had one as well. Attestations are lacking, but other Italian merchant groups probably followed suit.

Concentrating men and merchandise at the Fondaco aided surveillance. The men were the German merchants, of course, but also Hungarian merchants, who enjoyed a similar status. According to the sources, beginning in the thirteenth century the merchandise stored and traded there was highly varied and of wide-ranging origin. Metals and metallurgical products (silver, iron, copper, and more), along with pelts and leathers, came to the Rialto; products from the East (spices, silks, precious cloths) could also be purchased there. The account books of one flourishing late-fourteenth-century Nuremberg commercial society describe trade between north and south in which incoming gold and silver ingots and sheets of tin were exchanged for spices and Italian or Oriental silks.[65] Caravans of pack animals returned to German lands over the Alps carrying heavy loads of goods (olive oil, for example) purchased in northern Italy. Once the system was put into place, all German merchants passing through Venice were obliged to reside in the Fondaco, store both export and import goods there, and pass customs there. The city administration tightened its surveillance, charging special officials with enforcing internal regulations,[66] but in particular a draconian control was established on merchandise to make sure that taxes were paid on all products, imported or exported, bought or sold. The Fondaco provided an efficient means for centralizing customs receipts for commerce with northern lands.

The Fondaco dei Tedeschi stands out clearly on Jacopo de Barbari's map of Venice, where it appears after its reconstruction in the early fourteenth century and several subsequent renovations. It is a large building, two stories high, with three inner courtyards. On the map it appears to be almost as big as the current building, which was built in the early sixteenth century. Its system of communications with the rest of the city was considerably improved during the late Middle Ages with the enlargement of its canal frontage and the creation of *calli* leading to the neighboring parishes. It accounted for a truly impressive volume of business: in 1470 the chronicler Paolo Morosini evaluated its yearly gross at a million ducats; in 1499 a German pilgrim estimated the customs duties paid to the Signoria at a hundred ducats per day.[67]

In spite of stringent legislation (which on occasion led to bitter protests), the Fondaco dei Tedeschi became the obligatory center of commercial exchange between Venetian and German merchants. Attempts on the part of Genoa and Milan to capture at least a part of this commercial traffic came to naught.[68] For example, intense and flourishing business relations linked Venice and Nuremberg up to the sixteenth century. Both partners to the arrangement found advantages in it. The Venetians ran an efficient operation that enabled them to place the merchandise they unloaded from their ships and procure other cargoes of both raw materials and processed goods to ship overseas. They pocketed the fees levied on all transactions made within the Fondaco. "The Germans, on the other hand, were perfectly aware of the highly important role that they had come to play within the Venetian economy."[69] The development of many German cities, southern German cities in particular, benefited from these commercial relations. German businessmen built up veritable fortunes in Venice, as some family archives clearly demonstrate.

This brief summary should suffice to show how closely connected Venice was with a hinterland that was not only wealthy and active but the point of arrival of overland routes from northern European lands. The city, the port, and the Arsenal could not survive without the goods brought by Continental commerce. We shall look at one or two examples of these exchanges, beginning with agricultural products.

Continental Trade

We have seen how the earliest Venetian merchants bought grain in the *Regnum Italiae,* selling in exchange salt and products from the East. We have seen how Venice's penetration into the rural areas around Treviso, Padua, and Monselice also worked to provide it with indispensable grains. Postmortem inventories from well before the conquest of the Terraferma show that the Venetians, like everyone else, liked to stock their storage areas with reserves of wheat, wine, and produce from their lands. Local harvests were of course insufficient to cover the city's considerable and constantly growing needs, which meant that the city had to negotiate for foodstuffs or get them by constraint. Friuli and the patriarchate of Aquileia, which were soon placed in a situation of economic dependence, furnished massive amounts of wine, cheese, and pork products. When the cities in these areas began to expand and exert pressure on their own *contado,* Venetian maritime commerce worked to satisfy the need by importing massive amounts of grains, wine, oil, and other foodstuffs, which were consumed within the city but also resold at the Rialto to Italians from Verona, Mantua, or Cremona. Once again we find a turning point similar to the one we have already seen in the history of Venetian trade, and we see crisscrossing connections between long-distance trade, urban consumption, and goods in transit, between trade with distant ports and commerce with nearby areas.

The history of the war with Padua in 1234 displays these mechanisms in action. At the outset of hostilities Padua organized an alimentary blockade of the lagoon. Venice soon responded with a counterblockade, and Padua was forced to admit defeat. The Terraferma may have nourished the lagoon, but by that time the port of Rialto provisioned the Terraferma as well.

Raw materials followed a similar pattern. German merchants brought precious metals and copper from central Europe, as we have seen, thus providing commodities indispensable to long-distance trade. They were also the principal channel for iron imports, which arrived from Villach, in Carinthia, over the pass near Tarvisio. The Venetian market required considerable amounts of iron not only for the city itself (for tools, nails, kitchen implements, and barrel hoops) but in particular to satisfy the Arsenal's enormous needs for constructing and fitting ships. Moreover, we can explain the fear of penury that is expressed in the sources if we remember that Venice reexported metals. Iron departed, legally or illegally, toward southern Italy, the kingdom of Aragon, Constantinople, and the Levant. Despite pontifical interdicts, the sale of iron and weapons, even to the infidel, was a longstanding tradition in Venice.

The iron mines of the Alpine valleys had long been exploited, but far from serving the needs of Rialto alone, they had permitted the development of thriving metallurgical works around Belluno, Brescia, and Bergamo. Guaranteeing a secure supply of iron was a constant theme of the policies of the Republic, an aim that implied control of the route for carrying Carinthian iron through Friuli. It has been shown that on several occasions the route was threatened because of political vicissitudes: until the dissolution of the patriarchate of Aquileia, conflicts among competing seignories often troubled trade. Territorial expansion and the conquest of Friuli in 1420 later gave the Venetian Signoria control of this *strada dretta*. On several occasions after that date, however, the route was cut off or forced to follow detours, some of which are still traceable. Thus the conquest of the Terraferma did not change things radically. Although the Venetian administration now controlled the land route from Gemona to Portogruaro and from there to the Riva del Ferro, at the heart of the Rialto market, direct exchanges between regions continued to function, and they supplied the centers of metallurgy on the mainland, thus eluding Venetian taxation. This meant that Venice had to "resign itself to not playing the role in the redistribution of iron that it took on in other sectors vis-a-vis its hinterland."[70]

Venice also depended largely on that same hinterland for wood. The high figures for wood consumption are hardly surprising. Very early, for example, visitors remarked on the large number of chimneys in Venice. All sources of information confirm that heating was a comfort widely enjoyed in the city. Even though Carpaccio is far from always depicting the real Venice, his paintings show many roofs with curiously tall chimneys. Notarial acts, wills, and documents relating to the division of furnishings or to settling conflicts between neighbors show that fireplaces were so numerous, even outside the kitchens, that in the wealthiest houses some bedrooms had one. These thousands of notarial acts permit us to gauge shifts in material culture, the progress of comfort, and a rise in the standard of living in the city.[71]

The daily demand for firewood for heating and cooking was already heavy among the dense population of the city, but fuel was also needed for all the various ovens and furnaces in the city's bakeries, workshops, and the industrial enterprises that surrounded the city and polluted its air and water.[72] Finally, Venice used enormous quantities of logs for its dikes, its palisades, and its pilings, even though the use of wood declined somewhat in house construction, retaining walls, and bridges.[73]

The high-quality lumber that was indispensable to the immense Arsenal and the many private shipyards all had to be imported. This aspect of the timber supply has received the better part of historians' attention.[74] Where did the Venetians get the fir they needed for masts and spars, larch beams to frame their ships, and oak for the hull, ribs, keel, and planking? Fir and larch arrived from the Alps, to the north. As early as the thirteenth century sawyers' capitularies mention the evergreens of the Val Sugana and of Bassano. Logs, planks, and beams descended the valleys of the Adige and the Brenta. Venice had longstanding relations with Cadore via the basin of the upper Piave. The copious resources of the mountain hinterland provided an exportable surplus until the beginning of the modern age. They swelled a commerce that, once again, the popes prohibited when such cargoes were bound for Muslim ports. Two regions, Treviso and Friuli, traditionally provided Venice with oak, the most precious wood of all. With increased demand, Istria was added, but eventually these timber resources were depleted.

Once the Terraferma was placed under Venetian domination, the government responded to this threatened shortfall by elaborating, beginning in 1476, a systematic policy for the preservation of forestry resources. A policy was all the more urgently needed because deforestation was accelerating in the territories around Padua and Treviso and in Friuli. The very foundation of Venetian power was threatened. A first measure limited selective cutting and forbade deforestation. Wooded areas were protected according to a hierarchy of property rights: first came the forests of the Signoria, then those of the subject communes, and finally private domains. Other regulations covered the log trains that were floated down the various water courses. Above all, permission was required to cut oak trees earmarked for the Arsenal.

The city assemblies worked to enforce these policies, but infringements were many and the laws were so widely ignored that protection had to be increased in the years that followed. In the mid-fifteenth century a campaign was launched to inspect the state forests. The reports that emerged from such inspection tours clearly show the ravages that the forests had suffered: they describe deteriorated stands of trees, cuts carried out prematurely, and village communities that scoffed at the laws. A tighter protection of oaks was instituted, along with a program to replenish the supply by planting young trees. In 1479 even stronger measures were taken. Faced with an acute shortage of commercial-grade lumber, the city passed a law, completed by later texts, that extended the state monopoly to oaks outside the public domain in the wood lots of communities and private persons. Every village was commanded to take a survey of its oaks.

The efficacy of this kind of legislation was close to nil, and conflict with the village communities was incessant. The councils in Venice continued to pursue this forestry policy, largely in vain, throughout the modern age; deforestation continued unabated, abetted by illegal tree-cutting operations and abusive pasturage and encouraged by demand for wood from timber merchants and private shipbuilders.

We know that there was an acute shortage of wood in Venice, in particular of firewood for heating, during the 1440s. Faced with dramatically insufficient incoming supplies, the governing elites ordered a vast operation to evaluate wood reserves and study ways to procure more wood. The Senate tried to improve the entire supply circuit by setting up a classic controlled economy: a maximum price was set, and illegal practices (stocking wood to make prices rise) were violently condemned, but the assembly also attempted to attract firewood supplies to Venice. The majority of the government's efforts were directed at the thorniest aspect of the problem, which was difficulties arising from encumbered rivers and waterways. This led to a series of public-works projects aimed at improving navigation on the watercourses and the flat waters of the Terraferma and at dredging the channels in the lagoon.

The crisis abated in the decades that followed, but public vigilance did not flag. A new magistracy, headed by *provveditori,* was created to oversee tutelage of the forests and woods. Its jurisdiction and responsibilities were defined in a series of decrees, and various nobles were elected to fulfill this "mission useful to the honor of the city and to the life of the poorest."

Wood, whether in the form of kindling *(fassine),* firewood *(legna da ardere),* or precious oak, was part of a general picture of connections, exchanges, and movements affecting merchandise and men. Manpower was mobile, and both Venetians and provincials were involved in the commercial societies. Trade in oil, wine, hemp, and cheese followed similar patterns.

One observation emerges from all the case studies. In the first phase at least, the military conquest of the Terraferma simply ratified a long-established economic penetration and an ancient tradition of exchanges, encounters, and intervention.

The other Italian powers did not consider the Venetian conquest of the Terraferma to be a major turning point in Venetian politics. They too had long been engaged in the construction of a territorial state.[75] Hence they opposed those latecomers to expansion only when their own interests or territorial claims were directly threatened. This was the case with Milan. Moreover, as James S. Grubb has noted, not all Venetians shared either the fears or the principles of Doge Tomaso Mocenigo.[76] Few sources are explicit, of course, but we can sense that some families or networks were unenthusiastic about Venice's Continental policies and its expansionist spiral. Finally, and above all, even the contemporaries who subscribed to the notion that conquest was a necessity retained certain representations. Venice had founded its glory on the sea, and the sea was where it remained. As always, the state was one with the city. The shores of the lagoons truly marked a frontier in this respect.[77] Thus it is difficult to discern the turning point authenticated by an entire historiographical tradition. I might also note that contemporary chroniclers did not have particularly much to say about these events. The many authors who commented on Venetian institutions during the fifteenth century paid little attention to the *stato di terra,* its construction, or its administration. In short, Venetian political and historical culture does not seems to have been modified, or even marked, by the constitution of the *dominium di terra.*

Venetians nonetheless attempted to legitimate their conquest, and we need to examine their arguments. A first current of thought, favorably received by Florentine civic humanism and relayed in the subject cities of the Terraferma by Venetian sycophants, presented the Venetians as restoring an ancient Italian *libertas.* In this view the Venetians had been called to deliver the various populations from the oppression of local lords. A speech given by Lorenzo de' Monaci in 1421 to celebrate the millennium of the founding of the Venetian Republic emphasized this role of liberator.[78] As things turned out, the seignories were indeed struck down, but ancient liberties were not restored, and Venice pursued its advance, even attacking Milanese possessions. These incontestable events did not prevent Gasparo Contarini, in the early sixteenth century, from once again representing Venice as ridding cities of tyrants, but at the same time he appealed to a different current of thought and offered other justifications for Venetian conquest. Despite a vigorous Venetian tradition that had always rejected any notion of inheritance from ancient Rome, the mythic city that had dominated Italy and the world, Venice was henceforth presented as a new Rome. Because it had inherited Rome's ancient *virtù*, it followed logically that the ancient province of Venetia ought to be re-created under its tutelage.[79] Until the traumatic experience of Agnadello, however, the governing elites of Venice gave little indication of needing such humanistic arguments.

Long forgotten or neglected, crushed by layer upon layer of myth, the history of the Venetian domination of the Terraferma requires, first of all, an examination of what happened. We need to look at events before interpreting them.

One Paw on the Mainland

Venice took its first steps toward domination of the mainland early on by allying itself with Florence against Verona in 1336. Clearly, both allies had an interest in preventing the constitution of a strong state on the eastern plains of the Po.[80] The conflict ended in 1339 with the dismantling of the lordship of the della Scala family. Padua recovered its independence under Carrara domination, and Venice won a first possession, Treviso.[81] The lion had already placed one clawed paw on the mainland. It turned out not to be a very firm hold, however: when hostilities with Genoa began again in the last third of the fourteenth century, Venice had to withdraw. As we have seen, the years of war with Genoa also involved Padua and the king of Hungary. The Venetians managed to retain the lagoons and Chioggia, but among the losses ratified by the Peace of Turin, signed in 1381, was the loss of Treviso and its surrounding territory to the lord of Padua. In a classic scenario, subject only to local variation, a new coalition was formed in the years that followed in which Padua was the new rising power in the March of Treviso. Venice struck an alliance with the duke of Milan, Gian Galeazzo Visconti, against the lord of Padua, Francesco Novello II da Carrara. The Carrara lordship suffered the fate of the earlier della Scala regime,[82] and a large part of the March of Treviso passed under Visconti domination, with Venice recuperating Treviso itself.

The death of the duke of Milan in 1402 brought a recrudescence of troubles. Francesco Novello III da Carrara set himself to recuperating the territories that his father had lost. He became lord of Verona in 1404. Venice gained Vicenza from this move because in the spring of 1404 that city voluntarily handed itself over to the Venetians. Francesco Novello III, unable to tolerate a Venetian enclave between Padua and Verona, at the heart of his territory, launched hostilities. The campaign was hard fought. In June 1405 Verona finally opened its gates to the Venetians. Padua, besieged, fell in November of the same year, and as a vanquished city it suffered harsher conditions than Vicenza and Verona, who had given themselves up freely. To ensure public peace, Francesco Novello III da Carrara and his sons were tried and then strangled in their prison cells. At the same time, Venice pursued its eastward expansion. The first clash came with Sigismund, king of Hungary, king of the Romans, and later Holy Roman Emperor, who feared the Venetian advance toward Friuli and Istria. The war was suspended in 1413, began again, and ended in 1420 with the Venetians taking Friuli. From that moment on, Italian affairs took on increasing importance for Venice.

Against Milan

Italian affairs divided the governing circles in Venice. Some Venetians, Doge Tomaso Mocenigo among them, advocated peace in Italy and maintenance of the alliance with the duke of Milan. Others, under the leadership of Francesco Foscari, argued for a rapprochement with Florence against Milan and against the hegemonic policies of Filippo Maria Visconti.[83] The new alliance was finally signed in 1425, after Francesco Foscari became doge. A long and costly war against Milan ensued (1426–28). The war nonetheless enabled Venice to enlarge its territorial state, not just in nearby territories, where the Signoria of Venice could claim to exercise the rights of a dominant regional power, but in Lombardy. The new frontier between the Visconti Duchy of Milan and Venetian possessions passed through the heart of Milanese territory when the Venetians reached the Adda River and Brescia and Bergamo came under Venetian domination. The two powers now stood face to face. Hostilities with Milan were rekindled at regular intervals, and warfare broke out in 1431–33, 1436–41, 1446, and 1452. After the death of Filippo Maria, the last Visconti duke, the Venetians even hoped to take Milan itself,

The Venetian Terraferma

or at least to place the Milanese under their protection. During all these years, waging war placed a heavy burden on Venice's financial resources. Alliances changed, and Florence joined Milan. After the interval of the Ambrosian Republic, the Sforzas ruled the Duchy of Milan. Each change brought a new outbreak of hostilities, with an end result of something like a territorial status quo. With the Peace of Lodi in 1454, the rights of Venice, *La Dominante*, over Brescia and Bergamo were confirmed, and Crema too became a Venetian possession.

In 1467, when Venice supported the bellicose enterprises of the *condottiere* Bartolomeo Colleoni, Galeazzo Maria Sforza, the young duke of Milan, succinctly stated the anti-Venetian sentiments of a large part of Italy: "Sete soli, et havete tutto'l mondo contra" (You are alone, and you have the whole world against you).

"Tutto'l mondo contra"

The isolation of Venice was evident during the war with Ferrara. War broke out in 1481 because the Venetians were no longer satisfied with their (extensive) privileges in that city, traditionally its rival. Hostilities ended in 1484. The conflict, which was marked by Pope Sixtus IV's declaration of an interdict against Venice, was long and costly, and its results were mixed. Venice failed to take Ferrara, but at the Peace of Bagnolo it received Rovigo and the Polesine, the flatlands between the lower reaches of the Po and the Adige. This chronicle ends with the short-lived War of Rovereto in the spring of 1487 against Archduke Sigismund, count of the Tyrol. What it shows is that all the neighbors of the Republic of Venice (in this case, its neighbors to the north) were worried about its advance.

The first French "descents" into Italy led to still other shifting alliances and further encouraged Venetian territorial ambitions. Venice gained a foothold in Apulia; it attempted, without success, to gain control over Pisa and Livorno; and it occupied Cremona. The Venetian incursions into Romagna irritated Pope Julius II. Finally, the Venetians opened the route to the eastern part of Friuli by taking Trieste and then winning Fiume from the troops of Emperor Maximilian. Thanks to a skillful political opportunism and a firm expansionist policy, Venice played a winning game for some time. Then suddenly, with the formation of the League of Cambrai in 1508, the cards were reshuffled, and Venice began to lose. In May 1509 came the disastrous Venetian defeat at Agnadello. The Terraferma fell. The Venetians could see the watch fires of enemy troops camped by the shore of the lagoon flickering on the water. All the sources—chronicles, sermons, and records of Senate deliberations—reflect the Venetians' anxiety and the force of this shock. Evil times had come, signs were seen in the skies, processions circulated through the city, and the governing elites sought remedies. The balance was soon redressed, however, in an Italy that displayed a new realignment of foreign powers, and after a hard-fought campaign Venice regained its dominion over the Terraferma in June 1517.[84]

By the end of the fifteenth century Venice had thus become one of the principal territorial powers in Italy. The Venetian *stato di terra* stretched from Friuli to Ravenna and from Lombardy (Crema and Bergamo) to the Adriatic. Moreover, in order to conquer and defend this state, Venice, the "maritime republic," whose ships fought on the Po and on the Lago di Garda, also proved itself capable of putting a powerful army into the field. In the early fifteenth century some ten thousand to twelve thousand men fought under the banner of St. Mark. This figure grew when war became an almost permanent state. At midcentury Venice commanded some twenty thousand men; by the 1509 campaign that figure had risen to forty thousand, with a permanent army of some eight thousand. Nor did the Signoria stint in its efforts to hire worthy *condottieri*. One of these, Jacopo del Verme, a Veronese, was well rewarded for his role in the 1405 campaign; Bartolomeo Colleoni, who became commander in chief of the Venetian forces in 1454, received many seignories in the region of his native Bergamo.[85] It is easy to see why warfare dramatically raised the level of the public debt and why, in both Venice and its subject cities, high taxes prompted complaints and led to outbreaks of violence (at Verona, for example). It has been calculated that in 1512 Venice's military expenses reached 80,000 ducats a month. This was an enormous sum, even for a state whose annual revenues may have surpassed 1 million ducats.

The Stato di Terra

What are we to make of these events and these impressive figures? My objective throughout this chapter has been to demonstrate the lagoon area's reliance on its hinterland in order to show that what has been seen as a sharp break in Venetian policies in the fifteenth century was in reality something more complex. We need to recall other complicating factors: events on sea and on land were always intimately connected, and Venice continued to be active in the Mediterranean during the decades of the Continental wars. Moreover, no overall plan guided the Venetian conquest of the Terraferma. Defensive operations in its own hinterland much like operations the commune had conducted earlier with other allies led to the first Venetian interventions in the March of Treviso. At a later date Venetian policies become more clearly expansionist, and they changed pace when the Signoria attacked Lombardy. As John Law has remarked, we need to be on guard against anachronism and to avoid retrospective analysis. The constitution of the Venetian *stato di terra* does not explain the advance of the Turks. We cannot turn to an illusory and mechanical causality to make an abrupt turnaround in Continental policy responsible for the decline of Venice. Venetian power, far from declining in the sixteenth century, was in fact reconstructed on other bases.

For all that, the Venetian conquest of its Terraferma had consequences that we must not underestimate. Evolutions in political vocabulary are not the least significant of these. Foreign policy and expansion were at first been pursued in the name of the commune of Venice, a political organism that had changed greatly since its first appearance in the twelfth century. The old term *comune* finally disappeared, and after 1423 power in Venice was defined, with less ambiguity, as residing in the Signoria or the Dominium.[86] This seignory should not be confused with the lordship of men and families who exercised personal and hereditary power in other Italian cities, but it is not easy to define in simple terms how this city-state set in Italy of the princes administered its vast territorial state.

Before addressing that question, I might observe that historiographical clichés muddy any approach to the question. There are in fact firmly established representations of what the Venetian system of government was in subjected lands, whether in Romania or in Italy.[87] Such representations depict a centralized, coercive administration functioning smoothly everywhere. According to them, the Republic exerted its domination over Venetia and Lombardy swiftly and forcefully, and in only a few decades painted and sculpted images of the lion of St. Mark could be seen on columns, facades, gates, and walls everywhere. According to these same representations, power was tightly held, placed in the hands of a small number of rectors, chamberlains, or castellans who represented the central authority and were supported in the subject communities by restricted local oligarchies constituted on the model of the *Dominante*. These traditional interpretations have been seriously challenged, however, and recent research has shown them to be an integral part of a larger and more general Venetian political myth.

To return briefly to this dossier, we need to look first at the central problem of the provincial urban elites. Angelo Ventura's analysis of the general process by which societies in the cities of the Terraferma became more aristocratic remains by and large valid.[88] This change is not to be imputed to the *Dominante*, however: it had started before Venice began its territorial conquest, and it continued afterward with no Venetian intervention to favor or accelerate it. It has been established that Verona had a strong institutional continuity under three regimes—Visconti, Carrara, and the Venetians[89]—and an equally strong stability in its governing group.[90] In short, the urban oligarchies of the Terraferma became crystallized in the long term of the histories of each of these cities.[91] Moreover, the support the rural population of the *stato di terra* gave to Venice, also over the long term, can be explained largely by the hostility country people felt for the local oligarchies, their primary, closest, and oldest dominators. It is worth noting that the patrician elite of Venice did not open their ranks to these provincials. There were marriage alliances, of course, and Venetian nobility was granted to a few privileged persons as a reward for services rendered, but it was not until the seventeenth century that a crying need for money persuaded the Republic to distribute its titles of nobility more generously.

These local oligarchies spawned more or less violent forms of opposition to the capital city. For example, the dominant provincial groups were hostile to the system of appeals, much used by the Republic, that enabled certain private persons, but especially communes and communities of the *contado*, to express their desires and opinions.[92] In 1310 the Great Council instituted the magistracy of the *auditori nuovi*, whose officials traveled through the *dominium* precisely to receive appeals and hear complaints.[93] The local oligarchies resented having the Terraferma offered up to the appetites of Venetians avid for lands, posts, and ecclesiastical benefices.[94] Nor were they happy when they had to apply measures, fiscal ones in particular, that were unpopular. These elements all help to explain the eagerness of many families of the provincial aristocracy to rally to the cause of the new occupying force, for example, when Padua was taken in 1509 by the troops of Emperor Maximilian. This was something that Venice never forgot.

The attitude of this provincial oligarchy during the crisis of 1509, long considered a sign of the fragility of the Venetian state, needs to be examined case by case. The violent animosity of the aristocracy of Padua is beyond question. Hostility against the "Venetian tyrants" was ancient; it was in a sense cultural, given that it was rooted in a long tradition of clashes between the two cities. Heavy taxation and the large number of Venetian landholdings in the *contado* of Padua further exacerbated tensions. The events of 1509 gave the Paduans a chance to express themselves decisively. Treviso, in contrast, seems to have presented an example of tranquil loyalty in those same years. The oligarchy of Vicenza was divided; above all, it seems to have displayed opportunism.[95] Recent research has stressed the great diversity of societies and an area that Venetian domination could not possibly have rendered homogeneous in only a few decades.

It should be noted that in the Venetian system of government the subject cities kept their local prerogatives, their *privilegia*, as well as their own councils, magistracies, and statutes.[96] The *Dominante* retained the right of *arbitrium*. Many metaphors have been used to describe this organizational structure. One is the image of the body in which Venice is the head that commands the obedience of the various parts of the body, the cities of the *stato di terra*. Another image is that of the patron-client relationship, with Venice offering its protection to clients who are under obligation to it.[97] In any event, it was up to the city-state of Venice to send representatives out into its *dominium*. As it happened, and this is a fact worth noting, those representatives were few, though some Venetians thought them many in the somber years of the early sixteenth century. After Vicenza's voluntary surrender to Venetian domination, two rectors arrived to administer the city with a team of three judges, a chancellor, a chamberlain, and a handful of guards and servants. It is difficult given the conditions, to speak of a state technostructure, especially if we remember that Vicenza and its territory had a population of more than 100,000.[98] What is more, the example of Vicenza reflects common practice: in 1495 the Republic was represented by a corps of 130 officials scattered throughout the territorial state. The only nuance required to complete this picture is that, not surprisingly, Venetian law weighed heavier in nearby areas, around Treviso and Padua, and lighter in the more distant territories of the Trentino or around Brescia.[99] I might add that after reconquest, the restoration of Venetian power often consisted in a simple return to the structures that had existed before the war. For example, the privileges of the governing groups of the Terraferma were reconfirmed.

Another sizable correction to standard views of Venetian domination deserves mention. It has been shown that in the fiscal realm as well the *Dominante,* far from innovating, maintained and conserved existing structures in the fifteenth century. The various organs of the Venetian central government and local civic institutions shared responsibilities. The taxes that had been put into place under the seignorial regimes continued unchanged in both the forms and the amounts of the taxes levied. It is true, as Michael Knapton has noted, that certain changes did occur during the second half of the fifteenth century. At the time of the Turkish war and again at the time of the war with Ferrara, indirect taxes, the *dazi,* no longer produced sufficient revenues. The crisis led to repeated tax levies and highly unpopular direct taxes, such as the *datia lancearum.*[100] Venetian policy in fiscal matters was in general conservative, and the *dominium* was not bankrupt. In 1498, when the young Marino Sanudo started off with his fellow *auditori nuovi* on a tour of inspection of the *stato di terra,* he reported that they visited a fertile countryside and prosperous towns adorned with new monuments.[101] Was this patriotism? Or the pride of a Venetian traveling from Brescia to Friuli through conquered lands? It was not only that.

All of the monographs on these topics remark on the relative prosperity of the area on which they concentrate. We know better than to give principal credit to the Venetian administration during those decades of an overall upswing in the Italian economy. The fact remains that Venetian governance, perhaps inspired by an understandable egotism, was relatively benevolent.[102] In the fifteenth century we can see signs of a proto-mercantilism aimed at supporting the commercial activities of the capital city, but the merchants of the Terraferma do not seem to have abandoned their traditional positions, in particular in regard to commerce with Lombardy. Step by step, a regional market came to be organized, and during the fifteenth century networks already in place around Padua and Treviso for trade in wine and grains seem to have functioned rather well.[103] Finally, the port of Venice seems to have exported products from its active hinterland in fairly large quantities. It is known that at the end of the Middle Ages markets in the Near East were flooded by Western textiles. Some of these came from territories under Venetian domination: there was broadcloth from Venice, but there were also woolen scarlets, including the costly *bastardo di grana* manufactured in Padua. Fine cloth, at times dyed in Venice, was produced in Feltre, Vicenza, and Verona.[104]

Finally, it should be noted that revenues from landed property accounted for an increasing proportion of Venetian fortunes. Although not a complete survey, the 1514 *estimo* of personal wealth gives a preliminary notion of the size of these investments.[105] The Venetian penetration into the rural areas of the Terraferma had an effect on both the overall economy of the duchy and the old equilibrium in the lagoon basin.[106] In 1446 a third of the wealth of the territory of Padua appears to have passed into Venetian hands. The changes that resulted from the invasion of urban capital, not all of which was Venetian, into the countryside are well known. Peasant land ownership shrank, and sharecropping *(mezzadria)* contracts were imposed on areas that until then had resisted their introduction.[107] Proprietors gained a greater say in affairs, and their jurisdictional powers grew.[108] In certain zones, however, drainage and land-reclamation projects continued apace.[109] In some localities heavy concentrations of properties owned by Venetians elicited protest, as did administration by the dominant city, but the Venetian presence also fostered two-way exchanges and contacts.

It seems appropriate to end this chapter on the first century of Venetian domination, during the years that followed the Venetian reconquest of the Terraferma, with the image of flexibility suggested by recent research. Changes doubtless began to take place after 1530, but they are beyond the range of this book. Until 1797 the lion passant continued to exert his domination over large portions of these territories.

FOUR
Scenes of Daily Life

Thus far I have tried to evoke some of the basic scenic aspects of both the decor and the reality of Venice. My aim in associating the two has been to create a unified image of an equally unified life. After the brackish waters amid which Venice was built and from which the city drew its singularity, its odor, and the very rhythm of its days, we have seen the vast seas the Venetians sailed, which gave their landless city not only its original wealth but the first space over which it exerted sovereignty. Next came the land, which may have seemed to be simply a backdrop for the Venetian world but in fact was firmly bound to the city by rivers that operated like conduits for commerce and the earliest profits. Long before Venice turned to territorial conquest in Venetia, Friuli, and Lombardy, the land was just as vital to the city as the sea was: it nourished the lagoon, supplied the port and the shipyards, furnished an outlet for Venetian goods and services, and offered its routes for the transportation of merchandise that came to Venice by land and by sea and departed again from Venice.

Now I would like to penetrate the city itself. We have seen Venice being settled, built, and beautified by collective effort in a long-term creative process that was never truly finished. Thus far, all we have seen of this theatrical production is that process of construction; our static set design lacks the dynamics of change. The only actors on that stage have been the many writers, for the most part anonymous, who related the history of the city's growth, telling how a certain order and a certain aesthetic came to be defined. This city was not merely an icon, however; it was ceaselessly animated by acts, words, and movements. It was in equal measure a universe of stone, brick, and tile and a space in which men and women, acting in accordance with set rhythms, well-established codes, and accepted signs, fabricated history day by day, lived, produced, came together, and expressed their identities in specific practices and customs.

In order to put the city and its economic and social life into perspective I shall begin with the port and the market, the prime places amid the land, the lagoon, and the sea where a living, active society best expressed itself, the dual hub of its economic "adventures" and the areas in which Venice was most on display as an import-export capital.

The port comes first because all observers agreed that it reflected Venetian identity. One local chronicler saw water and *marchandise* as almost synonymous.[1] Commercial goods were as abundant as water; like water, they renewed themselves ceaselessly and flowed through the city. Foreign visitors also stressed the omnipresence of goods and marveled at their surprising variety. Everywhere—on the quays, in the storehouses and warehouses— products and rich wares were piled up, often in strange or downright exotic forms, such as sugar and cotton, silk and rugs, fruits and perfumes, gums and spices. The ships that were always present in images of the city were equally prominent in its daily life. On a more allegorical level, ships expressed the singularity of Venice and its functions. They provided a striking ideogram that expressed the nature of the city built on water, mistress of the Adriatic Gulf, and the power of the port whose presence was felt throughout a maritime world much larger than a vast empire.

AMID SEA, CITY, AND LAGOON: THE PORT OF THE VENETIANS

At the edge of the city two sectors functioned as a port. Although situated next to each other, they never formed a genuine quarter. Here the structures indispensable to trade coexisted with private and public centers for the construction and repair of ships.

Constructing Space

The docks and basins of the Arsenal lay at the eastern edges of the urban area. The public shipyards were founded in the late twelfth century in a marshy zone filled in and utilized as need dictated.[2] The site of the shipyards offered easy communication with both the southern shore of the lagoon and the commercial port, an advantage that in part explains their location. Beginning in the early thirteenth century, the sources describe increasingly focused activity, and by the end of the century the Arsenal had become a solid instrument in support of increasing Venetian intervention in the Mediterranean.[3] The busy state shipyards, which operated under the authority of powerful city magistrates, the Patroni all'Arsenale (Lords of the Arsenal), thus took on a decisive function in the formation of Venetian power even though the Arsenal held no monopoly on ship construction. Privately owned shipyards *(squeri)* produced a large number of ships and were indispensable to commercial shipping.

A second area that contributed to trade and to the life of the port was situated on the southern edge of the city, facing the lagoon at the end point of the channel that connected Venice to the passageway through the littoral islands at San Nicolò. The shoreline stretching between Castello and San Marco probably embraced the maritime vocation thrust upon it by lagoon geography early in Venice's history. It is known that the first customs office was constructed in the parish of San Biagio. Other public buildings (e.g., the first salt warehouse) were built nearby. In the second half of the thirteenth century the communal authorities made repeated attempts to organize activities in the area. Sailors, rowers, dockhands, and porters were everywhere. Merchandise had to be unloaded from the ships and brought to a shore that was not yet a proper quay. Space was bitterly disputed: bales of goods were piled high, bridges broke up the little available room, while men heated tar, caulked hulls, and repaired ships. The port was an indispensable part of the city and an original and eccentric locale, teeming with life and in constant transformation.

The layout of the port area encouraged a certain dilution of activities. The *porto* of San Nicolò, through which ships arrived from the sea, was some distance away, and the channel wound through the lagoon for several kilometers before it reached the moorings. Moreover, a network of canals penetrated deep into the built-up areas, making possible swarms of warehouse and storage areas and scattering operations related to ship construction. Shipbuilding in Venice long resisted topographical concentration. Some private shipyards were established near the port or the Arsenal, of course, but not all of them were. The hazards of documentation show the presence of *squeri* in various *contrade* within the city, some by the lagoon but others in the central area. One shipyard functioned for some time at Terranova, in the immediate vicinity of the Ducal Palace and the Piazzetta.

During the early decades of the fourteenth century, however, this organization of space was totally changed and the port area was concentrated, in successive stages, into an integrated whole. A first wave of public-works projects was focused on the Arsenal. In 1324–25, following a decree of the commune, a broad stretch of water and shoals known as the *lacus* of San Daniele was drained, thus enabling the shipyards to quadruple their surface area to the north of their original location. Some restructuring of the cordage works and their attendant warehouses had been carried out several years earlier.[4] Why were these projects necessary? There were in fact two reasons. Public works intensified during those years as the city improved or renewed its infrastructure, but maritime transport was also undergoing reorganization, as we have seen. The first convoys of merchantmen had been instituted, and when the system of lines of navigation was put into place, the commune took responsibility for fitting merchant galleys.[5] The Arsenale Nuovo was created to respond to these new needs. At the same time a series of measures improved connections along the port shoreline, which was paved in its entire length in 1324. Bridges were built or rebuilt, and the councils attempted to regulate boat traffic on the waterways, ship departures, and the unloading of cargoes in front of the communal grain-storage facilities at San Biagio. All of these various improvements, most of which were carried out during the first third of the fourteenth century, firmly connected the port to the center of the city. At the same time, other public projects made the city a more integrated whole.

One of the commune's projects was to restructure the small island of Terranova, next to Piazza San Marco. An old shipyard was demolished, and a quay, a street, and a bridge were put in. In the following year wheat-storage facilities were built next to the Mint, facing the basin of San Marco.[6] This was in 1339–40. The texts cite aesthetic considerations as playing a determinant role in these radical changes. This was the spot where foreigners disembarked and then, moving across the quay to the Piazzetta, discovered Venice, which should therefore be revealed to them in its full order and beauty. The city authorities acted to fashion its image by shaping the space that formed the center of the city. Merchant power was henceforth adorned in a monumental garb, domesticated in the Gothic constructions of Terranova, and used to assemble that image of order and beauty. The grain-storage facilities of Terranova were intended to communicate the idea that they overflowed with wheat brought by Venetian ships from lands from Italy to the Black Sea. Standing by the waters of the basin of San Marco, near Piazza San Marco and the Ducal Palace, these imposing buildings reassured some and impressed others: they expressed the wealth of the city and the excellence of its communal government.

Improvements were made on the far shore of the basin as well. The Punta della Trinità, which jutted out between the two major waterways of the Grand Canal and the Canal of the Giudecca, was shored up on a regular basis with loads of soil to protect it from erosion. This slow consolidation was halted when the commune ordered the construction of a stone quay to replace the old wood revetment. New salt warehouses were built with public funds, and a number of ordinances were passed to regulate the circulation and moorage of ships around the point and by the warehouses.[7]

What are we to deduce from all this? Port activities were expanding. They spilled over into new terrains in response to the fluctuations of an organic growth but above all keeping pace with the development of large public-works projects. The port infrastructure now lined the entire basin of San Marco, and the area was completely integrated into the city as a whole. The basin of San Marco, the point where the lagoon channel met the two principal canals, had been transformed into a real port. Stretching between the Punta della Trinità and Piazza San Marco, it was bordered by wharves, quays, and storage facilities but also by churches and the Ducal Palace. Charts drawn up to lessen the uncertainties of navigation in the lagoon channel by marking points of reference used the bell towers of the Monastery of San Giorgio and the basilica of San Marco to signal journey's end for ships arriving from the sea.

In only a few decisive decades Venice had become a commercial metropolis, adapting its morphology to its ambitions and to the difficulties of an unstable Mediterranean situation. The transformation was notable because the enlarged and restructured area devoted to the port and to commerce had been made truly functional. Deep within its physical space the urban complex had undergone changes just as sweeping as the economic and administrative ones that had affected maritime transport.

A long hiatus followed this period of communal efforts to optimize the operations of the port, but in the next century, when public-works projects began again in the city, they were discontinuous and did little more than echo earlier changes. In the decades during which historians agree that Venice reached a peak the city simply exploited or perfected a commercial and port organization that had been established a century earlier. The sea customs house (Dogana da Mar) built at the Punta della Trinità in the early fifteenth century, the land customs house set up at Rialto, and the demolition of the old customs house at San Biagio are examples of such improvements. The Senate complained incessantly about the confusion that reigned on the quays. In order to combat contraband operations, it decreed that only merchandise bearing a seal showing that the goods had passed through customs could be unloaded, after which the merchants had eight days to remove them from dockside. The chaos of cases and bales can easily be imagined. By setting up two customs houses, the Senate hoped to reorganize the process of getting ships moored and unloading their merchandise. Its aim was to redistribute these activities to both sides of the basin of San Marco by designating the market of the Rialto as the gateway for river traffic and Continental trade. Despite such efforts, the quays and customs warehouses continued to be overcrowded. Nor did contraband disappear, in spite of attempts to urge the customs administration to greater vigilance and to win the cooperation of numerous public offices. The smugglers were clever, and the guards were corruptible. In 1463 the storage facilities at La Trinità were enlarged and the Senate mandated the building of four new salt warehouses on land acquired by the city.[8]

The second half of the fifteenth century, after the fall of Constantinople, was a time of intense activity at the Arsenal. Buildings were repaired and reconstructed, old docks were roofed over, and new sheds were built. All these projects preceded a third enlargement, which began in 1473 and ended with the construction of the Arsenale Nuovissimo.[9] Three years later the first phase of construction was finished. Successive programs continued over a century, however, culminating in the building of two new dry docks about 1570. At the end of the fifteenth century all observers—and they were many— considered the Arsenal exceptional, a concentration of men and means unique within the Mediterranean world. The Arsenal, enlarged, reorganized, and embellished (the first Renaissance construction in Venice, its triumphal entrance, or Porta Magna, was built in 1460), had become one of the places where the Venetian state was on display, all the more so when its maritime power was under attack. Almost all visiting foreigners were taken to visit the dockyards and workshops, and almost all emerged wonderstruck: "Their arsenal . . . is even now the finest in the world."[10] Spectacular improvements were made in the naval shipyards, and work continued for a long time. With its massive bulk, its high walls, and its crenelated towers, the Arsenal dominated the entire eastern part of the city. Once again, changes in the maritime fortunes of the Republic were reflected in its urban space.

Elsewhere in the port area the pace of reorganization and renewal slackened, but changes did occur. Certain port-related activities began to move away from the center, thanks in part to a more general redistribution of industrial production and in part to problems related to the conservation of the site. Legislation to counter the noxious effects of maritime activities was enacted early on. For example, it was forbidden to take on or discharge ballast or to re-tar ships in certain zones judged to be endangered. In the fifteenth century, when there was a threat of the canals' filling in with silt, becoming too shallow for ship traffic, these ancient regulations were put back into effect and extended. Legislative texts repeated the prohibition to unload ballast, forbade the demolition of ships and galleys anywhere along the Grand Canal or the lagoon basin as far as Sant'Antonio, and relegated prohibited activities to the eastern edge of the city or the barrier islands. These laws simply reinforced an ongoing process. During the same decades, the *porto* of San Nicolò narrowed, making it obligatory, rather than simply frequent practice, to transfer men and merchandise to smaller craft.[11] Ships had to wait for hours, sometimes for days, for a favorable tide or wind that would permit passage through the littoral islands. All that traffic contributed to shifting certain activities to the outer islands.

The measures Venice took when the plague struck enter into this same picture of an enlarged organization of space. The first pesthouse was established on the island of Santa Maria di Nazaret, in the southern part of the lagoon basin, near the Lido. A second pesthouse was established, again near the barrier islands, on La Vigna Murata, where persons suspected of having been exposed to the plague were quarantined. Thus Venice reinforced its health defenses on the sea side. Further reinforcement came toward the end of the fifteenth century, when new public-health officials elected after 1485 redoubled the city's vigilance by requiring the admiral who commanded the *porto* of San Nicolò to enforce strict controls. Wealth came from the sea, but after the great epidemic of 1348–49 death arrived from the sea as well, and with inexorable regularity. The magistrates kept what amounted to a veritable map of the plague throughout the Mediterranean so that the councils could forbid exchanges with infected lands. The passageways through the littoral islands were supervised, and ships underwent careful inspection. Merchandise and ships arriving from lands where death lurked were burned, or at least the laws stated that they should be burned. By means of these procedures and these structures set up in outlying areas the city instituted quarantine.[12]

The geography of the lagoon dictated the location of the channel that stretched from the littoral barrier to the Punta della Dogana and on to the port, its winding way marked by the same clumps of oak pilings that can still occasionally be seen today. Along the shores that bordered the channel the life of the port and the opening to the sea made for a special atmosphere and a particular landscape, although in the fifteenth century shipping activities tended to become concentrated in distinct areas.

A Port Landscape

The background of that landscape is soon sketched: a forest of masts, dense or sparse according to the season and the rhythms of navigation, crowded when convoys departed or the cogs arrived carrying wine from Crete or cotton from Egypt. There are ships of all types and all sizes, riding at anchor more often than moored by the side of the quay, being loaded or unloaded by a mass of lighters that ply back and forth between the galleys and the warehouses and from the *barze* (round ships) to the granaries and the quays.

In the middle ground the shoreline of the basin of San Marco and the Grand Canal curves slightly from Piazza San Marco eastward to the Punta di Sant'Antonio. At one end passengers disembark a few steps from the Ducal Palace. Rowers await them at the quayside, their boats crowding the basin, vying for clients who might want to be ferried from ship to shore or be taken on a tour of the city or the lagoon.[13]

The wealthier foreigners lodged in inns on the Piazzetta or near the Ponte della Paglia; the others slept in the many hospices that lined the canal. Not only were there guides and boatmen to greet the foreign visitors but they could drink, gamble, listen to music, and otherwise amuse themselves in the inns. The Procurators of San Marco may have deplored the debauchery that reigned in these taverns, but the rent paid by those establishments went into the basilica's strongboxes. Despite repeated laws and regulations stating that prostitution "infringed on the dignity of the center of public power," prostitutes frequented the inns and taverns of San Marco.

The monumental quality of Piazza San Marco had its effect on the surrounding neighborhood, however. Fronting the lagoon, to the east of the Piazzetta, in the direction of the hospital of La Pietà, were a number of palaces (that of the Gabrieli family, for example) constructed or reconstructed in the Gothic style. Only further to the east, in the alleyways and the *calli* of San Provolo or Sant'Antonin, did the houses become more plebeian and did poverty become more obvious. Above all, the "port effect" was more evident there. Early-sixteenth-century tax declarations from the parish of San Giovanni in Bragora, for example, reveal a cosmopolitan but penniless population, which included many immigrants from the East, who lived crammed into ramshackle housing in one-room buildings that the records list as "old" or "in poor condition." Despite the proprietors' prohibitions, sailors, rowers, porters, dockers, and prostitutes lived crowded together eight or ten to a room. Although these tenants paid by the month (rather than by the year, as was customary elsewhere in Venice), they were often insolvent and skipped off, not only omitting to pay the rent but carrying off wooden bedframes, locks, and even doors. The structural crisis affecting the commercial shipping extracted a toll in social effects as well.

These parishes were thus full of foreigners, especially those who arrived by sea from Venice's far-flung possessions. Waves of immigrants arrived from a Balkan world shaken by wars and undermined by poverty, from an overseas empire becoming depopulated, from colonies impoverished by crushing taxes. Many of these uprooted people had passed through Venetian ports in Dalmatia, Albania, or western Greece before taking the great leap to the metropolis, which needed men for its armies and strong arms for its galleys. A first great wave of migration came in the 1430s. Turkish advances in the 1460s set in motion other population groups, who first landed on the Adriatic coast from Apulia to the Marches and moved north from there to Venice. Not all of these immigrants were poverty-stricken. Shipwrights and carpenters of Greek origin made considerable contributions to Venetian shipbuilding. Many foreigners, however, provided cheap labor and filled the ranks of the crews urgently needed by a rapidly growing fleet.[14] They were hard hit in the crisis of the early sixteenth century, when the maritime shipping lines suspended operations, merchant galleys were decommissioned, salaries plummeted, and the labor market collapsed, marking the end of full employment for seafaring men. The declarations for the 1514 *estimo* clearly reflect the harsh living conditions of this "seagoing proletariat," and from that time on there were fewer candidates for emigration to Venice from the towns of Greece, Albania, and Dalmatia.

Many foreigners from the Balkans lived in the *sestiere* of Castello.[15] In 1442 the Albanians in Venice, the majority of whom were Catholic, obtained permission to form a confraternity at the monastery of San Gallo, in the parish of San Severo.[16] A few years later their *scuola* was transferred to the church of San Maurizio. The Slavs grouped together in the *scuola* of San Giorgio degli Schiavoni. For some time the Greeks petitioned the Signoria in vain for a place of worship of their own. Orthodox services, at first held in various churches, were eventually offered at the church of San Biagio. Soon other concessions were granted: the Greek community received authorization to form a Greek confraternity and a Greek "nation" in 1498; in 1514 they were granted a church and cemetery of their own. Times were difficult, and the church was completed only in 1573, but it was the epicenter of a colony that left a permanent mark on place names, such as Rio dei Greci, Ponte dei Greci, and others.[17] Further to the east warehouses and lumberyards dotted the edge of the basin as far as San Biagio, where there was a warehouse for ship's biscuit for the fleet, and on to the Rio dell'Arsenale.

In the early sixteenth century most of the commercial shipyards were grouped beyond the Rio dell'Arsenale, the exception being the *squeri* of Santo Spirito on the Giudecca canal. Venetian shipbuilding was highly sensitive to economic change: during the first half of the fifteenth century recession had begun to affect certain branches of the industry, small-scale construction in particular. When timber began to come from mountain areas further and further away, small shipyards in Venice declined, moving to the Terraferma. The construction of high-tonnage ships remained active, and until the mid-fifteenth century it compensated for losses in other sectors. Depression spread after 1460, however, and construction reached a crisis in 1486–88, when competition from Ragusa increased sharply.[18] A slight upward turn in response to urgent legislation followed.[19] Both the production and the geography of private shipbuilding evolved, and the public shipyards exerted an attraction that was not only topographical but also social because the shipwrights from the private yards were called to work at the Arsenal's public shipyards in times of need. At the end of the fifteenth century the majority of Venetian shipwrights still worked in the *squeri*,[20] but as if by reflex, the private yards and their workers gravitated to the area around the public yards. The resulting concentration of men and labor defined a unique quarter within the economic and social fabric of the city. Here everything was organized around these dominant activities. Just outside the walls of the Arsenal, in the parishes of San Martino, Santa Ternità, and San Pietro, lay a mixed neighborhood of humble, low-rent housing, abandoned wood structures, workshops, and storage facilities. The people who lived in the area were carpenters, caulkers, sawyers, and seamen, blacksmiths, foundrymen, barrel makers, dockhands, and wine porters—men who worked at the Arsenal or the port in one capacity or another.

This made for a special population with strong roots in the eastern parishes of the city, and the socioprofessional homogeneity of the quarter, which was already greater than in the other *contrade* of Venice, probably increased with time. Relations remained close within the area. Here as elsewhere in the city, women lived within compartmentalized mini-neighborhoods where the baker's oven and the nearby well defined their daily itinerary and their relationships with others. For men too, social space seems to have been tighter than in other areas. Wineshops, both licensed and clandestine, that also provided food reflect the geography of a hardworking city. When these taverns were established near a *squero* or a caulking shop, they bolstered solidarities. An entire system of sociability operated on a daily basis to tighten connections made in the workplace, by marriage, during holidays, or in times of illness. Marriage rituals and bridal dowries as related by the gossips of the quarter tell us that endogamy seems to have been strong, with marriages contracted within the framework of the courtyard and the *calle*. Often the father and the husband shared the same line of work, at times the same geographical origin, and the bride did not change parish. The histories of the charitable institutions founded to aid seamen and *arsenalotti* present a similar picture: in the parishes of San Pietro di Castello or San Martino people lived, worked, and died without leaving the vicinity of the Arsenal. A decree of the Great Council in 1335 mandated the construction of a home for invalid seamen built at San Biagio.[21] At a later date private charitable institutions reinforced this assistance structure, and by the fifteenth century they formed a belt around the Arsenal. In the early sixteenth century the seamen's hospital of Gesù Cristo was founded on reclaimed land at Sant'Antonio.

This increasingly lively quarter of the city expressed its identity (unsurprisingly) with a full display of the urban "folklore" typical of the modern age. Games such as one in which two groups of combatants lined up at either side of a bridge for a ritualized "bridge war" were popular entertainments.[22] Originally linked to the winter festive cycle, they were organized in various parishes on special occasions, such as receptions for foreign visitors. The toponymy of Venice still reflects the winter games in the Ponte dei Pugni (Bridge of the Fists) near the church of San Barnaba. In that particular "War of the Fists" teams known as "Castellani" and "Nicolotti," for their home bases in the *sestiere* of Castello and the parish of San Nicolò, across the canal in the *sestiere* of Dorsoduro, fought with bats, later just with fists, for half an hour at a time, attempting to push each other off the bridge or into the canal. An entire historical and legendary prose tradition traces the origins of these collective fistfights and explains them in terms of game theory. It is worth noting, however, that the two factions came from two quarters of the city that had a strong socioprofessional orientation. Most men in the parish of San Nicolò were fishermen or fishmongers, occupations with an organizational structure sufficiently particular to create a community recognized by the city authorities, who granted it a variety of privileges.[23] In the *sestiere* of Castello it was the Arsenal and shipbuilding, as we have seen, that forged a common identity strengthened by the encouragement and flattery of the power structure of Venice. In a city in which crafts long played only a minor role and commerce ranked highest in the hierarchy of values and status, no other professional group was treated with greater circumspection or listened to and honored more than the shipwrights and other shipyard workers. We can surmise that the gibes and cheers exchanged by the combatants on the bridge in the heat of the *frotta* were full of fantasy and inspiration, but they also demonstrate the existence of a strong sense of community, of belonging to a group, on both sides.

At the beginning of the sixteenth century the Arsenal reigned over a vast quarter of the city with unique social, urban, and industrial characteristics. The "port effect" was felt throughout Venice, however. From the basin of

San Marco, where the public infrastructure required by trade was established, to the lagoon and the littoral islands, where certain specialized functions thrived, maritime activities shaped the urban landscape. They molded the image of Venice, making it shimmer with reflected wealth and power but also with exotic and foreign notes. Around San Marco and along the port at the basin's edge an entire cosmopolitan throng labored and passed amid the noise and the bustle of cargo being unloaded and merchandise being piled up, while the domes and the gold of San Marco and San Zaccaria provided a striking backdrop. That central space was thus overloaded with signs. At the heart of a truly symbolic urban hub and at the very place where Venice opened wide to the water, the sea, and the great beyond, it revealed itself as a city-world.

THE RICHEST SPOT IN THE WORLD

Venetian wealth was also made and exhibited in a second, complementary space. The great city market was established on the island of Rialto, at the geographical center of the city, where the Grand Canal makes a wide bend by the bridge that for centuries was the only span between the city's two shores. The market communicated with the port directly via the artery of the Grand Canal, but that same waterway also put it into contact with the lagoon and the nearby shores of the mainland. Marino Sanudo's description will help us to sense the importance of the market. Where did one go to board one of the *traghetti* that carried passengers to Padua, Treviso, Vicenza, Monselice, Este, or Portogruaro? To the quays of Rialto, near the Loggia or the Fondaco dei Tedeschi. After customs duties were paid at the land customs house on the iron, charcoal, and textiles that arrived from lands near and far, where was merchandise unloaded and stored? On the quays and in the warehouses of Rialto. This was the end of the routes that joined Venice to the Continent; this was where the terrestrial and maritime domains of Venice met. The island of Rialto became, in Marino Sanudo's words, "the richest spot in the world."

The Market: Area and Functions

A commercial area, a useful adjunct to any city in formation, seems to have taken shape at Rialto quite soon; butchers were concentrated there from the earliest centuries of the city's existence. In the times of the city's demographic and economic rise the first market infrastructure was built, financed, and controlled by powerful families. Next came a landmark event in the growth of the market, one that incidentally provides an excellent illustration of private interests merging with a constantly redefined common good. At the end of the eleventh century the Orio family, whose members had reached old age without descendants, made a solemn donation to the city of their properties at Rialto and the installations built on them.[24] In describing the area the act uses the term *market*. In the decades that followed, the role of the Rialto was confirmed, and its powers of attraction were enhanced by the transfer to the area of the magistracies that held jurisdiction over economic affairs and the installation of such structures indispensable to commercial exchange as the public scales. Revenues from the market guaranteed the war loans subscribed in 1164. Commercial transactions gradually occupied all the available space, then moved into the vast empty lots and marshy terrains that surrounded the first nucleus of shops. As early as the thirteenth century, increasing commercial specialization led the noble families who owned land on the island to abandon their houses there in favor of properties on the opposite shore, which tradition tells us was connected to the island by a bridge at the end of the twelfth century. It was on that opposite shore, as we have seen, that the Fondaco dei Tedeschi was built in the 1220s.

Next the commune launched ambitious public-works programs that abruptly changed the pace of the history of the market and transformed the commercial heart of Venice in only a few decades. The city's highest priority in the second half of the thirteenth century was to create freer access to the market and facilitate communications by both water and land. This meant opening up streets leading to and from the nearby parishes, clearing waterways and shorelines, and improving the circulation of boat traffic and docking installations. In 1288 the Great Council even made the first of many attempts to simplify the confusion of sales sites and create an ideal location for large-scale trade on the Campo San Giacomo, between the church, the Loggia, and the bridge. The square, called Rialto Vecchio, was to be reserved for major transactions and profitable and honorable exchanges. A second space, known as San Matteo or the Rialto Nuovo, was created, paved, and set aside for vendors of poultry, fruit, bulky merchandise, and the daily activities of an ordinary produce market. Later projects were inspired by similar aims: on the one hand, the city moved to rebuild and improve the market buildings (the butchers' hall, the fish market) that worked with the market at San Marco to supply the local population; on the other hand, it attempted to free up space and improve access to the old center. In text after text the communal government reiterated the importance and utility of the market. It multiplied inspections, ordered reports, drew up rules, and commanded renovations, explicitly declaring that the common welfare and the prosperity of the entire population were dependent upon accommodating the merchants who flocked to the market. Improvements were focused on the central area of San Giacomo, where functional remodeling was combined with attention to both ornament and didactic intent. On the walls of the central colonnaded structure scenic views and a map of the world recalled Venetian preeminence in trade and the connections between the Venetian marketplace and almost all the known world.

Regulation and renovation proved unable to keep up with growth, and there was so much confusion amid the many installations and so many impediments to circulation that a new inspection commission was named in 1341. It had the dual charge of combating general disorder in the market and facilitating transactions, but it was also expected to reconcile aesthetic imperatives with economic modernization. Although it sought an ideal city and a central market area organized for the common utility and propitious to business and profits, public policy also strove for harmony and beauty. As with the shoreline of the basin of San Marco, aesthetic needs determined urban policy and practical choices. The market of the Rialto was charged with enhancing the honor of the Venetian commune by participating in the creation of a representation of the city.

The commission presented its proposals, and they were put into effect. The streets at the heart of the market were cleared, and the stalls, ground cloths, and boards that had encumbered them disappeared, at least for a time. Shops were moved. Sales activities were once again redistributed around the two poles of the Rialto Vecchio and the Rialto Nuovo. Next, regulations were passed to eliminate the encroachment of private initiatives on the access routes to the market and to the Fondaco dei Tedeschi, the market's antenna on the other side of the canal. On the Grand Canal itself the city planned to build a public quay similar to the one at San Marco. This meant that public initiatives soon overflowed the city's original modest intent. Even before 1285 the commune had set aside a section of the public wharf area at the heart of the market, at the elbow in the Grand Canal between the bridge and the Loggia, and placed it under the authority of the magistrates of the Rialto. During the first decades of the following century the public area along the Grand Canal was further extended to reach from the palace of the communal officials to the public scales. All along this "Rialto Canal" free access and space on the quays for unloading goods were protected by the city magistrates. The commune used fees for renting water-side space to maintain the waterway and remove refuse.

By the mid-fourteenth century the city's efforts to organize the market space had by and large ceased. Here, as with the port area, the rise of commerce was inscribed in each phase of its growth in the stones, on the water's edge, and in the canals. A long pause followed, and further improvements were not made until the final years of the century. The first of these, in 1394, concerned the clock at the Rialto: the old mechanism was changed, and a bigger bell that "could be heard throughout the city" was installed in the tower. The commune reasserted its hold over the business center, over time at the market, and, by that token, over time in the entire city. The move was a symbolic preparation for further embellishment. "Nobles, merchants, and all the foreigners" came to Rialto. It was thus decided to pave the principal square. The ambitious works that were carried out in the months that followed, concentrated on restoring the financial and commercial center. The entire market area was outdated: some of the market buildings, the texts tell us, were shaky and threatened to collapse. Still, improvements were selective and highly focused. The Loggia of the Nobles was reconstructed; somewhat later a new one was built and a landing was installed for those same *zentilhomeni*. Some reconstruction or repair work was finally done in the early 1460s. The Rialto bridge underwent repair or reconstruction on a number of occasions throughout the century, but given the frequency of accidents and the number of texts that mention rotting wooden beams and the poor condition of the bridge's basic structure, these projects must have been patch-up jobs. In 1458, after lively discussion in the Senate, it was decided that for the enrichment of the Republic and its citizens, two rows of shops would be built on the bridge. They soon realized handsome profits.

This, then, was where merchants met other merchants and where the exchanges took place that guaranteed the prosperity of Venice in its role as a middleman. From the Byzantine world, the Islamic world, and beyond; from the distant horizons of Arabia, India, or China; from the Barbary Coast or Slavic lands there came spices and precious stuffs, medicinals, furs and jewels, and raw materials for the textile industry. The riches of the West—metals and cloth brought by the Venetian ship convoys or overland by Italian or German merchants—were also offered for sale at the Rialto. All of these products were traded "for the greater profit of the Venetian land." Doge Tomaso Mocenigo explained these mechanisms and the reasons for the exuberant health of the Rialto as a commercial center. The Venetians had made themselves masters of "the gold of the Christians" because all of Europe was directly or indirectly supplied from there. Once Venice had collected its customs fees and filled its warehouses with merchandise, long-distance trade items were reshipped by sea to the markets of the distant north (London, Southampton, Bruges) and the south (Languedoc, Spain, North Africa). The merchants of certain cities—Milan and other Lombard cities, Florence, and, beyond the Alps, Augsburg, Vienna, Nuremberg, Regensburg, Ulm, and Cologne—enjoyed privileged relations with Venice and operated at the Rialto, either directly or through their agents. Venetians thus became "superior to all," and a policy of a rigid commercial centralization transformed the Rialto into a gigantic storage facility that was necessary to all European lands active in trade. Tomaso Mocenigo stated, "The said Florentines bring merchandise of all sorts, to the amount of 150,000 ducats annually, and they buy French wool, Catalan wool, kermes [a red coloring agent] in grain, silks, waxes, gold and silver thread, sugars, raw silver, spices both large and small, rock alum, indigo, and jewels."

Something much resembling a permanent fair thus took place at the Rialto. The level of activity there varied throughout the year, though: the schedules of the shipping lines followed the calendar, as did relations with northern Europe. Both were subject to fluctuation, both were affected by accidents, and they set the pace for commercial exchange and strongly influenced the immediate economic situation. As we have already seen, the prosperity of this system depended on timing. The sale of cotton unloaded at the port in the month of June and readying convoys for departure toward Bruges or Beirut were transactions that were unlikely to involve the same backers or the same products. The arrival of the ships from their return voyage some-where between 15 December and 15 February (the merchant convoys of the Levant usually made their east-west voyage after mid-October, when the winds were favorable) signaled a period of feverish activity. For several weeks products from the East were bought and sold, then reloaded on the *mude* that sailed to the West in the spring. In March and April departures for Aigues-Mortes or Tunis set the city in motion. Another business peak came toward the end of May, when melting snow had made the Alpine routes passable once more and Germans flocked to Venice.[25]

Marino Sanudo and Marc'Antonio Sabellico provide descriptions that help to orient us among the mass of shops and warehouses of the Rialto, the endless welter of stores, stalls, porticos, and streets where, in spite of all the city's attempts to enforce regulations and improve structures, retail sales activities in a city produce market coexisted with locations for major inter-national trade transactions and the offices of scores of economic agencies.[26]

A Walk through Rialto

The Venice of wine and of iron began at the southern foot of the bridge and moved east toward the basin of San Marco. This was where the various *rive* began—one for iron, another for wine—and where the quays were crowded with barrels, sacks, and bales and besieged by boats and lighters jockeying for a mooring or for docking space so they could unload their cargoes, not only wine and iron but also oil and flour.[27] The great *fondaco* for oil was just down the way, and beyond it was the public flour warehouse, where city officials auctioned flour by lots. Just beyond lay the edge of the island of Rialto and the limits of the market. Docking and storage facilities lined both sides of the waterway, but in an attempt to discourage fraud the city had also located here all the offices responsible for supervising the merchandise unloaded and stocked in the area. The land customs office stood near the "Three Tables," the Ternaria, which controlled oil, wood, and iron. The wine customs office was also nearby, as were the offices of the *provveditori* who supervised customs operations and the magistrates of the salt office. At that date the latter not only supervised the sale of salt and the financing and execution of public works but also managed city-owned properties in the market, such as wharves and shop stands. We are told that the "waters of the canal" were thick with boats "from the bridge to the Riva di San Cassiano."

Beyond the bridge, moving toward Cannaregio, the market changed its aspect. Other quays lined the canal here, but these were reserved for the produce halls—the Erbaria, or vegetable market, and the Fruttaria, or fruit market—and, farther off, the Pescaria, the fish market, which had been moved from the central area of San Giacomo because of its smells and its noise, and the Beccaria, the butchers' hall. The latter was newly built in the early 1340s on land obtained after the demolition of the Querini family house following the conviction of the head of the family for conspiracy in 1310. The commune had profited doubly from this operation: by punishing the guilty family and razing its *domus* to the ground it had also recuperated a vast terrain big enough for one of the great market halls needed to feed the city.

In the fully populated Venice of the late Middle Ages the distribution of foodstuffs was organized according to a strict hierarchy. Almost every *contrada* had not only microsectors organized around a bake oven, for example, but also a main street, a *salizzada* or *ruga,* for retail commerce. Markets in each quarter were held on a specific day of the week on the *campo,* the small parish square. Markets in two of the larger quarters—at San Polo on Wednesdays and at San Marco on Saturdays—served a broader area of the city. Finally, there were the market halls. On both sides of the Grand Canal, at the Rialto but also at San Marco, they supplied the city and, in doing so, firmly linked two locations within the daily itineraries of Venetians.

This mixture of functions and uses continued to be one of the most striking features of the old city. Ships rode at anchor before the "marble shore of San Marco," as Petrarch called it in one of his letters. From the Piazzetta to the shore of Terranuova the way was lined with great halls, while a swarm of vendors hawking onions or cooked foods called out to passersby. Shops and stalls tended to invade all available space: we know that in the late fifteenth century ten stalls across from the Ducal Palace were rented to sellers of "herbs, melons, watermelons, and squash." The contrasts were just as striking at the Rialto: merchants long negotiated wholesale purchases of pepper next to the fishmongers' stalls, and throughout these years itinerant tradesmen and ambulant merchants were never fully controlled. Thus, these two central spaces, one of which was becoming the metaphorical locus of power, the other in theory reserved for large-scale trade, continued to be familiar, vibrant gathering places within the culture and the urban practices of the population at large.

South of the Rialto bridge lay the vast, ancient building of the Draperia, the cloth market. Shops on the ground floor sold local and foreign textiles, while the upper story served as a warehouse and housed some Rialto offices. A pedestrian continuing along the same street and moving further onto the island would find shop after shop selling all sorts of textiles, lengths of cloth, items of clothing, and furs. The apothecaries and the spice merchants had their shops on the same large street, which crossed the Ruga degli Orefici, another commercial street, while a network of smaller *calli* branched off toward the Grand Canal. Thanks to government-sponsored improvements and regulations, certain tradesmen—drapers, furriers, and goldsmiths, for example—were grouped in one area, but all descriptions state that confusion reigned.

It was precisely that confusion, the vast number of shops and stalls, and the juxtaposition of ordinary and costly merchandise that seemed extraordinary. In the fifteenth century the boats tied up to the quays became shops and could be rented as such. The market hall, piled high with fruits and greens, seemed a garden. Reality, already at a limit of believability, was beautified and transformed. Because of this gigantic display, all descriptions of Venice presented it as the city of profusion and plenitude. Foreigners marveled at a wealth unheard of in their age. Its market and the juxtaposition of so many men, goods, and activities within a limited area made Venice seem a mythical land of plenty, a world in miniature.

The loggia that stood at the foot of the bridge, on the right, served as a meeting place for merchants, but in the summertime magistracies with jurisdiction over economic matters—the Consoli sulla Mercanzia or the Savi sulla Mercanzia—often used it for hearings to settle controversies and suits.[28] Next to the loggia were the seats of other economic commissions and judicial bodies. The many treatises on the institutions and magistracies of Venice that started to appear in the fifteenth century, a time of increased interest in Venetian forms of government, delighted in providing long lists of such bodies. One such treatise, Marino Sanudo's *De magistratibus urbis,* although purely descriptive and hence perhaps not the most interesting of the genre, draws the distinction, fundamental in Venice, between the magistracies of Rialto and those of San Marco. The Rialto offices were located in two adjacent loggias in a building remodeled in the late fifteenth century. Behind this building was the small church of San Giacomo di Rialto, with a narrow *campo* beside it squeezed in between walls and porticos. This was the heart of the market, the place where the primacy of Venice was founded and refounded day after day.

Legend attributed particular antiquity to the church of San Giacomo. The chroniclers tell us that it was on the tiny island of Rialto, soon eponymous with the city of Venice, that the city was born. Human settlement of the lagoons was supposed to have begun with the founding of the church in 421. The writers of the great historical texts of the late thirteenth century, Martino da Canale and Marco, took this bit of information, fabricated not long before their time, and grafted it onto their narrations of the origins of Venice. Andrea Dandolo, who was both a doge and a chronicler, developed the myth to its full version. According to Dandolo, the people of Padua took refuge in the lagoons, which were not far from their city, in a period of repeated invasions. On 25 March 421 they chose the site that became Rialto and began to build: the church of San Giacomo was the first sacred edifice of the new community. This historical construct was destined to have a long life. Toward the end of the fifteenth century some skeptics challenged the notion of an inspired founding of Venice, precisely on the Feast of the Annunciation, but critical murmurs from humanist quarters did not prevent historians from continuing to repeat the story of Venice's founding in 421 until the end of the Republic and even beyond.[29] Among all the land areas in and around the lagoon, the island of Rialto was thus designated as the original shelter, the predestined asylum where Venice's history could begin. And within that island that formed the nub of the city the tiny area of San Giacomo was invested with particular luster.

The invention of the foundation of the city in 421 took its place, however, within the more complex fabrication of the legend of origins. The first purpose of that legend was to name the islands of Rialto, at the heart of the lagoon basin, and show them as predestined. It was not by chance that the *campo* of San Giacomo was reserved for the most prestigious sorts of trade or that the most honorable business deals were conducted at the most honored spot in the center of Venice. This was where Venetian and foreign merchants met, under the porticos and before frescoes representing the distant lands with which Venetians did business. A fourteenth-century decree states that no timber or other *cosa grossa* but only precious metals or titles to loans and properties could be auctioned at this site. It was prohibited to auction slaves there, although simple sales transactions for slaves were permitted at Rialto Nuovo. San Giacomo was where the moneychangers and bankers set up their tables, where "bargains involving very large sums were sealed with a 'yes' or a 'no.' "[30] Insurance contracts could be drawn up on the nearby Calle della Sicurtà. Marc'Antonio Sabellico tells us that although noise and frantic activity reigned elsewhere, at San Giacomo, "where all the business of the city—or, rather, of the world—was transacted," a place "full of all manner of men," one heard "no voice, no noise . . . no discussion . . . no insults . . . no disputes." Everything was discussed in low tones, for the proper way to do business was with few words.[31]

Public power also used marks and symbols to make its presence felt at the market. The seats of the various magistracies were distributed between the island of Rialto and San Marco, but many other signs of public authority and sovereignty, visibly inscribed in the area, made Rialto more than the merchant heart of a mercantile city. The island that had been the matrix of Venice soon became a place of power, thus gaining importance in the symbolic geography of the city. The column of the *bando*, a pillar topped by a platform from which the public crier proclaimed laws, stood in the Campo San Giacomo. The public scales that guaranteed that off-loaded merchandise would be weighed without fraud had stood at the foot of the Rialto bridge at least since the twelfth century, when it is first attested in the texts. Public authority asserted its presence in other ways as well: a prison stood beside the Grand Canal, next to the land customs office and the oil sellers' shops, and physical punishments were inflicted at both the Rialto and San Marco. Public floggings were administered on the steps of the bridge, in front of the offices of the island's magistracies. Sentences of public exposure were also carried out on the bridge, and on occasion a gallows bearing the body (at times a quarter of the body) of an executed criminal was set up near the Grand Canal, across from one of the market halls.

Nothing was lacking in that "well ordered" place, and all descriptions of the market end with a mention of the taverns and the public brothel. In 1358, a fairly early date in the overall chronology of the phenomenon,[32] prostitution was regulated by law in Venice.[33] Before that date prostitution, feebly combated rather than forbidden, existed in houses and taverns; although widespread, it was already to some extent concentrated in certain quarters. In 1358 the Great Council acknowledged what it called a "need": "It is necessary, given the multitude of men who continually enter and leave our city, to find an appropriate place where female sinners can live." The commercial vocation of Venice made it imperative to open a city-sponsored bordello. It was established in the market area, where prostitutes were already present in large numbers, in the parish of San Matteo del Rialto. The public house known as the Castelletto operated under the supervision of communal officials. Like all medieval houses of prostitution, the Castelletto was not closed; the women left it to find their clients, using nearby houses and continuing to frequent the inns and taverns. At night they returned to the Castelletto, which closed its doors until the morning bell pealed from the Marangona in the Campanile in Piazza San Marco to declare the beginning of a new workday. Like St. Augustine, the commune of Venice considered prostitution a necessary evil. It institutionalized it in order not only to control it but also to protect the prostitutes (though this was not its primary aim). Moral condemnation was to some extent effective, and the location of the public house on a side street, installed in humble buildings that were always badly maintained and at times in even worse condition, clearly shows how prostitution was regarded. The city's attempt to limit the flesh trade to one area almost immediately proved a failure. Prostitutes moved out beyond the boundaries of the island of Rialto, settling in large numbers in several parishes.

The fact remains that the Castelletto was the hub of a microquarter, and we know from the criminal archives that life there was often troubled. The area contained many inns, and the high rents realized by their owners prove that business was excellent. Besides the more reputable taverns and *ostarie*, there were many smaller drinking places, licensed and unlicensed. Foreigners passing through the city, city dwellers who had come to shop at the great market, and groups of young men and servants gathered in such places, which also catered to the shadier world of gamblers, the unemployed, petty thieves, and pimps. Their curses, disputes, and brawls, all duly noted in the judiciary records, set the daily pace in an area in which criminal activity was rampant.

This, then, was the other side of life at the Rialto, the seamier side of the theatrical decor, where the customs were not those of the lords of the pepper trade or even of the goldsmiths or the spice vendors on the commercial streets. Behind the image of profusion and plenitude in "the wealthiest place in the world" were sordid alleys teeming with a hardworking but miserably poor and at times dangerous people. The guards of course made regular rounds and patrols. Surveillance was redoubled around the Castelletto, and throughout the island vigilance was tightened at night with the aim of preventing theft, enforcing curfew, and diminishing the terrible danger of fire.[34] Sentences for crimes and misdemeanors committed within Rialto, that is, in the area bordered by the canals that marked its limits, were particularly severe, as they were at San Marco. The result was an objective concentration of police forces. Moreover, the guards and the many clerks who worked for the Rialto magistracies strengthened the presence of authority and increased the number of its representatives.

All to no effect. Day after day, the chronicle of criminality continued, enlivened by street brawls, by crowding and noise, and by the inevitable quarrels that broke out on the wharf or in the market hall over an affront, a push, a misplaced witticism, an economic disagreement, an inflated price, or an uncollected debt. Curses and scuffles, whether or not they were followed by *effusio sanguinis*, were common currency among the butchers and the cheese sellers. A shoving match between two men might degenerate, ending up in a battle royal in the market hall or the street between members of the two trade groups. A member of one of the magistracies of the Republic proclaimed, deploring such behavior with a certain hauteur: "Animals who live on the same feed naturally detest each other." Public officials who had come to inspect a shop, supervise a sale, or demand the removal of spoiled merchandise might be greeted by the shopkeeper with curses and even blows, even though such remonstrances were punished without mercy. Verbal and physical violence, omnipresent in the daily life of older societies, is a topic too well known to dwell upon.[35]

I prefer to recall another market and another world, those of the poor, the marginal, and the petty thief. Court records reveal the poverty and vagrancy that existed at the edges of Venetian society. Reports of hearings or sentences in the final decades of the fourteenth century give a glimpse of the homeless and of vagabonds from the mountains of Friuli or from German lands. In the daytime such men hired out as porters, but they also hung about, robbed passersby, or shoplifted from the stalls and shops; at night they formed bands to raid the warehouses, then slept on boats moored in the canal or in the shelter of doorways. Other, seemingly more stable lives might tip toward crime, and the market was one of the places where such accidents happened. In the urban society of the age, delinquency was not restricted to those immediately identifiable as excluded from the mainstream: an entire population seems to have lived on the border between work and poverty. Apprentices and servants did not always resist the temptation to appropriate a purse or a bit of money. Bands of freed slaves and boatmen *(barcaroli)* specialized in theft from ships. One man accused of cutting a purse admitted that hunger had urged him to it; another man caught shoplifting at the Rialto declared that he had wandered endlessly about the city.

Everything could be bought and sold in Venice, and everything had a price—a purse hanging from a belt or a piece of salt meat, a pair of shoes or a silver cup, a length of cloth or a mortar. A parallel economy provided a living for a second society, which was as reliant on the market as the first. There was no need to cross the lagoon to the pawnbrokers of Mestre to turn a theft into a few pennies. Receivers of stolen goods, occasional or not, were legion in Venice. The rag sellers of Rialto bought stolen clothes, and the dealers in secondhand goods accepted merchandise without inquiring into its provenance. Some dry-goods sellers and leather merchants showed a similar tolerance. Innkeepers accepted gages of all sorts. All of this life, barely concealed under the surface, emerged in the fracas of cries and invective from the sellers, the onlookers, and the guards intent on making arrests.[36] The pulse of the mercantile heart of Venice irrigated the city with wealth.

Out from the Center

The mercantile heart of Venice was inseparable from its complement, the port, but it was also connected to the warehouses and storage facilities lined up along the canal, occupying the ground level under the dwelling spaces, and it radiated out into the neighboring parishes. Proximity to Rialto raised property values near the market, in the parishes of the *sestiere* of San Polo. It was also proximity to the commercial center that created nuclei of Jews in the parishes of San Silvestro and San Cassiano in the fifteenth century. As is known, the ghetto was created in Venice in 1516, a move that was soon imitated in other cities.[37] The 1516 decree instituted a segregation that the commune had already experimented with in its colonial territories. Even before that date, except for a short period at the end of the fourteenth century, Jews were officially subject to exclusion and to many sorts of discrimination. They were obliged to live in Mestre, on the shore of the mainland, and could come into the lagoon area only for limited stays after a stipulated interval. The exclusion of Jews from Venice (one effect of which was a disproportionate amount of lending against gages in Mestre, a small town) was not inflexible, as can be seen by these very indications of a Jewish presence in the city.[38]

Across the Grand Canal from the market it was of course the Fondaco dei Tedeschi that most influenced the physiognomy of the city. As we have seen, various renovations of the building had led to changes in the surrounding streets, but its sphere of attraction reached well beyond its first setting to affect several *contrade*. Germans were everywhere in the parishes of San Bartolomeo, San Giovanni Grisostomo, San Salvatore, and Santi Apostoli. German merchants had their own chapel in the church of San Bartolomeo, and when it came to decorating the chapel in 1506, they commissioned a painting from their compatriot Albrecht Dürer, who was staying at Rialto at the time.[39] German settlement was less dense north of that area, becoming scattered in the parishes of San Canciano and Santa Maria Nuova. Germans did not remain grouped in one part of the city: as they came to Italy in greater numbers during the final decades of the fourteenth century they settled elsewhere as well. For example, many German workers of extremely modest social condition lived in the parts of the city where wool was worked.[40] Although it is inaccurate to speak of any genuine residential concentration of Germans in Venice, and although we must keep in mind differences in status and in conditions for assimilation, the fact remains that the Fondaco dei Tedeschi, one element among others that fixed the identity of these parishes, put a special stamp on its surroundings that included visible traces of a sizable foreign colony.

Thus the market had effects that radiated out to points near and far. Other, less evident effects followed the winding streets connecting Rialto and San Marco. The city had grown and become organized around those two poles, and that dual focus explains both the morphology of the city and many of its habits, itineraries, and practices, both individual and collective. The Mercerie started north of the Rialto bridge, at Campo San Bartolomeo. Passage along this series of commercial streets was soon facilitated by pavement and by bridges connecting its various segments, thus making it a major artery for the central parishes. At Piazza San Marco the monumental portal of the Bocha di Marzaria connected the square with the near neighborhood and the more distant market of the Rialto, which, although invisible from the streets of the Mercerie, was the end point of all routes. Thus, like Venice itself, Piazza San Marco, after the extension effected under Doge Sebastiano Ziani, was anchored in both land and water. Not only did the Piazza have a broad opening to the basin of San Marco at the meeting point of major waterways but it was firmly linked to the urban structure of Venice and its many buildings. Later works projects (e.g., the construction of the Clock Tower) were simply variations on the theme of the boundaries of the Piazza and the relations between that privileged space, the rest of the city, and the city's second center. The well-stocked shops that lined the Mercerie, from which the street got its name, were part of the exhibition of merchandise and wealth that made visitors from Nuremberg, Paris, or Douai think the stretch of the city from San Marco to Rialto a gigantic fair held every day of the year.

For a short period during the year the Piazza really did become a fair. This was in May, at the time of Ascension Day, when commercial activity was at its peak at Rialto. The fair, which was part of a program of entertainments and celebrations organized for the Feast of the Ascension, was yet another instance of the profound coherence of an urban system whose dual centers were endowed not only with a principal function but also with a whole range of rigorously symmetrical secondary functions. It was one of the duties of the Procurators of San Marco to oversee the preparation of a series of wooden booths that were set up in strict order all along the edge of the Piazza starting from the Ducal Palace and the porch of the basilica. The Captain of the Piazza and his men policed the shops and stalls, making sure that each one occupied its assigned place. On Ascension Day itself Venetians hastened to the celebration of the Sensa, along with pilgrims, some waiting to embark on a trip to the Holy Land and others come to Venice for the ceremonies and to receive the indulgences accorded to those who visited the basilica during the festivities. There were foreigners as well: Lombards came with textiles, the chronicler Malipiero tells us, along with Slavs selling woolen goods and merchants from the Marches.[41] Relations with those same areas of the Adriatic and northern Italy affected the decisions of the Venetian magistracies responsible for health and sanitation at the turn of the fifteenth century: when the plague was ravaging the Marches and Istria, they annulled the Sensa fair in order to avoid having the epidemic spread to Venice. The situation was reversed a few years later, when cases of plague had been found within the city. Should the fair be put off? It was known that the Dalmatians, ruined by the Turks, badly needed commerce. The public authorities hesitated for some time before the advisability of quarantine carried the day over mercantile interests.

Foreigners came to this fair with their products, but relatively few booths were reserved for them. First and foremost, the products sold at Piazza San Marco were local in origin, and they tended to represent the best in Venetian craftsmanship. A sixteenth-century list of the "arts and professions who must go to the Sensa" and a map of shops for the fair mention clothes sellers, carpenters, and blacksmiths, but above all it was the fine arts, luxury, and fashion trades that were on display in booths manned by goldsmiths, mercers, perfumers, glassmakers, comb sellers, chaplet makers, and merchants selling pearls, mirrors, shoes, majolica, and more. These products, offered for sale for a few days on Piazza San Marco, seem to have had sufficient power of attraction to guarantee the success of the fair and to turn handsome profits.

This annual fair with its few dozen stalls undoubtedly pales in comparison with the permanent market at the Rialto, and these exchanges undeniably occupied only a secondary place within the machinery of the Venetian economy. That is not what is important, however. Such lists of *marzeri, verier, oresi, spechier,* and *pettineri* reveal the dynamism of the luxury trades in a city that was not uniquely a maritime and colonial power, however brilliant its success in those domains.

IN SEARCH OF INDUSTRIAL VENICE

What in fact was produced in medieval and Renaissance Venice? What is there to be said about the working world in that metropolis? Many distinctive traits make it possible to postulate that Venice was a special case. Various authors, writing in different ages, praised Venice for its site, its mercantile wealth, or its singular political organization. Soon the characteristics that gave Venice a unique socioeconomic landscape and political setup were noted as well. Artisans and craftsmen were excluded from public life: here the guilds did not govern. Nor did Venice experience opposition or sedition fomented by the trades that were common occurrences in other urban milieus. According to some hypotheses, voiced with certain reservations, the social calm of which Venetians so often boasted—and even those who eschew myth have to admit that it was real—resulted from the surveillance of the working classes and the tutelage imposed on them. Crafts and artisan work (and this is another trait particular to Venice) made only a secondary contribution to the city's prosperity. Without going as far as Giorgio Cracco in suggesting that the merchant elites deliberately "sabotaged" crafts, most historians agree that industry arrived somewhat late in Venice, as "a compensation when the climate was unfavourable."[42] No one can deny that the Arsenal and the quarter organized around it represented one of the largest industrial concentrations of the time, but it was a very special sort of concentration in that it operated under the strict supervision of the state and its many workers labored to further maritime ventures and long-distance trade. The weakness of the wool industry in Venice in centuries in which the wealth of so many cities was based on the wool trade is perhaps the most obvious sign of the long undisputed primacy of merchant capitalism in Venice.

What are we to think of such interpretations? To say the least, they require some refinement. Venice, as we have seen, presented itself as a stage and as a performance. The port at the edge of the basin of San Marco, as we have seen in the texts, was where the city revealed itself to the foreign visitor. Piazza San Marco, those same texts tell us, was the most beautiful spectacle in the world. The island of Rialto was a treasure, the jewel that Venetians cared for, protected, and exhibited. Those two centers diffused a radiant, even a blinding light, which was that of the opulence of merchandise. Captivated by that light, by those successes, and by the hegemonic presence of trade in Venetian history and in the daily life of Venice, historians have long focused exclusively on the international dimensions of Venice's wealth and on its forms and objects of exchange. Recent studies have worked to correct that tendency and to bring other sectors of Venetian economic life out of the shadows. We will have to penetrate deeper into the life of Venice if we are to discern those lesser-known activities and find the less central areas where an entire laboring population was engaged in production.

Work and Its Worlds

Studying craft and artisan work takes us away from a celebration of "Venice the beautiful" toward an investigation of industrious neighborhoods, courtyards, and alleys, where poverty sometimes lurked, and to the utilitarian edges of the city, where workshops and construction sites were gradually infiltrated by hospices and socially inspired real-estate projects. The image of Venice as queen of the sea and sovereign of trade takes on a new shade of meaning here. Trade groups whose output exceeded local consumer demand operated in various quarters of the city. By the early sixteenth century an industrial periphery ringed the entire settled area.

The working world in Venice thus deserves further investigation. My first remarks concern the workers, but it might be more accurate to speak instead of various worlds of work. Condition and status were multiple, as in all the cities of contemporary Europe. How are we to compare the members of instituted and protected trade groups that had elected representatives, banners, confraternities, meeting places, and institutionalized solidarities in both life and death with the mass of mobile, ill-paid laborers whose names appear on no lists and whose physical strength fulfilled the city's devouring need for manpower? The same question might be asked of all the major manufacturing centers of the time, but it has a special pertinence in Venice, where artisan labor was subject to regulation at a particularly early date.

Let us start in 1173 with the process of administrative organization that began at that time. Under Doge Sebastiano Ziani a magistracy was instituted to supervise weights and measures. Its officials were responsible not only for the food-distribution system but also for the "arts." Their duties were so vast that in 1261 the agency was divided in two: the Giustizia Vecchia retained supervision of the guilds, while the Giustizia Nuova took on the task of supervising food supplies, taverns, and the wine trade. At the same time the wool guild came under the authority of a special magistracy, the Provveditori di Comun. It is clear even from this bare outline that these administrative changes reflect governmental tutelage. Later, in 1278, the Giustizia

Vecchia set itself the task of compiling texts to facilitate its operations. All the original documents that had been conserved in the agency's archives and all the guild statutes submitted to it were dutifully copied. This official register, which was then continued after 1278, forms a large dossier.[43]

What do these archives tell us? The first surprise they hold, one that accentuates the originality of Venice, is that this great commercial city had no merchants' guild. They also show that between 1218 and 1330 the Giustizia Vecchia registered the statutes of fifty-two guilds, a number that points to the extreme fragmentation of artisan activity in Venice compared with that in other major Italian cities.[44] That fragmentation was lasting. At the beginning of the fifteenth century workmen from no fewer than sixty-four different guilds helped to build the famous Cà d'Oro.[45] One consequence of this exaggeratedly fine division was that the guilds were roughly identical in size and importance, with no one guild dominating the others. Another consequence was a certain flexibility that guaranteed quality of production. For the rising luxury industries this was a major advantage.

In reality the many guilds in Venice did not include either the *grassi,* who in Venice were engaged in trade, or the *popolo minuto;* their members came instead from a population group of middling status. Figures on prices and salaries are lacking, so that socioeconomic analysis has little to go on. Still, we can suppose that state tutelage had positive aspects that would explain both the docility of workers as a group and their increasing contribution to Venetian wealth. All studies stress the absence of serious tensions between merchants and manufacturers and the importance of the guilds within the fabric of society. An examination of life in the *contrade* confirms that relative calm and also displays solidarities built around a shared trade or confraternity, even though social relations reached beyond the occupational framework to form more complex networks.[46] The guilds functioned under the joint authority of public officials and their own elected leaders. As was true elsewhere, they were subject to obligations and were governed by a prolix set of professional rules, but they were also carefully protected. The guild statutes took care to preserve an equilibrium within the individual branches of the labor force (e.g., by limiting the number of apprentices) and to keep productive units to a manageable size. The corporations could buy the raw materials they needed wholesale, thus eluding control by the merchants.[47] Some trades, such as the glass industry, were protected by regulations aimed at preventing foreign competitors from imitating the methods of Venetian manufacturing.

The social condition of the thousands of men and women who made up the labor force in Venice was just as varied as the groups to which they belonged.[48] According to lists of tenants, the poorest among them shared the daily life of the legions of unspecialized workers required by the economy of the age. Aside from the proletariat of the rowers and dockers whom we have seen at work in the port and in the market, this category included the *sottoposti,* the lowest category of industrial laborers, who performed such tasks as preparing raw silk and wool for processing, and the thousands of domestic servants in this urban world.[49]

Many of these workers were outsiders, foreigners or non-Venetians. Integration into Venetian society was not closed, and plague epidemics had left gaps in the population that made it easier to assimilate newcomers. Often a patronymic was the only sign of the Lombard, Albanian, or Dalmatian origin of someone who kept a shop in the parish or who was employed in one of the many public offices. The most recent arrivals were more likely to be unspecialized laborers. We have seen that the *sestiere* of Castello had a strong Balkan cast and that there were nuclei of German workers in wool-manufacturing areas. We have also seen that immigrants to Venice from the Brescian countryside or the mountains of Friuli settled at the edges of the city, in zones where the city gave way to water, where they lived among other poor people in simple shacks set among empty lots and vegetable plots surrounded by sheds, workshops, and warehouses. Ten or twenty years later those same immigrants had abandoned those indeterminate zones for more centrally located parishes and less ephemeral living arrangements, while other newcomers, attracted by the mirage of the metropolis, took their place at the periphery.[50]

Still other newcomers who arrived to swell the numbers of the lower classes or the ranks of domestic servants did not come to Venice voluntarily. The sources speak of slaves who worked for nobles, citizens, and craftsmen. An overwhelming majority of them were women. As we have seen, slaves soon counted among the sorts of merchandise that Venice traded. Sold throughout the Mediterranean world, slaves were also brought to Rialto, where they were bought by Venetians and Italians. The Slavic world was a first, nearby source of supply for the slave trade, and even long after the area had been Christianized it continued to furnish captives. Roman Catholic Albanians fleeing from the Turks were reduced to servitude in the fourteenth century, and until the fifteenth century the market for slaves included large numbers of Bulgarians, who were considered pagans and thus could easily be sold. For a time there were even Greek Christian slaves. In the years of Venice's struggle to gain overseas possessions, some Greeks captured in fighting along the coasts, in the islands, or in a variety of expeditions and raids were reduced to slavery. At a later date raids by pirates and even ship captains supplied the demand for slave labor, for example, in Crete. It is known that Candia had a flourishing slave market to which Venetian merchants went to replenish their supply. The slave trade was thus thriving, whether the human merchandise was destined for the metropolis or for other Mediterranean markets. Increasingly, however, questions began to be raised regarding the enslavement of Christians, even if they were schismatics.

With the growing reluctance to sell Christians, the slave trade shifted to the market centers of the Black Sea. In those ports, connected to active and long-established markets in the interior, Italians could stock up on slaves. Venetian ships departed from Tana, Trebizond, and even Constantinople carrying shipments of male slaves to Egypt, where they were sold at Alexandria; female slaves—Russian, Circassian, or Tartar women—continued on to Rialto, where they could be bought for forty to fifty ducats.[51] The wars of the final decades of the fifteenth century ruined the slave trade in those areas, and black slaves, more males than females, began to arrive in Venice.[52] Although trade in black slaves is reflected in Venetian painting, for example, in Carpaccio's *Miracle at Rialto* or Gentile Bellini's *Miracle of the True Cross at the Bridge of San Lorenzo*, it was much more limited in scope than the trade in black slaves organized first by the Portuguese and then by the Spanish.

Male slaves were thus a rarity in Venice. They were prohibited within the precincts of the Arsenal, but a few artisans owned slaves. Above all, slaves were part of noble entourages, in which they served their masters, escorted them, or acted as their gondoliers. Slave labor, which was principally female, was used within the household. Little information filters through from the sources, however. There are contracts stating the terms of a sale or a resale. When an occasional will mentions a small bequest to a female slave, it provides a rare glimpse of these many women, some of whom had been made pregnant by the men of the house. A few trial records mention foreign women suspected of concocting philters, plotting intrigues, or causing scenes and stirring up the sort of jealousies that "the domestic enemy" might inject into a large household.[53] The study of slavery has only a small number of slim facts to build on: we can discern only faint shadows of a few lives. Emancipations did occur, however, especially at the death of slaves' owners, and servile status was not transmissible. Thus, the Venetians' "stock" of slaves had to be constantly replenished. Freed slaves and the children of slaves melted into the mass of the *popolani,* identifiable only by surnames borrowed from their former masters.

Awkward and incomplete as this picture is, it shows the world of labor in Venice. Sources are lacking that might provide a clearer definition of hierarchies and lines of demarcation, and it is difficult to breathe life back into the actors of an economic chronicle that has long seemed somewhat flat compared with Venice's maritime adventure.

Silk, Woolens, Glass, Books

In the greater city of Venice, with its population of over 100,000 and its very high standard of living for the dominant classes, an entire series of trades worked primarily to nourish, clothe, shoe, shelter, and amuse the population and provide it with objects, both simple and refined. Venice had merchants and shipbuilders, but it also had butchers and pastry cooks, dancing masters and fencing teachers, cabaret owners and dry-goods sellers, barbers and apothecaries, candlemakers and gardeners, rag sellers and tailors, goldsmiths and furriers, shoemakers and weavers. The wills of even the poorest Venetians list a bed and some stools but also at least a few lengths of cloth and some simple furnishings—a pail, a stewpot and the chain with which to hang it over the fire.[54]

There were small-scale foundries in Venice, in the parish of San Barnaba in particular, but beginning in the fourteenth century competition from the mainland probably decreased their business.[55] There was even a cotton and fustian industry that worked some of the raw cotton imported in Venetian ships, but Lombard fustians and German cottons gave it serious competition beginning in the fifteenth century. Ceramic ware for everyday use was produced, probably in large quantities, in the form of dishes and vases prettily decorated in green and yellow. The many fragments and faded shards that emerge from the lagoon and the embankments bear witness to this industry. In Venice as elsewhere, certain sectors employed a large workforce. In the late thirteenth century the tanneries so polluted the water that the communal government decreed their removal across the Giudecca canal to the island of the same name. There is mention of the industry there as early as 1285, when the leatherworkers protested a decree of the public officials that limited their free access to water. Tanners were still active on the Giudecca, in the area around the Ponte Lungo, in the fifteenth century. It is impossible to imagine the palaces, churches, and houses of Venice that rise up out of the water or its many quays and bridges without recalling the men and masters of the building trades—sculptors, of course, but also swarms of workmen and day laborers, not to mention the people employed in the brick works that produced the bricks essential to buildings that were only faced with stone.[56] Nor would the picture be complete without the lumberyards at the edge of the city, where the timber that had been floated down the rivers was dried and stocked before being used to satisfy the city's needs. Timber merchants had long been established north of the parish of Santi Giovanni e Paolo, in the Barbaria delle Tole near the church of Santa Giustina, but there were also lumberyards on recently reclaimed plots of land near the candle works, the ironworks, or the sugar refineries. Sugar was a Venetian specialty, but the industry was in decline in the early sixteenth century as a result of growing competition from Atlantic sugar and refined sugar shipped from Cyprus.

For some time no single industrial activity seemed to rise above the rest. As we have seen, wool manufacturing has been considered symbolic of Venice's mediocrity as an industrial city. The rise of the Florentine textile industry in the thirteenth century is a familiar story; during the same decades, the *lanaiuoli* of Venice seem to have occupied a modest position, to judge from Martino da Canale's mention of wool workers in his chronicle as one among various trade groups participating in the celebrations for the election of the new doge, Lorenzo Tiepolo. The redaction of the statutes for the wool guild seem to have followed the institution, in 1244, of the Consuls of the Merchants. This first text concerns the weavers, the first group to become organized.[57] Regulation and prescribed manufacturing criteria were then extended to spinning, dyeing, and the other branches of the wool trade, all of which were placed under the supervision of the consuls. The communal government did its best to encourage an industry that it hoped would fill certain of the needs of the local market even if it could never compete with foreign cloth in international trade. One sign of Venice's dependence on foreign textiles was that throughout the fourteenth century the masters of the wool guild continued to meet in rooms in the warehouse for foreign-made textiles at the market of the Rialto, near the Draperia. We know little about wool working in the earlier period. Some legislative texts from the late thirteenth century seem to relegate wool working to the northern end of the lagoon, around the islands of Torcello,[58] but it is doubtful that such decrees were ever applied, and by the early fourteenth century wool workers seem to have practiced their craft freely in Venice. Before that date spinning, a source of employment for women, was probably based in Rialto. A final touch completes this less than brilliant scenario: the site of Venice made wool working difficult. From the outset Venice had turned to the mainland for technological support because the scarcity of fresh water in Venice meant that cloth had to be sent to Treviso, Padua, or Portogruaro to be fulled.

The story does not end there, however. In the fifteenth century wool working, which was concentrated around the Rio Marin, in the southwestern parish of San Simeone Profeta, began to leave a more visible mark on the topography of the city. The guild offices moved to the same area to facilitate the enforcement of manufacturing standards. In the early sixteenth century this genuine industrial concentration included the indispensable equipment, vast terrains (chiovere) containing racks for drying lengths of cloth after dyeing, and standardized housing constructed for the workers and weavers. Wool manufacturing spread out from this zone into the neighboring parishes, and by the early sixteenth century other nuclei demonstrated a genuine dynamism in the wool industry. A few smaller manufacturing units functioned north of there, amid the silk workers settled at the city's edge. More often, however, the various components of the wool trades were located near other industrial activities typical of the confines of the city. Dye works and their adjacent chiovere stretched along the shores of the inner lagoon. The communal government consistently tried to move dyeing and its polluting by-products far from the canals of the city center. It decreed in 1413 that dye works that used blood or indigo were to be moved "to the urban extremities," that is, to the shores of the salt ponds. At the beginning of the modern age its decrees were put into effect, and workshops and drying lots at the *caò* (outside edge) of Cannaregio, at San Girolamo, and at Sant'Alvise joined the other activities that exploited the periphery of the city.[59]

From then on the wool industry, which for decades had been almost invisible, made a real impact on the city and its economy. How can we explain this change? The spectacular rise of wool production during the sixteenth century is now counted as contributing to the revival of the Venetian economy in the period. During the last third of the sixteenth century Venice is thought to have manufactured between 20,000 and 26,000 lengths of woolen cloth per year, and in 1602 production peaked at 28,700 lengths. These figures clearly indicate a growing industry, given that even the most optimistic estimates set wool production in 1500 at some 2,000 lengths per year.[60] There are convergent indications of accelerated production at an even earlier date, during the latter half of the fifteenth century, when Venetian cloth of excellent quality was regularly exported to the markets of the East, in particular Constantinople, Syria, and Egypt. These were for the most part scarlet in grain, the famous *bastardi de grana*.[61] It seems clear that the know-how of the Venetian dyers, who were known for their reds, had much to do with the success of the Venetian wool trade.[62]

In fourteenth-century Venice the *arte della lana* was small in scale, fragile, and subject to recurrent crises. Often encouraged by protectionist laws that attempted to reserve at least a portion of the urban market for local production, wool manufacturing at that time seems to have been completely dominated by import-export trade. A century later wool manufacturing had made constant advances thanks to rigorous technical standards and the skill of the artisans, had captured a place in the export market, and had become a major industry.[63]

Other industries that have traditionally been considered secondary in the merchant economy of Venice have also been subjected to scholarly reexamination in recent years. The glass industry is one of these. Historians long considered glass manufacturing a curiosity specific to Venice and examined it in much the same spirit as the foreign visitors who were taken on the obligatory tour to Murano to wonder at the fragile objects that emerged from the furnaces. Both groups considered glass manufacturing exotic and duly noted it among the city's marvels; as early as the fifteenth century a mention of "Murano, where glass is made" had become a commonplace of descriptions of Venice.[64]

Beginning in the late thirteenth century glass manufacturing was in fact concentrated outside the city of Venice on the nearby islands of Murano. In 1291 the Great Council ordered the destruction of all glass furnaces situated within the city, but it authorized and even encouraged their construction within the greater lagoon area. This measure probably repeated previous decrees now lost, given that glassworks are attested on Murano before that date. The removal of the glass furnaces was part of more general legislation aimed at diminishing the danger of fire. The governmental decree was put into effect, and the owners of glassworks and their workers migrated to Murano, where they transformed its islands into an industrial suburb.

This is not the place to retrace the growth of the Venetian glass industry.[65] Suffice it so say that glass, in both noble creations and utilitarian objects, was produced at a brisk pace. Glass window panes were used fairly widely in Venice as early as the fourteenth century. In the fifteenth century shop inventories, such as, one prepared in 1496 at the death of Maestro Barovier, a highly regarded master glassmaker, list refined and costly objects sold on both the local and the international markets: chandeliers, chaplets, enameled drinking vessels, precious gilded vases. The better part of the trade, however, was in mass-produced pitchers, carafes, and other practical items. The records that contain page after page of authorizations to export glass objects reflect a flood of merchandise that emerged from the furnaces and was sent to the mainland, Germany, Istria, Dalmatia, and elsewhere. All efforts were made to guarantee the success and continued growth of a "trade of great commodity and useful to our city."

In the early sixteenth century the innovative glassworks concentrated on Murano provided one of the most active and most prestigious sectors of Venetian industry. Specialized products emerging from the workshops on the lagoon ranged from glass beads for chaplets to mirrors and eyeglasses (which were not invented in Venice, however). During the second half of the fifteenth century notable advances in crystal manufacturing revolutionized the mirror industry. For a century and more, in spite of competition from both Italian and European glassmakers who did their utmost to copy Venetian glass and to entice glassworkers to defect, Murano glass dominated the international market.

Venetians had know-how in many fields, and the rigid regulations imposed on the various trades indicates that very early the government attempted to protect Venetian specialties. The statutes drawn up in 1271 for the glassmakers forbade anyone not regularly matriculated into the guild from taking part in the trade. Later decrees further reinforced control over the labor force. Henceforth no glassmaker could leave the territory of the duchy, and fines for unauthorized departures soon rose precipitously as the authorities tried to keep pace with the problem of emigration and the divulgation of manufacturing techniques. Governmental decrees alternated between threats and clemency, punishing and then pardoning in the hope of attracting guilty fugitives back to the lagoons. This series of prohibitions, tempered by moments of greater flexibility, provides insight into at least one aspect of employment cycles in Venice.[66] Above all, trade secrets had to be safeguarded. In 1295 the Great Council, deploring the effect on the Venetian glass industry of the diffusion of certain technical procedures, noted that "the furnaces had multiplied at Treviso, at Vicenza, at Padua, at Mantua, at Ferrara, at Ancona and Bologna."

The same hope of an impossible monopoly explains the continued prohibition on the export of all products necessary to glass manufacturing. Execution of these rigorous measures was tempered, as usual, by trade in contraband goods. The ultimate decree, intended to put the finishing touch on such legislation, declared that only *Muranesi* or *Venitiani* were to be permitted to become glassmakers.[67] The difficulty of applying such drastic measures limited their Malthusianism. At the end of the fifteenth century the Senate attempted to restrict hiring to inhabitants of the islands, excluding even Venetians except in cases of urgent necessity. In 1501 the needs of the industry imposed a return to greater flexibility, and in times of labor shortages the master glassmakers could hire men from anywhere in the duchy.[68] Still, every attempt was made to combat competition. Local production was stimulated, trade secrets were preserved, and mastery of glassmaking techniques was restricted to an elite in Murano, Venice, or at least the duchy. Until the day when others mastered the techniques of making glass, Venetian expertise enabled the city to export a broad range of highly appreciated products.

What was true of glass and crystal was equally true of the silk industry. Beginning in the 1450s, Venetian-manufactured silks, both plain and worked, were sold throughout Europe but also in the Levant. Relatively low-cost unworked silks made up the major part of Venetian production. Richer and more costly silks were woven as well: damasks, lampas, satin brocades, and gold-figured velvets, including the famous *riccio sopra riccio* (curl on curl). Moreover, those damasks and the crimson *(paonazo),* polychrome, or gold velvets were exported to Constantinople, demonstrating that the direction of trade had reversed since Marco Polo's day. One of the advantages that the silk industry enjoyed in Venice was the availability of the raw silk and dyestuffs that passed through its port thanks to the city's traditional connections with the East. Oriental motifs long continued to be common in the West until local designers, at times in collaboration with prominent painters, enabled the principal silk-producing cities of Italy to develop their own styles.[69]

The arrival on the market of silks manufactured in Lucca in the early fourteenth century had a permanent effect on Venetian production, which was organized but modest in scale. Lucca had become established as the leading center of silk manufacturing in Italy in the thirteenth century, but recurrent political unrest encouraged emigration. Between 1307 and 1320 Lucchese silk workers and silk merchants were not only welcomed in Venice but given help to become established.[70] From that moment on, as the statutes of the silk guild indicate and the discourse of Doge Tomaso Mocenigo tells us, the trade grew: "The artisans of Lucca and its wealthy men came to Venice, and Lucca grew poorer."[71] In 1366 the city government demonstrated its interest in this growing industry by voting for protectionist measures.[72] Silk workers were forbidden to emigrate. Preparing the silk thread, the first phase in silk production, was for the most part done by women, *incannaresse* to spin the raw silk thread and *ordiresse* to warp it. Legislative texts describe the many steps of the silk-manufacturing process: the raw silk threads had to be drawn from the cocoons, then the silk thread had to be twisted and spun, then boiled, and so on. A perfect result, that is, a length of silk cloth *a perfectione,* passed from hand to hand through at least sixteen operations.[73]

By the end of the fifteenth century five hundred silk looms were operating in Venice. No precise figure can be determined for the number of workers, but three thousand seems reasonable. Many of these were immigrants; a good many weavers, for example, came from Bergamo. In any event, the silk industry contributed much to transforming the parishes of San Canciano,

Santa Maria Nuova, and Santa Marina into one relatively coherent socio-economic unit. There was some aristocratic investment in the quarter, as well as participation from newly rich members of the bourgeoisie, such as the Amadi family, who were active in international commerce. The tax declarations of some families who lived far from this quarter list among their properties not only a main building and production site but small houses to lodge varying numbers of silk workers, depending on the size of the operation. Industrial concentration also spread north of the parish of San Canciano, the limit of this large production area. A network of dye works completed the chain of silk-working activities in these parishes. Perhaps even more than for the production of wool cloth, the quality of the dye jobs achieved by the *tintori da seda* was a determining factor in the success of the Venetian silk industry.[74] Extensions of that homogeneous space reached out into the neighboring *contrade* of Santi Apostoli and San Giovanni Grisostomo, where scattered workshops and dye works are attested.[75]

Venetian silk production was subject to drastic regulation, enforced by the masters of the silk guild and the office of the Corte de Parangon, an agency instituted in the fifteenth century to ensure top quality. In spite of the sumptuary laws, the silk industry supplied a wealthy and demanding local market, but in the shops of the Rialto and the Mercerie it also furnished silks for foreign customers, and both the few samples that have been conserved and the many counterfeits of Venetian silks attest to a high level of quality. Specialists today disagree about whether Venice or Florence was the capital of Italian silk production in the late fifteenth century, and rivalry was not restricted to those two centers, since other Italian cities, such as Siena and Milan, were beginning to develop silk weaving, and the cities of the Venetian Terraferma soon demanded permission to produce certain types of silks. In the modern era a silk industry developed in France as well, and it soon gave Italian silks serious competition. Still, as late as the second half of the sixteenth century, when it began to feel the effects of that competition, the Venetian silk industry employed thousands of workers.[76]

We could go on, ticking off the list of luxury trades and the whole range of products that required a highly qualified labor force.[77] A glance at the interior of a wealthy patrician house would suffice to display the infinite variety of goods made in Venice. Postmortem inventories reveal a richness and a refinement of luxury that is at times confirmed by iconography. The goods that arrived in Venice from all parts of the world also satisfied local demand, and imports cannot be ignored since such documents repeatedly mention "Flemish-style canvases" or note paintings as *a la moderna* rather than in the older "Greek style" of panel paintings with a gold background. The first collections that were made also included precious objects from far away. Still, local looms wove the bed curtains, drapes, bedspreads, and counterpanes that are carefully listed in these documents as gold-embroidered, crimson, gold-edged, "with falcons," "with birds and fruits," or "with the family arms." It was also Venetian workshops that produced the enormous quantities of dishes, gold and silver flatware, enamels, and bronzes, as well as the jewels and furs stored in coffers in the bedrooms. There might also be tens of silver or gilt spoons and forks, silver knives with inlaid enamel work, or the even more costly crystal forks marked with the family crest. There would be silver and gold cups, saltcellars, large finger bowls, and enameled or engraved silver candy dishes. There might also be precious combs and silver scissors; small gold "alms purses" and other purses made of silk, leather, or velvet; gilded spurs and crested sleeve buttons; silver rings, chains, and belts; strings of pearls, medals, jeweled rings, crosses, and belt buckles, not to mention rubies, pearls, diamonds, and emeralds, both mounted and loose.

The workshops of Venice applied their skills to transforming everything that the merchant center imported. The metals the Germans brought to Venice departed for the East in the form of ingots or coins to pay commercial accounts, but they were also fashioned, worked, hammered, and engraved into fine objects. Furs, which made some merchants' fortunes, were sold in the shops of Rialto.[78] Ivory was used for the handles of small knives that the notaries describe along with everything else. Leather was used to make everyday articles but also fine shoes and gloves. The pharmacies and perfumers' shops stocked spices, herbs and simples, medicines, resins and gums. All of these unusual, dynamic crafts and trades gave fifteenth-century Venice a remarkable ability to renew its economy and its urban structure and to diversify their functions.

Printing offers another demonstration of Venice's talent for welcoming and developing innovation. Venice became a major center of printing at an early date. The cultural effects of the technological and commercial evolution of the book have been widely studied, but less has been written about the economic and social consequences of the extraordinary development of that new product.[79] The book trade began modestly in Venice: printing arrived there in 1469, almost fifteen years after its appearance in Germany, introduced (perhaps via Rome) by John of Speyer and his brother Windelin.

At the time Venice was far from being a cultural capital. A city with no court and no university, it was "far behind other Italian cities in the fifteenth century in the domain of the production of manuscripts."[80] It is true, however, that in 1362 Petrarch chose "St. Mark the Evangelist" as his heir, leaving his manuscripts to the city of Venice "for the consolation and the commodity of the nobles and scholars of the city." He stipulated that they were to be "conserved in some place in the city set aside for that purpose [and] protected from fire and rain." The bequest was accepted, but the project for a library, discussed for a time, never came to pass.[81] Humanism made slow gains in Venice even though famous professors gave lessons in philosophy or logic and clusters of intellectuals began to form, following the model of the circle that gravitated around the Camaldolese monastery of San Michele at Murano and its library. In 1469 Cardinal Bessarion's manuscripts, which he had given to the city two years earlier, arrived in Venice. Bessarion too had asked that a library be constructed to house his gift, and the Senate considered the idea and dreamed of the sovereign brilliance of Venice when such a monument would make it the *studium* of all of Italy. As is known, Venetians had to wait for Jacopo Sansovino and his transformation of Piazza San Marco before the Libreria was finally built. Nonetheless, with Cardinal Bessarion's legacy Venice received a priceless cultural treasure as well as confirmation that it was the heir to the lost capital of the Christian East.

In September 1469 John of Speyer obtained a five-year monopoly of printing in Venice, but his untimely death left the way open to other printers, ten or more of whom set up shop within the next two or three years. This was the beginning of an era of rapid and sustained growth, even though brief but violent market crises regularly shook this new and fragile industry. The history of the development of the book trade in Venice stresses the importance of the Venetian, Italian, and German investors who made possible improvements in printing presses and who subsidized such ambitious early publishing ventures as the great canonical texts printed by Nicholas Jenson.[82] In the 1480s, thanks to veritable editorial teamwork and collaboration between the printers and the schools, Venetian books conquered a major part of the European market. Later innovations increased book circulation and gave books an increased economic importance. More and finer woodcuts provided illustrations for such works as Euclid's *Elementa* and medical texts. Inexpensive editions could appear only a few months after the publication of a famous text; lower prices led to press runs of considerable size. Musical scores began to be printed, as did books in other languages than Latin: Greek texts began to appear on the market. Then Aldus Manutius published Aristotle and invented italics.

All of lettered Europe looked to Venice. The growth of the book trade also had a remarkable effect within the city. At the beginning of the sixteenth century Venice had between one hundred and two hundred print shops. The overall number of volumes produced during the two final decades of the fifteenth century has been estimated at 1,125,000. Hundreds of workers were employed in the print trade, and tax declarations for the 1514 *estimo* show many booksellers grouped around the Rialto and a certain number of printers of widely varied socioeconomic status scattered through the parishes.

Thus, by the early sixteenth century Venice, the city of trade set in what Marino Sanudo called "the bosom of the Adriatic," had become a lively industrial center.[83] Many sectors of the Venetian economy displayed a strong capacity for innovation and adaptation. The Republic's maritime power in the Mediterranean had been shaken, but the sweeping project to improve the Arsenal with the building of the Arsenale Nuovissimo was intended to restore that power. Efforts to reorganize administration and modes of production in the shipyards and to introduce technological improvements in ship construction had been under way for decades. The glass industry continued its tradition of providing a livelihood for a large worker population in Murano,[84] and improvements in the manufacturing process and the inventiveness of the master glassmakers guaranteed domination of the European market through the sixteenth century. Printing was established in Venice in only a few short years, a new activity that revived both the Venetian economy and Venetian cultural life.

Renovation was the order of the day, whether it was set in motion by the state and its decision makers or it sprang from the daily labors of individuals. At a time when trade routes were being reorganized despite setbacks in the Mediterranean and when economic hegemony was slipping toward other cities and northern markets, some gloomy souls complained, but the power and the wealth of Venice—differently composed, perhaps—were still there. The city had reached maturity, but because it was still able to change, innovate, and create, it warded off decline. Venice lost its primacy in the sixteenth century, but the harvests were good in the countryside of the Terraferma, and in the city crafts and trades were prosperous. Venice did what the epoch expected of it, and its opulence remained.

Paolo Veneziano's altar panel of 1345 commemorates the saving of Venetians
from the lagoon's treacherous high tides by St. Mark, whose relics were brought
from Egypt to Venice in 828 (detail). (Cameraphoto/Art Resource, NY)

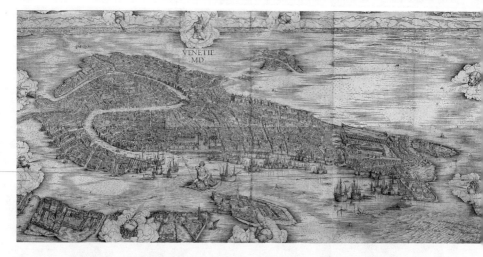

Jacopo de Barbari in his 1500 map showed a Venice where its watery world was completely integrated into its built environment. (Cameraphoto/Art Resource, NY)

Early dwellers of the lagoon learned to live off resources of the marshes and watery environment, as shown here by fifteenth-century painter Vittore Carpaccio in *Hunting on the Lagoon*. (The J. Paul Getty Museum, Los Angeles; © The J. Paul Getty Museum)

The mosaics of the Cathedral at Torcello give evidence to early Byzantine contact and influence. (*Last Judgment,* west wall; Alinari /Art Resource, NY)

Top: Torcello was one of the earliest settled islands in the lagoon.
(A. Ammerman)
Bottom: The Franciscan monastery on the island of San Francesco del
Deserto reminds the viewer of the Venetians' effort to wrest land from the
water. (A. Ammerman)

Timber, essential for construction and the shipbuilding industry, came to Venice from mainland forests via the Brenta River, another waterway important to the city. (Etching by Mortimer Luddington Menpes. Arthur Ross Foundation; photo: Jim Strong, Inc.)

San Marco's piazza has long been a central gathering place for the city, as seen
in this detail from a fifteenth-century painting by Lazzaro Bastiani.

Gentile Bellini's fifteenth-century painting *Procession on the Piazza San Marco* celebrated the elaborate processions that drew together Venice's civil and religious hierarchies. (Alinari / Art Resource, NY)

Even into the eighteenth century, San Marco's piazza had lost none of the vitality and urbanity that attracted travelers from other parts of Europe, as shown in *The Square of Saint Mark's, Venice,* by Canaletto. (Gift of Mrs. Barbara Hutton, Photograph © 2002 Board of Trustees, National Gallery of Art, Washington, D.C.)

Gaspar Van Wittel's seventeenth-century painting of the Doge's Palace captured the remarkable impression of a city of stone afloat upon the water. (Scala / Art Resource, NY)

Venetians built their wealth on the production and consumption of luxury goods drawn from the lands bordering the Mediterranean, as evidenced in this detail from Giovanni Mansueti's *Miraculous Healing of the Daughter of Benvegnudo of S. Polo.* (Cameraphoto / Art Resource, NY)

The Rialto, one of the major centers of the city, brought together commerce and leisure and people of all social classes, even as late as the eighteenth century, as seen in Francesco Guardi's *Grand Canal with the Rialto Bridge*. (Widener Collection, Photograph © 2002 Board of Trustees, National Gallery of Art, Washington, D.C.)

Gentile Bellini captured the city's monumental decor and theatricality of what its dwellers considered a normal urban scene in his *Miracle of the True Cross at the Bridge of S. Lorenzo*. (Alinari / Art Resource, NY)

By the sixteenth century, the Great Council, which originally had broad authority, was reduced to a body of aristocratic families who elected officials to staff the city's complex bureaucracy. (Gasparo Contarini, *Della Repubblica*, 1578)

FIVE

The State in Motion

A few names have stood out in this examination, suddenly marking the course of Venetian history. A few scenes have also emerged, rescued from the muddle of time to give precise and fresh illustrations of collective action: there is Agnello Partecipazio transferring the seat of the duchy to Rialto; Pietro II Orseolo and the fleet departing under the protection of St. Mark the Evangelist to conquer Dalmatia; Sebastiano Ziani ordering the enlargement of Piazza San Marco and the rebuilding of the Ducal Palace; Enrico Dandolo refusing the imperial title but winning a Mediterranean empire for his city; Tomaso Mocenigo exhorting Venice not to betray its destiny. But there is also Francesco Foscari setting Venice resolutely on a path to greater involvement in Italian affairs and territorial expansion.

After the city of stone and the various settings in which Venetians carried on their business, after the group and the many actors, famous and obscure, whom we have observed engaging in commerce, sailing the seas, working, and fighting, the time has come to consider "famous men." This implies a closer focus on the power structure, which so far we have seen only in its general manifestations, on the various agents who executed its directives, and on its successive forms of organization: the doge, then the commune, then the Signoria. Like that of any political organization, the history of a city, even a city-republic, can in fact be understood by identifying a certain number of individual trajectories that in their singularity crystallize the reality of a common adventure. In short, I shall spotlight the political elites in their various capacities for public action but also in the symbolic capital that gave them a place and a prominence in the political sphere.

First we need to examine those elites in their number and their mass and observe them as they renewed their ranks in both the middle term and the long run. My analysis is anchored in such events as the Serrata, or "closing" of the Great Council, which defined a governing class, and subsequent revisions of the "inner circle." In other words, we will investigate the system of distinction within the dominant group. Our topic will be the minorities who were identified as being of superior social, economic, political, and even cultural status. It also seems important to rescue a few men, a few lives, from the anonymity of what might be called traditional social and political history. To that end I shall accompany a descriptive history of collective political events with a brief study of a few individual figures. Individuality does not prohibit a phenomenological approach to the history of the community of which individuals are a part, and to some extent that history can be narrated through them. This is the method I shall follow. It would in fact be a betrayal of the way Venetian society represented itself not to recognize its mistrust of praise or commemoration of the individual and its decided preference for collective portraits. Venetian painting and sculpture only rarely show an individual, and when they do portray a doge or a high magistrate who stood out as illustrious for one reason or another, they also depict the collectivity the sitter served: they portray the honor of the Republic and of the noble group that was one with the state.[1]

Before we turn to the men, however, we need to describe the institutions and the general rules and customs of politics. The group and the single actor were in fact united by a structured field of action through which everyone had to pass, one defined by a set of institutions, laws, and practices. One cannot understand the language of the Venetians' commitments without first studying what I shall call the *grammar* of politics. That grammar—and this is my first observation—has traditionally been presented as both unique and admirable because it was capable of guaranteeing the existence of Venice as an organism through the centuries and of giving it an astonishing stability. My opening question is thus, How was that model formed and diffused?

THE REPUBLIC OF THE VENETIANS

In order to try to understand that process we need to return to the early decades of the sixteenth century and the moment when Gasparo Contarini's celebrated *De magistratibus et Republica Venetorum* was written, published, and then translated.[2]

The dedication of the French translation of Contarini's work, published in 1544, offers a first answer to our question. It states the somber fact that governments and institutions are unstable, a verity that dominated political philosophy after Machiavelli.[3] There was no lack of examples of republics that had come unraveled: Sparta, Athens, Thebes, Carthage. In a historical landscape of change and ruin only one city seemed to have halted "the movable wheel of fortune": Venice persisted; the Republic endured. The reader of the age of François I could undoubtedly find in Contarini's analysis of the institutions of his native city a way to pierce the mystery of Venice's singular resistance to the vicissitudes of history. The French translation of Contarini's work was only one of the many possible manifestations of profound interest in the Venetian political system in a Europe whose ruling powers were facing the immense consequences of the breakdown of Christian unity, an event that produced a sharp break with history and threatened to affect the institutions of even the most solidly established states.

Three decades later Jean Bodin's *Six livres de la République,* although sharply critical of Venice, attributed much of its success to its form of government. As a state, Venice was "aristocratic but governed by harmonious proportion."[4] Although the Venetian Republic did not represent the most perfect form of political regime, which according to Bodin was hereditary monarchy, it nonetheless reconciled mixed institutions, associating some popular elements with an aristocratic government. That combination was the gage of the "conservation" of the "fine and flourishing" Republic.

Conservation is in fact the central characteristic of all analyses of the political order of Venice and one that they attempt to explain in a variety of ways. Authors felt no need to evoke the convulsions of the ancient world; instead they sought reasons for the astonishment (and often the admiration) that they felt before the lasting power of that order in phenomena close to their own time, in particular in the vicissitudes of recent Italian history. In the troubled geopolitical landscape of the Italian peninsula in the fifteenth and sixteenth centuries Venice was a case apart. As early as the final decades of the fifteenth century the crisis in Florence—the fall of the Medici, Savonarola's republic, the return of the Medici—provided ample matter for theoretical reflection and elicited comparisons that were flattering to Venice's inviolable institutions.[5] Whereas the ancient republics had foundered, the Republic on the lagoon seemed unique in its ability to defend the values of the antique "Italian liberty."[6] The texts proclaimed that an apparently immutable Venice resisted; it had withstood the severe shock of the Italian wars and the disasters of the War of the League of Cambrai, when all the powers of Europe were allied against it. Moreover, the institutional structures of Venice explained and guaranteed that duration.

Beginning in the early sixteenth century, Venice's official historians were indefatigable in their elaborations on the theme of the extraordinary historical longevity of their city, ever free and sovereign despite successive attacks. Venice "for one thousand fifty years has shone with firm and stable liberty";[7] "For one thousand two hundred years, the free Venetians have commanded."[8] The only imaginable ending to this state of affairs was the end of the world: Venice had lasted, lasted still, and would last, free, triumphant, and happy, as long as the world itself.[9]

For decades the Venetian model, which in theory was founded on a harmony between the three forms of domination—monarchy, represented by the doge; democracy, by the Great Council; and aristocracy, by the Senate and the Council of Ten—provided fodder for theoretical reflection.[10] Traces of an interest in Venice and its role in the political education of Europe can be found in the political philosophy of the age in Italy, France, England, and Poland.

This paradigm did not last forever. When decline could no longer be denied, the image of the constitutional equilibrium of the Venetian regime faded. The city's power to last was no longer imputed to the virtue of its institutions; rather, it tended to be equated (according to one trend in the literature on the Republic) with the triumph of a system of coercion, the overweening power of a small police force, and a widespread system of police informers. In the nineteenth century, when the Republic was no more and the lagoon area was under another domination, the Signoria still figured as a terrifying power in both representations and memory. According to romantic drama,[11] as well as certain contemporary historical works, that power and that terror were based on limitations on free speech in the city and the state, thanks to a seamless collaboration between the police and the judiciary that relied on an absolute and secret power that knew all and made all decisions.

It is thus possible to reconstitute the major stages of the genesis of the political idea of the "Republic of the Venetians," even if a bumper crop of treatises and the spread of modern institutions have to some extent obscured the fecundity of the imaginary of earlier centuries. The "myth" of Venice has a long history. The passages that follow attempt to revive those often forgotten representations.

I should first remark that the history of Venice, starting from when a history of Venice first began to be written, has always been described as atypical. Consequently, and this has primary importance for our concerns, the political history of Venice has been dissociated from that of the other cities of Italy, as if a unique destiny had been reserved for the unique city in the middle of the lagoons. Moreover, not only local chronicles and histories emphasized that singularity. It was also reflected outside the lagoon area: the chronicle of Rolandino, a "veritable incunable of the myth of Venice," bore witness to it in the thirteenth century.[12] Attestations to an admiration of peaceful social relations in Venice and to Venetian institutions can thus be found at an early date, but there were also sharp criticisms of the community's policies and the first signs of a darker sort of legend.[13]

The creation of the myth concerning Venetian institutional structures really dates from the fifteenth century. The process was quite obviously closely connected with new historiographical demands and with a slow development that led, in the early sixteenth century, to the creation of the post of official historiographer.[14] Along with an increasing number of general histories that described the bases of Venetian liberty and praised the wisdom of Venetian laws, more analytical works—reflections and treatises on the government of Venice and its organization—were also produced in the final years of the fifteenth century. Marc'Antonio Sabellico published his *De Venetis magistratibus* in 1488. In the last part of his *De origine, situ et magistratibus urbis Venetae* (1493), a work dedicated to Doge Agostino Barbarigo, Marino Sanudo presented a practical description of local institutions. Finally, although his text does not explicitly equate Venice with his model for an ideal republic and although he expresses a number of severe criticisms, the theoretical construction that Domenico Morosini elaborates in his *De bene instituta re publica* is in many ways close to the Venetian institutional system.[15] Although that line of thought triumphed in the next century, its theoretical foundations were firmly in place at the end of the fifteenth century.[16]

This brought a change in how the various elements of the history of Venice were organized. The themes of liberty, duration, equilibrium, and concord, which had been created and developed by the medieval chronicles, still remained, but henceforth they were subordinated to a new theme. Methodically and consistently, historians described the state in order to praise it. All of Venice's qualities were henceforth seen as products of the excellence of the regime. We might even conclude that political eulogy was born in the fifteenth century, served both by both local theory and by reflection on the nature of Venetian institutions that was produced elsewhere in Italy.[17] There was also a significant change in vocabulary: earlier texts speak of "Venice" or "the city of Venice," but a shift to "the commune" and then to "the Signoria" denotes stages in political evolution. Henceforth, however, treatises and public acts used the term *Republic*. The forms used by the political regime reflected the essence of the city.

To summarize: At the end of the fifteenth century the history of the city of Venice began to be organized around a new achievement, the Venetian state. The foundations for the political myth had been laid. Once the first shock of the crises of the early sixteenth century had passed, it was clear that they had determined a new course of events, prompting changes within the regime and launching the Venetian myth throughout Europe.

One question remains before we penetrate the complexities of Venetian institutions and examine the workings of political decision making and administration: Why place this rich and lively apologia of the Venetian state at the head of our investigation?

When Myth Encounters History

In the first place, it was long impossible to dissociate reality from an eminently flattering and distorted image.[18] For centuries the Venetian political myth skewed all approaches and all analyses. At least until the nineteenth century the myth strongly influenced the writing of history because the principal goal of that history was to support the myth. Those historiographical times have passed, but the mold has not been completely broken. The myth itself has become an object of study.[19] It has continued to hold in its sway, this time indirectly, a portion of recent historical production aimed precisely at showing the myth to have been myth and at reexamining the merits of the Venetian regime stressing crises or breakdowns in the system.[20] Venetian historians as a group seem to have emerged only very recently from a long and at times ingenuous pursuit of abuses, corruption, and intrigue (broglio).[21]

There is a second, more pertinent justification for this detour through representations of politics. The rhetoric of praise blossomed precisely when Venetian institutions became truly singular on the Italian political scene. As we have seen, expansion onto the mainland and the constitution of a vast territorial state did not change the nature of either the political regime in Venice or an order that had been constructed through the centuries. Milan became a duchy, and Tuscany underwent thoroughgoing political and administrative reorganization, but Venice remained a city-state. The stato di mar was completed by a stato di terra that was indispensable to the power and the wealth of the Republic. Moreover, the Venetian community cultivated special ties with at least some of the colonial possessions. Still, the state derived its primordial meaning and its physical being from within the confines of the city, in the minds of both its governing class and the governed from Grado to Cavarzere. The state was one with the terra, where the original group had taken refuge, where the community had grown, and with which, as we have seen, it had good reason to be closely identified. Elsewhere, power was held by a prince or a king. In Venice the councils survived, and with them the mechanisms of aristocratic decision making. This is why contemporaries were so deeply fascinated by the institutions of Venice, but it also explains the originality, even the incongruity, in modern Europe of an urban republic that survived so long that it ultimately became fossilized.

The notion of political myth suggests a final series of reflections. In a general manner it probably served to enhance the brilliance of the name of Venice and the reputation of Venetian power, which by the sixteenth century was beginning to be eclipsed by the constitutions of the great monarchies and empires. However, the political myth seems to have been most persuasive among the community gathered between land and sea, revealing to it what it believed to be the truth of its own history. We have seen how deep-rooted the providentialist conception of history was in representations of Venice. At first the image of the city of divine election, the city to which, from its first settlement on a predestined site at the heart of the lagoons, God "had always lent a protective hand," triumphed. During the fifteenth century the dream of Venice as a city divinely brought to power and glory began to fade, and it was seen as the task of the Republic—of the state—to assure the prosperity of the community and guarantee it a perpetually happy destiny. The new dialogue the community initiated with itself, by means of the words that created the myth, produced a meaning and a legitimacy for the state; it aimed at sparing Venetians all anguish, all doubt about their future, and placing them—and their city—at the summit of power, the place they believed had always been rightfully theirs. Thus, one might propose that the myth functioned to depoliticize the community.

Venetian historical discourse consistently denied all possibility of decline. One need cite only a few examples to show how this denial operated. The year 1514, when the Dominant was facing grave military difficulties, began badly. On 10 January several shops at the Rialto caught fire; there was a strong wind, and the fire spread through the market as far as the Pescaria. The heart of the city was ravaged. Although some complained of the many misfortunes that had befallen them, most Venetians displayed a "hardened soul," and the senators went right on discussing the war and providing for the city's needs.[22] To cite another example, there are various accounts of a fire that devastated the Arsenal in 1569. Paolo Paruta and Andrea Morosini relate the event in their histories and inventory the damage. They write first in glowing terms of the size and wealth of the naval shipyard, the number of ships that were built there, and the number of shipwrights who worked there. Their description of the catastrophe is on the same grandiose scale as the picture that precedes it. The fire is as great as the Arsenal, and words fail to depict its violence. The stores of gunpowder blow up, walls collapse, and the citizens of Venice run to see the fire spread to burn down an entire neighborhood.[23] News of the disaster reached all Europe. As far away as Constantinople there was talk of the damage to the Arsenal. The community squarely faced the challenge, however, and "in a few months it had rebuilt the towers and the walls of the Arsenal and had returned it to its former splendor."[24]

Natural calamities were surmounted; oppositions and conflicts were erased. Always miraculously overcome, they hardly ruffled the surface of Venetian life.[25] Thanks to the excellence of its government, Venice could enjoy concord and peace, flourishing solidarities, and full employment in a harmonious and active society where everyone labored in his proper place

and for the common good. Venetian historians stated, and Venetians probably believed, that Venice had reached a privileged state of development. As a
body that had achieved total fulfillment, the city could never know decrepitude or senescence. It had excluded itself from time and from becoming.

Of course no serious investigation can be satisfied with certitudes of this
sort, and later writers made it their business to trace the inevitable troubles
or instances of resistance and even conflict that disturbed this apparent
quietude, identifying the men, powerful or obscure, who were unconvinced
by the dominant ideology or who did not meet its criteria. It should be kept
in mind, however, that the words and the culture of that ideology were
widely shared, and the discourse supporting the logic of Venetian identity
had a broad circulation that helped to provide a lasting structure for the
Venetian world. The political myth that followed the earlier mythic motif of
the providential city turns out to be essential to an understanding of the very
fact of the much-praised Venetian equilibrium. It set the city within an
imaginary of happy times and peaceful continuance in a world in which
everything else seemed swept away by swiftly moving events.

This was the way the Venetian community lived its history and im-
parted it to others, quite naturally making use of the decor of the city.
The entire city, in its order and in the harmony of its beauty, was presented
as a commentary on, even an explanation of, the history of the state and of
the group. There was no discontinuity between the organization and arrangement of the city and the writing of a history that was, consequently,
simply that duplication, that doubling, in written form. The effect sought
and produced was that of a mirror. At the center, in Piazza San Marco, the
mirror effect was further enhanced since the primordial function of that
civic space was to stand as a figure for the city as whole. On that piazza,
which the official texts stated was "el piu bello spectaculo di questa città,"
the city was presented and represented; it was there that the myth was
dramatized.

At San Marco: "The Closely United and Carefully Composed Body of the Republic"

The figures, symbols, and virtues of the Republic were displayed and
brought to life at San Marco in a frequently repeated spectacle whose rep-

lication was a sign of the serene immutability of institutions and politics. Although the Piazza was richly functional, it also served as the metaphorical locus of Venetian power.

We have followed the waves of construction and reconstruction that created the Piazza, modeled it, and adorned it from Venice's earliest days to Sansovino's vast projects. To understand how political power put its stamp on that eminently public space, it is not enough to list the monuments that surround it—the Ducal Palace, the Procuratie, the Clock Tower, later the Library and the Fabbriche Nuove. An anecdote from the late fifteenth century helps to illustrate the care Venetian governments took to protect the image of the Piazza. At a time when other cities were adorning their great civic squares with statues symbolic of the power of the prince, the Venetians cheated on the dispositions of Bartolomeo Colleoni's will. That famous condottiere bequeathed some of his fabulous wealth to the Republic, expressing his desire that an equestrian statue honoring him be placed in Piazza San Marco.[26] The Signoria adroitly twisted the terms of the bequest, and in 1496 the equestrian statue, begun by Andrea del Verrochio and finished by Alessandro Leopardi, was placed, not on Piazza San Marco, but on the Campo Santi Giovanni et Paolo, the "piazza" facing the buildings of the confraternity of San Marco. The work was judged praiseworthy, and all Venice went to admire it. Above all, no monument lessened the impact of the political message and the reference to the collective entity of the *terra* in the real Piazza San Marco.

A few dates show that Piazza San Marco quite soon played a major role in ceremonial occasions in Venice. That the political and the religious—the Ducal Palace and the basilica—shared space on the square counted for much in its early prominence. The description of the twelve principal ceremonies of the year in Martino da Canale's chronicle tells us that by the end of the thirteenth century many festivities took place within the confines of the square. Venetians undoubtedly continued to respect the custom of processions that moved through the city as well. To cite one example, beginning in 1310 a procession was held yearly on 15 June, the feast day of St. Vito and St. Modesto and the anniversary of the failure of the Tiepolo-Querini conspiracy. The procession to the church of San Vio at Dorsoduro commemorated the victory of order over one of the rare attempts to alter the course of Venetian politics by force.[27] In 1509, two centuries later, a procession was instituted to render thanks for another happy event, the anniversary of the retaking of Padua, by connecting the occasion, the church of Santa Marina, and the feast day of its patron saint, 17 July.[28]

Piazza San Marco also figured in other processions and was the site of other celebrations. We have seen the ceremonies of the Sensa on Ascension Day, and the square was used for other festive occasions, such as the solemn ceremonial entry of an important foreign visitor. Venice's site in the lagoon did not offer the walls and gateways that other cities used to organize symbolic welcoming ceremonies, but it possessed several thresholds where land and water met: the frontier between the duchy and the city itself, the Adriatic at the outer islands, and the debarkation point on the Grand Canal at San Marco. When the city displayed its honor and reputation to outsiders, it made use of these various confines, playing on its profoundly "aquatic" nature. For the most honored guests and for official visits, fifteenth-century Venice, represented by its highest magistrates, its Senate, its nobility, and a throng of inhabitants, moved onto the lagoon. The order of the cortege and its itinerary as it advanced over the water gradually became fixed. The Bucintoro, the doge's ceremonial barge, went as far as the island of San Clemente. As the boat procession wound its way from that "gateway to Venice" back to the Grand Canal, visitors and notables were entertained by spectacles, allegorical figures on some of the boats, and a succession of theatricals and amusements.[29]

It was at Piazza San Marco, however, that the "closely united and carefully composed body of the Republic," as Gasparo Contarini called it, was repeatedly put on show in ritual events. The description of the strict order of march of processions within the space of the Piazza given in an official text dated 1459 seems to clarify the network of connections between the doge and the state, the honor of the state and the reputation of Venice, and the state and its honor. Since the glory of the state reflected on all of its members, on St. Mark's Day and on all solemn religious feast days the Procurators of San Marco were expected to join the cortege of the doge and the Signoria as it formed on the Piazza.

Let us now move, without going into the history of the elaboration of the various rituals,[30] to the early decades of the sixteenth century, when their components had become formalized.[31] They will show us the "most Serene Republic" in both action and in representation. One such occasion was the expression of collective joy that heralded the election of a new doge. The bells would begin to ring. Throughout the city, work stopped, shops closed, and everyone moved toward Piazza San Marco. There bonfires would already be burning, to be followed by illuminations and fireworks after nightfall. The rituals of the coronation of the doge took place here as well, also before a large crowd. First the doge would be shown to the people from the marble balcony of the basilica. Until 1423, when Francesco Foscari became doge, this presentation was accompanied by the formula, "Here is your doge, if it pleases you." Acclamations followed, thus preserving the fiction of collective assent and the participation of the popular assembly, the Arengo, which originally had chosen the doge. The new formula, "We have chosen as doge . . ." put an end to that last remnant of a popular voice and reduced the assembled populace to spectators. After mass had been said, the doge received the banner of St. Mark, thus publicly showing that he had received guardianship, for as long as he might live, of the absolute and eternal authority from which legitimate governance derives. The second phase of the ceremonials followed. The doge, two of his close kin, and the admiral of the Arsenal took their places on a wooden platform that was then carried all about the Piazza by twenty-four *arsenalotti*, while other workers from the naval shipyards opened a path for them through the crowd. This was accompanied by a display of largesse, with coins thrown into the crowd from the platform. The third phase of the ceremonies, the crowning of the doge, had at one time taken place inside the Ducal Palace, in the Hall of the Senate, but with the election of Marco Barbarigo in 1485 it was moved to the open courtyard of the Ducal Palace, where it gained in both pomp and publicity by taking place at the top of the monumental staircase, the Scala dei Giganti.[32]

A procession followed. Its order of march was so perfect that it remained unchanged throughout the sixteenth century, thus projecting an image of continuity and harmony that concealed the realities of power struggles.[33] At the head of the procession came standard-bearers carrying the eight banners of St. Mark; they were followed by heralds and six musicians, then squires of the foreign ambassadors and the doge's squires, followed by more musicians. Next came citizen officeholders, and after them, six canons of San Marco (joined on the most solemn religious occasions by the patriarch), then the doge's chaplain or an acolyte bearing a white candle. At times a squire carrying the doge's crown came next. Bringing up the rear in this first segment of the procession were citizen officeholders, secretaries, members of the chancellery, and the Grand Chancellor. The doge was the most prominent feature of the second segment of the procession. He was preceded by the *ballottino,* a young man who received the *ballotte,* balls used to vote in a ducal election, and by two squires, one carrying the doge's folding throne, the other a cushion for the doge's feet. Then the doge himself appeared, flanked by two of the most prestigious foreign ambassadors and escorted by a patrician holding over his head the baldachin known as the *umbrella,* by other ambassadors, and by a noble bearing the ducal sword. Holders of the major offices in the Republic formed the third and last part of the procession. First came the *giudici del proprio,* followed by the doge's counselors, the procurators, the heads of the Quarantia, the *avogadori di comun,* the heads of the Council of Ten, and so on.

The procession moved within the space of Piazza San Marco, but at times that setting, splendid as it was, seemed insufficient and was supplemented by a marvelous, ephemeral decor that we can imagine thanks to iconographic evidence and travelers' descriptions. The Piazza was decorated with lengths of white cloth held up by poles anchored in stone bases and topped by chandeliers, so that hundreds of white- and red-flamed torches lighted the scene and amplified its brilliance. At times the poles were decorated with leafy branches, making them resemble trees or an oak forest, through which the torches flickered. The outside edge of the Piazza, thus illuminated, decorated, and transfigured by the procession (which typically lasted for hours), became even more theatrical. Foreigners repeatedly stated that it displayed the triumph and the wealth of Venice and its Signoria.

THE GRAMMAR OF VENETIAN INSTITUTIONS

The figure of the doge occupies a central place in this ritual, thus it is with that figure that our voyage into the complexities of Venetian institutions must begin.

The "Most Serene Prince," or, Venetian Ambiguities

The figure of the doge provides a focus for an analysis of changes in Venetian institutions. That said, a host of questions arise. How much real power did the head of the state hold? He reigned, but did he govern? The series of scenes that accompanied his coronation required the presence of the people and of representatives from the councils in order for the political drama to operate. What role did they effectively play in the designation of the "most serene" head of government? How are we to summarize the evolution, through ten centuries of history, beginning with the master of the soldiers, a Byzantine magistrate and the servant of the emperor, to the patrician who, surrounded by the members of the Signoria, embodied the Venetian state?

As early as the Renaissance outsiders asked similar questions. One visitor, Philippe de Voisins, wrote, "And he holds the said duchy for his lifetime, if they find nothing for which he must be undone," adding, "he can do nothing out of the presence of his counselors."[34] One could hardly find a better summary of the ambiguities of the ducal function. The person who is shown in the spectacle of his full power is in fact supervised and controlled by councils who have the power to depose him. The evolution of institutions produced that "paradoxical prince," a "republican prince" who, although clothed in gold and coiffed with the *corno* (as he is solemnized in Titian's great portraits), was nevertheless subject to many constraints.[35] This process merits further investigation.

Rather than follow the reconstructions of Venetian local history or the myth of an original liberty at the origins of the Venetian community, I prefer to recall the early submission of the lagoon basin to Byzantium. Before the institution of a doge the population was governed by a high functionary, the master of the soldiers, delegated to the post by the exarch of Ravenna. The first indigenous *dux* was probably elected about 725–30, in the troubled times of the iconoclast controversy, but until the Lombards took possession of the exarchate in 750 the doge and his successors remained subject to imperial authority. For some time during the march toward independence the doges bore the Byzantine titles with which the emperors honored them. It should be stressed that the *dux* who governed the islands and the *lidi* with his tribunes held unlimited powers. Moreover, as the history of the Partecipazio or the Candiano dynasties shows, young family members' close association with power long threatened to institute the hereditary principle. Fierce struggles arose among the dominant families, and the space of San Marco near the first ducal palace and the basilica was their battle ground.

That was where the doge reigned, where the relics of the patron saint and guardian of Venetian identity were kept, and where the Arengo elected the doge by acclamation and approved new laws. I prefer to insist on the convulsions that marked those early centuries rather than accept the thesis of a civil concord consubstantial with Venetian society. We have already seen the bloody events that marked the fall of Doge Pietro IV Candiano; one might also cite the earlier assassination of Doge Piero Tradonico, who fell victim to a conspiracy in 864, or the later uprising that put an end to the domination of the Orseolo doges.

The doge governed in this fashion, surrounded by a few powerful persons, the *primates,* until 1032. Then things began to change. After the fall of Ottone Orseolo, the last Orseolo doge, two counselors were elected along with the new doge, Domenico Flabianico. In the decades that followed, the city pursued its growth, its enterprises diversified (foreign ventures in particular), and the entourage of the doge grew in both numbers and visibility to include *giudici* from families who had long served as tribunes: Badoer, Giustiniani, Michiel, Morosini, Contarini, and others.[36] There is also evidence of other counselors, *boni homines,* members of the Arengo and thus by definition drawn from throughout the duchy. Still, the most prominent families of Rialto, men of great wealth who wielded obvious influence over a vast and maneuverable clientele network, dominated that *curia ducis.* Those same families, together with families enriched and raised to prominence by trade, provided the membership of the Council of the Sapienti *(Consilium Sapientum),* instituted in 1143 under the dogeship of Pietro Polani.[37] This was thus a council elected at regular intervals, probably chosen by the Arengo; it met from that time on, was consulted by the doge, and might on occasion oppose him.

These were the institutional changes that transformed Venice into a commune. The first mention of the commune is in an act dated 1144. It was profoundly different from the communes of other cities of Italy, but with it Venetian forms of government lost something of their earlier specificity.[38]

The Commune, the Doge, and the Arengo

The commune soon occupied much of the political landscape and captured sovereignty. It limited the power of the doge, who lost his regalian prerogatives one after the other. After the Council of the Sapienti assumed the power to legislate, the commune also absorbed the powers of the Arengo.[39]

An irrepressible dynamic had been launched, and the history of the doges was henceforth connected with that of the commune. Diplomatic ties bear this out, as after that date the texts always portray the doge flanked by *iudices* and *sapientes*. This new formula replaced the combination of *dux* and *populus* that had been customary in public acts up to the eleventh century. A first step in the process in which the council (later the councils) took on ever greater importance came in 1172, when the doge, Vitale II Michiel, was assassinated because he was held responsible for a military loss to Byzantium. Recent studies of this crisis tend to interpret it as the defeat of the old institutional order rather than as a struggle among families brought to a head by the central question of trade.[40] The commune emerged the victor over the doge and his power, thanks to the joint efforts of the dominant families of the first commune, both the older families and those more recently risen to prominence. An electoral commission (modified in 1178) was created to designate a successor to the doge, in part because the question of hereditary transmission of the dogeship had been revived with the Falier and Michiel doges. The electoral commission still emanated from the Arengo, but henceforth it was controlled by the Rialto aristocracy.[41] From that time on, the choice of the doge lay in the hands of powerful council members, who selected, successively, two newly enriched (and fabulously wealthy) men, Sabastiano Ziani and Orio Mastropiero, who were followed by a member of a very old family, Enrico Dandolo, the doge of the Fourth Crusade.[42]

Once the delicate problem of ducal election had been settled, the commune took care to limit the doge's prerogatives (which it took to itself) and his personal role. That it did so swiftly can be seen from the text of the *promissio* sworn in 1192 by Enrico Dandolo.[43] New restrictions were added to the oath in 1229, when Giacomo Tiepolo became doge. Several decades later the doge no longer governed; moreover, at the death of each doge a commission considered possible additions to the next *promissio* and devised new means for ducal supervision.[44]

In the final stage in this process mechanisms for the election of the doge were complicated to an extreme, and the Arengo was stripped of its power to choose the electors. This reform, carried out at the death of Doge Riniero

Zeno in 1268, was a masterpiece of the genre. The Great Council drew lots to choose 30 men from among its members; those 30 chose 9 of their number, again by lot, who then nominated 40 "electors." Twelve of that group, again chosen by lot, chose 25 representatives, who drew lots to reduce their number to 9. Those 9 in turn named 45 men, 11 of whom, again chosen by lot, selected the 41 electors who voted to choose the first magistrate of the Republic from among the candidates. As this procedure operated at the time, it was ponderous (taking several days) but efficacious. Much can be learned from it. In the first place, it shows that the commune feared factions, schemes, and secret understandings. The pyramid of collegial bodies that it set up and the alternation of drawing lots and direct nomination was intended to circumvent the risk of collusion. It also shows, however, that in spite of the complicated machinery that was put into place, competition was intense among the great families for control of determining who became doge.

In support of that notion one might cite the turbulent elections of the thirteenth century, the election of 1229 in particular. The electors (forty at that point) split their votes equally between two candidates. They drew lots to settle the question, and fortune favored Giacomo Tiepolo over Marino Dandolo. Not only did Tiepolo's dogeship cap the meteoric career of an exceptional man—he had been duke of Crete, *bailo* at Constantinople, and *podestà* on several occasions—but it illustrates the rise of the popular classes in Venice, a movement that had begun at the end of the twelfth century.[45] With the election of the second Tiepolo doge, Lorenzo (1268–75), the older citizen families, the *populares veteres*, reinforced their position at the side of the ancient aristocracy, although (and I shall return to the topic) it is not easy to interpret the political maneuverings of those years. Under the Contarini, Dandolo, and Gradenigo doges the *case vecchie* later took back the dogeship, retaining control of the office until 1382, but infighting by no means disappeared. (Here I shall spare the reader the complexities of a tortuous political chronicle.) After 1382 and the election of Antonio Venier, sixteen families—the *case nuove*, who were soon also known as the *case ducali* or the *Curti*—dominated the *Longhi* to elect an uninterrupted stream of doges from among their own until 1612.[46] One example of these tensions was the conflicts that marked the unsuccessful attempt of the *case vecchie* to take back control of the dogeship in 1486, when they backed one of their own, the chronicler and statesman Bernardo Giustiniani.

As these changes demonstrate, the doge had become the first magistrate of the Republic. Closely supervised and held to scrupulous respect of the *promissio*, he was also subject to a long list of prohibitions: he could not leave Venice without authorization, receive foreign ambassadors privately, or even open or send official letters if his counselors were not present. He could not abdicate without authorization. Deposition was the ultimate threat, reminding the "most serene" doge that even though he had been elected for life, he held power through the councils. Once the troubles of the earlier centuries had passed, doges tended to die in their beds—the exception was Marino Falier, who was executed in 1355 for conspiracy—but the list of doges who were forced to abdicate is fairly long. The best-known deposition is probably that of Francesco Foscari in 1457, an act reeking of a vendetta nourished by centuries of family hatreds.

Accidents aside, men of prestige, competence, and tested personal qualities were chosen to personify the Venetian state. What is more, again with certain exceptions, the doges benefited from a long tenure. Magistrates were usually appointed for a one-year term in the Republic; the doge alone remained and knew the city's secrets. He presided over the councils and possessed the right to propose laws and defend suggested legislation. His ability to influence events was strong in spite of all, and he held considerable potential power, many examples of which are reported in the chronicles. When Venice was fighting the French in 1495, many Venetians joined with the memorialist Marino Sanudo to regret the illness that kept the doge, Agostino Barbarigo, from attending council meetings, which tended to be indecisive when he was absent. Some years later the Venetian gerontocracy suffered another reversal when Antonio Grimani's absence because of illness had a similar effect on events.[47] It is clear that the power of the *primus inter pares* was at least equal to that of a magistrate.

Finally, the doge represented the state in its continuity, as demonstrated by the political ritual that staged that continuity. Edward Muir has shown that after the power of the doge expanded in the twelfth century and after Sebastiano Ziani and his successors elaborated a first symbolic system, ducal power was subjected to a veritable process of sacralization in the thirteenth century.[48] The doge acquired a central place in the imaginary order of the city, and myth credited him with being the source and historical origin of political decision in Venice. An entire apparatus charged the doge with signs of sovereignty and positioned him at the center of ceremonies intended to resolve tensions inherent in the mechanisms of politics. The festivities following the election of Lorenzo Tiepolo, for example, surrounded the person of the doge with a genuine ritual of unity. This evolution reached a peak in Giovanni Bellini's priestly and somewhat ethereal portrait of Doge Leonardo Loredan, a work that offers an excellent visual translation of the notion that the dignity of the doge's function had become more important than the man himself.[49] Politics operated on two levels. On one level the doge was the agent of a symbolic system, and by his presence he maintained the pertinence of that system in the sociopolitical sphere. On a second level, however, Venetian equilibrium depended on the complexity that he added to action and decision making. The strength of the system probably lay in this active dialectic between the symbolic and the real.

Any remaining traces of the former sovereignty of the Arengo would have to be sought in the realm of the symbolic. As we have seen, the emergence of the commune upset the old equilibrium, by then outdated, and gave Rialto and its dominant lineages supremacy in political institutions. The creation of the Council of the Sapienti and the reform of the mechanisms for electing the doge transformed the earlier delegation of powers into a veritable dispossession, and soon what once had been the popular assembly retained only the right to a purely formal approval. It was for just such an approval that the Arengo was convoked in the basilica of San Marco to attend a reading of the electoral reform of 1268. The members of that body were told that henceforth the Great Council, and only the Great Council, which generated the various collegiate bodies that chose the electors of the doge, would hold sovereignty. In light of this history the 1423 modification of the ritual for presenting the new doge was a foregone conclusion.

With the history of the *dux* and the *populus* we have followed the curve of a dispossession. It remains for us to trace the same dynamic in another way, with a brief description of how the commune gained strength and how, as both institutions and the exercise of power became more complex, the various councils emerged out of the original Council of the Sapienti.[50] At the election of Orio Mastropiero in 1178 a six-member Minor Council was formed to serve along with the first and larger assembly (later known as the

Castello
1. San Pietro
2. San Biagio
3. San Martino
4. San Giovanni in Bragora
5. Santa Ternità
6. Santa Giustina
7. Sant'Antonin
8. San Giovanni Novo
9. Santa Maria Formosa
10. Santa Marina
11. San Lio

San Marco
12. San Marco
13. San Basso
14. San Giuliano
15. San Geminiano
16. San Moisè
17. Santa Maria Zobenigo
18. San Maurizio
19. San Vitale
20. San Samuele
21. Sant'Angelo
22. San Benedetto
23. San Fantino
24. San Paterniano
25. San Luca
26. San Salvatore
27. San Bartolomeo

Cannaregio
28. San Geremia
29. San Leonardo
30. San Marcuola
31. Santa Maria Maddalena
32. Santa Fosca
33. San Marziale
34. San Felice
35. San Sofia
36. Santi Apostoli
37. San Giovanni Grisostomo
38. San Canciano
39. Santa Maria Nuova

Dorsoduro
40. San Gregorio
41. San Vio
42. Santa Agnese
43. San Trovaso
44. San Basilio
45. San Raffaele Arcangelo
46. San Nicolò dei Mendicoli
47. San Barnaba
48. Santa Margherita
49. San Pantaleone
50. Santa Eufemia

Santa Croce
60. Santa Lucia
61. Santa Croce
62. San Simeone Apostolo
63. San Simeone Profeta
64. San Giovanni Decollato
65. San Giacomo dell'Orio
66. San Stae
67. Santa Maria Mater Domini
68. San Cassiano

San Polo
51. San Tomà
52. San Stin
53. Sant'Agostino
54. San Boldo
55. San Polo
56. Sant'Aponal
57. San Silvestro
58. San Matteo
59. San Giovanni di Rialto

Venetian Administrative Divisions

Great Council). New magistracies were created: an *advocator comunis* acted as public prosecutor, *curie iudicum* assumed functions of justice, *visdomini* were charged with police functions, *camerarii* managed the city's finances, and the Procurators of San Marco controlled the city's treasury. An administrative and topographical reform based on the various circumscriptions determined the new system of government. The smallest divisions in the city were the *contrade,* which corresponded to parishes.[51] These *contrade* were then grouped by twos to form approximately thirty *trentaccie.* Finally, six larger districts, called *sestieri,* were created, three on either side of the Grand Canal.[52] The *contrade* provided the framework for the convocation of the Arengo; in 1207 Doge Pietro Ziani set rules for nomination to the various magistracies based on the *trentaccie* and the *sestieri.* Three *trentaccie* took turns designating a "college" of three "electors," who then chose the members of the councils and the various officials.[53] Six Procurators of the Commune, one from each *sestiere,* were elected and served on the Minor Council, and one representative per *trentaccia* sat on the Great Council.

Institutional refinements continued to be made, "pro proficuo et utilitate Comunis Venecie." By the mid-thirteenth century the Great Council tended to be the principal legislative organ of government. The number of its members grew, and henceforth they were selected by an electoral college chosen by the Great Council from among its members. Major compilations of the statutes were drawn up, the most important of them in 1242 under Doge Giacomo Tiepolo.[54] The courts and offices on which this constantly expanding political armature was constructed continued to proliferate, setting up an extremely complex organization, frequently remodeled, that contained many overlapping responsibilities and conflicts of jurisdiction.[55]

De magistratibus urbis venetae

In the early years of the fourteenth century, when this process of construction was completed, the Great Council was the sovereign organ of government and the keystone of the system. After a period of tension, laws connected with the Serrata (1297) once again rewrote the modes of election of the Council, in the process defining the group that made up the governing families. The Great Council appointed the immense majority of the officials who held posts in the various magistracies and councils. It held legislative power and granted pardons. It was no longer the only legislative body, however, because it had delegated some of its functions and powers to other councils. The oldest of these was the Council of the Forty, the Quarantia, instituted between 1207 and 1220. That body was presided by three heads *(capi)*, who were automatically members of the Minor Council. The Council of the Rogati (or Pregadi), also called the Senate, was of more recent date. It was made up of sixty members, all of whom also sat on the Great Council. At first the *rogati* had jurisdiction in matters of commerce and navigation, but in the early fourteenth century their responsibilities were enlarged to include international affairs, diplomacy, and defense. By successive delegations the Senate absorbed certain of the responsibilities of the Great Council, and it also replaced the Quarantia, whose role became limited to the judiciary domain. The Senate enjoyed great authority since the highest magistrates of the Republic were de facto members.

Contemporary texts describe the structure of this system. The collegial direction of the Venetian state was entrusted to the Signoria, which was also the formal summit of the state. The Signoria was made up of the doge, the six members of the Minor Council (one for each *sestiere*), and the three heads of the Quarantia. It was superior to all the councils, and it possessed the right to propose legislation *(metter parte)*. It set the agenda for the Great Council, which it could convoke in extraordinary session, and it resolved conflicts of jurisdiction among the various judiciary and administrative organs. Legislative functions were held by the various assemblies. The *officia*—the offices of the Ducal Palace, Rialto, and the foreign offices— handled administrative and judiciary functions. This three-part distribution of functions was practical as well as geographical. The courts of justice, the administrative offices, and the police headquarters were installed at San Marco, as were the offices of the Procurators of San Marco, the Patroni all'Arsenale, and the ducal chancellery, which kept the state archives. The magistracies that governed the city's economic and financial life and its commercial activities had their headquarters at Rialto, near the exchanges. Venetian officials—*podestà, castellani,* consuls, *rettori, baili,* and *camerlenghi*—were dispersed throughout the duchy, on the islands, and in the marketplaces and Venetian outposts in the Mediterranean from Chioggia to Zara, from Istria to Crete, and from Constantinople to Tyre.[56]

One example will suffice to illustrate the complexity of the communal bureaucracy and show how offices, superimposed on one another in the name of a growing demand for control but also reflecting a certain empiricism, had invaded all sectors of public life in Venice: the magistracies charged with supervising urban development were characterized by increasing numbers of officials and overlapping permanent and extraordinary agents. The first judges of the Piovego were elected in 1283, but from 1224 until that date five or six offices that exercised tutelage over the canals and the public domain (functions later assigned to the Piovego) appeared, disappeared, and reappeared. Soon after the new court inherited responsibility for the conduct of urban policies the system changed: the Signori di Notte and the *capisestiere* were invested with responsibilities that they shared within the smaller geographical area of the *contrada* with *capicontrada*. Moreover, within the limits of their jurisdiction the Procurators of San Marco and the officials of the Rialto held similar powers. Finally, provisory delegations, temporary nominations of commissions of experts or specially delegated officials, and *savi* designated to a specific construction project or report complicate the description further and reinforce an impression of institutional fertility, even if at times the result was conflicting or overlapping jurisdictions. Two centuries later, in that city of continuity where institutions were thought remarkably consistent the picture had changed. The Republic preferred to duplicate rather than destroy, which meant that the old medieval magistracies had survived, but many of them were losing momentum. Their responsibilities were gradually taken away from them and redistributed. The administrative machinery was transformed and refined with the appearance of new collegiate bodies such as the Savi agli Ordini, which had jurisdiction over maritime affairs.[57] Perhaps this frequent reshuffling of the institutional cards was what enabled Venice to live in an apparently stable political order.

This example prompts a more general question: How are we to evaluate the roles of permanence and change in the Venetian political system? Thus far we have discussed two trends. First, with the formation of the commune I have traced a movement that shifted power to the members of the councils, hence to a group of families. Within this history the event of the Serrata—the closing of the Great Council and the definition of a governing elite—is traditionally presented as a major milestone and a sign of the victory of the aristocracy. But I have also insisted on another process, that of an increasing complexity in the mechanisms of political decision making and the many bureaus and offices of the administrative machinery. For some time these two questions dominated analysis of Venetian politics. The fifteenth-century disappearance from the Venetian political vocabulary of the term *comune* to the profit of the term *Signoria,* along with the constitution of the territorial state, seemed to sanction an aristocratization of power that had begun long before. Similarly, historians have tended to read Venetian history in its continuity, as if it reflected only organic growth, the vigorous development of Venetian institutions, and an impressive administration by means of which the state was constructed. Such an approach probably reflects the influence of the permanent paradigm of the modern state.

Mobility, transfers, and transformations seem to have been much stronger than has been thought, however. The governing circle, which grouped the protagonists of Venetian history, shows proof of a certain fluidity in the successive changes in its composition. These two points will be taken up in order.

Anyone who surveys Venetian institutions in the early fifteenth century is struck, first of all, by their continuity. Political geography and systems of domination changed elsewhere, but around the lagoon nothing seems to have budged. A doge was elected and reigned, surrounded by his counselors. The Great Council met every Sunday afternoon; the Senate met three or four times a week. The Republic, serene and constant, was governed according to wisdom and its ancient laws. This false immutability is a snare, however.

In a trend that had already begun, the power of the Senate was extended until, in the fifteenth century, it became the principal legislative organ and the council that governed the state, as Marino Sanudo tells us. As its political, legislative, and financial responsibilities increased, its membership swelled. An adjunct commission, or *zonta,* was added to it during the dogeship of Lorenzo Celsi (1361–65), and it became a permanent body in 1450, when its membership, extended several times, rose to sixty nobles. The 120 senators (the Senate itself and its *zonta*) were joined by the doge and his counselors, the members of the Quarantia, the chief magistrates, and ambassadors returned from duty, all of whom were members of the Senate by right of office, and by the *savi* of three commissions that prepared proposed legislation but whose members did not have the right to vote. These three commissions that aided the Senate in its legislative activities were the Savi del Consiglio, or Savi Grandi (six members); the Savi di Terra Ferma (five members); and the Savi agli Ordini (five members), all of which were instituted as the Senate's business and its dossiers grew more specialized. With its adjunct members, the Senate numbered as many as 230 men, who directed the defense of Venice, conducted international affairs, supervised the Arsenal, regulated the economic life of the city, and passed statutes regarding shipbuilding and surveillance of the waterways. They also appointed extraordinary magistrates, as well as the various *provveditori* and *savi,* persons charged with special embassies and missions, experts, inspectors of the rivers and shores, of hospitals and public health, of wood and grain supplies—officials who were named by the Senate and reported back to the Senate—as well as making appointments to the ordinary magistracies, naming ambassadors, and of course appointing the *savi* of the three commissions.[58]

With the institution of the three commissions of *savi* we come to one of the major innovations of the governmental system in Venice of the early Renaissance. In his analysis of Venetian magistracies Marino Sanudo states that the Savi del Consiglio were "six of the first and principal [men] of the Land," and indeed, in the hierarchy of honors and dignities they followed directly after the doge, the six ducal counselors, and the *capi* of the Quarantia.[59] This speaks volumes about the extraordinary rise of this recently created magistracy, which prepared the legislative work of the Senate and executed its decisions. It was created in 1380, during the difficult years of the war with Chioggia, and in only a few years its six seats became among the most prestigious posts in the Republic. It goes without saying that they were reserved for patricians from the most prestigious families. Second in importance in the hierarchy of dignities was the Savi di Terra Ferma (or della Guerra), perhaps first organized in 1420, whose responsibilities soon extended beyond the domains of war and the territorial state, broad as those were. The third commission to be added, the Savi agli Ordini, was charged with responsibility for maritime affairs.[60] The sixteen "sages" of these commissions and the Signoria formed the Collegio, also known as the Pien Collegio, whose twenty-six members thus included some of the most prominent representatives of the urban nobility. Whether they were "sages" of the Terraferma or the doge's counselors, these men were among the most honorable and the most experienced of the Venetian gerontocracy, thus shifting the locus of power in the fifteenth century.

It shifted again when a new council, the Council of Ten, rose to power, thus complicating the division of jurisdictions and upsetting the equilibrium among the various organs of government. The Council of Ten, instituted as a temporary measure after the Tiepolo-Querini conspiracy in order to assure peace and public order, originally had a mandate for two months at a time, which was later extended to five years before the body was permanently instituted on 20 July 1355, following the Marino Falier conspiracy. Its responsibilities gradually broadened. In 1355 it had seven members by virtue of office (the doge and his six counselors), plus ten council members chosen from among the most prominent senators (who had to be from different families, however). Attached to the Ten there was an *avogador di comun,* who acted as public prosecutor and did not have the right to vote. The reasons for establishing this new office in the politically troubled times of the early fourteenth century explain its responsibility for state security. An extremely broad interpretation of that charge justified its increasing intervention in diplomatic affairs and police matters, and it made successive and repeated encroachments into realms outside its initial responsibilities (control of the corporations and the flagellant confraternities, economic tutelage of such strategic resources as mines and forests, supervision of the Mint).

Because the Council of Ten was charged with secret business and because its agents, its special funding, and the many informants who served it made it appear omnipotent and omniscient, it often seemed to cast a disquieting, even tragic shadow over Venetian life. Without indulging in sensationalism, it is fair to say that the power of the Ten reached a peak in the fifteenth and sixteenth centuries.[61] At that point a *zonta* was attached to it to handle affairs of exceptional gravity; it also created and controlled such offices as the Executors against Blasphemy and the famous Inquisitors against the Propagation of Secrets, a body that preceded the institution of the State Inquisitors.[62] This led to conflicts of jurisdiction with the Senate. On several occasions the Great Council passed statutes to settle difficulties and controversies and reassure those who were alarmed by the Ten's growing hold over public life. The momentum was irreversible, however, and during the course of the fifteenth century Venetian power tended to function in increasing secrecy. Too many patricians sat on the Great Council, whose sessions became boisterous as clientism, maneuvering, intrigue, and even fraud occurred on election days. The mechanisms of decision were gradually remodeled, and the Council of Ten played a fundamental role in the new political landscape.

At the start of the sixteenth century Venetian power functioned in the following manner: the Senate deliberated and voted, its members relying on their experience and authority to turn the heavy political and economic machinery of a state that operated in many spheres. The minutes of the Senate's deliberations, which are divided into series according to specific areas, demonstrate the breadth of its jurisdiction and interests. However, a narrow, exclusive, even restricted governing circle crystallized and took over the direction of the state's business. This smaller group included the Signoria, the Ten, the Savi Grandi, and the Savi di Terra Ferma.[63]

The final evolution of the institutional system in Venice can be deduced from the picture that we have just seen. It may have been true, as Marino Sanudo stated, that the Great Council remained the "Signor della Terra." It was on that foundation that the Republic and its many institutions had been built and were based. Sovereignty emanated from the Council, even the sovereignty invested in the narrow, exclusive, and restricted highest governing circle. Laws, including those that had been deliberated by other bodies such as the Senate, were voted by the Great Council. It was from within the Great Council that the consuls who represented Venice on the Terraferma and the officials of many of the principal magistracies were elected. The Great Council filled 131 posts, among them those of the senators, the Procurators of San Marco, and the members of the Council of Ten.[64] It is hardly surprising that all chroniclers and all the foreign visitors should offer long descriptions of the hall in which the Great Council met, dwelling on its paintings and its gilded ceiling.[65] An entire iconography, including a series of portraits of the doges,[66] defined the place of the political, not so much diffusing the abstract idea of power as stressing the destiny of a Christian community directed by the best it had to offer. We have seen the extent to which this rich decor, ceaselessly preserved and restored, contributed to the representation of Venice and its history.

In the early sixteenth century, however, the rowdy debates, conflicts, and even crises that often troubled the sovereign assembly of the Republic hardly conform to that representation and those mythical pronouncements. A growing mistrust can be discerned among the elite whom Sanudo called "i primi della terra."[67] Moreover, feelings of resentment of those same *primi*, not to mention explicit demands and expressions of opposition, on the part of the many nobles on the Great Council who were less noble, less powerful, and less glorious often filter through in the records of debate.

What are we to conclude from all this? It is customary to consider these successive shifts as signs of an increasing aristocratization of the regime, a greater closing of Venetian society, and a progressively tighter control over public life and the state. I do not contest those interpretations, except to note that we should approach the concept of aristocratization with extreme caution since it leads to illusory or anachronistic images of the Arengo of the early centuries or of the Great Council in its original form. As if power had not always been in the hands of the few; as if a few families, in both the twelfth and the fifteenth century, had not kept firm control over some offices. Quite simply, the families changed and the positions to be monopolized changed even more. If we want to reconstruct what Venetian institutions actually were, we must follow the dynamics of the constitution of a state and a system of power. This will enable us to identify some of the things that made Venice unique, in particular its surprising conjunction of empiricism and efficacy, its mix of ad hoc procedures and competence, and its consistent habit of making the provisory definitive. We can grasp the role of Byzantine legacies and Italian adaptations, and we can observe how the center of power shifted, one move at a time, in this republic of councils. But we can also discern more general evolutions, such as the extraordinary development of the Venetian bureaucracy in the communal age or, later, the tightening of the decision-making circle and the move to secrecy that launched the fundamental mechanisms of modern politics. In conclusion I might add, without making the usual judgments regarding social and ideological change that such an evolution implies, that movement was acutely present in that republic of order and stability: it commanded the ability of institutions to adapt, and it presided over shifts within the Venetian political class.[68] As long as that movement persisted the Republic lasted, renewing itself, and its history continued. During the sixteenth century the system still had a relative flexibility that made it supple enough to use its institutions and judiciary procedures to ward off a certain number of conflicts.

"UNO STATO FERMO E TERMINATO"

The political society and the aristocracy on which the Venetian state was founded were singular.[69] Historians often find it difficult to define elites. They set up multiple criteria of selection in order to isolate the group of men and families that were placed, at a given time, in a situation of political, economic, and cultural dominance. Very early in Venetian history the governing class itself defined those who were authorized to govern, and for decades it continued to refine the procedures for identifying that group. It is a prime fact of Venetian sociopolitical organization that the closing of the Great Council defined a governing class.[70] A second particularity immediately follows the first. The history of the dominant group is still often confused with the study of mechanisms for constructing and dismantling political society, thanks to the apparent strength of the almost biological process of renewal that makes new levels of society emerge, while others just as inexorably seem destined to fade and disappear. Venice presents the contrary example of continuity in its society and government, though we must guard against exaggeration. "Among the 144 noble houses that, according to the chronicler and historian Marino Sanudo, made up the nobility in 1527, there were sixteen whose eponymous ancestors had been doges and *judices* in the tenth and eleventh centuries and fifty others who had acceded to the patriciate before the year 1200."[71] It is easy to see why an entire historiographical tradition founded on the histories and treatises of the fifteenth century has chosen to connect these two phenomena and to explain the longevity of the Republic by the stability of the aristocracy in power.[72] I prefer simply to observe that in the years following the Serrata, power games in Venice were narrowly conditioned by a process of authenticating a noble governing class.

"*I primi della terra*"

Before 1297–98 nobility in the lagoon area was identified by blood, memory, and reputation. Nobility was manifest in the family name, and it was displayed by banners, emblematic devices, and coats of arms. The longevity of any given family was common knowledge. Local chronicles listed the various tribune families and narrated the origins of the most famous *case,* thus helping to establish that memory and its store of legends. One can draw up a list of the houses that rose to an early position of hegemony and trace promotions, enrichments, and the emergence of new names. All political and social analysis of the Venetian thirteenth century is based on a study of the relative status, importance, and influence of the various families, as well as on examination of changes occurring in the group of those who mattered and made decisions. During the course of that century the governing class grew and was renewed under the pressure of the *populares,* some of whose members had acquired extraordinary wealth. The governing group of the first commune, which had already been refashioned on several occasions, held power almost exclusively until the early 1220s. After 1225 pressure from the *homines novi* increased. The commune developed its administrative apparatus, employing more and more people. This process can also be observed in other Italian communal cities of the time, but in the case of Venice the conquest and then the administration of a trade empire required a larger number of offices and men and a more concentrated effort. Spontaneous or organized, the emigration of Venetians and their families to Crete or Negroponte created gaps at home, and many who had recently risen to wealth and prominence were waiting for just such an opening. They exploited it, and a new equilibrium was instituted with the election of Giacomo Tiepolo. Next, the old merchant bourgeoisie of the *populares veteres* took advantage of the election of Lorenzo, the second Tiepolo doge, under whose tenure (1268–75) they firmly established their position beside the older aristocracy.

The statistical tables published by Gerhard Rösch are eloquent witness to this process. A count of elections shows that 55 percent of the men elected to the Great Council during the latter half of the thirteenth century bore "new" names.[73] The increasing number of Council members is even easier to demonstrate. At the time of the Ziani reform that assembly had thirty-five members, one for each of the *trentaccie;* a half-century later it had several hundred members, designated according to changeable, complex, and "somewhat haphazard" procedures.[74] These were de facto members, heads of magistracies chosen yearly by a special commission. This system engendered tensions and pressures and encouraged factions and patron-client networks. Several proposals were offered (in 1286 and again in 1296) to reform these procedures and institute better control over the composition of the Council. They were rejected.

The proposal for a general reform backed by Doge Piero Gradenigo in 1297 was not rejected, however. This was the famous Serrata of the Great Council, which sanctioned the sociopolitical mutations that had taken place in recent decades, among them a redistribution in the relative importance of

Venetian families and the growing power of the Council itself. Henceforth only members of families that had sat on the Great Council in the four years preceding the reform of 1297 were eligible for membership.[75] A new procedure permitted the admission of a few "new" men, however, providing that their names were proposed by a commission and approved by twelve members of the Quarantia. The 1297 law was made permanent in 1299. After the Serrata, membership in the Great Council signified nobility.[76] Playing a political role expressed lineage status; it defined a nobility of function, transmitted by patrilineal filiation.

These are the facts. How are we to interpret them? As we have seen, it was long thought that the Serrata marked the victory of the oligarchy over the "populars" because the Great Council was almost completely closed to the "new men."[77] According to Frederic C. Lane, whose interpretation is still dominant today, in reality the Serrata represented a division of power among the powerful. It may well have concealed a certain broadening of the governing class, but beginning in the final decades of the thirteenth century a narrow circle of men monopolized the most important offices and responsibilities, thus constituting an early example of a group of what might be regarded as professional politicians.[78] Various factors in the years of the second Genoese war, first among them a desire to lessen the political and social risks of factional strife, explain why consensus was reached, thus permitting the redefinition of procedures for gaining access to Venice's principal assembly. At the end of the thirteenth century and the beginning of the fourteenth century the Great Council swelled to a high point of eleven hundred members. There was an incontestable influx of new members during those years, a phenomenon that worked to moderate tension and, precisely, to permit acceptance of the hereditary principle and the creation of the new system.[79] The families that could demonstrate that members had sat in the Council before 1293 were included; some of the families that had been excluded successfully argued their rights; the doge backed the candidacy of some "popular" families; and in some cases admission was used as a reward for exceptional service. This provided enough ways to be elected to explain the more than doubled size of the Great Council but also the bitterness of families that failed to gain admission. It may also explain the 1300 conspiracy of Marino Boccono, a member of the *populares* (or at least this is the interpretation suggested in the later Trevisan chronicle) and the convulsions of the early fourteenth century. It would be a mistake, however, to rely too readily on the Serrata to explain the Tiepolo-Querini conspiracy, which had other causes in the papal interdict during the War of Ferrara, the heavy economic consequences of Venetian defeats in that conflict, ancient hatreds, and family and personal rivalries.[80]

The increase in its membership reflects the new function and importance of the Great Council, which now gathered together the political class of Venice rather than representing it.[81] The division or shared responsibility for political authority within a much enlarged governing community was aimed at avoiding the temptations of tyranny and the disorders of factionalism.[82] The mechanisms of the Serrata encompassed a search for a balance of forces among the various families and a distribution, within a situation of mutual surveillance, of rights and privileges among an elite that was designated as such. The system of domination set in place was thus dual, combining an obvious control of the dominant over the dominated with a more complex control over the dominant themselves by means of their global integration into the structures of public governance.

Analysis of the Venetian governing class does not come to an end with consideration of the Serrata. Two chronologies stand opposed where the constitution of the Venetian dominant group is concerned. One of these is short, ending in the 1320s with the definition of the hereditary aristocracy thanks to the series of laws enacted between 1297 and 1323.[83] The other prolongs that process until the War of Chioggia[84] and even beyond.[85] Some facts support the first view, which is close to the traditional interpretation. After the Tiepolo-Querini conspiracy the procedures for admission to the Great Council became narrower and more complex. After 1319, in a move to assure control and supervision of the Council, the Avogaria di Comun passed on claims to eligibility from families who were not members of that body. Other facts support the second view. When the colonial nobility began to return to the Venetian homeland, the younger branches of the "autochthonous" nobility were gradually included among the families whose members sat on the Great Council. Above all, the patrician regime evolved slowly.

In my opinion, two sets of considerations are relevant here. First, the legislative and juridical substratum put in place beginning with the Serrata was definitive. The laws voted in those decades created a nobility of function; membership in the dominant group became hereditary. During those same years the policy of economic protectionism and restrictions aimed at guaranteeing commercial rights only to Venetians reinforced the coherence of that chronology and introduced a new rigidity into Venetian society.[86] Throughout the history of the Council, hereditary recruitment to the largest governing assembly and limiting access to its membership to the nobility continued to define the character of Venice as an aristocratic republic. In 1403, for example, in a move to combat the effects of the natural process of biological extinction,[87] the Quarantia proposed (without success) that when a family died out it might be replaced in the Council by another family.[88] Proposals of the sort continued to be rejected, even at a much later date when Venice seemed sunk in torpor. A degree of flexibility had indeed been won after the troubled times in 1310, and a few men who had distinguished themselves in the repression of the Tiepolo-Querini conspiracy were received into that assembly.[89] In 1381 thirty-one new families, the *case nuovissime,* were admitted as a reward for exceptional contributions to the war effort against the Genoese.[90] In both cases the danger had been extreme, and the Republic knew how to show its gratitude.

I might add that on the ideological level, Venetian historical narration aimed at clearly displaying the beneficent effects of the organization of a power structure of the sort. It was the duty of the elect who governed the city to see to it that the providential success willed by God came to pass. When the city became a state, it was their task to attempt to maintain the power of the Republic even when that power faltered. Consequently, it seems useless to demonstrate and repeat that the Venetian elites were corrupt, ignorant, or incompetent. It is likely that they were all of these to some extent, as were all political elites of the time, and it is equally likely that there were periods when vacillation and disarray increased. I do not deny that such analyses should be pursued, given that the "myth" of Venice long described the patriciate as honest, inflexible, and constant. But these necessary corrections and this search for a "truth" that was not difficult to find should not prevent us from seeing something more important, which is the constitution, thanks to the Serrata and the texts of the legislation consequent to that event, of an identity of domination and a discourse of justification, hence the creation of a series of procedures that legitimated and concealed the ongoing reality of the relation of force that founded social domination. By defining and "closing" a dominant class, the aristocratic republic admittedly employed violence (at least symbolic violence) and worked to produce obedience. Similarly, there are many obvious reasons for the elites' appropriation of domination, and they should not be ignored. But although the elites may have displayed unbridled ambition, sought profits, and been guilty of corruption, pulling wires, and even political crime, that does not mean that some of those who were rewarded with civic honors did not display their awareness of the common good. Whether or not they acted on that awareness, it was what urged the elites to reproduce themselves and to last, just as the city and the state had lasted. We thus have to recognize that the discourse the dominators elaborated to justify themselves may have been a mirage, but it shaped the meaning of Venetian history. It operated in perfect counterpoint to legal measures to found the nobility as a unified group whose members shared rights and privileges but also, as they themselves declared, duties and a mission.

On the other hand, and here I am following the argument of Stanley Chojnacki, the Serrata did not fix the definition of the governing group once and for all.[91] For decades the social and symbolic identity of the nobility continued to be refined and defended. Various measures stated the conditions for membership in the aristocracy and regulated relations within the patriciate. Measures voted in 1319, 1323, and 1376 established criteria for admission to the Great Council—age, legitimate birth, direct descent from a member of the Council, and so on. Their effect was simple: the "collective identity of the nobility" was gradually encompassed within an extremely constraining legal framework.[92] The laws passed in 1376 heralded a growing interest in a "purity" of the governing class; the honor of the *dominium* was not to be sullied by the presence of men of dubious birth within the nobility. In the early fifteenth century procedures instituted for registering for the *Balla d'Oro* brought these concerns to a peak. In Stanley Chojnacki's view, the new mechanisms of supervision put into effect on that occasion and with the laws that followed were equivalent to a second Serrata.[93] All adult Venetian patricians, with the exception of those who embraced an ecclesiastical career, were de facto members of the Great Council. But before they could take their seats they had to show proof of an acceptable patrilineal filiation and, after 1376, of their mother's social condition as well. The *Balla d'Oro* added to these strict requirements a ritual that marked the entry of young men into the political career. On St. Barbara's Day the names of a certain number of *juvenes* were drawn by lot, with winners as young as twenty years of age gaining immediate admission to the Great Council.[94] Unless fate smiled on them at the next *Barbarella,* the others had to wait until they were twenty-five to occupy the seat in the Council to which their birth gave them a right. It should be added, and this is the important point for our purposes, that requirements for proof of patrician condition became much more rigid. More often than not, the magistracy responsible for their verification, the Avogaria di Comun, refused petitions, and the archives (*quaternus*) kept by that body after 1414 completed the system, serving as the first truly official lists of Venetian nobility. Examination of the *quaternus* reveals, incidentally, that in the early fifteenth century these government agents were not well acquainted with the nobility. Restrictions continued to be added during the fifteenth century; in an attempt to avoid contamination and stain, they focused on the all-important act of marriage. Laws voted in 1506 and 1526 sanctioned this process, and henceforth the Avogaria kept the registers in which noble births and marriages were entered, the famous *Libri d'Oro.* It should be noted that although the nobility coincided with the membership of the Great Council (in its various definitions), distinctions were of course drawn within that group.

"Le casade de zentilhomeni de Venezia"

Just how many nobles were there? In his *De origine* Marino Sanudo tells us that in 1527 there were 144 "houses of gentlemen" in Venice.[95] These noble houses produced 2,570 men who sat in the Great Council and competed for the available government posts. A century later their numbers had decreased and there were only some 1,500 patricians, which had probably been their number at the end of the fourteenth century as well. There was thus a certain coefficient of numerical variability of the elites within Venetian society. They were always in sufficient number, however, not to be homogeneous.

The noble houses of Venice were ranged in a shifting hierarchy according to their relative antiquity, wealth, influence, and size. In the years in which the Serrata was voted it was clear that one could not compare the illustrious *case* that had produced the Contarini, Michiel, Falier, or Dandolo doges in the eleventh and twelfth centuries with families who succeeded, only with interruptions and difficulties, in having a sole representative elected to the

Great Council. It was equally impossible, in the final third of the fourteenth century, to equate the prolific houses that occupied a large portion of the urban space (the Morosini, for example, whose presence was felt in twenty-three parishes, or the Contarini, named on the property rolls in all the six *sestieri*) with families that seemed doomed to extinction because their name and their wealth were in inexorable decline.[96]

The sons of some noble families chose to serve the Church rather than to pursue a political career. As is known, the role of the Church was soon circumscribed in Venice, but we should not forget that certain *case vecchie* traditionally held ecclesiastical benefices. Biographical studies reveal that at times family strategy or individual inclination accounted for a career in the Church.[97] Certain nobles became involved in society through other means than a political career, as Gentile Bellini's portrait of Lorenzo Giustiniani amply demonstrates.[98] Bellini painted Giustiniani, the first patriarch of Venice and a man born into one of the oldest lagoon families, who was beatified in 1524 and canonized in 1690, standing with his right hand raised in a gesture of eternal benediction.

With time these differences within the patriciate increased, causing tension even though by law the Venetian nobility was one group, one class, in appearance one and united because born to govern, and even though the procedures for verification of nobility instituted in 1414, which applied to all young nobles, put all noble houses on the same plane, at least juridically. In practice, however, there were strong contrasts within a highly segmented nobility.

Certain venerable *case* whose names universally evoked the finest hours of the Venetian adventure enjoyed a legacy of prestige and an enormous symbolic capital. It is hardly surprising that in Venice the head of the house did not keep a family memoir. Chronicles stamped with the arms of the *cà* that narrated the history of the city and bore marginal annotations by their noble owners played a role similar to the family books of other cities. In Venice family history merged harmoniously with the history of the community.[99] When it happened that the author of a chronicle bore a name like Giustiniani or Sanudo and belonged to the social universe of the *case vecchie*, it was even easier to construct a narrative and a logical demonstration that equated the destiny of the city with that of its major houses. Those houses may have lost political supremacy by the Renaissance, but their prestige remained, and the registers of the Segretario alle Voci, in which the results of the elections to the various councils and offices were entered, always show them present in good numbers at the summit of the Venetian state.

Other houses, often of more recent origin, might possess considerable wealth. Here in brief is the story of Andrea Vendramin, who married Regina Gradenigo and was elected doge in 1476. As a youth he entered into trade in association with his brother Luca, and he made his first profits at Alexandria, following the conventions of Venetian economic and social history. During the second quarter of the fifteenth century he returned to the lagoon and, still in partnership—*fraterna*—with Luca, amassed an imposing fortune.[100] The Vendramin brothers specialized in real-estate operations, acquiring properties in a number of parishes. Rental properties, a grocery store, a recent lot development, warehouses; four houses here, five houses there, at San Cassiano, San Moisè, Santa Maria Formosa, San Geremia, San Stin, San Salvatore, even at Chioggia—the acts show the Vendramins buying, bargaining, and making use of the full arsenal of Venetian law. If their strategy was impressive, the results of this concentration of real estate were equally so. The dowries of the daughters of the family are clear proof of the Vendramins' power and their lavish standard of living.

Many similar examples might be cited. I have already described the construction, in the late fifteenth century and the beginning of the sixteenth century, of the imposing buildings that lined the Grand Canal, including great palaces like those of the Loredan and Grimani families. We have also observed that the Venetians were avid consumers, and we have seen the luxury of their interiors and the precious objects they accumulated and soon began to collect.[101] Their homes contained gilded and sculpted marble mantlepieces and painted, encrusted, and highlighted beams, pilasters, and ceilings. Gold was everywhere. Decor and ornament joined to create a sumptuous, magnificent setting, as we can see from the interior of the palace of Ser Nicolò Benvegnudo as it appears in a painting by Giovanni Mansueti.[102] There is no need to insist further on the extreme opulence of those who dominated this wealthy city with their wealth. Other nobles, however, were poor, even very poor. Some patrician fathers could afford to dower their daughters with shares of the state funded debt, promissory notes, and real estate worth several thousand ducats (in spite of the many laws attacking dowry inflation, which the senators held responsible for the dissipation of patrimonies, the failure of many marriages, and, along with other causes, the spread of the sin of sodomy); other noble fathers found it impossible to scrape together even a meager dowry or the few indispensable goods—linens, clothing, table ware—with which to send their daughters off to a new life.[103] Tax declarations show the precarious economic condition of certain nobles who bore an illustrious name but rented space on a top floor, where they lived with their family in just a few rooms.

In other words, there were disparities among noble families, but this is hardly surprising. Venetian great families split into various branches at an early date, so that a Morosini might be rich or poor, well- or ill-housed, learned or ignorant, patron or client. These diversities are well known, and as early as the fifteenth century generous aid was provided to impoverished nobles by the more fortunate members of the same clan. Aid was also dispensed by the state, especially in the form of lodging, such as in the houses constructed in the parish of San Barnaba.[104] Many nobles who never descended to that level of indigence lived meagerly, and lacking other revenues, they depended on state service to survive. This made the chase for magistracies, a condition of political life in the Republic, all the more feverish. In this connection I might also recall the importance of the constitution of the *stato di terra* and the additional administrative opportunities that it provided. The size of the Venetian administration should not be exaggerated, however: at the end of the fifteenth century, conditions combined to make appointments difficult. In spite of the high number of posts to be filled and their rapid turnover (appointments were limited to six months, eight months, twelve months, sixteen months, or two years), competition seems to have been strong. The Great Council had altogether too many members, which created increased pressure. Sessions buzzed with client-patron negotiations, favors being exchanged, and bargaining for votes, all of which troubled the election process. Moreover, as I have noted, such practices cast a certain discredit on the city's major assembly.

These differences undermined solidarities and created fractures within the nobility as a group, not because they fed genuine political conflict but because they encouraged dissension, maneuvering, hatred, and struggles for power and influence. The age qualification for membership in the Great Council created an additional subgroup. As Stanley Chojnacki has shown, it was difficult to integrate young Venetian men into public life.[105] As is known, the *juvenes* in these societies elicited strongly negative reactions, and in its institutions the Venetian Republic, like Florence, was a gerontocracy. The law restricted access to the most important posts by enforcing strict minimum age limits: thirty, thirty-five, forty, and even forty-five years.[106] A few more rapid and prestigious careers aside, the *cursus* was aptly named: the race was long, and it was won one step at a time. In the fourteenth and fifteenth centuries certain posts were reserved for those at the beginning of their careers in a shifting hierarchy of magistracies. Above all, such newcomers were met with genuine suspicion and continued to be called *juvenes* for years. Doge Tomaso Mocenigo attempted to warn the governing elite against the "youth" Francesco Foscari, who was fifty when he became doge, judged to be hardly a responsible age.[107] The fact that fifteenth-century Venetian chronicles speak of many occasions when *nobiles juvenes,* some of whom were already members of the Great Council, brawled and rioted within the confines of the Ducal Palace demonstrates that young aristocrats were indeed turbulent, seeming to justify their elders' fear of their *impetus* and their associations, meetings, and conspiracies.

The *Balla d'Oro* provided a procedure, new in the fifteenth century, for ritualizing the entry of young nobles into political life. Its dual aim was to create a firmer basis for patrician status and provide a way to initiate these young men into public affairs as early as possible. It formalized a veritable rite of passage that served to integrate the *juvenes* into society, discipline them, and help them to accept, share, and defend the rules and values of the oligarchy in power. The postulate of a youth full of folly and tumult gave legitimacy to this concrete and symbolic organization of entry into political life.[108]

Venetians were different in other ways as well. It was of course commerce that defined the Venetian once and for all. Whether Italian sources were flattering or scornful, satirical or descriptive, they long described the Venetian as a seafarer and a trader, an accountant and a courtier. He counted up his bales of merchandise; he warehoused his pepper and his cotton; he lent and invested; he sailed the seas or wrote to his agents and commissioners abroad. A specialist in tables of rates of exchange and always watching for shifts in the market, he threw himself at the mercy of *la ventura*—the hazards of the sea—and heedless of caricatures, he took to the wind more readily than he mounted his horse.[109]

The first and most illustrious figure in the gallery of portraits of Venetian nobles is thus Marco Polo. A trader and a son and nephew of traders, a traveler and discoverer of unknown lands, he was more than a conduit for the transmission of a description of the marvels of Asia and the astonishing tale of the adventures of some Westerners who had gone to the end of the world. He made a dream breathe and live, and he narrated astonishing fables, but he also had a taste for figures, and he was attentive to commodities and their price. He managed his affairs according to the normal rules of family capitalism; he took on the risks and suffered the disillusionments of all businessmen. His voyages, which began from Venetian trading posts in the East, show us the colonies that Latins had established everywhere from the Mediterranean to the Black Sea, an entire system of trade, exchange, and men moving ever farther toward the East. Later, on his return to Venice, Marco Polo returned to being a reasonably affluent merchant who owned a large house and a sufficiency of material goods and who was well integrated into the society of his time.[110]

At the other end of the same gallery of portraits there is another sailor, merchant, and discoverer: Alvise Cà Da Mosto. Born in 1432, he spent his childhood in Venice, then sailed between the English Channel and the Mediterranean in an apprenticeship typical of young merchants. In 1454, at the age of twenty-two, "in order to bring back some profit from this expedition, acquire some goods, [and] attain some degree of honor," he embarked on the Flanders galleys commanded by Marco Zeno. The rest, as they say, is history. The adventure of the great voyages of discovery was born of his meeting with Henry the Navigator, prince of Portugal. Cà Da Mosto described his reasons for setting out for more distant seas: "Being assured of everything, feeling myself young and well disposed, desirous of seeing some of the world and of discovering things that never came into the ken of anyone of my nation, also combined with the hope of the gain that I thought to bring back."[111] A first voyage in 1455 took him as far as Cape Verde; the following year he sailed out again, this time as far as the Casamance River. His exploration was scientific, and his narration is no less so. Alvise Cà Da Mosto observed and described in minute detail the mores of the inhabitants, the birds, the diameter of the trees, the local fauna, what he ate, and the quality of the air he breathed. His chapters follow one another in orderly fashion, dealing with agricultural resources, then animals, markets before horses or the customs of the women. But Alvise was not merely an explorer; he became interested in the products that the Portuguese and the natives were trading—in the slave trade (a horse for fifteen slaves) and, at the edge of the land of the Blacks, in the commerce that consisted in bartering gold for salt. He financed his second voyage with the profits that he realized selling the slaves he had bought in Guinea.

There is little difference between the stories of the two exceptional men that I have chosen to illustrate the Venetians' relationship with merchandise and with distant horizons, even though one traveled in the thirteenth century and the other in the fifteenth century.[112] Admittedly, during the fifteenth century some prosperous patricians who were also businessmen had a less daily and less immediate physical contact with merchandise. The commercial activities of Guglielmo Querini, which have been reconstituted thanks to his will and to various private documents, bear witness to a clear decline of the *colleganza*. Querini made broad use of agents, which enabled him to run his business from Venice, leaving only to go to his lands in the Polesine, near Rovigo, or to take a trip to Ravenna.[113] There are many indications, which I will not go into, that the nobility diversified their investments and that Venetian capital moved into nearby rural areas. In two generations of the Barbarigo family, for example, the relative value of investments in lands and holdings in movable goods reversed from one generation to the next.[114] It would be a mistake to exaggerate these changes, however: in his later years, when his fortune had been made, the noble merchant undoubtedly preferred to live in his house in Venice. For many, however, youth was the time to sail as a crossbowman on the galleys of the Republic or to serve a commercial apprenticeship in the family firm, working with correspondents, relatives, or friends at Candia or Alexandria. Others rejected the sedentary life and remained active as ships' masters well into their mature years. We have seen Andrea Vendramin's merchant years. Before him, Nicolò Tron (who later became doge) spent fifteen years trading at Rhodes, where he built up his fortune. Another future doge, Antonio Grimani, also rose to prominence through trade.

Trade predominated, but some patricians specialized in public affairs. They give us valued insights into the ways in which Venetian political society operated. Nobles of function were many in Venice, but of those who had the right to hold office at least a third—a conservative estimate—did not occupy their posts regularly because they were out of the city either for business reasons or because they occupied an official post elsewhere. I have noted that the Great Council would inevitably have to delegate powers as soon as an enlarged nobility and its many de facto members brought that assembly to a size that made it impossible to fulfill all the tasks required of it with any degree of efficiency. Events thus combined to create a political elite whose talents and experience increased over time. We saw in chapter 1 how Marco Corner honed his competence and shaped his career. He provides us with a known name and enough information to reconstitute a life, but many others mentioned in the records of debates or listed as named to a post in the records of the preparatory commissions indicate a broad variety of genuine talents, and we often learn that a certain patrician was asked to prepare a note or draw up a report to a council because he was *optime informatus.*

Clearly, certain nobles became administrators or technicians. Moreover, the monetary gain—the *utilità*—attached to the posts is insufficient to explain this aristocratic investment in the smooth operation of the state. One might risk the hypothesis of a tension within the elite itself that led some members of the most distinguished lineages to seek superdistinction by adopting a career, a process that tended to produce genuine political professionals. These were the men who were selected time after time to fill certain responsibilities and posts, but public service did not prevent them from also continuing to manage their properties or participate in trade or the financing of trade.

If many of these nobles acquired their expertise in the course of appointments and a life spent in making sure that the political and administrative machinery functioned smoothly, others sought to supplement their experience with learning, combining an intellectual preparation with the practice of power. Margaret King has demonstrated, following Vittore Branca, that humanism was not uniquely Florentine.[115] The humanist movement began in the early fifteenth century, and it continued throughout the century, penetrating the patriciate and the spheres of power. Manuscripts circulated, libraries were formed, and despite the presence of a few bookseller-printers in Venice, learned nobles felt the need to stock their shelves with books bought elsewhere. The libraries of such men as Francesco Barbaro, Pietro Barbo, Pietro Barozzi, and Domenico Morosini bear witness to the passion for learning, as well as elucidating their relations and epistolary exchanges with other Italian humanist circles.[116] The list is long of the masters who formed that community, that *ordo litterarorum*. Suffice it to say that it included, among others, Guarino Veronese, Vittorino da Feltre, and George of Trebizond.[117] When schools were opened, they supplemented the teaching of preceptors. The will of Tommaso Talenti, a Florentine who became a Venetian citizen, provided for the first school of logic and philosophy, which opened at Rialto in 1408.[118] From 1420 to 1454 Paolo della Pergola taught in the school, and its success under his guidance was so great that he envisioned opening a general *studium*. The Council of Ten was opposed to its founding, following the lines of a policy already established at Vicenza, Verona, and Treviso to locate the only institution of higher learning at Padua. Another school, the third if we count that of the ducal chancellery (which prepared administrative personnel and to which we shall return), opened near the Campanile on Piazza San Marco in 1446. Marino Sanudo's chronicle describes the success of humanist pedagogy at the end of the fifteenth century: "Here [at Rialto] one reads philosophy and theology in the morning and after dinner, for those who want to go to it, and the lessons are paid by San Marco. At present the most excellent philosopher, our patrician Antonio Corner, whose reputation is celebrated in many schools, teaches there, and daily he gives many lessons, in law as well as in logic, philosophy, and theology."[119] Sanudo adds, "Furthermore, at San Marco, near the Campanile, there are two masters paid by San Marco, very learned in humanity, who give their lessons publicly to anyone who wants to hear them, without having to pay. At present there are Giorgio Valla from Piacenza, who knows Greek perfectly . . . and Marco Antonio Sabellico."

Certain names, works, and authors stand out during the century. One of the best-known men, Bernardo Giustiniani, was a figure highly emblematic of this world of Venetian humanism. The author of *De Divi Marci Evangelistae vita* and *De origine urbis Venetiarum,* Giustiniani put his stamp on Venetian historical narrative; his *Orationes* recall that his eloquence was particularly appreciated; his correspondence demonstrates his interest in everything of importance in the humanism of his time. His achievements were not limited to his many writings and his patronage of George of Trebizond and Giovanni Mario Filelfo: he also pursued a political career at the highest levels. Repeated ambassadorships took him to Rome, Naples, France, and Milan; on his return to the lagoon he was elected to the Council of Ten, and throughout his career he was a *savio grande*. He became Procurator of San Marco, and he participated in all but one of the elections for doge in the latter half of the fifteenth century. Although these achievements would have been enough to fill a long and rich life, Bernardo never abandoned trade, and his commercial activities are well known.[120] Not all careers were as brilliant as his, and not all of the growing number of people imbued with humanist culture wrote.[121] Still, generation after generation, the political elite of Venice was won over by humanism, with perhaps all that such an acquisition might imply for the construction of an imaginary of individual virtue in the service of the *res publica*.[122] Thus it was not only influence or wealth that produced divisions within the nobles as a group.

Our picture of Venetian political society would not be complete, however, if it failed to take into account the emergence of the *cittadini*.

"The Second Crown of the Republic of Venice"

The "second crown" of the Republic[123] was worn by a bourgeoisie that was excluded from the institutionally created elite and consequently from access to the highest administrative posts, but beginning in the late fifteenth century that bourgeoisie gradually took over a multitude of offices that provided the framework of the Venetian state.[124] Thus by the side of the elite, whom we have seen filling posts that consecrated their dominant status and their honor, a large number of offices were reserved for non-nobles.[125] The need for a larger administration may have led to the constitution of this group with a bureaucratic vocation. The creation of the territorial state certainly also played a determining role in this development: even if Venice left a high degree of autonomy to its subject cities and communities, as we have seen, that vast collection of territories still needed to be governed. A number of recent studies have seen broader sociopolitical implications in the phenomenon of the *cittadini*, however.

In the first place, it has been observed that the process of distinguishing the original citizens of Venice began in the years following the War of Chioggia. That conflict, its cost, and the context of economic crisis had upset the hierarchy of wealth in the city. Moreover, the wealthier *popolari* had contributed generously to the war effort through the mechanism of forced loans. Some of them were rewarded by admission to the patriciate; others (a greater number) gained a chance for a career in the bureaucracy. Some interesting nuances have been added to this general line of interpretation. A variety of measures designed to revive the economic machinery after the War of Chioggia changed life in Venice. The restriction on trade with the Levant, which traditionally had been reserved to nobles and "original citizens," was eased somewhat.[126] Concessions were extended to foreign craftsmen.[127] In that context, "the increasing role given to the original [citizens] in the administration in the fifteenth century resulted from a process of re-establishing an equilibrium aimed at compensating for the reduction of their commercial privileges."[128]

It may be useful to summarize the main stages in the creation of this "second crown," a group whose identity within the history of the Republic became clearer as time passed. In order to accede to the "graces and benefits" that the city offered, candidates had to prove, first, that they were of legitimate birth and, second, that their origins were "honorable."

Recruitment of personnel for the ducal chancellery began to be reorganized in 1442. Soon a school was opened to instruct twelve young men in grammar and rhetoric in the hope that "many honorable citizens would have their sons study there."[129] In 1478 access to the ducal chancellery was reserved to original citizens.[130] Other laws followed that increased the privileges of those same citizens in their quest for intermediate or minor posts. Then, during the early decades of the sixteenth century, increasingly selective criteria attached conditions to the recognition of the status of *cittadino originario*. These criteria, first imposed for candidates for positions in the chancellery, were extended to the rest of the bureaucracy. Thus, with time, continued high-level service within certain families created an "order of secretaries" and, on a lower level, a group of specially privileged persons who had access to posts in the Venetian bureaucracy based on the fact of their birth but not on their social status.

In all these cases a corps was formed that was no more homogeneous than the nobility, but like the nobility, it was endowed with a particular, even exclusive identity. It has been estimated that at the end of the sixteenth century the *cittadini* made up 7 percent of the population, while the nobles accounted for some 3 percent to 4 percent.

According to the discourses that celebrated the Venetian system of government, this was how the virtues of a mixed state were instituted and how the ground was laid for an aristocratic republic that tempered the political exclusion of the "people" by conceding notable rights and privileges to the most "honest" and "honorable" of that "people." We can recognize in this hymn to the qualities of Venetian institutions the hand of Gasparo Contarini, who systematically presented Venice in the most flattering light. A certain number of political theorists thought that the concession of areas of liberty to the people was one explanation for the stability of the Republic.

There is one, and to my mind only one, truly important fact to be deduced, recognized, and emphasized in all this. Throughout the evolutions of the Venetian system of government, which were concealed under an apparent and fictive immutability, Venetians always managed to fabricate, diffuse, and gain fairly broad acceptance for the discourse that legitimated the various reforms of that system. Our analysis thus ends as it began, at the level of representation, of all the representations. At the beginning of the sixteenth century the group of the "illustrious men" of Venice was no longer made up of a few great figures of doges or particularly rich and enterprising patricians. High-level state functionaries appeared on the scene, some of whom—Andrea Franceschi, for example—were painted by Titian as they rose to join Venetian political society and become a part of the great imaginary fresco of those in the past centuries who had assumed a civic "honor" that was also the honor of the city.

SIX

The People of the City

I have assembled and described the components of the environment in which Venetian life took place. Patient labors built a city where there had been marshes. The Venetians traded on the sea, and their power grew until the greater part of the West was supplied through the Venetian market. On the side of the land, which the Venetians long claimed to ignore, they launched economic ventures, in particular commercial exchanges and real-estate investments. At the same time, and by no means autonomously, a series of political events created other relations and other involvements because Venice was never uniquely open to the sea or to the East. This complex situation made for an environment and a set of factors that shaped Venetian history. It is this framework that we must keep in mind because it is inseparable from historical reconstitution and from the images that such a reconstitution spontaneously recalls: a convoy of galleys en route to Alexandria, cogs loaded with wine after the grape harvest in Candia, Venetians fighting under the walls of Ferrara. This was how a unique history was set in motion, a history constructed by a community—probably because at the time it believed that Providence had assigned it a special destiny—that enjoyed a remarkable success, fashioned with the passage of time.

In the early chapters I considered, within the context of the necessities imposed by the site, the relative weight of exogenic factors and the Venetians' own choices and the working out of historical events that were integrally connected even when they seemed to belong to different economic, cultural, political, or religious categories. The presentation this approach requires deliberately merges the imaginary of the sea and an analysis of maritime power; it seeks out the city's economy where it left its most visible marks—in the marketplace, along the canals where dyed cloth was rinsed, in the courtyards where silk was spun. Next I examined political institutions and their transformations, but also their human component, within a political society that proved to be less inflexible than its hereditary nature might lead one to expect, a political society riddled with tensions and quite diversified in spite of its exclusiveness.

The people of Venice, in groups or as individuals, have never been absent from this study. We have looked at entire swaths of Venetian society, but also narrower segments of the population, in their socioprofessional groups, in light of their criteria of differentiation, and in their various levels of wealth and degrees of integration. Thus we have considered the governing class, the organized craft and trade groups, occasional workers in the port or the market, slaves, foreigners, recent immigrants, men and women. Some of the traditional criteria of social analysis have already been touched upon, but in order to render that society intelligible and to complete those first parameters, other things remain to be said.

The history of urban societies is usually written by examining how they were segmented into categories determined by wealth, work, and status, by who was dominant and who was dominated. Consequently, the city is treated as a place of passive, if not inert, construction of identities. People exist, but in a statistical fashion; their lives are limited to how they fit into collective portraits that risk becoming disembodied because their only logic is socioeconomic. It has become current practice to round out this first approach by stressing relational networks—all of the various ties that operate, both horizontally and vertically, among the inhabitants of a given city. At times an investigation of how people lived, prayed, ate, and married their sons and their daughters is added; in short, the categories of honor and feelings about life and death are included. I shall of course attempt to describe those realities.

My principal aim is to describe and present the men and women of Venice within the framework of their lives and the relations they experienced on a daily basis, to give them speech and permit them to move. Rather than attempting an exhaustive (and probably illusory) reconstitution of a complex society and all of its shifting mechanisms, I hope to evoke Venetians and the ways in which they lived together and constituted an urban community. A society generally exists within a logic of the living. My task will require an archaeology of behaviors, practices, acts, and even, within the limits of the possible, words. A society is not just a group of human beings who fall into hierarchies of activities and honors in the ways that they populate, animate, or govern the city. Any society functions by means of language, which interprets the logic (or logics) of its identity. It is by studying such signs that we can grasp the specificity of an urban culture in the context of its relations with social, economic, and political forms of conditioning, forms that representations show as presumably undifferentiated.

In other words, now that we have seen the Venetians trading, investing, and serving as *castellano, bailo,* or *rettore* somewhere in the Venetian empire or in the country areas around Padua, it is time to return to the capital city and the handful of islands with which we began. I shall not consider the societies that functioned in Modon or Verona in the age of the Venetian Republic, although that is one possible way to understand Venetian history, as recent historical studies have shown.[1] As stated at the outset, a totalizing history is not my aim: I have chosen to focus on the city. What do we see in Jacopo de Barbari's sweeping view of the Venice of 1500? He draws the circuit of the waters and notes some of the land areas that form the world of the lagoon around the Rialto archipelago. He shows the near shores of the lagoon. But thanks to a deliberate focus that operates on us as we view the scene, it is the urban space of Venice that incontestably dominates by the sheer size of its development, the density of its buildings, and its central position. The representation may claim to be faithful, but its immediate meaning is to express an absolute hegemony of Venice over the islands of the lagoon, the waters, and the nearby mainland, all shown as modest satellites of Venice, their hub. The present book began with the construction of a city and a chronicle of how men toiling in both public and private projects created order out of mud flats and wasteland and fashioned an urban universe. It will end with a description of the men and women who labored and lived in that universe and gave it meaning. After the ecosystem and the various processes for dominating space, we must turn to historical anthropology.

I shall describe these men and women within their normal context and their usual networks, concentrating on their relations with their milieu and with all the manifestations that make up the "culture" of a group. Thus, I shall seek evidence of harmony and the marks of serene operation just as much as traces of conflict or of the shocks and moments of violence that punctuate the organization of daily life, explicitly or symbolically. Nothing in a society is unconnected. The ways in which a society functions or malfunctions fit together within interlocking dialectical mechanisms that must be identified, not through a binary opposition of order and disorder, law and anarchy, morality and deviance, but according to the logic of a signifying movement that produced the Venetian "equilibrium." It was in that dialectic and its capacity for integrating conflict and its resolution, contestation and its appeasement, that the city found its sticking power. The historian must avoid both an anthropology unattached to time and a "cultural history" just as unmindful of chronology and take into account the constant that moves from social regulation to deregulation but always reproduces a regulation and deregulation in transformed, even inverted guises. Social phenomena have two faces, but we must study them as integral wholes. That is the only way they can be explained.

MEN AND FAMILIES

For some decades now, family history has profoundly renewed the study of older societies. The reconstitution of kinship structures and the study of the ideology and the imaginary of kinship have been used to distinguish various social configurations and determine "models." This has led to the identification of an urban Mediterranean model. It should be recognized, however, that the abundance of Florentine sources and their exceptional nature, reflected in both that abundance and the outstanding quality of the studies they have inspired, have strongly conditioned the elaboration of that model.[2] After a period of filiation, if not of imitation, Venetian studies have finally broken free of that model and multiplied. To be sure, they cannot rely on a rich harvest of family record books like the Florentine *ricordanze* to aid in the reconstruction of a real world of familial tensions and emotions. Furthermore, probably because the documentation lent itself to that sort of investigation, Venetian family studies, particularly in a first phase, have tended to privilege the noble, wealthy, and dominant families. Within these limitations and recognizing these grey areas, it can be said that Venetian studies have taken on a personality of their own and repeopled the houses, courtyards, and parishes of Venice.[3]

To comprehend the importance of membership in the first circle of relatives one need only read a will or a witness's deposition and observe how men and women present themselves and state their identity. For men, both nobles and commoners, the patrilineal reference that defined them as the son, even the grandson, of someone was of course of primary importance. Women often remain mute or are difficult to classify as long as they remain unmarried; their identity is stated in relation to the men who make them wives or widows. This is a first gender difference. It operates forcefully and directly, signaling other, equally radical cleavages and pointing the way to two types of life experience and two systems of representations.

When we look at Venetians in the aggregate and include the humbler social categories that are sometimes concealed by the patrician dynasties, we see the conjugal couple clearly delineated in the documentation. From the top to the bottom of the social scale, marriage sets up the first norms of social integration, and domestic values are praised by the moralists and theoreticians of the family who present an ideal familial model.[4]

Taking a Wife

In the name of that order and its preservation, marriage was concluded according to rules that imposed constraints in all social milieus. It is quite evident that seeking a good match was a serious matter among the families who counted the most.[5] Still, on occasion a more laconic archival text reveals confabulations and meetings regarding the comparative merits of marriage-able daughters that end in an agreement taking place in the city of court-yards, shops, small houses, and narrow streets. It is also clear that in spite of all the legal limits imposed on dowries, they rose astronomically.[6] It is an easy task to inventory the components of the dowries of the daughters of the aristocracy and the bourgeoisie: cash, state loan shares, movable goods, and a trousseau. During the final centuries of the Middle Ages the dowry system penetrated the entire social system, however, to the point that there seem to have been no marriages without dowries.[7] In popular milieus lists of wom-en's dowry goods—more accurately, the inventories of the dealers in sec-ondhand clothes who evaluated the *donora*—and the depositions of the intermediaries in the marriage—relatives, women friends, or neighbors so-licited, in the absence of documents, to testify to the price and the composi-tion of the dowry—permit us to reconstitute lists of a variety of movable goods.[8] The bed, the sheets, and kitchen utensils (in greater or lesser quan-tity) made up the better part of what a wife brought to the marriage. In some cases the entire dowry was made up of these modest goods symbolizing female roles; if they constituted only a minimal portion of the worth of the dowries of the wealthiest women, they were all there was among the poorest.

It was good policy for a father to provide in his will for dowries for those of his young daughters who were not destined for the religious life and to stipulate amounts. If the father failed to do so, the task fell to the girls' brothers, along with exclusive rights to the father's landed property. But the dowry was not just a family affair: the public powers had an interest in it as well. An imposing array of statutes regulated the operation of the dowry system.[9] We have access to abundant particulars because charitable institutions had a stake in dowries as well. Some people left money in their wills to provide a small dowry for poor and meritorious young women of their parish or to assure an honorable establishment for nubile girls of their neighborhood or circle of friends. Dowry practices thus cast and recast the order of society, and dowries were obligatory.

Love also makes an appearance in the judiciary archives and the mass of notarized acts.[10] One trial for adultery came to naught because the guilty parties were in flight: a witness stated that they had disappeared one night on a canal that opened onto the broad lagoon, and no one had seen them since. In another case, a noble drew up a will in which he named none of his relatives or friends but, contrary to all the rules for the transmission of property, left his modest fortune to his wife, who was clearly of popular origin. The social price for such transgressions of the rules was always high. Marriage outside the norms was rare and entailed exclusion from the group. Adultery was more frequent; committed "in scorn of God, justice, and the state," it was severely punished.[11] The literature of the times—for example, the tales of Franco Sacchetti, Gentile Sermini, and Giovanni Sercambi—is full of stories that show the drama and dishonor that a seducer brings when he pollutes the domestic space. Such tales prove both that real tensions existed and that adultery and its scandals were feared.[12]

In this sort of society taboos of female purity were, or at least were supposed to be, maintained. Virgins were protected and closed in within the domestic space.[13] Foreign visitors, in particular those from Flanders, were struck by how little freedom young Venetian women, or at least young women of a certain social standing, enjoyed. They rarely left the house, and when they did they were wrapped in voluminous garments and wore a veil over their heads. They might be seen very early in the morning, on their way to the nearby church accompanied by a servant woman. When those same women became wives and took up the roles that had been assigned to them, they remained closed in within the family space, and they were still closely watched by the household and the neighborhood, were seldom seen outside the house, and were protected from danger, to the point of keeping them away from the windows. "A pillar for the husband and the family," they bore children and raised them and helped "the husband in the diligent direction of the house [and] in the conservation and multiplication of goods."[14] They lived, removed from public space, in honor and the enjoyment of a good reputation.[15]

More than individuals, marriage connected families, promising them social and biological continuance. It provided a framework for sexuality; it perpetuated civic and Christian life. It was in this aim that transfers of persons and goods were regulated by statute and an imposing formal apparatus was constructed and ritualized, thus marking the basic importance of the union and the passage of the woman from one state to another. Moreover, a marriage that placed an inexperienced and submissive young woman under the authority of a much older husband also had the result of establishing tight control of female sexual identity,[16] stabilizing it and circumventing the irrational desires with which the imaginary obsessively imbued the female, a figure of latent desire, of weakness and temptation, and, precisely, a figure of the intrusion of amorous disorder that could only break the order of social continuity. Marriage was thought of and organized as a technique for the neutralization and appeasement of the phantasms that a particular society had developed regarding its female component.

The Worlds of the Family

In the popular milieu,[17] unless death or life's vicissitudes disturbed this conjugal structure or made it difficult to perceive, the couple occupied a prominent place and the children appear between the two figures of the father and the mother.[18] Children often remain indistinct, however, appearing only when a birth is recalled, a baby is put out to a wet nurse, a dowry is arranged, or a son inherits. On occasion, when a family of artisans or small shop owners disposed of a certain amount of wealth and there were no direct heirs, a woman might inherit at least use of the income on the estate.

It goes without saying, however, that men of this group (and all groups) preferred to follow the rules for the division of wealth that were backed by the local statutes: a dowry for the daughters, the goods to the sons. They operated within a narrow social universe, however; a testator might mention his children and his wife, on rare occasions his mother, but typically the other people mentioned were not blood relatives. Work, a common geographical origin, or "friendship" created ties that completed the first circle of the immediate household and at times made up for what it lacked. People close to the testator by affection or habit also provided services that would normally be done by kin, such as seeing to it that the clauses of the will were carried out, accompanying the funeral cortege, or distributing personal effects.

Nonetheless, the family remained an ideal, and the individual moved more easily within the community when he was surrounded by his blood kin and his relatives by alliance. The couple was less clearly defined among the nobility because the domestic group was often larger, and the individual, both in the ordinary and the exceptional acts of his life, always appears surrounded by the network of his kin and those who were close to him.[19] That network was extensive, a fact that may well have contributed to giving the nobility a measure of its self-confidence. Studying it thus raises questions regarding the strength of solidarities, the size of kinship groups, and how kinship affected daily life.

The Casa

Any attempt to reconstruct family structure in Venice must first turn to the *casa,* the group of people who bore the same name. We have already seen some of those *case*—Contarini, Morosini, Dandolo—and noted that the course of their history was often intertwined with Venetian history. Still, unlike the families of Genoa, Florence, or Bologna, in Venice the group represented by the *casa* soon divided into various branches, or *rami*. The documentation permitting, we can follow the process of segmentation in the oldest houses—in the Badoer family, for example—from the tenth to the thirteenth century, as well as the parallel process of geographical dissemination within the urban space of Venice.[20]

In practical terms, until the fifteenth century the parish of residence enables us to distinguish among these *rami;* after that time the introduction of distinctive signs in family crests, which for centuries had remained common to all branches, began to reflect the ancient divisions. In certain cases the split seems to have been so longstanding that a common surname was no longer an impediment to marriage, and even a brief perusal of the marriage registers will show patrician marriages between members of the same *cà.* A man and woman both named Querini or Venier could thus marry as if they were totally unrelated.

It should be noted, however, that marriage within the *cà* was far from common because a form of recognition functioned among these quite distinct filiation lines that sometimes bound them with tenuous symbolic ties. Independent *rami* could not quite consider themselves genuine relatives of the main lineage, and it would have been out of the question to maintain social relations or follow the norms of social and affective comportment that all Venetians agreed were signs of kinship. In Venice as elsewhere, kinship was not only maintained and recognized but also named and practiced.[21] Still, there was a lingering notion that the entire *casa* had descended from a common ancestor. The trunk of the family tree, as one noble Dandolo declared in the fifteenth century, might have been split long before, but that trunk had existed (or was supposed to have existed), and it remained as a sign of antiquity and a proof of vigor for the various Dandolo lineages and for all the men of the *cà* who shared that theoretical common ancestor in an immemorial past.

It followed that even when the connection was weak, the *casa* retained a meaning within the texture of society, and solidarities might exist among those who shared no more than the family name. Largesse dispensed at the hour of death displays the psychological reality of the imaginary of a group with a large membership. Among these liberalities were cash bequests to be distributed among the poorer men and women of the *cà.* Even more symbolically, a clause in a testament might stipulate the distribution of objects bearing the family crest among the many people who bore the name. Membership in the *cà* thus presumed, at least for its wealthier and more powerful representatives, an awareness of duties toward the whole of the patronymic group. Although that awareness was not equally felt by all, it did tend to crystallize relations and obligations, first among them assistance to the poor. It also explains why services were exchanged more willingly among those who shared the same name even if they were not of the same blood.

Lineage

Nonetheless, the noble recognized his own lineage and his kin, and he distinguished between his blood relatives and others who bore the same patronymic. His existence was played out within the society of his close kin, whom he saw daily, whether or not they lived in the family dwelling, whether or not their business was in *fraterna*. When he went to his eternal rest, his body was placed in the tomb of his lineage.[22] This makes it difficult to establish a hierarchy among the various social functions of lineage. In the Venetian Republic birth determined political status and the right to sit in the Great Council. Membership in a lineage was expressed in many other ways as well, however. Throughout a man's career, support from kin continued to work to advance the lineage. The limitations and prohibitions imposed on the deliberations of the assemblies and on election procedures show how hard the Venetian regime tried (without great success) to avoid partisan votes and to control the negotiations that enabled families to assert their positions collectively and provided individuals the only path to advancement.

In business as well, whatever its scale, the same relations of mutual assistance and trust were mobilized. Within the family exchanged services were the rule: assistance and support were dispensed as a matter of course. The local statutes recognized the vitality of these solidarities in economic life. Kin who lived under the same roof and who conducted business together were fully recognized as associates. No formal contract, written documents, or *carte* like the ones that accompanied all the other acts of Venetian life were needed. Many sorts of economic enterprise were managed under such *fraterne*.[23] The example of certain large "fraternal" partnerships in the fifteenth century shows that the mechanisms of "family capitalism" continued to be more important to economic decision making than individual strategies, although some individual entrepreneurs carved out careers outside such family businesses.[24]

Property was firmly controlled by brothers, uncles, nephews, or first cousins, and within an estate real property was the most zealously managed. The dispositions of last wills and testaments favored the rights of the male members of the family, in the name of the kinship group and its interests and of a strict respect of the dominant patrilineal values. Complex dispositions functioned to ensure that dwellings would remain in the family for centuries and that the men of the family would inhabit them. The desire for continuity and for anchoring the lineage that this custom reflects shows that it took more than time to construct a genealogy. It also required close spatial ties and ties to the physical *cà*, the house, be it great or small, beautiful or plain, of brick, stone, or wood. Laws governing succession thus elaborated an ideal model in which the family house, never sold, never divided, would be transmitted from one male generation to another, in collateral devolution in the absence of sons or grandsons. Daughters were dowered and did not inherit. Steps were taken to ensure their exclusion from inheritance, to remedy breakdowns in the system, and to see to it that real property did not pass into female hands.[25] Wills repeat identical clauses, one after the other; they organize the transfer of real property, especially the most precious holding, the family dwelling, from male to male.[26] In a similar spirit, the statutes regulated the real-estate market, recognizing the rights of preemption of relatives,[27] even stipulating preferential terms for closer kin. Special provisions were made for kin and for safeguarding the integrity of property, and the texts demonstrate that they were often invoked. The law offered the instruments of conservation indispensable for combating discontinuity, time, and the death of men, should these threaten to undo the family and weaken its deep roots in the city.

An image will help us visualize this process. In the 1540s Titian painted the Vendramin family gathered around a reliquary of the True Cross. This canvas commemorating the Vendramin lineage shows only male family members. In it Andrea Vendramin is surrounded by his seven sons, with his brother Gabriele at his side but figured somewhat less prominently. None of his daughters appear. Moreover, the devotion of the True Cross recalls their ancestor, another Andrea Vendramin, and his special connection to the relic and its miracles.[28]

Lineage had an equally strong influence in matters that did not concern participation in public life or the family wealth. Once again, our best informants are the men of the time. When they describe kinship relations, they tell of words, gestures, and feelings; they evoke minute details, a constant frequentation, and rules of social conduct that clearly established kinship ties and stated the degree of proximity. A family member was called kin and was summoned for both daily affairs and such major events in family life as weddings and funerals.

Affines

Consanguinity shaped a first active network within the governing class, but a second circle, that of kin by alliance, operated at its side. A good marriage procured another circle of relations, a reserve of support, intermediaries, and guarantors active in both the economic and the political sphere. In Venice, however, a woman's ties to her family of birth remained particularly close. Married into another house, the woman nonetheless continued to *tenir gran parentado* with her blood relatives. The sources depict or suggest exchanges, visits, and a lively sociability. Thus the will of a Venetian noblewoman will usually include a certain number of bequests to members of her lineage of origin.[29] The amount of the bequests of course varied according to the socioeconomic position and the age of the testatrix, but other criteria were just as important: the presence or absence of male descendants or daughters who needed to be dowered, for example. Whether these bequests were modest or sizable, they reveal a continuing connection between the woman and her family of birth. Big or small, this return of the wife's goods to her lineage of origin was always real, adding a nuance of its own to the Venetian patrilineal social model. In other words, blood and alliance helped to construct a broad relational network around women. The lineage acquired, animated, and maintained an entire capital of acquaintances, support, and aid thanks to women but for the benefit of men.

During the fifteenth century certain changes began to take place that favored the progeny of one individual over collaterals. To cite only one example from the highest ranks of Venetian society, Doge Agostino Barbarigo chose his grandsons, the children of his daughters, as his heirs. Such dispositions were still rare, and Venetians resorted to them only to remedy a difficult situation, but they reveal a trend, the gradual appearance of a private sphere, that also occurred in comportment, in representations, and in the domestic space of the house.[30] For all that, and while the configuration and functions of the family in the Italian Renaissance have been hotly debated in recent years,[31] these real shifts and this mobility in practices and concepts, which left their mark on an equally mobile history, did not prevent the operation of lineage solidarity or keep individual strategies from taking their customary place at the heart of collective strategies. What is more, the ideology of lineage conditioned life among the bourgeoisie of Venice just as much as within the nobility.

Citizen Families

In a search for honorable status the families of the original citizens of Venice adopted crests, cultivated favorable marriage alliances, and built houses that gave them roots and prestige within their quarter and their city. It could be said that this was a reproduction of the values of the dominant class, to the point of blatant imitation. But why should that surprise us? The great families of Venice not only controlled trade and politics but by their dominance they determined the structure of those spheres. Anyone who wanted to rise in society or consolidate his status had to procure the necessary instruments and fashion a personal identity in tune with the preponderant models. This meant that marriages were concluded with great care. With the exception of hypergamous unions for the daughters of the very wealthiest commoners, the milieus of commerce and the bureaucracy reveal a certain tendency toward endogamy. Marriages among the families of government functionaries helped the milieu of the administration to became increasingly well defined during the sixteenth century. On the other hand, physicians, lawyers, and notaries practiced exogamy, and the size of the dowries that such families received compensated for the socially honorable status that was their part of the bargain.[32]

Family crests enter into this picture. The leading bourgeois families had a crest and displayed it sculpted over a gateway, at the entrance to a courtyard, or at the curve of a wall, just like the patrician houses. Crests served to demonstrate geographical stability; they put a durable stamp on the physiognomy of the city; they provided part of the social text of the urban grammar and guaranteed duration and memory. One example of a citizen house that made its mark among noble dwellings is Palazzo Dario, the *cà* of the citizen Giovanni Dario. It still stands facing the Grand Canal, where it contributes to the beauty of what Philippe de Commynes called "la rue la mieux maisonnée" (the most finely housed street) in the world. The example is extreme, as is the richness of the dwelling, but many parishes in Venice still retain the memory of the houses of "honorable citizens."

The Venetian bourgeoisie thus displayed a degree of conformity in its comportments, and it attempted—more or less successfully, depending on the age of the family, its wealth, and its honor—to define and operate in accordance with a politics of the family. Venice stands out as different, however, in both practice and the family's idealized image of itself. As we have seen, the family literature abundant in Tuscany is absent in Venice. It is probably not by chance that the few family chronicles that have been conserved were written by members of citizen families. The first of these, that of the Amadi family, is not really a "family book." It offers no in-depth recital of family history, and it presents no detailed account of domestic events, great or small. Instead, it recounts the story of a miraculous Virgin and the construction of the church that sheltered the image, Santa Maria dei Miracoli. Not only did the Amadi family own the statue but from start to finish they controlled the wave of Marian devotion that the statue inspired, and it was their role in that event that brought them to prominence and established their memory.[33] The Freschi family provide a second example and another way to imagine family biography.[34] They began to note down family births and marriages toward the middle of the fifteenth century. About 1500 the manuscript of this chronicle is even illustrated: three generations of couples are represented, each one with the crests of its respective families. Zaccaria, the third of the Freschi line, is depicted wearing the red toga of a secretary of the Council of Ten and standing at the side of his sumptuously dressed wife.[35] In a third example, the Ziliol family chronicle contains a brief reconstruction of family history and displays a certain interest in genealogy. Andrea Ziliol (1457–1544) began keeping the chronicle for the edification of his descendants, one of whom, Alessandro, continued it in the early decades of the seventeenth century.[36]

Why should these writings have existed? And why should citizen families have felt the need for such excursions into the history, long or short, of their ancestors? The past of the aristocratic houses was, as we have seen, largely identical to the past of a city characterized by political stability. Historical narrative thus maintained family memory and served to keep the glory of the family bright. There were also specialized family chronicles, called *caxade de Veniexia*, that narrated the histories of patrician *case* from their mythical origins and composed veritable group portraits. Moreover, it was among the duties of the Avogaria di Comun to record births and marriages, a task that the father of the Florentine family fulfilled in his *ricordanze*. For all of these reasons, in Venice the identity of the individual noble and of the lineage of which he was a part tended to merge with the more global identity of the family among the patricians.[37]

Just as *cittadini* were by law refused access to membership in the governing class, they were refused such means for preserving their memory and affirming their status. Those families, or at least certain of them, thus invented other ways to found their honor and assert their longevity.[38] In doing so they elaborated specific forms of expression more than they sought a recognition that, in any event, was not forthcoming.

Recent historical studies focusing on this long-neglected milieu have brought to light an entire repertory of practices. Writing a family document was one of these, and it was not by chance that they appeared during the second half of the fifteenth century, a time of major change when citizens, or at least a portion of that group, were identified as such and gained entry to city offices. *Cittadini* were also active in the flagellant confraternities, in which major posts were assigned exclusively to native citizens beginning in the early fifteenth century. They filled these posts, then moved on to occupy whatever positions of power were open to them. Special ties were created among these families and, to an even greater extent, among some of the confraternities.[39] The episode of the founding of the sanctuary of Santa Maria dei Miracoli had resonances that illustrate such strategies. The Amadi family dramatized its role in these events and its patronage of the miraculous image. A wealthy bourgeois family but with no particular prestige, they exploited and directed the wave of Marian devotion for several years in a row. When they found themselves promoted to the first rank of parish notables, they used the devotions to reinforce their weight and influence in the quarter, but their new prominence also brought them to the forefront in the greater urban scene.[40]

Such practices enable us to discern functions of substitution, modes of symbolic compensation, and the existence of specific practices within this milieu of the *cittadini* of Venice, if not of a genuine culture unique to them.

These in turn throw light on the sociopolitical system of Venice and help to explain its stability. The Venetian bourgeoisie may not have been able to accede to the center of power, but it enjoyed privileges and posts reserved to it that distinguished it from the mass of commoners and installed it in an intermediary position. Far from dreaming of destabilizing the hierarchy of power or contesting the Venetian system of representations, the *cittadini* accepted and supported them, working to multiply their moorings in Venetian time and space and helping to define their identity and their place between the nobles and the people.

All categories of the Venetian population lived within fixed primary social horizons. For some, the family group was apt to be limited to spouse and children; for others, it was more flexible and more broadly defined. In all cases, families were absorbed within a veritable nebula of kin and affines. Individuals were set within families. When, to the delight of the historian, a father who "strays" from his status draws up a contract with an equally detached future son-in-law and the contract stipulates the amount of the girl's dowry, we can see the entire social specter revealed in its respect for a conformity shared by both parties.

Some Venetians did not fit into the model of the nuclear family, however. Thus we need to ask how, in this complex society, forces of violence and disorder worked to combat the common desire for equilibrium and continuity; how systems were ceaselessly decomposed, upsetting families and unsettling men.

THE ISOLATED, THE EXCLUDED, AND THE REBELLIOUS

Woes

Repeated waves of plague attacked the social edifice at least until the first third of the fifteenth century.[41] It is certain that on the demographic level Venice, like other cities of northern Italy, was never as hard hit by epidemics as Florence or Tuscany in general. The capital city of the lagoons continued to attract a flow of immigrants, who at least partially replaced those who had died. Population figures are not the only data to be considered, however: at the height of the epidemics of the 1380s the social landscape of the *contrade* of Venice appears to have been strongly revised.[42] Houses stood empty, entire families were swept away, and continuity was interrupted. In the universe of daily life relations with neighbors and ties of sociability were realigned.

When deaths had peaked and the crisis had subsided, Venice began to revive, but the plague continued to be an ever-present danger. Within the city there were sporadic outbreaks, which the authorities did their best to combat, working with increased efficiency as the fifteenth century advanced, in particular after the constitution of the Provveditori alla Sanità, a magistracy charged with responsibility for public health.[43] Death returned with fair weather, however, and almost every summer its threat was visible in a city that the rich and powerful tended to desert and where guard patrols were reinforced out of fear of theft in a general social climate described as anxiety-ridden.

The plague was not the only cause of widespread death in an urban area that was at times overpopulated, where we can sense that in some quarters people lived tightly packed in poverty-stricken courtyards and in the promiscuity of tiny, crowded alleyways. In the central parishes, which were also the first to be urbanized, there are many signs of housing shortages and pressure on the existing lodgings. The high death rate, which reached at least two peaks in the early fourteen century, created a pressing need to find new burial places in the lagoon, thus giving evidence of little-known waves of death that struck hardest at the poorest and most ill-lodged segment of the population.[44] Epidemics, poverty, and the many vicissitudes of a fragile existence threatened not only the physical family but also a family continuity, transmission, and memory that men had worked hard to construct.

For this very reason, and although it may seem paradoxical in these societies where historians tell us, somewhat schematically, the ideals of solidarity were so strongly developed, many people lived isolated lives. Their numbers become clear the moment the distorting screen of dovetailing solidarities crumbles. Among the wealthier and the more socially secure Venetians were prodigal sons who perturbed the course of family history, as well as some whose destinies escaped the common behavior patterns. Exclusion might also strike those who failed to follow the rules of the group. Usually, however, the kinship group, which was larger and sufficiently cohesive to surround and protect individuals, softened bad blows and prevented the black sheep from straying. Who, then, were the men and women whom we glimpse for a moment in the tax declarations of the proprietors of their lodgings, appearing for an instant before they fall back into obscurity? They were the many poor women who had no dowry or were past the marriageable age; or they were widows, and the widow was a common figure in every narrow street and courtyard. Widows were particularly numerous in societies in which a large age gap separated husband and wife and definitive widowhood came relatively early.[45] Most isolates were men, however, and in these decades of demographic discontinuities and replacement men flocked from the nearby countryside or more distant horizons to swell the contingent of social misfits in Venice. We should of course avoid generalizations: integration functioned, and we can find Germans or Greeks of a certain substance who were well settled into their street or their quarter. Still, at the edges of the city and near the port areas and the market there were immigrants who existed at the limits of poverty and found assimilation difficult. They lived side by side with other men born in the lagoon area, workers with a lamentably low standard of living, old or disabled seamen, all the unknowns in Venice triumphant about whom we know only that they were alone and often poor. Solitude might thus result from a number of structural factors characteristic of medieval life but also from a current situation of unfavorable circumstances. Moreover, the very order that reigned within the family and within society might secrete internal contestation and endogenous violence.

Disorder, Violence, and Resistance

In order for marriage, along with the social ties that it engendered, to exist there had to be some who were excluded from it or were either temporary or definitive misfits—surplus men who were difficult to integrate into the system because they were too young, too poor, or unstable. In Venice these were apt to be seamen, porters, apprentices, or day laborers. Even within the dominant lineages, however, not all life histories included marriage. It is known that in order to avoid the burden of multiple dowries on family fortunes, a certain number of daughters were destined for the convent, and others became tertiaries by choice.[46] It has been remarked less often that celibacy was imposed on some sons as well, both in the name of economic considerations and in order to limit the creation of collateral branches of the family.[47] These wifeless men developed modes of behavior that fell outside the practices that were the general rule. We can imagine that they all had liaisons with consenting partners: in the tradition of the novella, the seducer who intrudes on the conjugal space is always young. They might also patronize the public bordello, and the wealthier young men might have escapades with courtesans.[48] As far as we can tell, however, the clientele of the public houses always included a high proportion of foreigners and outsiders.[49] Seamen and merchants passing through Venice might pause in their business to visit the public house of prostitution or the baths, institutions whose clientele included foreigners and out-of-towners, as well as some of the poor and many of the unconnected men employed in the construction or shipbuilding industries.

Finally, there were frequent instances of sexual violence, although it should be emphasized that others besides young men unable to marry might be responsible for them. Women were often sexual prey and were chased, raped, and beaten. Some of these women were servants and slaves employed in the houses of nobles, bourgeois, or artisans, especially since, in practical terms, slaves and servant women had no recourse to law for protection against rape.[50] Women of popular milieus were also exposed to aggression day and night, in the street or in their houses, and attack on the part of an unknown, an acquaintance, or a neighbor was not limited to isolated women struggling with a harsh daily life with no family and no support. Many an attacker was the woman's putative husband or her father, and because these women were of the lower classes, they were obliged to frequent the streets and squares, which might prove dangerous. They were hardly any better protected in their small, one-room houses or in the open bedrooms of popular lodgings. A knife was all it took to open a door lock; a window could be broken with a push of a shoulder; boards could easily be removed from the thin partition walls of the houses.

Such repeated instances of disorderly conduct and common violence came to form an image in which the female body, far from being the object of attentive protection, became fragile, exposed to violence from individuals or groups determined to "know it by force." A totally different female identity appears here, revealing a different form of male domination. Even if that global explanation is insufficient to explain all rapes, the operation of the matrimonial market and its demographic, economic, and social constraints were clearly at the heart of the phenomenon. Young men, or in any event men excluded from marriage, were responsible for many of these violent acts. We must guard against anachronism, however, and take care not to interpret this sort of violence as arising from pure impulse or the "savage" side of men, young or less young. Admittedly, the laws defined rape as a crime, but the frequency with which the courts refrained from applying the severe statutory punishments is striking.[51] This leads me to the hypothesis that there very probably existed a subculture of rape within which the immediate possession of a female body by force was within the range of male sexual behavior in Venice.

The authorities in Venice, as in other Italian cities, also had to deal with transgressions that they considered much more serious because they challenged the very order of Creation, in which the city saw itself playing a role. Sodomy was a widespread, manifest sexual practice, or at least it was described as such in active attempts to repress it in the fifteenth century.

I shall not repeat descriptions of that combat, especially because trials for sodomy, which resulted from investigations and arrests of persons caught in flagrante delicto but also from denunciations, conceal a broad range of sexual behaviors. Attacks on children and adolescents came before the judges, and certain cases would have to be classified as pederasty, but perusal of the registers also shows instances of durable homosexual relationships. There were also cases of male procuration, and some genuine networks of male prostitution were broken up, but single individuals were charged as well. The practices that came before the courts were habitual in some cases but occasional in others; moreover, the judges distinguished between "active" and "passive" partners. Heterosexual sodomy, which was more frequently pursued in the courts in the late fifteenth century, fell under the same set of laws. The figures speak volumes: according to Guido Ruggiero, in Venice the Council of Ten brought close to five hundred cases before the courts in the fifteenth century.[52] Also according to Ruggiero, a homosexual "subculture" flourished in fifteenth-century Venice, whereas until that date "networks of homosexuality" had remained "at the bottom and margins of society."[53] Whatever one might think of this interpretation, the fact remains that the "abominable vice" was actively pursued by the new repressive institutions that all the major Italian cities put into place in the early fifteenth century.[54]

What are we to deduce from all this? The Church and the city invented a matrimonial order that tended, ideally, to subject sexual behaviors to rules and to work indefatigably to perpetuate the social body within that order. This model was less all-embracing than it seems, however, and a range of refractory sorts of conduct and transgressions of the rule developed. In marriage the woman was considered an object of exchange, an economic and symbolic capital to be mastered and protected, dominated and controlled. One result was the creation of a group of men who, for a variety of demographic, economic, and social reasons, were excluded from this institutionalized sexuality or who were still unmarried, given the customary age gap between husbands and wives. These men thus found an outlet for their sexual desires in violence toward women or, on occasion, in homosexual acts. It was the high status of women and marriage that directly or indirectly fed practices that denied female identity. It is clear that homosexuality may have functioned as a rejection of the woman or as a form of misogyny encouraged by representations of the woman as a distant and disquieting object.

These anomalous behaviors were lodged deep in the secret heart of the mechanisms of society. They and certain violent, bloody acts and practices of defiance were a part—or at least this is my hypothesis—of a broad range of symbolic rebellions that confronted the powers of Italy in the fourteenth and fifteenth centuries and that came to be neutralized because they were perpetual.[55]

The world of young males generated forms of opposition, rejection of a system of values, and a muffled criticism of a society in which old men exerted a domination that primarily concerned the state but also controlled patrimonies and women. These young men formed groups that are not well known but that were aimed at strengthening age solidarities and displayed a strong social homogeneity. The judges pursued them in the interest of repressing what they called a *mos juvenum*.[56]

There is evidence of youth bands and associations of young males, perhaps organized spontaneously. They usually met at night. Their members participated in rowdy gatherings and riotous behavior; they committed acts of vandalism and goaded the police forces into well-planned confrontations; they harassed the few nocturnal passersby with pleasantries that often degenerated into violence. They spared neither the order of the city and its

decor, which they vandalized, nor the order of the state and its representatives, the patrols of the Signori di Notte or the guards of the Council of Ten,
nor the order of a society whose rules they contested by their many violent
acts, sexual and other.[57]

It is customary to stress the youth companies' function of social integration, for example, in noisy and festive rituals. Perhaps. I do not contest that
role, which is well known.[58] The fact remains that the scope of their behavior
was a good deal broader than that. The members of these associations
displayed a sociability that had its own forms, rules, and rites, which the
judges—and this is a point I would like to stress—interpreted as proof of
intent to cause mischief. We must resist the temptation to view social interplay in those centuries with rose-colored glasses. These practices were not
simply the pranks of fun-loving, turbulent youths or new products of an
urban culture in formation. Nor were they society's only means for guiding
behavior. Young men (and children) were invested with ritual roles, and they
acted out those roles in organized groups.[59] Nonetheless, young males seem
to have caused trouble and committed violent acts in order to have their
own say; they used admittedly traditional means, including noisy and rowdy
behavior, to emit their own messages.

Far from being exclusive to the popular classes, some dangerous bands
were made up of young nobles, accompanied by their slaves or servants. In
the fifteenth century young patricians joined *compagnie della calza*, festive
brigades supervised by the Signoria that existed to organize entertainments
and festivities but on occasion also met for less official and more violent
amusements.[60] The roles of the young were thus not simply divided between
some young males who belonged to a joyous company or youth society and
others who were excluded from them, nor can we assign socialization to the
former and violence to the latter. Disorders and conflicts might contaminate
ritual occasions, but there were times when the *juvenes* spoke for themselves,
invading the public scene from which they were usually excluded. We find
here an exact equivalent of the troubles and tensions discussed above in the
context of political society. The "elders" found support for their solid command in other places than the highest levels of Venetian society. On all levels, young males who were accused of lacking restraint and moderation
attempted—without restraint and without moderation—to conquer a place
for themselves.

What can we conclude at the end of this brief excursion into the history of the *juvenes*? Some men acted and met together outside the boundaries of the family, either because they were trying to liberate themselves from their family of birth or because they had not yet established a new family. When they did so they assumed a number of functions of social mediation, but they also engaged in practices that were exclusive to them. Tolerance toward them wore thin. It is thus hardly surprising that the public powers made it their business, during the second half of the fifteenth century in particular, to subject the most precious of these young people, the young nobles, to increased discipline through *compagnie della calza* that were a genuine emanation of the patrician state. Nonetheless, three points should be kept in mind. First, the texts of the time reflect a singularly negative, even fearful image of youth, as if the *juvenes* represented a concrete danger. Second, when the criminal archives mention youth brigades, they seem to justify society's worst representations of them, thus proving at least the existence of conflict and capacities for indiscipline. Third, the example of the youth groups is enlightening because it shows how circles of friendship and sociability made up for the insufficiencies of the family (or the absence of a family) and provided the individual with needed support.

Such circles existed for everyone. They might be large or small, loosely organized or highly active, and they might undergo sweeping changes. In considering the various socially and geographically based nuclei that organized daily life, my discussion will center on the notion of a fragmented city. I shall attempt to answer a number of questions. Were neighborhood relations part of the life experience of everyone in Venetian society? Did most Venetians hold the neighborhood to be a primordial reference and the determining space of daily interaction? Did certain people also operate on a broader spatial scale? Above all, who were the social actors in these larger configurations? Were they all among the dominant? In short, can we determine different forms of the city and different cultures within the city?

THE CULTURES OF THE CITY

Such questions imply that the first thing we must do is examine the reality of the neighborly relations that historians often simply postulate or take as unvarying. As we have seen, the house inscribed in time the longevity of the most notable families. The dwelling had been constructed by the ancestors, in the past; it was bequeathed to the descendants, in the future. For individuals or families who maintained more modest relations with duration, the house at least established them within an area, a neighborhood, a social space. What relations pertained within this context? How can we define this establishment within a precise locality and discern the exchanges that it implied?[61]

The Fragmented City: Men and Women

It should be noted at the outset that locality did not place the same constraints on everyone. More than social position, gender imposed a first difference, because for men, whether artisans, wealthy commoners, or nobles, economic activity soon enlarged this first space of reference. One's trade or profession implied associations that reached beyond the immediate neighborhood. Often a group of adjoining parishes was enlivened by activities and exchanges of services. A particular quarter might be known and unified by its dominant economic activities, as was true of the silk-processing areas on the perimeter of Venice. Noble families had even broader networks, often mobilizing relatives, friends, and acquaintances throughout the city or at least in several *sestieri*. Male networks took different forms and varied in their scope. Both in theory and in practice such relational networks provided an executor of a will, a witness, a guarantor, an intermediary, the host for a wedding banquet, a godfather, and more. Depending on the individual case, everyone enjoyed flourishing and intertwined relations based on trade or profession, on membership in the same confraternity, on serving as godparent, or on a shared geographical origin.

Relations within the neighborhood quite certainly formed one such network, and when it coincided with another, for example, when a specific craft or trade was concentrated in one *contrada,* two solidarities might be merged. The evolution that began during the fifteenth century and eventually created some quarters with a high degree of socioeconomic homogeneity, as was the case in the area surrounding the Arsenal, operated in this fashion, creating a growing differentiation by position and status in relations among males. Even if the patrician did not neglect his capital of more modest local clients, dependants, and favor-seekers, it was no longer on the scale of the quarter that he measured his prestige and influence. On the other hand, some workers found that their urban horizons narrowed when social topography grew more fixed and life came to be organized within the borders of a few neighboring *contrade*. A man who worked in the nearby shipyard or bake oven might walk along the central *salizzada,* stopping for a drink at the corner tavern, which might serve contraband wine. In doing so he might encounter people he knew, taking the opportunity to pause to exchange news across a small canal, while crossing a bridge, or while waiting for the *traghetto.*[62]

Men were thus well aware of the local community, and even though the sources rarely mention day-to-day neighborhood relations or the spaces in which they existed, there were games played on the *campo* or in the *calle,* passing exchanges, even friendships born of proximity and of wine drunk in company under the shade of a fig tree or by a boat tied up at the water's edge. Other, more lively circles were grafted onto this first circle of neighborhood relations. Social interactions are complex affairs, and a distinction should be made between those arising out of work, sociability, leisure, and residence.

Female networks offer a different model. The wills of Venetian women of the popular class are repetitious to the point of banality. After the obligatory phrases and a few pious remembrances, they list the husband and the children, who receive the better part of the estate, but they also reflect another way of organizing social relations. Females from the immediate vicinity appear, and a next-door neighbor, a friend, or the marriageable daughter of an associate is often remembered with a gift of a little money, an article of clothing, or perhaps a length of cloth. Female generosity depicts the narrow spaces of neighborly relations and traces tight nuclei of sociability. The topographical details given for the benefit of the executors describe the buildings around a courtyard, the houses lining a *calle,* or a clutch of lodgings in the same housing unit. These brief touches reveal the social microgeography of a *contrada.*

Certain networks display vertical solidarities. Noble women and wealthy non-noble women acted as patrons for neighborhood women. Their testaments gave them an opportunity to repay a small debt, reward a midwife, and perpetuate beyond the tomb circles created by patronage, by living in proximity, and by friendship. Instead of leaving money for a purely mercenary posthumous pilgrimage to certain of the churches of Venice, some of the wealthier women preferred to combine alms and penance by assuring themselves, at the cost of a few ducats, the pious devotions of a poor neighbor woman. In turn, some women of modest, even obscure condition preferred to charge a powerful neighbor woman with responsibility for their meager estate rather than have someone of a status equal to their own take on the task, thus increasing their own honor and that of the living patroness. Such a search for postmortem patronage was practiced even outside the limited category of female servants and freed slaves. All of these acts, hierarchical exchanges, and thoughtful little gestures within the female community demonstrate the warmth of relations that were established within the quarter and a common desire to recognize the duties inherent in social position. This sociability was reinforced by membership in parish female religious organizations, by holiday meals, and by ritual entertainments. Banquets and gatherings of women accompanied the Festival of the Twelve Marys, for example, at least as it was celebrated until the end of the fourteenth century.[63]

Such small bequests stipulated in the nonreligious clauses of women's wills, of which we have tens of examples, show that an entourage of females surrounded the wealthy testatrix. These bequests diminish in number and in size only in the wills of women of a more modest condition. Only the wills of the poorest women omit them. They had nothing to bequeath, but did this mean that they were without friends? I think not. These exchanges gave cohesion to the territory of the *contrada*, and they throw light on forms of sociability and on the contours of a hidden world that suddenly springs to life.

Still, this world of female loyalties and solidarities was not wholly contained within the parish. Women at the high end of the social scale moved in a vaster space. After bequests to members of their lineage of origin, their wills often list gifts that reach beyond the area of residence to show the geographical and social range of their friendship network. These remembrances evoke a varied society: an old nurse, a former servant woman, a "friend." With the help of such indications we can trace some of the testatrix's itineraries in the city as, accompanied by a chaperone or servant, she visited relatives; they reflect a lasting attachment to the microquarter of her birth.

At the lower end of the social scale we find more consistent mention of nearby parishes. Female relationships transcended the immediate borders of the *contrada* to be inscribed in a larger territory that in many cases was their quarter of origin. In the absence of sufficient data or representative samples, we can only formulate hypotheses regarding marriage alliance among the common people. Parish endogamy does not seem to have been particularly strong. Marriages were concluded instead within a group of parishes, a larger area defined by daily exchanges and the constraints of getting from one place to another. By their visits to one another and by the routes they took as they moved through the city, women maintained connections and strengthened old relationships. In all cases, although women may also have operated in a second social space (large or small, nearby or distant), the framework of the *contrada*, conceived not so much as a whole but rather as a group of compartmentalized areas of neighborly relations, played a strong role in women's lives and determined their social customs.

We have seen throughout this discussion how alliance, spiritual kinship, and even the exercise of the same trade might at times bring together even more closely people who were already united by living in close proximity. In Venice the *contrada* coincided with the parish, and the confusion of these two contexts undoubtedly reinforced their effectiveness, but it also complicates any examination of local society and its modes of life.

The Fragmented City: The Parish and the Quarter

In the *contrada* that coincided with the parish friends also saw one another at church, and they met again in the cemetery. The circle of one's friends and relations was one and the same as the group of the faithful. The neighborhood community became the spiritual community as it was united, even fused, in prayer and in the Christian rites accompanying life and death. Venetians joined together to honor the patron saint to whom the parish church was dedicated. Together they participated in the festivities that marked the Christmas cycle or the Carnival season; lingered after mass to hear the public crier make such announcements of interest to the life of the *contrada* as real-estate sales or delays accorded in tax payments; and frequented the meetings of a parish confraternity. All of these many occasions, these many acts of listening, acting, and talking, created connections or sanctioned and reinforced the fabric of society on the local scale.

Christians had a special attachment to their church, its bell tower, and its surrounding area. Practices evolved, however, and in the fifteenth century Venetians' relationship with their parish tended to vary with social status, displaying many subtle variations. To trace these changes briefly, in the fourteenth century membership in the spiritual community of the parish church was all-important. The immense majority of the masses endowed at a testator's hour of death were celebrated in the local church. If a confraternal group was remembered in a will, it was the parish confraternity. More detailed bequests to support the church building or provide candles also went to the nearby church. Parish members were buried in the parish church, with no need of prior arrangements. Death recreated the same space as life. In this usual course of affairs, this widespread mode of living and dying, it is difficult to separate the part played by habit, the influence of the priest (who was often also the notary), and the strength of a group attachment to the local church and its bell tower. To die was to remain within the spaces of one's life and one's relationship with God; it was also to remain near one's own. A few notables, nobles or wealthy commoners, had begun to reach out toward a larger sacred space, leaving a bequest, for example, to one of the great mendicant friaries or to a confraternity outside the parish. What such dispositions show, however, is the pull of the quarter and the power of attraction exerted by the nearest great mendicant friary over a number of parishes.

During the fifteenth century such shifts accelerated as the city's physical growth slowed, and Venice tended to present itself as one sacred unit. To be sure, local pious institutions did not disappear, and the parish was not forgotten in this moment of change. Still, step by step, pious donations shifted. More and more frequently, testators specified other places of burial than the parish cemetery or the parish church and its portal. Bequests for masses, once numerous, tend to thin out. A simple list of the churches cited in wills enables us to evaluate the scope of this change. Where the sacred landscape had been organized around the nearby church and one of the great mendicant churches, a century later wealthy testators name ten or twenty sacred buildings to which they leave bequests. There is a clear tendency toward diversifying one's options; in a more unified city, testators at the hour of death generally left money to a larger variety of intercessors. Differences still existed: the nobles and the wealthiest commoners made their most generous bequests to the great monasteries and friaries. The remembrance given to the parish church and its chapter was by then seen as a traditional pious act. For others, their primary place of worship came first. It is not surprising that women and certain commoners generally retained the traditional attachment, and this was even more consistent among the poorest parishioners and the newcomers, for whom finding a place in the community was of prime importance. Their wills stand out from the mass of acts that have been conserved by explicitly stating an intention to set down roots and a desire to be integrated into the spiritual family of the parish.

Shifting charitable practices confirm these metamorphoses. Hospitals began to receive a greater share of bequests, while other forms of assistance declined. Fewer bequests are listed for charitable distributions within the *contrada,* for the funeral meal (a rarity by the fourteenth century), or for distributions of alms in the form of clothing or coin. When wills do retain clauses benefiting local charities, which assisted known poor who lived nearby and were members of the community, such bequests reflect the desire of a few parishioners to bolster their social position by returning to symbolic practices that were slowly being abandoned. Such bequests often come from the newly rich or the formerly powerful.

What are we to make of these scattered bits of information? Everyone, or nearly everyone, had a soft spot in his or her heart for the parish bell tower, the *campanile.* For men, it signaled their life within a community of which they were a part. It symbolized their ties to a known territory defined both by their daily movements and by a sentimental geography, and it reminded them that their individual and family history was incorporated into the history of that society. Ordinary acts and daily exchanges but also most of the rites in the life of a Christian took place within these familiar places, in a relation of at least physical proximity to neighbors. On certain occasions that same familiar space might spring to life as the entire local community assembled to celebrate a feast day, commemorate a series of miracles, or attend celebrations in the church. On such occasions the community insignia—banners, boats, relics conserved in the church that was dedicated to the local patron saint—played their accustomed role and reasserted collective identity. If some conflict should arise opposing that society to the society of the neighboring islet, ancient rivalries and old solidarities spontaneously sprang back to life.[64] Within each parish society the *campo,* a small square in front of the church that often had a markedly residential atmosphere, operated as the natural center of the urban nucleus, a role based on both its importance as an empty space in a crowded city and its multiple functions.

It is clear, though, that life in Venice was not totally circumscribed within these boundaries. Certain of the larger *campi* took on other functions and served a broader area, sometimes for a while, sometimes permanently. These were meeting places, spaces to live in and share. Once again sites fell into a hierarchy, spaces dovetailed, and practices were superimposed on one another; once again an area came to be formed, presided over by a church.

The open spaces around the churches of the great mendicant orders, Santa Maria Gloriosa dei Frari (for the Franciscans) and Santi Giovanni e Paolo (for the Dominicans), illustrate this process. Processions and funeral corteges made their way around these squares; boats bearing the dead tied up at a landing on the nearby canal. The masses said and the sermons preached in these imposing churches had a broad resonance, setting the tone for devotions that increased in intensity during Advent or Lent. Day after day the candle vendors did a brisk business, selling their wares to passersby from near and far. The many chapels of these immense churches held the tombs of lineages and confraternities. Relatively obscure confraternities met in these churches, but they also served as the headquarters of the great flagellant *scuole*. One of these was the Scuola Grande di San Marco, which rebuilt its quarters next to Santi Giovanni e Paolo after its former building was destroyed by fire. The strange and lovely facade of the Scuola, decorated with sculptures and bas-reliefs and encrusted with colored marble, was begun about 1487 by Pietro Lombardo and Giovanni Buora and finished in 1490–95 by Mauro Coducci. Another major confraternity, the Scuola Grande di San Rocco, had its quarters near the church of Santa Maria Gloriosa dei Frari.

In short, the larger squares, churches, and *scuole* were major centers whose gravitational pull embraced an entire quarter and at times an even larger section of the city. Less illustrious monastic institutions also provided urban and social spaces that energized a group of parishes and served all who came to the church to listen to a sermon or who drew water from the cistern in their *campo*.

The threads of our discourse are thus tangled. The myth of the neighborhood was active in the contemporary imagination, and its effects have touched the imagination of historians as well. As a result, the local community is often considered an immutable model, a normal and constant context in older societies, as if the village had necessarily been recreated within the city. Neighborliness was not a permanent state of the social organization, however; it was simply one form of the possible, and in the Venice that we are investigating its importance varied according to the gender and socioeconomic position of the individual, customs, and periods. Moreover, this particular form of social organization seems to have lost some of its clarity, at least in some people's minds, toward the end of the Middle Ages.[65] History does not advance simply or in linear fashion, however. During the sixteenth century a contrary trend arose among a good portion of the Venetian population that reemphasized neighborhood relations and local modes of existence.[66] Finally, the reality of a first, local level on which life was lived and relational networks were structured does not exclude other levels on which social relations operated.

From the Fragmented City to the City Recomposed: Venetian Confraternities

Brian Pullan has written that the ordinary devotional life of good Catholics in medieval and Renaissance Venice was strongly influenced, if not dominated, by the confraternities.[67] The vitality of the confraternal movement was nothing new. Such associations multiplied in the West in the fourteenth and fifteenth centuries, and their broad distribution shows that they responded to a genuine need, filling a gap left by other support structures. I shall not repeat here the history of the rise and dissemination of these brotherhoods, nor shall I insist that in Venice as elsewhere they constituted a response to a need to join a corporate body, a palliative and a defense, and an insurance policy against poverty, loneliness, and the anguish of a solitary death. The confraternities carried on charitable and cultural activities, with each member contributing to the salvation of the others as well as to his own. They encouraged social integration, both horizontally and vertically; they imposed rules for living collectively; and they reinforced solidarities in the name of an ideal of fraternity.

Confraternities might be wealthy or poor, ephemeral or durable, prestigious or relatively obscure, and their members were both influential and humble. These organizations were many and varied, but all of them were subjected—and this is a first common trait—to strict public surveillance. Everywhere, the public powers and the ecclesiastical authorities worked concurrently, occasionally condemning confraternal associations, always limiting their activities to a few carefully defined areas. In Venice, however, the state exercised much more control over the confraternities than did the Church hierarchy. Public tutelage could be extremely strict, although, as Richard Mackenney remarks, we must take care not to take too lofty a view of their history and see them only through the distorting prism of public documentation.[68]

The role of the *scuole piccole* should not be underestimated in our reconstitution of the social framework of Venice. The earliest of these were trade brotherhoods. Many appeared in the late thirteenth century, in association with the crafts but distinct from them, and they proliferated all the more easily because several brotherhoods might serve the same trade.[69] There were also a large number of devotional companies, which evolved as forms of piety changed.[70] A new wave of Marian piety, for example, gathered the faithful together around the practice of the rosary.[71] It was in Venice, in 1506, that Albrecht Dürer painted *The Virgin of the Rose Garlands*, a much-admired work, for the Confraternity of the Rosary in the church of San Bartolomeo. There were also *scuole* of the *Santissimo Sacramento* and *scuole del Venerabile*, founded in growing numbers during the sixteenth century to promote the cult of the Eucharist.[72] In fact many associations worked together within the framework of the ordinary life of the parish, including some that served the foreign communities. Among the Italians, the Milanese placed their brotherhood under the patronage of St. Ambrose, whose altar was in the Church of the Frari; the Florentines, who also gathered at the Frari, dedicated their association to the Virgin and St. John the Baptist.[73] Brothers from Bergamo congregated at San Silvestro, the Lucchese met at San Giovanni di Rialto, and so on. Germans had their own associations, often linked to their professions, as did the many "nations" that peopled the cosmopolitan city of Venice.[74] There were men's associations, women's associations, and mixed groups; there was no end to the refinement of their categories and no limit to the list. According to Marino Sanudo, there were perhaps two hundred such societies in Venice in 1500. One person might have different reasons for joining several groups: defense of professional interests, a search for intercessors, a felt need to join several companies. The *scuole piccole* proliferated, often with memberships of several hundred. They appealed to the majority of men and women rather than to a lay elite that practiced a more intense piety. Commentators have stressed their role in supporting the established order, seeing in this large number of groups that fragmented the social body but also incessantly welded it together an instrument for maintaining control, peace, and discipline.

Many of these confraternal nuclei reached beyond their immediate locality to recruit members from the entire city. Among these, the flagellant confraternities amply demonstrate that these societies ceaselessly strove to construct cohesion.[75]

More than simply visible, the flagellant confraternities were downright conspicuous in Venetian life. Texts and images depict them occupying a prominent place in the hierarchical order of march in processions. Their buildings in the various quarters of the city—reconstructed, decorated, and enlarged—dot the monumental landscape.[76] Because these societies were wealthy, they commissioned grandiose decorative programs for their quarters, works that in many cases still exist and are counted among the best-known examples of Venetian painting.[77] Their memory lives on in these works, aided by voluminous archives and a painstaking historiography.[78]

Let's take the chronology first: Santa Maria della Carità seems to have been the first confraternity, and tradition states that its statutes, which date from 1260, served as a model for subsequent *scuole grandi.* Thus it appeared in the same year in which flagellant processions flourished throughout Italy, spreading from Perugia, and the prophecies of Joachim of Fiore inspired a strong penitential tension and eschatalogical enthusiasms. Other confraternities—San Giovanni Evangelista, Santa Maria della Misericordia, and San Marco—were founded soon thereafter. These four *scuole* later became six (as many as the *sestieri* into which the city was divided) with the constitution of the companies of San Rocco (1489) and San Teodoro (1552). The flagellant confraternities were originally known as *scuole dei battuti,* a name they retained until 1467, when the Council of Ten, their supervisory body, began to designate them as *scolae magnae,* or *scuole grandi.*[79]

The statutes stipulated that the members of the *scuole,* who were exclusively adult males, were to "discipline themselves" during processions and on a number of ceremonial occasions. Soon, however, the *scuole* began to accept members who were dispensed from rites of self-flagellation, and as their membership changed their ideal model of fraternal life changed as well. Patricians were what we would call "honorary members": they were exempt from the obligation of flagellation and could join a *scuola* without requesting permission from the Council of Ten or paying an initiation fee.[80] By the fifteenth century a hierarchy had been established among the brothers. The chapter, now reserved to the *fratelli da capitolo,* ceased being a plenary assembly, and the "chapter brothers," dispensed from ritual flagellation, had exclusive responsibility for the administration of the *scuola.*[81] The other members, known as *fratelli alla disciplina,* continued to practice self-flagellation during processions; in accordance with a carefully regulated exchange, they were also the ones who benefited from the *scuola's* generous distributions of aid.

The forms of that assistance merit examination. These societies of *battuti* quite naturally emphasized meditation on the Passion; equally naturally, attending the dead was one of their missions. Their aid at the moment of that great journey, the massive presence of confraternity members at the funeral ceremonies, and prayers for the dead were unquestioned duties. With time, however, charitable works and activities tended to have the highest priority. Following a widespread model, these companies first turned to supporting a hospital and caring for the poor. At different dates they built, enlarged, and transformed "the place of the poor of the *scuola,*" but such institutions could provide only limited support, as one example will suffice to show. After its move near the church of Santi Giovanni e Paolo, the confraternity of San Marco charged several of the brothers with responsibility for a hospital, specifying that it would have a capacity of from eight to twelve beds.[82] The *scuole* used their real-estate holdings for public assistance, and they gradually became genuine charitable institutions.

The economic base of the *scuole* permitted this shift of focus because they were soon able to attract a large membership. Officially, these companies were supposed to have between five hundred and six hundred members, but as early as the fifteenth century their actual membership was higher. The reason for this rise in numbers was simple: the *scuole* urgently needed money. Rivalry among them was keen, particularly in processions, in the creation of tableaux vivants, and in the richness of their decor and illumination. Moreover, the *scuole* had taken on major commitments to reconstruct and adorn their meeting rooms, their *albergo*. None wanted to be outdone. It has been calculated, to cite one example, that between the end of the fifteenth century and the beginning of the seventeenth century Santa Maria della Misericordia invested some 32,000 ducats in the building and decoration of its new headquarters.[83] The Scuola Grande di San Rocco was luckier: Tintoretto painted his first canvas there free of charge, and after he became a member of the confraternity, he devoted the rest of his life to the decoration of the building.[84] This meant that all the *scuole* used the obvious expedient of admitting supplementary members who were able to pay the initiation fee, the *benintrada*. Postulants were never lacking, because one could expect profits, both spiritual and material, from membership in a *scuola*. Before the severe plague epidemic of 1576 the Scuola Grande di San Giovanni Evangelista had some 1,800 members; in 1585 the Scuola di Santa Maria della Misericordia had 1,500 members. Most of the brothers remembered the *scuola* to which they belonged in their wills, and some left sizable bequests in the form of public loan shares, houses, warehouses, and lands. As a consequence, all of the *scuole* had a stock of properties, which increased overall at the end of the fifteenth century.[85] Houses might be bequeathed to found a charity, but the chapters also used cash gifts and bequests, income on properties, and their ordinary resources to pursue a policy of real-estate purchases and sales. Although some of these houses had rental tenants and brought in additional revenue, many were given *amore dei*, "for the love of God," to poor confraternity members.

Not all aid in Venice was channeled through the *scuole*. The city had a growing network of hospitals, and Venetians' generosity at their hour of death was regularly channeled into institutions such as San Lazzaro, La Pietà, or, later, Sant'Antonio. At times a larger bequest that left a perpetual legacy could found a charitable institution, administered by the Procurators of San Marco.[86] Hospices were set up and financed for "twelve poor men," "eight impoverished widows," or "four women in need." Still, in an age in which the older tradition of charitable works within the parish was in decline, the *scuole grandi* assumed an increasing role in assistance in the form of bread distributions, dowries for poor young women, lodgings given *amore dei,* and so forth. Their charitable works were no longer addressed exclusively to their own members, and the confraternities even found themselves constrained to take on assistance to prisoners and their families.[87]

At the end of the sixteenth century the confraternities faced financial difficulties. State levies, contributions for the navy in particular, had become heavier and heavier. As a consequence the *scuole grandi* lost some of their appeal, while new institutions of public aid increased their audience. The *scuole* had nonetheless had a moment of glory during the decades when the citizens of Venice jostled for the privilege of administering them and they were a powerful stabilizing factor in Venetian society.

These associations have traditionally been credited with several qualities, first among them that they contributed to social peace, as both native and foreign observers of the Venetian scene often noted from the sixteenth century on.[88] After all, did their management of the system for doing good works not grant the citizen class a notable area of power? Nothing could be truer, at least as long as the state refrained from attacking the forms of patron-client relations that they encouraged. Thus the *scuole grandi,* along with many other elements in Venetian society, are seen as having participated in maintaining institutional and social equilibrium. The charity they dispensed was real, however, all the more so because their largesse was distributed throughout the urban area.[89] In zones of strong urban growth with a high concentration of popular housing, that is, in places where the demand for aid was high, the confraternities fulfilled what seems to have been an essential mission.

The *scuole grandi* were not neighborhood institutions, though. One need only examine the membership lists or collect data from wills to sense their wide appeal, even though most *scuole* tended to concentrate their efforts on one side or the other of the Grand Canal. Often, in fact, *da capitolo* members joined a particular *scuola* for family reasons or other personal reasons.

We can conclude that the *scuole grandi* operated, in the late Middle Ages and at the beginning of the modern age, as broadly defined assistential societies. They operated in the name of a clear awareness of economic disparities, and thanks to a division of the functions and duties among their members they encompassed other groups and associations and brought large segments of the social body into one heterogeneous but united group.

One final form of the possible remains to be examined; one last map of how Venice functioned, this time on the scale of the city as a whole. With it my analysis of the city's dovetailing operations ends.

The City Recomposed: The Centers of Venice

Certain practices confirm the reality of Venice as an urban space interlaced with streets and canals and organized around a few great centers. They show how Venetians moved within their city and the relations they maintained with the physical framework of their lives.

Everything indicates that the customs on display in any larger city space were primarily male customs. The very structure of the city, with the early crystallization of a commercial zone at Rialto, made that qualification inevitable. What can we learn from the detailed indications of time and place given in sources that describe daily economic life? Men, both nobles and commoners, who appear as witnesses to a contract or who report a conversation describe going from one quarter to another to negotiate an agreement, witness a document, or serve as guarantor for a loan. The settings they depict are above all the market and Piazza San Marco. What are we to make of this? The principal city market created the objective conditions of such meetings by the functions granted to it, but the area of Piazza San Marco, although strikingly invested with power and its signs, also served as a familiar community space, standing as it did at the point of convergence of the main city itineraries. In their habits Venetians recognized the attraction exerted by the centers that animated the city. Nor was it just the wealthy, the actors directly engaged in broad-based economic operations, who developed this culture of the city. Often for very ordinary matters, because they hoped to find work there or because they enjoyed frequenting places where they met others, men found things to do in public space.

This does not mean that women were radically excluded from such spaces. Some women went to the Rialto or to the market halls of San Marco because they worked there selling bread, fruit, eggs, or greens; peasant women brought baskets of salad greens, plums, or melons to the markets from the edges of the city or from the islands of the lagoon and the duchy. They did not challenge men's right to their special preserves—the fish market and the butchers' hall. Other women may have frequented the markets to buy things. Evidence is lacking, and images of markets and squares usually portray a universe peopled almost entirely by male figures. Still, servants and women of modest means were not the only ones who risked leaving the domestic space or a familiar home territory. Sumptuary legislation bears witness to this. A fourteenth-century decree restricted the sale of jewels to the market of the Rialto, but in the face of protests from members of the goldsmiths' guild, who complained of a decline in business because honorable women refused to venture into a business quarter and an area where prostitution flourished, the prohibition was lifted in 1394 and the sale of jewelry was once more permitted at San Polo and San Marco.[90] We are led to believe that it was above all the proximity of prostitutes that limited the liberty of movement of Venetian women. If women of the better classes were loath to subject themselves to male gazes at Rialto, they apparently minded less if this occurred on Piazza San Marco or at the market at San Polo!

Still, the particular organization of economic life in Venice is insufficient to explain the phenomenon of the city's unity. Genoa was at least as deeply engaged in trade and commerce as Venice, but its urban space continued to be narrowly compartmentalized. The evolution of governmental structures greatly influenced this difference. In Venice, the progressive construction of a strong central authority led to weakening systems of local influence, or at least to limiting their importance. The fact that noble families lived permanently in one place did not produce any immobility either in spatial terms or in social relations within the *contrada*. Rather, local bases of power gradually dissolved as the patrician political regime was constructed. The relationship between political authority and its area of exercise was transformed, and that change was abetted and accelerated by urban-renewal projects that worked to modify the city's morphology, reversing the original fragmentation of communities and facilitating relations with distant or out-of-the-way islands. The aim of the city's urban policy was of course to enable Venice to adapt to its role as a commercial marketplace. This meant that public spaces to serve the market and the port had to be created, and the infrastructure indispensable for all types of exchange had to be installed or enlarged. Improvements also responded to the new demographic conditions of the city and to the circulation needs of a constantly expanding urban complex. They also had the goal of consolidating a regime, putting into place a political and social order, and translating forms of power into spatial terms. Reference to the local scene thus tended to become secondary, or rather the long reach and the power of attraction of the greater community's spaces superimposed another reference on the local one.

It is easy to stress the functions that civic spaces assumed in Venice, and the topic has received a good deal of scholarly attention. We have seen just such an inventory in the discussions of Piazza San Marco and the market at the Rialto in previous chapters. Great political rituals, religious celebrations, the spectacle of justice and its sentences—nothing has been omitted. I have shown that these places served as a stage and also as the almost obligatory receptacle into which festivities, ceremonies, and all the many manifestations of identification and unification flowed. We have also seen how important such ritual occasions were to a representation of the city and the creation of its image. Still, it is not enough to describe official rituals and stress their connection with a prestigious topography marked by the signs of public power. A study of society needs to grasp the role of the group in such manifestations. Thus it has become customary to take the pulse of the processions and their spectacles of harmony and cohesion; to depict the trade guilds and the confraternities as they parade by; to recompose the hierarchy of "estates" and assert the defeat of the threat of dissociation and the unity of the urban body thanks to the participation of all these groups. Anyone who is not content to remain within the classic analyses of the cortege and its composition finds that further information is more tenuous. Some indications do crop up, however, in fragmentary notations scattered in highly disparate sources. One text tells us that two lagoon dwellers from Murano donned their best clothes to attend a celebration in San Marco. Or our text might be a well-known but eloquent painting: Gentile Bellini's depiction of the procession of the relics of the True Cross shows not only the marchers but the people watching the cortege. There are also letters and relations of foreigners, unanimous in their insistence that men and women, rich and poor, nobles and commoners, participated in such ceremonies. Finally, there is Marino Sanudo's description of Piazza San Marco on Palm Sunday 1495, when the customary procession also celebrated the formation of the Holy League to combat the French invaders. As Sanudo describes the scene, the entire city seems to have gathered on the Piazza: Venetians were so tightly crowded on the square, in the church, and on the balconies that they could hardly budge.

All Venice marched in procession, everyone in his proper place; all Venice watched the marchers parade by in perfect harmony. In this moment of collective celebration the witnesses—the spectators—also became actors. The community played and replayed one of the essential scenes of its cohesion. Such remarks, which are banal and in part conventional, probably contributed to fix even more firmly the image of a society of concord and unanimity. They nonetheless deserve comment since they indicate that it was not only men or the dominant classes who felt the attraction of the major centers of San Marco and the Rialto.[91] Upper-class women were present, and the descriptions take care to note their luxurious attire. The sumptuary laws were in abeyance on such occasions, and the law texts that codify public rituals, the *Cerimoniali*, state that female dress was an explicit sign of wealth that brought additional honor to the city. There were of course other women present who had no need of laws limiting the number of pearl necklaces they might wear or how long their sleeves should be.

The group gathered. The chronicles relate these circumstances of collective life, these times of happy tension and festivity when all, or almost all, Venetians abandoned their houses, streets, or shops to converge at the center of the city. To be sure, there were many feast days on the calendar throughout the year, and not all celebrations were of equal importance. Nor was their attraction identical: each had its own resonance. Undoubtedly the Feast of the Twelve Marys and the Sensa, both of which were mythic expressions of the Venetian past, made all hearts beat faster. The first of these occasions evoked the young people of Rialto; the second, the origins of Venice's grandeur. Together they forged a closer union and manifested the uniqueness of the lagoon. There are many indications that Venetians of all walks of life subscribed to and participated joyfully in these celebrations.

Only by insisting on the importance of the devotions rendered to Venice's patron saint can we understand the emotional pull of San Marco. Civic religion deeply affected the history of Italian cities, as is known,[92] but in Venice the power structure's early and victorious appropriation of the values of celebration and legitimation inherent in the cult of the patron saint carried civic religion to an extreme. The Evangelist and the community on the lagoon, St. Mark and the Venetian Signoria, were one. The lion of St. Mark was portrayed on the basilica, on the palace of government, on the Campanile in Piazza San Marco, and on the Clock Tower. Represented in various ways, the lion served as an almost exclusive symbol of the city, eclipsing all other figurations.[93] He holds an open book that displays the words on which Venice's *praedestinatio* was founded. At the very center of the city the divine election conferred on Venice and the Venetians is repeated in the form of infinitely redundant images.

Finally, there was the basilica of San Marco, the true epicenter of the sacred space of Venice, which means that the evolution of the sacred geography of the city and of Venetian devotions also counted for much in the definition of the city as one unit. The basilica radiated over this territory, well protected by the watery wall of the lagoon, made sacred by a host of religious buildings and precious relics, surrounded by great churches that created new spatial coordinates. The cathedral of San Pietro di Castello, situated far away at the eastern edge of the city, played only a minor role in urban devotions. One Milanese pilgrim who passed through Venice on his way to Jerusalem gives a particularly lucid description of the marginal setting of the city's "mother church": "The patriarchal Church or Cathedral is called the Church of San Pietro. It has not many ornaments. I think that Saint Mark, who was his disciple, must have stolen them."[94] Nothing could be truer. The basilica was built in imitation of the Church of the Holy Apostles in Constantinople. It was twice reconstructed on the Byzantine model, and it continued to receive decorations, trophies, spoils of war, and the wealth of the East. The quadriga of gilded bronze horses stands above the portal; the southern facade contains the porphyry group of the Tetrarchs, two sculpted columns called the Pillars of Acre, and Byzantine bas-reliefs. Inside the church, there are other marbles from the East and hundreds of imported columns, surrounded by medieval copies.

No important occasion was celebrated without a mass at San Marco or without having the faithful crowd into that monument, where everything expressed not only an infinite richness but also the privileged role of Venice in glorification of the faith. The Pala d'Oro, a gold altar screen 3.15 meters wide and 2.10 meters high, dazzles the viewer with silver and gold leaf decorations, precious stones, and cloisonné enamels set into a host of panels surrounding the image of the Pantocrator.[95] The treasury contains other marvels, many of them the spoils of pillage: enamels, worked gold pieces, precious reliquaries and their holy contents.[96] On the vaults, the cupolas, and the upper surfaces of the walls the grand iconographic schemes in mosaic against a gold background constantly reiterate the theme of Venice as

God's chosen city. Prime examples of this are the Descent of the Holy Ghost, which occupies the center of the ceiling in the nave, and the biblical scenes in the narthex.[97] The legend of St. Mark, represented in ten medallions on the Pala d'Oro, reappears here in colorful scenes against a gold field; again in the mosaics of the galleries and the Zen chapel; yet again on the six bas-reliefs of the lower galleries, along the *presbyterium,* and in several of the scenes that decorate the gothic altar. St. Mark, surround by other saintly protectors, is pictured once more in the central apse of the presbytery.[98] A mosaic at the entry to the basilica after a cartoon probably by Titian (1545) shows the saint dressed in pontifical vestments and preparing to celebrate mass, replacing the Christ Pantocrator. Upon entering the basilica, the first thing the faithful see is the face of the patron saint.

Aside from solemn moments when the cult of the saintly protector of Venice tended to merge into a cult of the city itself, there were many other times when people gathered in Piazza San Marco. There were always exceptional festive occasions, religious or profane, such as a tourney, a joust, or a mystery play. On some such occasions a platform stage would be set up and arrangements made for an audience. Other gatherings were spontaneous, with no previous organization. News of a Venetian victory brought the population running joyfully to the Piazza. Bad news had the same effect: if the Venetian fleet had been defeated or a far-off base had been lost, Venetians gathered in Piazza San Marco to hear the news and lament in company.

Ceremonies took place there, and Venetians made their way there at critical moments. All civic spaces, but Piazza San Marco in particular, for a time became the metaphorical loci of the community, the spaces of all (or almost all) citizens.

This is an ideal vision, and we should not give in to it unresistingly. It had strict counterpoints. Deviant and antagonistic rituals aimed at contestation, for example, occurred in spaces that were equally deviant in relation to this official public stage. I am thinking of Marino Sanudo's harsh descriptions of certain penitential processions that formed spontaneously behind an incendiary preacher and wound their way in disorder and with "fury" through the streets and over the bridges at the edges of outlying parishes. Another culture probably functioned on both the margins of society and the edges of the city. In its most ambitious projects the Venetian government of the late fifteenth century aimed at transforming the urban periphery and reshaping the "extremities of the city" in the image of the center. It would be a mistake to think that aesthetic impulses alone inspired such projects. The desire to impose better control over the uncertain confines of the city, where the poor and the last arrivals congregated, was also ideological. The documentation regarding these "other" cultures or cultures of contestation is far from abundant, and it is always indirect, given that its source is the "haves," or at least the solidly installed. The few indications we do have reveal that for Venetians of the central city there were "places far off and incommodious" in the sestiere of Santa Croce or at the caò of Cannaregio, frontier areas whose urban status the inhabitants of the center city were far from fully recognizing.[99] It is logical to suppose that for the people in those "places far-off and incommodious" the distant culture of the center was just as foreign.

The fact remains that the mirage of the center had an extraordinary force. Very probably most people shared a desire to take part in the common experiences, to be involved in the culture of the city that so naturally superimposed itself, on certain occasions, on the culture of the neighborhood and the quarter. There were of course exiles and rebels in the history of Venice, but multiple instruments were used to produce unity and enhance the common dream, to bring the community to life, imagine it, and represent it as an organic, firmly cohesive whole.

The city was thus its own imaginary, its own mythology. This was how the Venetian identity, in a constant mirror effect, fashioned the Venetian system in the centuries of the Middle Ages and the Renaissance.

Conclusion

It is thus on Piazza San Marco and with a final image suggesting that the imaginary had the function of dictating or forging an awareness of reality that this series of evocations of the historical spaces of Venice in the Middle Ages and the Renaissance comes to a close.

The rosy hues of the Ducal Palace and the gold of the basilica provide a broad range of chromatic effects. Thanks to its domes, mosaics, and vaults, the basilica reconstitutes the splendor of Byantium. The Gothic of the Ducal Palace proudly displays Moorish elements. The Porta della Carta, another Gothic monument, teems with decorative sculptures and ornamentation. St. Theodore tops one of the monumental columns that define the limits of the Piazzetta; the lion of St. Mark stands on the other. Like the city itself, the entire decor of San Marco plays back and forth between East and West. It recalls the Byzantine past and the city's longstanding ties with the Levant just as much as it reinterprets the Western tradition. It suggests Venice's connections with Italy and the Mediterranean and, even beyond its empire of islands, trading stations, and naval bases, with distant and marvelous horizons. And because that decor is so strange and so composite, it becomes unique. The Piazza opens onto the basin of San Marco, onto water and light; through the immense windows of its upper story the Ducal Palace breathes in the sun and the sea. Boats are moored at the water's edge. Across the basin, on the opposite shore, merchandise is being unloaded at the storehouses of the Punta della Dogana and men are scurrying along the quay. Everything speaks of wealth and the omnipresence of commerce, but everything also speaks of the ordered existence of the community under the guidance of a sovereign Signoria. Banners floating from the tops of masts bear the lion that is the emblem of the city, while the basilica, an immense reliquary, recalls the pact of the city's founding and its providential creation.

The sacred and the profane, holiness and wealth, commerce and relics, duration and serenity—Piazza San Marco expresses it all.

Whether it is a feast day or an ordinary day, texts and pictorial representations repeatedly show Venetians on the Piazza, coming and going, walking and talking as if drawn there by the social and symbolic charge of a space that is their identity. A space whose meaning it was to be the space of all the spaces of their city.

NOTES

ONE   *A City Born in the Water*

1. Philippe de Commynes, *Mémoires,* in *Historiens et chroniqueurs du Moyen Age,* ed. Albert Pauphilet, Bibliothèque de la Pléiade (Paris: Gallimard, 1952), translated under the title *The Memoirs of Philip de Commines, Lord of Argenton,* ed. Andrew R. Scroble, 2 vols. (London, 1856), 2:169: "I was extremely surprised at the situation of this city, to see so many churches, monasteries, and houses, and all in the water."

2. Patricia Fortini Brown, *Venetian Narrative Painting in the Age of Carpaccio* (New Haven: Yale University Press, 1988).

3. The history of Venice as an urban complex has given rise to two different sorts of analysis in recent years. A certain number of studies have taken architecture as a starting point for their examination. These include Saverio Muratori, *Studi per una operante storia urbana di Venezia* (Rome: Istituto Poligrafico dello Stato, 1960); Paolo Maretto, *L'edilizia gotica veneziana* (Rome: Istituto Poligrafico della Stato, 1960); and Giorgio Gianighian and Paola Pavanini, eds., *Dietro i palazzi: Tre secoli di architettura minore a Venezia, 1492–1803* (Venice: Arsenale, 1984). Other studies have concentrated on reconstituting the social topography of the city: Ennio Concina, *Structure urbaine et fonctions des bâtiments du XVIe au XIXe siècle: Une recherche à Venise* (Venice: UNESCO and Save Venice, 1982); and for the modern age, idem, *Venezia nell'età moderna: Struttura e funzioni* (Venice: Marsilio, 1989).

4. Aldo Contento, "Il censimento della popolazione sotto la Repubblica veneta," *Nuovo Archivio Veneto,* 2d ser., 19 (1900): 5–42, 179–240; Giulio Beloch, "La popolazione di Venezia nei secoli XVI e XVII," ibid., 3d ser., 3 (1902): 5–49, esp. 46–49; Reinhold C. Mueller, "Peste e demografia: Medioevo e Rinascimento," in *Venezia e la peste, 1348–1797,* exh. cat. (Venice: Marsilio, 1980), 93–96. Basing their estimate on the number of men of an age to bear arms, Contento and Beloch put the population of Venice at between 100,000 and 130,000 in the early fourteenth century. Mueller's somewhat lower estimate—between 100,000 and 120,000—is taken today as roughly accurate (see, e.g., Maria Ginatempo and Lucia Sandri, *L'Italia delle città: Il popolamento urbano tra Medioevo e Rinascimento [secoli XIII–XVI]* [Florence: Le Lettere, 1990]).

5. Antonio Carile and Giorgio Fedalto, *Le origini di Venezia* (Bologna: Pàtron, 1978); Antonio Carile, "Le origini di Venezia nella tradizione storiografica," in *Dalle origini al Trecento,* ed. Girolamo Arnaldi, vol. 1 of *Storia della cultura veneta* (Vicenza:

Neri Pozza, 1976), 135–66; Elisabeth Crouzet-Pavan, *La mort lente de Torcello: Histoire d'une cité disparue* (Paris: Fayard, 1995), 36–60. For the narrative sources, see Giovanni Monticolo, ed., *Cronache veneziane antichissime*, Fonti per la Storia d'Italia, 9 (Rome, 1890); Roberto Cessi, ed., *Origo civitatum Italiae seu Venetiarum: Chronicon altinate et chronicon gradense*, Fonti per la Storia d'Italia, 73 (Rome: Tipoografia del Senato, 1933); and Giovanni Diacono (John the Deacon), *La cronaca veneziana*, ed. with commentary by Mario De Biasi, 2 vols. (Venice: Ateneo Veneto, 1988).

6. Wladimiro Dorigo, *Venezia origini: Fondamenti, ipotesi, metodi*, 3 vols. (Milan: Electa, 1983).

7. Dorigo's argument depends on the preliminary observation that the Venetia described by Pliny should not be confused, as it usually is, with the territory of the same name that made up the tenth region of Augustus. For a reinterpretation of Pliny's description of the tenth *regio*, see Santo Mazzarino, "Il concetto storico-geografico dell'unità veneta," in Arnaldi, *Dalle origini al Trecento*, 1–28. According to this theory, that ancient and smaller Venetia was in fact the size of the present-day lagoon basin. The entire zone was then occupied by wide stretches of *stagna*, plots of land covered by water only periodically, when the rivers spewed floodwaters into the lagoon or, in lesser measure, with exceptionally high tides. In spite of the hydrological disorder brought on by the "floods" of the seventh century, and in spite of the first and exceptional *acque alte* (high tides) of the eighth century, the lagoon basin still had not been formed at the end of the eighth century. The old equilibrium between land and water began to change in the ninth century. The final phase of the transformation came later (still according to Dorigo), in the eleventh and twelfth centuries. A few authors, Giuseppe Marzemin among them, had already suggested that what is now the Venetian lagoon was prosperous agricultural land, part of the territory of Altino or Padua (see Giuseppe Marzemin, *Le origini romane di Venezia* [Venice: Fantoni, 1936], 19–24).

8. Giacomo Filiasi, *Memorie storiche de' Veneti primi e secondi*, 9 vols. (Venice, 1796–98), 3:329, 4:208 ff.

9. Recent measurements suggest that the ground level in Venice has sunk from four to six meters since prehistoric times, about three meters since Roman times, and about eighty centimeters since the thirteenth century. Subsidence is apparently increasing today: according to the latest estimates, the rate of sinkage has increased from thirty centimeters per century to about fifty (see Louis-Jacques Rollet-Andriane and Michel Conil Lacoste, *Sauver Venise* [Paris: Robert Laffont, 1971], 46–48).

10. Paolo Delogu, André Guillou, and Gherardo Ortalli, *Longobardi e Bizantini*, Storia d'Italia, ed. Giuseppe Galasso, 1 (Turin: UTET, 1980); Lellia Cracco Ruggini et al., eds., *Origini-Età ducale*, vol. 1 of *Storia di Venezia* (Rome: Istituto della Enciclopedia Italiana, 1992); Claudio Azzara, "Fra terra e acque: Equilibri territoriali e assetti urbani nella Venezia dai Romani ai Longobardi," in *Venezia: Itinerari per la storia della città*, ed. Stefano Gasparri, Giovanni Levi, and Pierandrea Moro (Bologna: Il Mulino, 1997), 23–40.

11. Cassiodorus (ca. 470–80—ca. 570–75) was successively consul, *magister officiorum* (chief of civil service), and praetorian prefect. A high-ranking Roman functionary, he had the confidence of the Ostrogothic king, who charged him, as Byzan-

tine forces were preparing to attack Ostrogothic Italy, to arrange for supplying Ravenna with wine, oil, and wheat. The purpose of the 537–38 letter was to negotiate such transactions with the leaders of Venice (the "tribunes of the maritime population"), who appear to have had a monopoly over transporting and forwarding merchandise to Ravenna by Venetian ships.

12. *Corpus Christianorum,* series latina XCVI, *Magni Aurelii Cassiodori Senatoris opera,* pt. 1, *Variarum Libri XII,* ed. A. J. Fridh (Turnhout: Brepols, 1973), 491–92, quoted below from *The Letters of Cassiodorus,* trans. Thomas Hodgkin (London, 1886), 517. On Heinrich Kretschmayr's analysis of this letter as a source for the history of the earliest economic activities of Venice, see Kretschmayr, *Geschichte von Venedig,* 3 vols. (1905–34; reprint, Aalen: Scientia, 1986), 1:67–69.

13. See Andrea Dandolo, *Andreae Danduli Ducis Venetiarum Chronica per extensum descripta,* ed. Ester Pastorello, new ed., Rerum Italicarum Scriptores, 12, pt. 1 (Bologna: Zanichelli, 1942), 53, 54, 59, 60.

14. Oderzo was taken in 639 by Rothari, king of the Lombards. Given that Oderzo was destroyed in 667, the population probably fled to Eraclea and Cittanova even before their city fell.

15. Donald M. Nichol, *Byzantium and Venice: A Study in Diplomatic and Cultural Relations* (Cambridge: Cambridge University Press, 1988), 8–9.

16. Roberto Cessi, *Venezia ducale,* vol. 1, *Duca e popolo* (Venice: Deputazione di Storia Patria per le Venezie, 1963), 71–72.

17. Pierandrea Moro, "Venezia e l'Occidente nell'alto medioevo: Dal confine longobardo al pactum lotariano," in Gasparri, Levi, and Moro, *Venezia,* 41–57.

18. Grado, to the north, and Cavarzere, on the Adige River to the south, continued to mark the outside borders of the Duchy of Venice.

19. The inscription is now in the basilica at Torcello, on one of the walls near the high altar.

20. This inscription has a long bibliography, including Vittorio Lazzarini, "Una iscrizione torcellana del secolo VII," *Atti del R. Istituto Veneto di Scienze, Lettere ed Arti* 73 (1913–14): 387–97, reprinted in Lazzarini, *Scritti di paleografia e diplomatica,* 2d ed., enl. (Padua: Antenore, 1969); Roberto Cessi, "L'iscrizione torcellana del secolo VII," in *Le origini del ducato veneziano* (Naples: Morano, 1951); idem, *Venezia ducale,* 1:69–70; idem, "Alcune osservazioni sulla basilica di Santa Maria di Torcello e sulla chiesa di San Teodoro di Rialto," *Atti dell'Istituto Veneto di Scienze, Lettere ed Arti* 119 (1960–61): 665–74; and Agostino Pertusi, "L'iscrizione torcellana dei tempi di Eraclio," *Studi Veneziani* 4 (1962): 9–39. For an analysis of the debate regarding this inscription and of the various interpretations of it, see Crouzet-Pavan, *La mort lente de Torcello,* 91–93.

21. Various large religious buildings, such as Santa Maria delle Grazie, the cathedral of Grado, dedicated to St. Eufemia, were built or rebuilt in the area during the sixth century. A study of these constructions enables us to discern the architectural model that would have been familiar to the refugees from Altino who settled at Torcello. On this question, see Mario Brunetti et al., *Torcello* (Venice: Libreria Serenissima, 1940).

22. Scholars usually date to the seventh century some fragments belonging to the

earliest mosaics preserved. It seems highly likely that these works were executed by artists who came to Torcello from Ravenna. Archaeological excavations have also indicated the existence of a kiln at Torcello during the same decades (see Lech Leciejewicz, Eleonora Tabaczynska, and Stanislaw Tabaczynsky, *Torcello: Scavi 1961–62* [Rome: Istituto Nazionale di Archeologia e Storia dell'Arte, 1977]; and Lech Leciejewicz, "Alcuni problemi dell'origine di Venezia alla luce degli scavi a Torcello," in *Le origini di Venezia: Problemi esperienze proposte* [Venice: Marsilio, 1981], 55–64).

23. Luigi Lanfranchi and Gian Giacomo Zille, "Il territorio del ducato veneziano dall'VIII al XII secolo," in *Dalle origini del Ducato alla IV Crociata*, vol. 2 of *Storia di Venezia* (Venice: Centro Internazionale delle Arti e del Costume, 1958), 3–65.

24. Two works by Flaminio Cornaro are fundamental to an understanding of this topic: *Ecclesiae venetae, antiquis monumentis nunc etiam primum editis illustratae ac in decades distributae,* 13 vols. (Venice, 1749), and *Ecclesiae Torcellanae antiquis monumentis nunc etiam primum editis illustratae, pars prima* (Venice, 1749). On the history of settlement in the lagoon, one can also read with profit Gabriele Mazzucco, *Monasteri benedettini della laguna veneziana* (Venice: Biblioteca Nazionale Marciana and Arsenale, 1983); Luigi Lanfranchi, "I documenti sui più antichi insediamenti monastici nella laguna veneziana," in *Le origini della chiesa di Venezia,* ed. Franco Tonon, Contributi alla Storia della Chiesa di Venezia, 1 (Venice: Studium Cattolico Veneziano, 1987), 143–50; and Giovanni Spinelli, "I primi insediamenti monastici lagunari nel contesto della teoria politica e religiosa veneziana," ibid., 151–66.

25. I borrow the phrase "invention of a city" from Elisabeth Crouzet-Pavan, *Venise: Une invention de la ville, XIIIe–XVe siècle,* Collection Époques (Seyssel: Champ Vallon, 1997).

26. The material summarized here is developed more fully in Elisabeth Crouzet-Pavan, *"Sopra le acque salse": Espaces, pouvoir et société à Venise à la fin du Moyen Age,* 2 vols., Collection de l'École Française de Rome, 158 (Rome: Istituto Storico Italiano per il Medio Evo, 1992), 1:57–139. For a brief overview of the topic, see Giorgio Bellavitis and Giandomenico Romanelli, *Venezia,* Le Città nella Storia d'Italia: Grandi Opere (Rome: Laterza, 1985).

27. On the physical expansion of Venice, see Bartolomeo Cecchetti, "La vita dei veneziani nel 1300. Parte 1. La città, la laguna," *Archivio Veneto* 27 (1884): 5–54, 321–37; 28 (1884): 5–29, 267–96; 29 (1885): 9–48, reprinted as Cecchetti, *La vita dei Veneziani nel 1300* (1885–86; reprint, Bologna: Forni, 1980).

28. Crouzet-Pavan, *"Sopra le acque salse,"* 1:116–25.

29. Ibid., 97–116.

30. Ibid., 72–96.

31. Although urban expansion in Venice took unique forms, its history should be seen within a more general context and compared with the great phases of urbanization in other contemporary Italian cities of the age of the communes. For examples, see Franek Sznura, *L'espansione urbana di Firenze nel Dugento* (Florence: La Nuova Italia, 1975); Mario Fanti, "Le lottizzazioni monastiche e lo sviluppo urbano di Bologna nel Duecento," *Atti e Memorie della Deputazione di Storia Patria per la Romagna,* n.s., 27 (1976): 121–43; Francesca Bocchi, "Suburbi e fasce suburbane nelle città dell'Italia medievale," *Storia della Città* 5 (1977): 1–33; Étienne Hubert, *Espace urbain*

et habitat à Rome du Xe siècle à la fin du XIIIe siècle (Rome: École Française de Rome, 1990), 134–40; Giancarlo Andenna, "Il monastero e l'evoluzione urbanistica di Brescia tra XI e XII secolo," in *S. Giulia di Brescia: Archeologia, arte, storia di un monastero regio dai Longobardi al Barbarossa*, ed. Clara Stella and Gerardo Brentegani (Brescia: Grafo, 1992), 93–118; Enrico Guidoni, "Un monumento della tecnica urbanistica duecentesca: L'espansione di Brescia del 1237," in *La Lombardia: Il territorio, l'ambiente, il paesaggio*, ed. Carlo Pirovano, 5 vols. (Milan: Electa, 1981), 1:127–36; and Gian Maria Varanini, "L'espansione urbana di Verona in età comunale: Dati e problemi," in *Spazio, società, potere dell'Italia dei Comuni*, ed. Gabriella Rossetti (Naples: Liguori, 1986), 1–26. For a brief summary of these problems, see Elisabeth Crouzet-Pavan, "Entre collaboration et affrontement: Le public et le privé dans les grands travaux urbains," in *Tecnologia y sociedad: Las grandes obras publicas en la Europa medieval* (Pamplona: Gobierno de Navarra, 1995), 363–80.

32. Crouzet-Pavan, *"Sopra le acque salse,"* 1:265–85.

33. Ibid., 212–14. See also Giuliana Mazzi, "Note per una definizione della funzione viaria a Venezia," *Archivio Veneto*, 5th ser., 134 (1973): 6–29.

34. Crouzet-Pavan, *"Sopra le acque salse,"* 1:194–214.

35. Ibid., 86–88.

36. For a comparison with solutions adopted in other Italian cities, see Duccio Balestracci, "La politica delle acque urbane nell'Italia comunale," *Mélanges de l'École Française de Rome, Moyen Age* 104, no. 2 (1992): 431–79; and idem, "Systèmes d'hydraulique urbaine (Italie centrale, fin du Moyen Age)," in *Le contrôle des eaux en Europe occidentale, XIIe–XVIe siècles/Water Control in Western Europe, Twelfth–Sixteenth Centuries*, ed. Elisabeth Crouzet-Pavan and Jean-Claude Maire Vigueur (Milan: Bocconi, 1994), 115–22.

37. For an anecdote that throws light on the problem of the taste and quality of water in Venice, see Crouzet-Pavan, *La mort lente de Torcello*, 309–10.

38. Crouzet-Pavan, *"Sopra le acque salse,"* 1:237–43, 296–98, 308, 311.

39. G. Boldrin and G. Dolcetti, *I pozzi di Venezia, 1015–1906* (Venice, 1910); Massimo Costantini, *L'acqua di Venezia: L'approvvigionamento idrico della Serenissima* (Venice: Arsenale, 1984).

40. Lorenzo Seguso and Angelo Seguso, *Delle sponde marmoree, overe dei pozzi e degli antichi edifizii della Venezia marittima* (Venice, 1859); Giuseppe Tassini, "Tre celebri vere di pozzo in Venezia," *Archivio Veneto* 2 (1871): 442–47.

41. Costantini, *L'acqua di Venezia*.

42. Crouzet-Pavan, *"Sopra le acque salse,"* 1:445–46, 483.

43. Ibid., 518–19, 520–22.

44. Ibid., 244–52.

45. Juergen Schulz, "The Printed Plans and Panoramic Views of Venice," *Saggi e Memorie di Storia dell'Arte* 7 (1970): 13–37; idem, "Jacopo de Barbari's View of Venice: Map Making, City Views, and Moralized Geography before the Year 1500," *Art Bulletin* 60, no. 3 (1978): 425–74. See also Giuseppe Mazzariol and Terisio Pignatti, *La pianta prospettica di Venezia del 1500 disegnata da Jacopo de Barbari* (Venice: Cassa di Risparmio di Venezia, 1962); Teresio Pignatti, "La pianta di Venezia di Jacopo de Barbari," *Bolletino dei Musei Civici Veneziani* 1–2 (1964): 9–49; and Giocondo Cas-

sini, *Piante e vedute prospettiche di Venezia (1479–1855)* (Venice: Stamperia di Venezia, 1971). For a new reading of Jacopo de Barbari's *View* and comments on the manipulation of the image, see Deborah Howard, "Venice as a Dolphin: Further Investigations into Jacopo de' Barbari's View," *Artibus et Historiae* 35 (1997): 101–12. For an analysis of the various cartographic representations of Venice, see Giandomenico Romanelli, "Venezia tra l'oscurità degli inchiostri: Cinque secoli di cartografia," introduction to *Venezia, piante e vedute: Catalogo del fondo cartografico a stampa, Museo Correr,* ed. Susanna Biadene (Venice: Stamperia di Venezia, 1982); and Juergen Schulz, "Maps as Metaphors: Mural Map Cycles in the Italian Renaissance," in *Art and Cartography: Six Historical Essays,* ed. David Woodward (Chicago: University of Chicago Press, 1987), 97–122, 223–29. To end the list, an essay indispensable for the history of iconographic representation is David Rosand, " 'Venezia figurata': The Iconography of a Myth," in *Interpretazioni veneziane: Studi di storia dell'arte in onore di Michelangelo Muraro,* ed. Rosand (Venice: Arsenale, 1984), 177–96.

46. Crouzet-Pavan, *"Sopra le acque salse,"* 1:218–36.

47. Ibid., 131–37.

48. Ibid., 142–64. These decisions have in part been published: see *Codex Publicorum (Codice del Piovego),* ed. Bianca Lanfranchi Strina, vol. 1 (1282–1298), Fonti per la Storia di Venezia, sec. 1, Archivi Pubblici, Monumenti Storici, n.s., 22 (Venice, 1895).

49. Crouzet-Pavan, *"Sopra le acque salse,"* 1:165–94.

50. Ibid., 265–86.

51. Jacques Heers, "Les villes d'Italie centrale et l'urbanisme: Origines et affirmations d'une politique (environ 1200–1350)," *Mélanges de l'École Française de Rome, Moyen Age* 101, no. 1 (1989): 67–93; Jean-Claude Maire Vigueur, "L'essor urbain dans l'Italie médiévale: Aspects et modalités de la croissance," in *Europa en los umbrales de la crisis (1250–1350)* (Pamplona: Gobierno de Navarra, Departamento de Educación y Cultura, 1995), 171–204; Elisabeth Crouzet-Pavan, "Politique urbaine et stratégie du pouvoir dans l'Italie communale," in *Enjeux et expressions de la politique municipale: XIIe–XVe siècle,* ed. Denis Menjot and Jean-Luc Pinol (Paris: L'Harmattan, 1997), 7–20.

52. Roberto Cessi and Annibale Alberti, *Rialto: L'isola, il ponte, il mercato* (Bologna: Zanichelli, 1934); Donatella Calabi and Paolo Morachiello, *Rialto: Le fabbriche e il ponte* (Turin: Einaudi, 1987); Crouzet-Pavan, *"Sopra le acque salse,"* 1:174–75.

53. Crouzet-Pavan, *"Sopra le acque salse,"* 1:174 ff.

54. Gregorio Gattinoni, *Il campanile di San Marco* (Venice: Fabbris, 1910); Giacomo Boni, *Il campanile di San Marco riedificato* (Venice, 1912).

55. Umberto Franzoi, "Le trasformazioni edilizie e la definizione storicoarchitettonica di Piazza San Marco," in *Piazza San Marco: L'architettura, la storia, le funzioni,* by Giuseppe Samonà et al., 3d ed. (Venice: Marsilio, 1982), 43–77, esp. 75–77.

56. The church had stood on the other side of the Rio Batario.

57. The chroniclers all speak of the great effort and immense difficulty involved in unloading the columns and placing them at the threshold of the Piazzetta, where they stand today.

58. Silvano Borsari, "Una famiglia veneziana del Medioevo: Gli Ziani," *Archivio Veneto*, 5th ser., 145 (1978): 27–72.

59. Antonio Quadri, *La piazza di San Marco considerata come monumento d'arte e di storia* (Venice, 1831). Piazza San Marco measures 176 meters by 82 meters on its longer side, 57 meters on the shorter side; the Piazzetta measures 96 meters by 48 meters (40 meters on the side nearest the basilica). These dimensions made a strong impression on contemporaries. On the highly significant decoration projects of the thirteenth century—the quadriga of horses surmounting the basilica, the Tetrarchs, the sculptures added to the two columns of the Piazzetta—see Michela Agazzi, *Platea Sancti Marci: I luoghi marciani dall'XI al XII secolo e la formazione della piazza* (Venice: Comune di Venezia, 1991). For a consideration of precisely what Venetians may have known of the various sites in Constantinople, see Juergen Schulz, "Urbanism in Medieval Venice," in *City-States in Classical Antiquity and Medieval Italy: Athens and Rome, Florence and Venice,* ed. Anthony Molho, Kurt Raaflaub, and Julia Emlen (Stuttgart: Steiner, 1991), 419–45, esp. 438–40. See also idem, "La piazza medioevale di San Marco," *Annali di Architettura* 4–5 (1992–93): 134–56.

60. Ennio Concina, *L'Arsenale della Repubblica di Venezia: Tecniche e istituzioni dal Medioevo all'età moderna* (Milan: Electa, 1984), 9. Older works on the Arsenal include Costantino Veludo, *Cenni storici sull'Arsenale di Venezia* (Venice, 1869); and Mario Nani Mocenigo, *L'Arsenale di Venezia* (Rome: Filippi, 1938). See also Ennio Concina, ed., *Arsenali e città dell'Occidente europeo* (Rome: La Nuova Italia Scientifica, 1987).

61. Crouzet-Pavan, *"Sopra le acque salse,"* 1:125–31; Giorgio Gianighian and Paola Pavanini, "Terreni nuovi di Santa Maria Mazor," in Gianighian and Pavanini, *Dietro i palazzi,* 45–57.

62. Among these projects were San Michele and Santa Maria dei Miracoli (see John McAndrew, *Venetian Architecture of the Early Renaissance* [Cambridge, Mass.: MIT Press, 1980], 134–43, 160; Crouzet-Pavan, *"Sopra le acque salse,"* 1:664–65; and Manfredo Tafuri, *Venezia e il Rinascimento: Religione, scienza, architettura* [Turin: Einaudi, 1985], 24 ff.).

63. Manfredo Tafuri, ed., *"Renovatio urbis": Venezia nell'età di Andrea Gritti, 1523–1538* (Rome: Officina, 1984); Concina, *Venezia nell'età moderna.*

64. Crouzet-Pavan, *Venise,* 141–42.

65. Calabi and Morachiello, *Rialto.*

66. Deborah Howard, *Jacopo Sansovino: Architecture and Patronage in Renaissance Venice* (New Haven: Yale University Press, 1975); Tafuri, *Venezia e il Rinascimento.*

67. Manfredo Tafuri, *Jacopo Sansovino e l'architettura del '500 a Venezia* (Padua: Marsilio, 1972); Howard, *Jacopo Sansovino;* Donatella Calabi, "Un nouvel espace public," in *Venise 1500: La puissance, la novation et la concorde: Le triomphe du mythe,* ed. Philippe Braunstein (Paris: Autrement, 1993), 72–93.

68. To cite only a few titles among an immense bibliography: Bruno Zevi, *Biagio Rossetti, architetto ferrarese, il primo urbanista moderno europeo* (Turin: Einaudi, 1960); Enzo Carli, *Pienza: La città di Pio II,* 2d ed. (Rome: Editalia, 1967); Leonardo Benevolo, *Storia dell'architettura del Rinascimento* (Bari: Laterza, 1968), trans. Judith

Landry under the title *The Architecture of the Renaissance*, 2 vols. (London: Routledge & Kegan Paul, 1978); Giorgio Simoncini, *Città e società nel Rinascimento*, 2 vols. (Turin: Einaudi, 1974); *Mantova e i Gonzaga nella civiltà del Rinascimento* (Mantua: Arnaldo Mondadori, 1977); Vittorio Franchetti Pardo, *Storia dell'urbanistica dal Trecento al Quattrocento* (Bari: Laterza, 1982); *Ludovico il Moro: La sua città e la sua corte, 1480–1499* (Milan: Archivio di Stato di Milano, 1983); Enrico Guidoni, *La città dal Medioevo al Rinascimento* (Rome: Laterza, 1989); Giovanni Cherubini and Giovanni Fanelli, eds., *Il palazzo Medici Riccardi di Firenze* (Florence: Giunti, 1990); and Giorgio Cerboni Baiardi, Giorgio Chittolini, and Piero Floriani, eds., *Federico di Montefeltro: Lo Stato, le arti, la cultura* (Rome: Bulzoni, 1986).

69. For a history of the Ducal Palace, which I shall not review here, several titles might be cited from a large bibliography: Leopoldo Cicognara, Antonio Diedo, and Giannantonio Selva, *Le fabbriche più cospicue di Venezia misurate, illustrate e intagliate dai membri della Veneta reale Accademia di belle arti*, 2 vols. (Venice, 1840); Francesco Zanotto, *Il Palazzo Ducale di Venezia*, 4 vols. (Venice, 1853); Antonio dall'Acqua Giusti, *Il Palazzo Ducale di Venezia* (Venice, 1864); Gambattista Lorenzi, *Monumenti per servire alla storia del Palazzo Ducale di Venezia* (Venice, 1869); Pietro Paoletti, *L'architettura e la scultura del Rinascimento in Venezia: Ricerche storico-artistiche*, 2 vols. (Venice, 1893); Vittorio Lazzarini, "Filippo Calendario: L'architetto della tradizione del palazzo ducale," *Nuovo Archivio Veneto*, 2d ser., 7 (1894): 429–46; Max Ongaro, *Il Palazzo Ducale di Venezia: Guida storico artistica* (Venice: Borin & Dal Poz, 1927); Giovanni Mariacher, *Il Palazzo Ducale di Venezia* (Florence: Del Turco, 1950); Elena Bassi and Egle Renata Trincanato, *Il Palazzo Ducale nella storia e nell'arte di Venezia* (Milan: Martello, 1966), translated under the title *Palace of the Doges in the History and Art of Venice* (Milan: Martello, 1966); Elena Bassi, "Appunti per la storia del Palazzo ducale di Venezia," *Critica d'Arte* 54 (1962a): 25–38 and (1962b): 45–53; Elena Bassi and Egle Renata Trincanato, "Il Palazzo Ducale nel '400," *Bollettino del Centro Internazionale di Studi di Architettura Andrea Palladio* 6 (1964): 181–87; Teresio Pignatti, *Palazzo Ducale* (Novara: Istituto Geografico De Agostini, 1964); Nicola Ivanoff, "I cicli allegorici della Libreria e del Palazzo ducale di Venezia," in *Rinascimento europeo e veneziano*, ed. Vittore Branca, Civiltà Europea e Civiltà Veneziana, 3 (Florence: Sansoni, 1967), 281–99l; Samonà et al., *Piazza San Marco*; and Wolfgang Wolters, *Der Bilderschmuck des Dogenpalastes: Untersuchungen zur Selbsdarstellung der Republik Venedig im 16. Jahrhundert* (Wiesbaden: Steiner, 1983).

70. Balestracci, "La politica delle acque urbane"; Pierre Racine, "Poteri medievali e percorsi fluviali nell'Italia padana," *Quaderni Storici*, n.s., 61 (1986): 9–32, esp. 31.

71. Crouzet-Pavan, *Venise*, 19–21.

72. For an analysis of contemporary reactions, see ibid., 157–58.

73. For examples of neighbors' petitions in other cities, see Duccio Balestracci and Gabriella Piccinni, *Siena nel Trecento: Assetto urbano e strutture edilizie* (Florence: Clusf, 1977), 17.

74. Crouzet-Pavan, *Venise*, 89–102.

75. McAndrew, *Venetian Architecture of the Early Renaissance*, 194; Deborah Howard, *The Architectural History of Venice* (London: Batsford, 1980).

76. There is an inexhaustible but somewhat uneven bibliography on this topic.

One older study of the noble palace in Venice, Léon Beylié's *L'habitation byzantine: Recherches sur l'architecture civile des Byzantins et son influence en Europe* (Geneva: Falque & E. Perrin; Paris: E. Leroux, 1902), focuses on the problem of origins. For a more recent work on the same topic, see Giuseppe Fiocco, *La casa veneziana antica* (Rome, 1949). For an overall view, see Duilio Torres, *La casa veneta* (Venice, 1933). On the constitution of a residential zone along the Grand Canal, see Antonio Quadri and Dionisio Moretti, *Il Canal Grande di Venezia* (Venice, 1828); Giorgia Scattolin, *Contributo allo studio dell'architettura civile veneziana dal IX al XIII secolo: Le casefondaco sul Canal Grande* (Venice: Nuova Editoriale, 1961); and Giuseppe Mazzariol, *I palazzi del Canal Grande* (Novara: Istituto Geografico De Agostini, 1981). Two articles by Egle Renata Trincanato that previously appeared in the *Giornale Economico della Camera di Commercio di Venezia*—"La casa patrizia e il suo rapporto con l'ambiente," 1952, 5–26, and "L'ambiente veneziano," 1953, 5–25—have been reprinted in Trincanato, *Appunti per una conoscenza urbanistica di Venezia* (Venice: Filippi, 1954). For an analysis of the morphological evolution of the Venetian house and its successive floor plans, see Maretto, *L'edilizia gotica veneziana*, and idem, *La casa veneziana nella storia della città dall'origine all'Ottocento* (Venice: Marsilio, 1986). For a case study, see Elena Bassi, *Palazzi di Venezia: "Admiranda urbis Venetae"* (Venice: Stamperia di Venezia, 1976). An older work useful for its close examination of a certain number of palaces is Giuseppe Tassini, *Alcuni palazzi ed antichi edifici di Venezia storicamente illustrati* (Venice, 1879). For the Cà Pesaro, see Agostino Sagredo and Federico Berchet, *Il Fondaco dei Turchi in Venezia: Studi storici ed artistici* (Milan, 1860). There are also several more specific studies: Giuseppe Tassini, "Quattro palazzi di Venezia," *Archivio Veneto* 3 (1872): 120–25; idem, "Palazzo del doge Marino Falier," *Nuovo Archivio Veneto*, 2d ser., 6 (1893): 269–70; Luca Beltrami, *La "Cà del Duca" sul Canal Grande ed altre reminiscenze sforzesche in Venezia* (Milan: Allegretti, 1900); Richard Goy, *The House of Gold: Building a Palace in Medieval Venice* (Cambridge: Cambridge University Press, 1992); and Juergen Schulz, "The Houses of the Dandolo: A Family Compound in Medieval Venice," *Journal of the Society of Architectural Historians* 52 (1993): 391–415. On stylistic aspects and for the publication of a certain number of accounts and documents concerning construction, see Paoletti, *L'architettura e la scultura del Rinascimento in Venezia;* Bartolomeo Cecchetti, "La facciata della Cà d'Oro dello scalpello di Giovanni e Bartolomeo Buono," *Archivio Veneto* 31, no. 1 (1886): 201–4; and Richard Goy, "Architectural Taste and Style in Early Quattrocento Venice: The Facade of the Cà d'Oro and Its Legacy," in *War, Culture, and Society in Renaissance Venice: Essays in Honour of John Hale,* ed. David S. Chambers, Cecil H. Clough, and Michael Mallett (London: Hambledon Press, 1993). For an overall picture, see Norbert Huse and Wolfgang Wolters, *The Art of Renaissance Venice: Architecture, Sculpture, and Painting, 1460–1590,* trans. Edmund Jephcott (Chicago: University of Chicago Press, 1990). One might also mention Franco Valcanover and Wolfgang Wolters, eds., *L'architettura gotica veneziana* (Venice: Istituto Veneto di Scienze, Lettere ed Arti, 2000). See also the monographs *Palazzo Ziani: Storia, architettura, decorazioni,* ed. Giandomenico Romanelli (Venice: Albrizzi, 1994); and Marta Tortorella, "Zattere al Ponte longo: Da Cà Graziabona a palazzo Zorzi (1458–1780)," *Studi Veneziani,* n.s., 31 (1996): 51–110.

77. As early as the fifteenth century, Philippe de Commynes noted that many Venetian palaces were painted (*Memoirs of Philip de Commines*, 2:169–70).

78. Here too there were exceptions to the rule: the Palazzo Contarini del Bovolo, built at the very end of the fifteenth century, is famous for its superb external spiral staircase.

79. Maretto, *La casa veneziana*; Crouzet-Pavan, *"Sopra le acque salse*," 1:499–503, 509–14, 522–23.

80. Tafuri, *Venezia e il Rinascimento*, 8.

81. Felix Gilbert, "Venice and the Crisis of the League of Cambrai," in *Renaissance Venice*, ed. J. R. Hale (London: Faber; Totowa, N.J.: Rowman & Littlefield, 1973), 274–92, esp. 277.

82. Ralph Lieberman, *Renaissance Architecture in Venice, 1450–1540* (New York: Abbeville, 1982).

83. Buildings now attributed to Coducci include Palazzo Zorzi, on the Rio San Savero, and Palazzo Corner-Spinelli (constructed for the Lando family), on the Grand Canal, as well as Palazzo Vendramin-Calergi, originally the same Palazzo Loredan to which Gritti objected.

84. Crouzet-Pavan, *Venise*, 289–90.

85. Here the problem of the real-estate market and how it functioned enters into the picture (see Crouzet-Pavan, *"Sopra le acque salse*," 1:410–62, 464–79, 509–25).

86. The phrase "so many stately churches in the sea" is taken from Commynes, *Memoirs of Philip de Commines*, 2:169.

87. See, in general, André Vauchez, ed., *L'antichità e il Medioevo*, vol. 1 of *Storia dell'Italia religiosa*, ed. Gabriele De Rosa, Tullio Gregory, and André Vauchez (Rome: Laterza, 1993); and André Vauchez, *Ordini mendicanti e società italiana, XIII–XV secolo*, trans. Michele Sampaolo (Milan: Il Saggiatore, 1990). See also *La coscienza cittadino nei comuni italiani del Duecento*, Centro di Studi sulla Spiritualità Medievale, 11 (Todi: Accademia Tudertina, 1973).

88. For a general study of Arabic influences, see Ennio Concina, *Dell'arabico: A Venezia tra Rinascimento e Oriente* (Venice: Marsilio, 1994).

89. On the various meaning of the term *terra*, see Robert Finlay, *Politics in Renaissance Venice* (New Brunswick, N.J.: Rutgers University Press, 1980), 55–58.

90. The bibliography on the lagoon is immense but not of uniform quality. Among the older works one might cite are Giulio Rompiasio, *Metodo in pratica di sommario, o sia Compilazione delle leggi, terminazioni & ordini appartenenti agl' illustrissimi & eccellentissimi Collegio e Magistrado alle acque, opera dell'avvocato fiscale Giulio Rompiasio; riedizione critica a cura di Giovanni Caniato*, Strumenti per la Ricerca Archivista, Sezione 1, Repertori Antichi, 1 (1733; facsimile reprint, ed. Giovanni Caniato, Venice: Ministero per i Beni Culturali e Ambientali, 1988); Cristoforo Tentori, *Della legislazione veneziana sulla preservazione della laguna: Dissertazione storico-filosofico-critica* (Venice, 1792); Bernardino Zendrini, *Memorie storiche dello stato antico e moderno delle lagune di Venezia e di quei fiumi che restarono divertiti per la conservazione delle medesime*, vol. 1 (1811; reprint, Sala Bolognese: Forni, 1998); Camillo Vacani, barone di Forteolivolo, *Della laguna di Venezia e dei fiumi nelle attigue provincie: Memorie* (Florence, 1867); and Antonio Averone, *Saggio*

sull'antica idrografia veneta (Mantua: Aldo Manuzio, 1911). More recent titles reveal a quite different historiographical approach. One example is the texts in *Mostra storica della laguna veneta,* exh. cat. (Venice: Stamperia di Venezia, 1970), in particular Bianca Lanfranchi and Luigi Lanfranchi, "La laguna dal secolo VI al XIV," 74–84; Maria Francesca Tiepolo, "Difesa a mare," 133–38; Paolo Selmi, "Politica lagunare della Veneta Repubblica dal secolo XIV al secolo XVIII," 105–15; and G. A. Ravalli Modoni, "Scrittori tecnici di problemi lagunari," 169–73. See also *Laguna, fiumi, lidi: Cinque secoli di gestione delle acque nelle Venezie* (Venice: La Press, 1985). The studies of Giuseppe Pavanello and Roberto Cessi are still highly useful: see Giuseppe Pavanello, "Di un'antica laguna scomparsa (La laguna eracliana)," *Archivio Veneto Tridentino* 3 (1923): 263–307; idem, *La laguna di Venezia (Note illustrative e breve sommario storico)* (Rome: Provveditore Generale dello Stato, 1931); idem, "Della caduta dell'Impero romano alla costituzione di nuovi centri politici e della laguna veneta propriamente detta," in *La laguna di Venezia,* ed. Gustavo Brunelli et al., pt. 3, *La storia della laguna fino al 1140* (Venice: Ferrari, 1935), chap. 28, 53–73; Roberto Cessi, "Il problema della Brenta dal secolo XII al secolo XV," in ibid., vol. 1, pt. 4, t. 7 (Venice: Ferrari, 1943), fasc. 1, pp. 1–77; idem, "Lo sviluppo dell'interramento nella laguna settentrionale e il problema della Piave e del Sile fino al secolo XV," in ibid., vol. 1, pt. 4, t. 7, fasc. 1 (Venice: Ferrari, 1943), 79–108; and idem, "Evoluzione storica del problema lagunare," in *Atti del Convegno per la conservazione e difesa della laguna e città di Venezia* (Venice: Ferrari, 1960), 23–64. Finally, let me recall the monumental and stimulating Dorigo, *Venezia origini.*

91. Crouzet-Pavan, *"Sopra le acque salse,"* 1:344–57.

92. This 1324 plan was the first to attempt to separate fresh water and salt water. On the persistence of these problems and the various decisions to make the system of dikes more flexible, to open or close gates in the dikes, and to modify the course of the Brenta, see ibid., 358–59.

93. Marco Cornaro, *Scritture sulla laguna,* ed. Giuseppe Pavanello, vol. 1 of *Antichi scrittori d'idraulica veneta* (Venice: Ferrari, 1919).

94. Giuseppe Gullino, "Corner, Marco," in *Dizionario biografico degli Italiani* (Rome: Istituto della Enciclopedia Italiana, 1983), 29:254–55.

95. After Marco Corner Paolo Sabbadino suggested a program of radical diversion of the rivers in the late fifteenth century, but the writings of Sabbadino's son Cristoforo best exemplify contemporary thought on the problems of the lagoon basin.

96. The streams of sea water that enter the lagoon through the various breaks in the littoral islands, impelled by the incoming tide, do not mix in the lagoons, nor do they retreat by chance paths. The lagoon separates into basins of unequal size; the water that enters through one *porto* spills into its own basin; when the tide turns, the currents reverse to carry water back to the sea through the passageway by which it entered the lagoon. This means that the various basins hold varying volumes of water. Moreover, the pace at which the sea water circulates and the rate of the currents depend on the relationship between the area of the basin within the lagoon and the distance from the outlet. The bigger the surface of the basin, the faster the current (see Crouzet-Pavan, *"Sopra le acque salse,"* 1:355–57).

97. Sambo *père* had directed a series of projects to divert the water of the Brenta away from Lizzafusina to the Corbola canal. The Venetian mainland continued to suffer from hydrographic disorder and the flooding of its capricious rivers.

98. Roberto Cessi and Niccolò Spada, eds., *La difesa idraulica della laguna veneta nel secolo XVI: Relazioni dei periti*, vol. 3 of *Antichi scrittori d'idraulica veneta* (Venice: Ferrari, 1952), 5–8; Salvatore Ciriacono, "Scrittori d'idraulica e politica delle acque," in *Dal primo Quattrocento al Concilio di Trento*, ed. Girolamo Arnaldi and Manlio Pastore Stocchi, vol. 3 of *Storia della cultura veneta*, pt. 2 (Vicenza: Neri Pozza, 1980), 491–512.

99. For a detailed description of such operations, see Crouzet-Pavan, *"Sopra le acque salse,"* 1:319–33.

100. Cessi, "Lo sviluppo dell'interramento."

101. Crouzet-Pavan, *La mort lente de Torcello*, 326–35.

102. The question of the Brenta made relations with Padua even more conflicted than they had been (see Cessi, "Il problema della Brenta"). One particular bone of contention was a water-deviation project carried out by Padua in 1142 that increased the risk of sand deposits in an area of importance to Venice.

103. For examples of inspections under such guidance, see Crouzet-Pavan, *"Sopra le acque salse,"* 1:362–63.

104. On the institution of this magistracy, see Antonio Favaro, "Notizie storiche sul magistrato veneto alle acque," *Nuovo Archivio Veneto*, 3d ser., 9 (1905): 179–99.

105. Salvatore Ciriacono, *Acque e agricoltura: Venezia, l'Olanda e la bonifica europea in età moderna* (Milan: F. Angeli, 1994), 162–70.

T W O   *A City Wed to the Sea*

1. The first painting in this cycle, placed in the Sala dello Scrutinio, was in fact commissioned to represent the legendary victory of the Venetians over the Carolingians in 809. For the text of the 1587 commission, see Wolfgang Wolters, *Der Bilderschmuck des Dogenpalastes: Untersuchungen zur Selbstdarstellung der Republik Venedig im 16. Jahrhundert* (Wiesbaden: Steiner, 1983), 308–12.

2. The Hall of the Great Council was completely reconstructed after the fire. It was dominated by Tintoretto's vast *Paradise*. After a competition, the commission had been given to Veronese, who had died in 1588 before even beginning his painting. Tintoretto replaced him, painting the immense composition that occupies the entire wall before which the doge and his councilors sat (see Umberto Franzoi, Teresio Pignatti, and Wolfgang Wolters, *Il Palazzo Ducale di Venezia* [Trevisio: Canova, 1990]).

3. To recall briefly the stages of the construction of the myth of Pope Alexander III, some parts of the legend seem to have sprung up in the thirteenth century as a way to disguise the effective neutrality of Venice during the hostilities between the emperor and the pope in 1176 (on the Peace of Venice, see Paolo Brezzi, "La pace di Venezia del 1177 e le relazioni tra la Repubblica e l'Impero," in *Venezia dalla prima crociata alla conquista di Costantinopoli del 1204* [Florence: Sansoni, 1965], 51–70). The legend of the donation was really fabricated, however, between the end of the

war with Ferrara (1308) and the beginning of the Scaliger War (1336–39) in an effort to counter bitter anti-Venetian sentiment by asserting Venice's long and solid devotion to the Holy See, incidentally confirming the legitimacy of Venetian sovereignty in the Adriatic Gulf (for a description of this chronology, see Gina Fasoli, "Nascita di un mito," in *Studi storici in onore di Gioacchino Volpe per il suo 80° compleanno*, 2 vols. [Florence: Sansoni, 1958], 1:445–79, esp. 473–75). Bonincontro de' Bovi, notary of the ducal chancellery, redacted a first version of these events in 1317. The first frescos depicting the *trionfi* were also in the Ducal Palace, in the chapel of San Nicolò di Palazzo (see Agostino Pertusi, " 'Quedam regalia insignia': Ricerche sulle insegne del potere ducale a Venezia durante il medioevo," *Studi Veneziani 7* [1965]: 3–123; Edward Muir, *Civic Ritual in Renaissance Venice* [Princeton: Princeton University Press, 1981], 103 ff.; and idem, "Idee, riti, simboli del potere," in *L'età del Comune*, ed. Giorgio Cracco and Gherardo Ortalli, vol. 2 of *Storia di Venezia* [Rome: Istituto della Enciclopedia Italiana, 1955], 739–60). The *trionfi* symbolized the independence of Venice and were carried through the streets during the *andate*, the principal processions of the doge.

4. The naval battle of Punta Salvore, which the Venetians were supposed to have won over Otto, Frederick Barbarossa's son, was depicted in the Hall of the Great Council. Giovanni and Gentile Bellini restored the scene in 1474.

5. In the abovementioned fresco by Tintoretto the artist put aside the theme of the pontifical privileges that justified Venice's domination over the seas in favor of the notion of a celestial legitimation. Some Venetians backed Paolo Sarpi in opposing the tradition of pontifical privileges, insisting instead that Venetian rights had been acquired over the years (see Wolfgang Wolters, "Les miroirs du palais ducal," in *Venise 1500: La puissance, la novation et la concorde: Le triomphe du mythe*, ed. Philippe Braunstein [Paris: Autrement, 1993], 19–38).

6. Franzoi, Pignatti, and Wolters, *Il Palazzo Ducale di Venezia*.

7. Wolters, *Der Bilderschmuck des Dogenpalastes*. These projects involved Antonio Veneziano, Pisanello, and Gentile da Fabriano in 1422, then, in the late fifteenth and early sixteenth centuries, Gentile and Giovanni Bellini, Alvise Vivarini, Vittore Carpaccio, and Pietro Perugino.

8. One example is a painting by Francesco Bassano that shows Pope Alexander III giving the blessed sword to the doge; another is the *Siege of Constantinople* by Palma il Giovane.

9. Lina Urban Padoan, "La festa della Sensa nelle arti e nell'iconografia," *Studi Veneziani 10* (1968): 291–353.

10. For examples of pilgrims' reactions, see Elisabeth Crouzet-Pavan, *"Sopra le acque salse": Espaces, pouvoir et société à Venise à la fin du Moyen Age*, 2 vols., Collection de l'École Française de Rome, 158 (Rome: Istituto Storico Italiano per il Medio Evo, 1992), 2:725–26.

11. Gina Fasoli, "Liturgia e cerimonia ducale," in *Venezia e il Levante fino al secolo XV*, ed. Agostino Pertusi (Florence: Olschki, 1973), 1, pt. 1: 261–95.

12. Alberto Tenenti, "Il senso del mare," in *Il mare*, ed. Alberto Tenenti and Ugo Tucci, vol. 12 of *Storia di Venezia* (Rome: Istituto della Enciclopedia Italiana, 1991), 7–70.

13. Ibid., 34.

14. Giuseppe Cappelletti, *Storia della Repubblica di Venezia dal suo principio sino al giorno d'oggi*, 13 vols. (Venice, 1848–55), 4:168–71. See also the painting *The Presentation of the Ring to the Doge* by Paris Bordone; and Muir, *Civic Ritual in Renaissance Venice*, 88–89.

15. Tenenti, "Il senso del mare," 46–47.

16. Marcantonio Coccio Sabellico, *Degl'istorici delle cose veneziane, i quali hanno scritto per pubblico decreto*, vol. 1, *Istorie veneziane latinamente scritte da Marcantonio Coccio Sabellico* (Venice, 1718), 15–21.

17. Paolo Morosini, *Historia della città, e repubblica di Venetia, di Paolo Morosini senatore veneziano distinta in libri vintiotto* (Venice, 1637), 7–12.

18. Cappelletti, *Storia della Repubblica di Venezia*. Cappelletti remarks, however (4:45–49), that although Morosini states his intention to write a "good and true history," he follows the legendary chronology.

19. Giacomo Filiasi, *Ricerche storico-critiche sull'opportunità della laguna veneta pel commercio sull'arti e sulla marina di questo stato* (Venice, 1803), 3–8.

20. Fabio Mutinelli, *Annali urbani di Venezia dall'anno 810 al 12 maggio 1797* (Venice, 1841).

21. Once again, see Tenenti, "Il senso del mare," 56–57.

22. See Reinhard Lebe, *Quando San Marco approdò a Venezia: Il culto dell'Evangelista e il miracolo politico della Repubblica di Venezia*, trans. Luciano Tosti, rev. Virginia Cappelletti and Franco Tagliarini (Rome: Il Veltro, 1969).

23. Patrick Geary, *Furta Sacra: Thefts of Relics in the Central Middle Ages* (Princeton: Princeton University Press, 1978), 108–11. Geary stresses the role of the *translatio* as a weapon in the struggle against Carolingian influence. According to him, Frankish intervention had set off the conflict between the two patriarchates. The patriarch of Aquileia, who had already obtained an extension of his jurisdiction over Istria, laid claim to Venetia, which, if recognized, would have deprived the patriarch of Grado of his authority over the area. In 827 the Synod of Mantua affirmed that Aquileia, founded by St. Mark, was to enjoy authority over all of the province of Istria-Venetia. The transfer of the saint's relics occurred one year after that synod.

24. Hans Conrad Peyer, *Stadt und Stadtpatron im mittelalterlichen Italien* (Zurich: Europa, 1955), 9–11, analyses the situation as part of a phenomenon of independence taking place in a certain number of cities at that time. Still, one must insist, as Patrick Geary does, that the Venetian operation occurred at a much earlier date.

25. For a summary of this historiographical debate, see Silvio Tramontin, "Realtà e leggende nei racconti marciani veneti," *Studi Veneziani* 12 (1970): 35–58.

26. The basic text in this connection is Nelson McCleary, "Note storiche ed archeologiche sul testo della 'Traslatio sancti Marci,'" *Memorie Storiche Forogiuliesi* 27–29, nos. 10–12 (1931–33): 223–64.

27. In theory, the chronicler John the Deacon used this account (see Tramontin, "Realtà e leggende," 50–51 nn. 39, 40).

28. Manuscripts from at least as early as the tenth century helped to circulate this information.

29. Fasoli, "Nascita di un mito."

30. Some in Venice remained faithful to the cult of the city's first patron saint, St. Theodore (see Antonio Niero, "I santi patroni," in *Il culto dei santi a Venezia*, ed. Silvio Tramontin, Biblioteca Agiografica Veneziana, 2 [Venice: Studium Cattolico Veneziano, 1965], 75–98).

31. On the mosaics in the basilica of San Marco depicting the arrival of the relics, see Silvio Tramontin, "San Marco," in ibid., 41–73, esp. 63–69.

32. The two fundamental texts on which I base my analysis are the wills of Doge Giustiniano Partecipazio and Orso Partecipazio, bishop of Olivolo (see Roberto Cessi, *Documenti relativi alla storia di Venezia anteriori al mille*, vol. 1, *Secoli V–IX*, new ed. [Padua: Gregoriana, 1942]; and Antonio Carile and Giorgio Fedalto, *Le origini di Venezia* [Bologna: Pàtron, 1978], 34–36).

33. Here I am following Lebe, *Quando San Marco approdò a Venezia*, 68–74, who in turn cites Peyer, *Stadt und Stadtpatron* regarding the *vexillum*.

34. Agostino Pertusi, "Ai confini tra religione e politica: La contesa per le reliquie di S. Nicola tra Bari, Venezia e Genova," in *Saggi veneto-bizantini*, ed. Giovanni Battista Parenti (Florence: Olschki, 1990), 139–86.

35. "Molte vi sono. E queste e quelle che mantien la città nostra, ch'è senza muraglie" (see Marino Sanudo, *I diarii di Marino Sanuto [MCCCCXCVI–MDXXXIII] dall'autografo Marciano ital. Cl. VII codd. CDXIX–CDLXXVII*, ed. Rinaldo Fulin, Federico Stefani, Nicolò Barozzi, Guglielmo Berchet, and Marco Allegri, 58 vols. [Venice: Visentini, 1879–1903], vol. 20, col. 99).

36. It seems important to integrate these determining factors within an economic analysis and, above all, not to reduce them to a caricature of "mentalities," as certain economists have done (see, e.g., Charles P. Kindleberger, *The World Economic Primacy, 1500 to 1990* [New York: Oxford University Press, 1996]).

37. Philippe Braunstein and Robert Delort, *Venise: Portrait historique d'une cité* (Paris: Seuil, 1971), 51.

38. Yves Renouard, *Les hommes d'affaires italiens du Moyen Age* (Paris: Colin, 1949), 3–13.

39. Michel Mollat, Philippe Braunstein, and Jean-Claude Hocquet, "Réflexions sur l'expansion vénitienne en Méditerranée," in *Venezia e il Levante fino al secolo XV*, ed. Agostino Pertusi (Florence: Olschki, 1973), 1, pt. 2: 515–39, esp. 520.

40. There is thought to have been another route, by both land and water, in the early centuries of the Common Era for carrying local traffic, salt, and agricultural products through the lagoons from Ravenna to Altino.

41. Andrea Gloria, *Codice diplomatico padovano dal secolo sesto a tutto l'undecimo*, Monumenti storici pubblicati dalla deputazione veneta di storia patria, vol. 2, ser. 1, Documenti (Venice, 1877), 12–16.

42. Gino Luzzatto, *Storia economica di Venezia dal XI al XVI secolo* (Venice: Centro Internazionale delle Arti e del Costume, 1961), 5.

43. See Constantine VIII Porphyrogenitus, *De administrando imperio*, ed. Gyula Moravcsik, translated into English by R. J. H. Jenkins, new rev. ed., Dumbarton Oaks Texts, 1 (Washington, D.C.: Dumbarton Oaks Center for Byzantine Studies, 1967), and, from the original edition, vol. 2, *Commentary* (London, 1962). This work, which is usually known under the title given above, was a manual written by the emperor

for the education of his son and heir. See also Donald M. Nichol, *Byzantium and Venice: A Study in Diplomatic and Cultural Relations* (Cambridge: Cambridge University Press, 1988), 20–21; and Paolo Delogu, André Guillou, and Gherardo Ortalli, *Longobardi e Bizantini*, Storia d'Italia, ed. Giuseppe Galasso, 1 (Turin: UTET, 1980).

44. Comacchio was sacked in 933 by Pietro II Candiano (see Frederic C. Lane, *Venice, a Maritime Republic* [Baltimore: Johns Hopkins University Press, 1973], 24).

45. Ibid. Lane describes Venetian control of the middle Adriatic south of the Ravenna-Pola line and north of a line running from the mouth of the Kotor River (north of Lake Scutari) to the Gargano peninsula.

46. Freddy Thiriet, *La Romanie vénitienne au Moyen Age: Le développement et l'exploitation du domaine colonial vénitien, XIIe–XVe siècles*, 2d ed. (Paris: Boccard, 1975), 35.

47. Gerhard Rösch, "Mercatura e moneta," in *Origini-Età ducale*, ed. Lellia Cracco Ruggini et al., vol. 1 of *Storia di Venezia* (Rome: Istituto della Enciclopedia Italiana, 1992), 549–76, esp. 566–67.

48. The Venetians were exempted from nearly all customs fees in all markets, but the other merchants from the Latin world were taxed, Pisans at the rate of 4% Genoese at the rate of 10% (see Gerhard Rösch, "Lo sviluppo mercantile," in Cracco and Ortalli, *L'età del Comune*, 131–51, esp. 133).

49. This fact confirms the incontestable prosperity of the Hellenic economy in the twelfth century (see Thiriet, *La Romanie vénitienne*, 44; and Vera Tchentsova, "Le commerce vénitienne en Grèce du XIIIe siècle à la première moitié du XVe siècle d'après les données prosopographiques," in *Le partage du monde: Échanges et colonisation dans la Méditerranée médiévale*, ed. Michel Balard and Alain Ducellier [Paris: Publications de la Sorbonne, 1998], 287–96).

50. Thiriet, *La Romanie vénitienne*, 42–43, gives an analysis of various Greek chroniclers.

51. Lane, *Venice, a Maritime Republic*, 35–36.

52. My periodization follows the traditional one in Luzzatto, *Storia economica di Venezia*.

53. Donald M. Nichol, "La Quarta Crociata," in Cracco and Ortalli, *L'età del Comune*, 155–81. Nichol states: "It may quite possibly be true that at the time the Greeks were right to suspect that it had been the doge of Venice, Enrico Dandolo, who brought the Crusaders to Constantinople, later maneuvering things in such a way as to give them a moral pretext for conquering it" (180).

54. Lebe, *Quando San Marco approdò a Venezia*, 154–55.

55. "Si riche ville"; "ces haux murs et ces riches tours, ces riches palais et ces hautes églises"; "la ville qui de totes les autres ere soveraine" (Geoffroi de Villehardouin, *La conquête de Constantinople*, in *Historiens et chroniqueurs du Moyen Age*, ed. Albert Pauphilet, Bibliothèque de La Pléiade [Paris: Gallimard, 1952], 99, quoted in the English translation by Frank T. Marzials under the title *Memoirs of the Crusades* [London and Toronto: J. M. Dent; New York: E. P. Dutton, 1908], 31).

56. Agostino Pertusi, "Le profezie sulla presa di Costantinopoli (1204) nel cronista veneziano Marco (c. 1295) e le loro fonti bizantine (Pseudo Costantino Magno, Pseudo Daniele, Pseudo Leone il Saggio)," *Studi Veneziani*, n.s., 3 (1979): 13–46.

57. For the history of trade in the Black Sea, see Sergej Pavlovic Karpov, *L'impero di Trebisonda: Venezia, Genova e Roma (1204–1461): Rapporti politici, diplomatici e commerciali,* trans. Eleonora Zambelli, ed. Virginia Cappelletti and Franco Tagliarini (Rome: Il Veltro, 1986).

58. David Jacoby, "La colonisation militaire vénitien de la Crète au XIIIe siècle: Une nouvelle approche," in Balard and Ducellier, *Le partage du monde,* 297–314.

59. For a study of this conquest, see Thiriet, *La Romanie vénitienne,* 74 ff.; and Giorgio Ravegnani, "La Romania veneziana," in Cracco and Ortalli, *L'età del Comune,* 183–233.

60. For an overall picture of the scene in the Black Sea area, see Karpov, *L'impero di Trebisonda.*

61. Gerhard Rösch, "Il gran guadagno," in Cracco and Ortalli, *L'età del Comune,* 233–62.

62. David Jacoby, "L'expansion occidentale dans le Levant: Les Vénitiens à Acre dans la seconde moitié du XIIIe siècle," in Jacoby, *Recherches sur la Méditerranée orientale du XIIe au XVe siècle: Peuples, sociétés, économies* (London: Variorum Reprints, 1979), 225–64.

63. Eliyahu Ashtor, *Levant Trade in the Later Middle Ages* (Princeton: Princeton University Press, 1983); idem, "Observations on Venetian Trade in the Levant in the XIVth Century," In *East-West Trade in the Medieval Mediterranean,* ed. Benjamin Z. Kedar (London: Variorum Reprints, 1986), 533–86.

64. Lane, *Venice, a Maritime Republic,* 175.

65. Venice also was obliged to cede the mainland territories of Treviso and its region to the duke of Austria. On the situation in Dalmatia, see Barisa Krekic, "Venezia e l'Adriatico," in *La formazione dello stato patrizio,* ed. Girolamo Arnaldi, Giorgio Cracco, and Alberto Tenenti, vol. 3 of *Storia di Venezia* (Rome: Istituto della Enciclopedia Italiana, 1997), 51–85, esp. 65–66.

66. It has been shown that when the earlier trade routes declined, trade with the Levant enjoyed a period of growth during the final third of the fourteenth century. Both the Venetians and the Genoese were forced to focus on the southern routes, Syria and Egypt. During the two next decades, Venetian traders gained preeminence. See Ashtor, *Levant Trade in the Middle Ages,* 104–6. See also Michel Balard, *La Romanie génoise: XIIe–début du XVe siècle,* Bibliothèque des Écoles Françaises d'Athènes et de Rome, 235, 2 vols. (Rome: École Française de Rome, 1978), 868.

67. Gabriella Airaldi, *Genova e la Liguria nel Medioevo* (Turin: UTET, 1986); Giovanni Petti Balbi, *Una città e il suo mare: Genova nel Medioevo* (Bologna: CLUEB, 1991); Geo Pistarino, *Genovesi d'Oriente* (Genoa: Civico Istituto Colombiano, 1990); idem, *I Signori del mare* (Genoa: Civico Istituto Colombiano, 1992); Roberto Sabatino Lopez, *Storie delle colonie genovesi nel Mediterraneo,* 2d ed. (Genoa: Marietti, 1996).

68. Michel Balard, "La lotta contro Genova," in Arnaldi, Cracco, and Tenenti, *La formazione dello stato patrizio,* 87–126, esp. 116–17.

69. Nor should we forget the Genoese naval expedition to Cyprus commanded by Marshal Boucicaut, which went on to attack several Muslim ports and then fought a Venetian fleet commanded by Carlo Zeno off Modon.

70. On negotiations with the king of Naples and on the 100,000 ducats paid by the Venetian Republic, see Krekic, "Venezia e l'Adriatico," 79–82.

71. Bernard Doumerc, "Il dominio del mare," in *Il Rinascimento: Società ed economia*, ed. Alberto Tenenti and Ugo Tucci, vol. 5 of *Storia di Venezia* (Rome: Istituto della Enciclopedia Italiana, 1996), 113–80.

72. For an example of such discussions, see Jean-Claude Hocquet, *Le sel et la fortune de Venise*, vol. 2, *Voiliers et commerce en Méditerranée, 1200–1650*, 2d ed. (Lille: Presses Universitaires de Lille, 1982), 11–18.

73. For a survey of bibliography on this topic, see Kindleberger, *World Economic Primacy.*

74. Benjamin Arbel, "Colonie d'oltremare," in Tenenti and Tucci, *Il Rinascimento: Società ed economia*, 947–85.

75. Lane, *Venice, a Maritime Republic*, 358, 246, 248.

76. See Fernand Braudel, *Civilisation matérielle, économie et capitalisme, XVe–XVIIIe siècle*, vol. 3, *Le temps du monde* (Paris: Colin, 1979), 117–18, trans. Siân Reynolds under the title *Civilization and Capitalism, 15th–18th Century*, vol. 3, *The Perspective of the World* (New York: Harper & Row, 1984), 148–50.

77. Robert Finlay, "Crisis and Crusade in the Mediterranean: Venice, Portugal, and the Cape Route to India (1498–1509)," *Studi Veneziani*, n.s., 28 (1994): 45–90.

78. Frederic C. Lane, "The Mediterranean Spice Trade: Its Revival in the Sixteenth Century," *American Historical Review* 45 (1940): 581–90, reprinted in Lane, *Venice and History: The Collected Papers of Frederic C. Lane* (Baltimore: Johns Hopkins University Press, 1966), 25–34.

79. The Gulf Squadron was instituted in 1301; its task was to patrol the Adriatic as far south as the Strait of Otranto "ad custodiam culfi" (see Bernard Doumerc, "La difesa dell'impero," in Arnaldi, Cracco, and Tenenti, *La formazione dello stato patrizio*, 237–50, esp. 240).

80. Lane, *Venice, a Maritime Republic*, 44–55, 336–53; Ugo Tucci, "La navigazione veneziana nel Duecento e la sua evoluzione tecnica," in Pertusi, *Venezia e il Levante fino al secolo XV*, 1, pt. 2: 821–41.

81. Frederic C. Lane, "Merchant Galleys, 1300–34: Private and Communal Operation," *Speculum* 38 (1963): 179–205, reprinted in Lane, *Venice and History*, 193–226.

82. Frederic C. Lane, "Tonnages, Medieval and Modern," *Economic History Review*, 2d ser., 17 (1964): 213–33, reprinted in Lane, *Venice and History*, 345–70.

83. Bernard Doumerc, "Le rôle ambigu de la *muda* vénitienne: Convoi marchand ou unité de combat," in *Histoire maritime: Thalassocraties et période révolutionnaire* (Paris: CTHS, 1991), 139–54.

84. On the question of piracy in the Levant, see Alberto Tenenti, "Venezia e la pirateria nel Levante: 1300–c. 1460," in Pertusi, *Venezia e il Levante fino al secolo XV*, 1, pt. 2: 702–71.

85. This was the case in 1378 (admittedly a period of demographic depression), when Vettor Pisani commanded only fourteen galleys; in 1470, at the fall of Negroponte, Vettor da Canal had fifty-five galleys under his command.

86. Hocquet, *Le sel et la fortune de Venise*, vol. 2, *Voiliers et commerce*, 109.

---

87. Ennio Concina, "Le plus grand chantier de l'Occident: L'Arsenal," in Braunstein, *Venise 1500*, 40.

88. Alberto Tenenti, *Cristoforo da Canal: Le marine vénitienne avant Lépante* (Paris: S.E.V.P.E.N., 1962).

89. On the war of 1499–1503 and the destiny of Antonio Grimani, who paid for the reversals suffered by the Venetian fleet, see Lane, *Venice, a Maritime Republic*, 359–60.

90. Sanudo, *Diarii*, vol. 3, cols. 4–5.

91. Doris Stöckly, *Le système de l'incanto des galées du marché à Venise (fin XIIIe–milieu XVe siècle)* (Leiden: Brill, 1995).

92. Ugo Tucci, "Le commerce vénitien du vin de Crète," in *Maritime Food Transport*, ed. Klaus Friedland (Cologne: Böhlau, 994), 199–211.

93. Balard, "La lotta contro Genova"; Mario Gallina, *Una società coloniale del Trecento: Creta tra Venezia e Bisanzio* (Venice: Deputazione Editrice, 1989). For an original viewpoint, see Sally McKee, "Women under Venetian Colonial Rule in the Early Renaissance: Observations on Their Economic Activities," *Renaissance Quarterly* 51, no. 1 (1998): 34–67.

94. On the power of the Corner family on Cyprus and its role in the development of sugar production, see Marie-Louise von Wartburg, "Production du sucre de canne à Chypre: Un chapitre de technologie médiévale," in *Coloniser au Moyen Age*, ed. Michel Balard and Alain Ducellier (Paris: Colin, 1995), 126–31; and Bernard Doumerc, "Gli armamenti marittimi," in Arnaldi, Cracco, and Tenenti, *La formazione dello stato patrizio*, 617–40. For the general context, see also Jean Richard, "Chypre du protectorat à la domination vénitienne," in Pertusi, *Venezia e il Levante fino al secolo XV*, 2, pt. 2: 657–77.

95. Arbel, "Colonie d'oltremare," 966–68.

96. Ibid.

97. Giuseppe Stefani, *L'assicurazione a Venezia dalle origini alla fine della Serenissima*, 2 vols. (Trieste: Assocurazioni Generali di Trieste e Venezia, 1956), trans. Arturo Dawson Amoruso under the title *Insurance in Venice from the Origins to the End of the Serenissima*, 2 vols. (Trieste: Assocurazioni Generali di Trieste e Venezia, 1958); Gino Luzzatto, "Tasso d'interesse e usura a Venezia nei secoli XIII–XV," in *Miscellanea in onore di Roberto Cessi*, 3 vols. (Rome: Editizioni di Storia e Letteratura, 1958), 1:191–202; Claudio Schwarzenberg, *Ricerche sull'assicurazione marittima a Venezia: Dal dogado di Pasquale Cicogna al dogado di Paolo Renier* (Milan: Giuffrè, 1969); Karin Nehlsen–von Stryk, *Die Venezianische Seeversicherung im 15. Jahrhundert* (Ebelsbach: Gremer, 1986).

98. Reinhold C. Mueller, " 'Chome d'ucciello di passagio': La demande saisonnière des espèces et le marché des changes à Venise au Moyen Age," in *Études d'histoire monétaire, XIIe–XIXe siècles*, ed. John Day (Lille: Presses Universitaires de Lille, 1984), 195–219.

99. A simple *colleganza* united a moneylender *(socius stans)*, who remained in Venice, and a merchant, who made the voyage that produced the profits on the capital invested. As a rule, three-fourths of the profits went to the party who furnished

the capital and one-fourth went to the merchant. In the bilateral *colleganza* one-third of the capital was furnished by the merchant *(socius porcertans)* (see Adolfo Sacerdoti, "Le colleganze nella pratica degli affari e nella legislazione veneta," *Atti dell'Istituto Veneto di Scienze, Lettere ed Arti* 59 [1899–1900]: 1–45; and Gino Luzzatto, "La commenda nella vita economica dei secoli XIII e XIV con particolare riguardo a Venezia," in *Atti del convegno di studi storici del diritto marittimo medievale* [Naples: Meridionali, 1934]).

100. Gino Luzzatto, "Les activités économiques du patriciat vénitien (Xe–XIVe siècles)," *Annales d'Histoire Économique et Sociale* 1 (1937): 25–57, reprinted in Luzzatto, *Studi di storia economica veneziana* (Padua: CEDAM, 1954), 125–65.

101. "Perhaps Venice's easily-acquired riches imprisoned the city within a set of strategies determined by ancient custom, whereas other cities, with less assured fortunes, were sooner or later obliged to become more cunning and inventive?" (Braudel, *Civilisation matérielle, économie et capitalisme*, vol. 3, *Le temps du monde*, 105; in English, *Civilization and Capitalism*, vol. 3, *Perspective of the World*, 128).

102. On the *fraterne*, see Frederic C. Lane, "Family Partnerships and Joint Ventures," *Journal of Economic History* 4 (1944): 178–96, reprinted in Lane, *Venice and History*, 36–55.

103. Ugo Tucci, "Monete e banche nel secolo del ducato d'oro," in Tenenti and Tucci, *Il Rinascimento: Società et economia*, 753–806; Reinhold C. Mueller, "The Role of Bank Money in Venice, 1300–1500," *Studi Veneziani*, n.s., 3 (1979): 47–96; idem, "I banchi locali a Venezia nel tardo Medioevo," *Studi Storici* 1 (1987): 145–55; Frederic C. Lane and Reinhold C. Mueller, *Coins and Moneys of Account*, vol. 1 of *Money and Banking in Medieval and Renaissance Venice* (Baltimore: Johns Hopkins University Press, 1985); Reinhold C. Mueller, *The Venetian Money Market: Banks, Panics, and the Public Debt, 1200–1500*, vol. 2 of *Money and Banking in Medieval and Renaissance Venice* (Baltimore: Johns Hopkins University Press, 1997).

104. John Day, "Les instruments de gestion du monde," in Braunstein, *Venise 1500*, 142–56.

105. Pierre Sardella, *Nouvelles et spéculations à Venise au début du XVIe siècle*, Cahier des Annales, 1 (Paris: Colin, 1948). Sardella studies the effects of "news" on the wheat market and the market for spices, on marine insurance, and, in the domain of finance, on the areas that were economically the most sensitive to events. See also Ugo Tucci, "Alle origini dello spirito capitalistico a Venezia: La previsione economica," in *Studi in onore di Amintore Fanfani*, 6 vols. (Milan: Giuffrè, 1962), 3:545–57; and Frederic C. Lane, "Ritmo e rapidità di giro d'affari nel commercio veneziano del Quattrocento," in *Studi in onore di Gino Luzzatto*, 4 vols. (Milan: Giuffrè, 1949), 1:254–73, reprinted as "Rhythm and Rapidity of Turnover in Venetian Trade of the Fifteenth Century" in Lane, *Venice and History*, 109–27.

106. The people of Ragusa, for example, had obtained the same rights as Venetian citizens, which meant that they could load their merchandise and sail on Venetian ships (see Krekic, "Venezia e l'Adriatico," 61).

107. Thiriet, *La Romanie vénitienne*, 304–5.

108. Jean-Claude Hocquet, *Le sel et la fortune de Venise*, vol. 1, *Production et monopole*, 2d ed. (Lille: Presses Universitaires de Lille, 1982).

109. Jean-Claude Hocquet, "Le sel supporte les épices," in Braunstein, *Venise 1500*, 124.

110. Alberto Tenenti and Corrado Vivanti, "Le film d'un grand système de navigation: Les galères marchandes vénitiennes, XIVe–XVIe siècle," *Annales E.S.C.* 16 (1961): 83–86.

111. On the beginnings of this system, see Doumerc, "Gli armamenti marittimi," 622–25.

112. Bernard Doumerc, "La crise structurelle de la marine vénitienne au XVe siècle: Le problème du retard des 'mude,' " *Annales E.S.C.* 40 (1985): 605–23.

113. Frederic C. Lane, "The Crossbow in the Nautical Revolution of the Middle Ages," in *Economy, Society, and Government in Medieval Italy: Essays in Memory of Robert L. Reynolds*, ed. David Herlihy, Robert S. Lopez, and V. Slessarev, Explorations in Economic History, 7 (Kent, Ohio: Kent State University Press, 1969), 161–71, reprinted in Lane, *Studies in Venetian Social and Economic History*, ed. Benjamin G. Kohl and Reinhold C. Mueller (London: Variorum Reprints, 1987), sec. 6.

114. Freddy Thiriet, "Les itinéraires des vaisseaux vénitiens et le rôle des agents consulaires en Romanie gréco-vénitienne aux XIVe–XVe siècles," in *Venezia e le grandi linee dell'espansione commerciale* (Venice, 1956), 188–215.

115. Marino Sanudo, *De origine, situ et magistratibus urbis Venetae, ovvero, La Città di Venetia (1493–1530)*, ed. Angela Caracciolo Aricò (Milan: Cisalpino–La Goliardica, 1980), 28.

THREE   *The Lion and the Land*

1. Tomaso Mocenigo, in Marino Sanuto, *Vitae Ducum venetorum*, Rerum Italicorum Scriptores, ed. Ludovico Antonio Muratori, vol. 22 (Milan, 1733), cols 399–1252, esp. 949–58.

2. Sanuto, *Vitae Ducum venetorum*, cols. 958–64.

3. Lemaire de Belges states: "When and as long as they will be lords of navigation on the sea, they will have hardly any controversy with the Christian Princes, but instead will prosper with great wealth: which is signified by the first Lion; but every time and as many times as they lose the said navigation and put themselves to usurping on solid land, they will move against them the indignation of the great princes, by whom they will be totally undone and sprung upon: which is told to them by the second Lion" (quoted in Antonio Medin, *La storia della Repubblica di Venezia nella poesia* [Milan: Hoepli, 1904], 161). Lemaire de Belges may have seen these mosaic depictions of lions during a trip to Venice in 1506, when he may have learned the prophetic meaning that Joachim had given to them (see John Easton Law, "The Venetian Mainland State in the Fifteenth Century," *Transactions of the Royal Historical Society*, 6th ser., 2 [1992]: 153–74; and Marjorie Reeves, *The Influence of Prophecy in the Late Middle Ages: A Study in Joachimism* [Oxford: Clarendon Press, 1969]). I might note that this description of the lions, which Lemaire de Belges wrote for the benefit of Louis XII, mocks not only the animal that symbolized the patron saint of Venice and the Republic itself but more specifically the lion in the passant position, figured in profile, standing with one forepaw placed on the open Gospel and the

other resting on the ground. In Lemaire's *Legende des Venitiens* the second lion's two rear paws are in the water, and the lion is focused on the land. I might also recall Carpaccio's famous painting of the lion of St. Mark (1516, commissioned by the government). Jacobello del Fiora had painted a first lion passant a good deal earlier (in 1415), which means that the representation and the political and territorial claims it clearly expressed were a familiar theme (see Marco Pozza, "I proprietari fondiari in Terraferma," in *L'età del Comune,* ed. Giorgio Cracco and Gherardo Ortalli, vol. 2 of *Storia di Venezia* [Rome: Istituto della Enciclopedia Italiana, 1995], 661–80).

4. Girolamo Priuli, *I diarii di Girolamo Priuli,* vol. 4 *(aa. 1499–1512),* ed. Roberto Cessi, Rerum Italicorum Scriptores, n.s., 24, pt. 3 (Bologna: Zanichelli, 1938–41), 30–31.

5. Ibid., 19–24.

6. This version of events explains the idea, which had an astonishing longevity, that in the great migration each of the mainland bishops abandoned his former seat and established a new one. In reality it was some time before the religious organization of the lagoon became stable. Thus the bishop of Altino managed to maintain his title even though he resided in Torcello. This is at least a commonly accepted hypothesis. The diocese of Oderzo disappeared, probably in the late seventh century, at the death of its last titulary.

7. It is interesting that according to the official version of Venetian history, from the very founding of Venice the Venetians and the people of Padua fought for control of the river mouths (see Paolo Morosini, *Historia della città, e repubblica di Venetia, di Paolo Morosini senatore veneziano distinta in libri vintiotto* [Venice, 1637], 3–4).

8. Marcantonio Coccio Sabellico, *Degli istorici delle cose veneziane i quali hanno scritto per pubblico decreto,* vol. 1, *Istorie veneziane latinamente scritte da Marcantonio Coccio Sabellico* (Venice, 1718).

9. Pompeo G. Molmenti, *La storia di Venezia nella vita privata, dalle origini alla caduta della Repubblica,* new ed., 3 vols. (Trieste: Lint, 1978).

10. One might cite other interpretations that seem to differ from Molmenti's but in fact take the same vision of Venetian history as their point of departure. One such is Heinrich Kretschmayr, *Geschichte von Venedig,* 3 vols. (1905–34; reprint, Aalen: Scientia, 1986). According to Kretschmayr, Francesco Foscari understood that because the foundations of Venetian power had been shaken in the East, the Venetian state needed to strengthen its power on a different base, that of territorial expansion.

11. Marino Berengo, *La società veneta alla fine del Settecento: Ricerche storiche* (Florence: G. C. Sansoni, 1956); Angelo Ventura, *Nobiltà e popolo nella società veneta del Quattrocento e Cinquecento,* 2d ed. (Milan: UNICOPLI, 1993).

12. Giorgio Chittolini and Elena Fasano Guarini, "Gli stati dell'Italia centro-settentrionale tra Quattro e Cinquecento: Continuità e trasformazione," *Società e Storia* 21 (1983): 617–40.

13. James S. Grubb, *Firstborn of Venice: Vicenza in the Early Renaissance State* (Baltimore: Johns Hopkins University Press, 1988).

14. Joanne M. Ferraro, *Family and Public Life in Brescia, 1580–1650: The Foundations of Power in the Venetian State* (Cambridge: Cambridge University Press, 1993).

15. Giorgio Borelli, Paola Lanaro Sartori, and Francesco Vecchiato, eds., *Il sistema*

fiscale veneto: Problemi e aspetti, XV–XVIII secolo (Verona: Libreria Universitaria, 1982).

16. Exceptions to this clear division are the works of Philippe Braunstein, cited below, and those of Gerhard Rösch, in particular *Venedig und das Reich: Handels- und Verkehrspolitische Beziehungen in der deutschen Kaiserzeit* (Tübingen: Niemeyer, 1982).

17. I quote the introduction to Freddy Thiriet, *Histoire de Venise*, Que sais-je? 522 (Paris: Presses Universitaires de France, 1969), 5.

18. There is evidence of Venetians on the major waterways of northern Italy—including the Po, where they competed with the people of Comacchio—as early as the eighth century (see Gino Luzzatto, *Storia economica di Venezia dal XI al XVI secolo* [Venice: Centro Internazionale delle Arti e del Costume, 1961], 4). Boatmen distributed salt and fish in the valleys of the Adige, the Brenta, the Piave, and the Tagliamento. Their boats went upriver as far as Pavia, carrying merchandise from the East as well as the products of the lagoon. There should be no need to repeat the familiar quotation from the *Honorantiae civitatis Papiae*, a famous text of Lombard law, stating that the Venetians did not cultivate the soil and did not sow but harvested salt. For a survey of the meager resources of the lagoon, see Giorgio Cracco, *Un "altro mondo": Venezia nel Medioevo dal secolo XI al secolo XIV* (Turin: UTET, 1986), 5 ff.

19. There is brief reference to the exploitation of salt before the foundation of the city of Venice in Jean-Claude Hocquet, "Le sel supporte les épices," in *Venise 1500: La puissance, la novation et la concorde: Le triomphe du mythe*, ed. Philippe Braunstein (Paris: Autrement, 1993), 112–13.

20. Comacchio, which competed with Venice in the salt trade, was leveled twice by the Venetians, once in 882–83 and again in 933 (see chap. 2).

21. Hocquet, "Le sel supporte les épices."

22. The high price of Venetian salt encouraged the development of several competing centers of production in the late twelfth century. There were saltworks in the Alps, on the Istrian coast (at Capodistria and Piran), at Cervia, and in Romania.

23. Jean-Claude Hocquet, *Le sel et la fortune de Venise*, vol. 2, *Voiliers et commerce en Méditerranée, 1200–1650*, 2d ed. (Lille: Presses Universitaires de Lille, 1982); idem, "Expansion, crises et déclin des salines dans la lagune de Venise au Moyen Age," in *Mostra storica della laguna veneta*, exh. cat. (Venice: Stamperia di Venezia, 1970), reprinted in Hocquet, *Chioggia, capitale del sale nel Medioevo*, trans. Carla Neri (Padua: Libraria Editrice, 1991); idem, "Le saline," in *Origini-Età ducale*, ed. Lellia Cracco Ruggini et al., vol. 1 of *Storia di Venezia* (Rome: Instituto della Enciclopedia Italiana, 1992), 515–48.

24. For examples of these aquatic domains, see Hannelore Zug Tucci, "Pesca e caccia in laguna," in Cracco Ruggini et al., *Origini-Età ducale*, 490–514.

25. *Codex Publicorum (Codice del Piovego)*, ed. Bianca Lanfranchi Strina, vol. 1 (1282–98), Fonti per la Storia di Venezia, sec. 1, Archivi Pubblici, Monumenti Storici, n.s., 22 (Venice, 1895).

26. For techniques for lagoon fishing and the economic and social aspects of fishing, see Elisabeth Crouzet-Pavan, *La mort lente de Torcello* (Paris: Fayard, 1995), 179–96.

27. For a study of one of these parishes, the Venetian community of the Nicolotti, see Roberto Zago, *I Nicolotti: Storia di una communità di pescatori a Venezia nell'età moderna* (Padua: Francisci, 1982).

28. Roberto Cessi, ed., *Origo civitatum Italiae seu Venetiarum: Chronicon altinate et Chronicon gradense,* Fonti per la Storia d'Italia, 73 (Rome: Tipografia del Senato, 1933), 32–34.

29. Sante Bortolami, "L'agricoltura," in Cracco Ruggini et al., *Origini-Età ducale,* 461–90.

30. Crouzet-Pavan, *La mort lente de Torcello,* chap. 5.

31. See Bortolami, "L'agricoltura"; and Gérard Rippe, *Padoue et son territoire, Xe–XIIIe siècle: Société et pouvoir,* Bibliothèque des Écoles Françaises d'Athènes et de Rome. Rome: École Française de Rome, forthcoming.

32. Marco Pozza, *I Badoer: Una famiglia veneziana dal X al XIII secolo* (Padua: Francisci, 1982), 60–63. On these holdings and on the Badoers' matrimonial alliances with powerful families of the Terraferma, see Pozza, "I proprietari fondiari in Terraferma."

33. Elisabeth Crouzet-Pavan, *Venise: Une invention de la ville, XIIe–XVe siècle,* Collection Époques (Seyssel: Champ Vallon, 1997), 198–99.

34. Gino Luzzatto, "Capitale e lavoro nel commercio veneziano dei secoli XI e XII," in Luzzatto, *Studi di storia economica veneziana* (Padua: CEDAM, 1954), 89–116; Giorgio Cracco, *Società e stato nel Medioevo veneziano (secoli XII–XIV)* (Florence: Olschki, 1967), 3.

35. Pozza, "I proprietari fondiari in Terraferma." For Venetian possessions in the Treviso area, see Marco Pozza, "Penetrazione fondiaria e relazioni commerciali con Venezia," in *Il Medioevo,* ed. Daniela Rando and Gian Maria Varanini, vol. 2 of *Storia di Treviso,* ed. Ernesto Brunetta (Venice: Marsilio, 1991), 299–321.

36. Cracco, *Società e stato nel Medioevo veneziano,* 211–43.

37. Giorgio Cracco, "Mercanti in crisi: Realtà economiche e riflessi emotivi nella Venezia del tardo Duecento," in *Studi sul medioevo veneziano,* ed. Giorgio Cracco, Andrea Castagnetti, and Silvana Collodo (Turin: Giappichelli, 1981). For the political utilization of a miracle that occurred in 1265, in a climate of crisis in trade, see Debra Pincus, "Christian Relics and the Body Politic: A Thirteenth-Century Relief Plaque in the Church of San Marco," in *Interpretazioni veneziane: Studi di storia in onore di Michelangelo Muraro,* ed. David Rosand (Venice: Arsenale, 1984), 39–57.

38. For the situation of the lagoons "between the empires," see Philippe Braunstein and Robert Delort, *Venise: Portrait historique d'une cité* (Paris: Seuil, 1971), 31. For this period, see also Gherardo Ortalli, "Venezia dalle origini a Pietro II Orseolo," in *Longobardi e Bizantini,* by Paolo Delogu, André Guillou, and Gherardo Ortalli, Storia d'Italia, ed. Giuseppe Galasso, 1 (Turin: UTET, 1980), 339–438.

39. Otto did not reconstitute the Empire at Rome until 962.

40. Roberto Cessi, *Storia della Repubblica di Venezia,* new ed. (Florence: Giunti Martello, 1981), 74. Pietro III Candiano had already served the kings of Italy and asked for their aid. Cessi states that already everything "seemed to compromise the fortunes of a healthy sea life to attempt the adventure of continental politics" (73). I might nonetheless remark that the conquest of the Gulf of Venice, that is, the zone

delimited by an imaginary line drawn from Pola to Ravenna, had already been accomplished by Pietro II Candiano (932–39) and Pietro III Candiano (942–59).

41. See Paolo Brezzi, "La pace di Venezia del 1177 e le relazioni tra la Repubblica e l'Impero," in *Venezia dalla prima crociata alla conquista di Costantinopoli del 1204* (Florence: Sansoni, 1965), 51–70.

42. Gerhard Rösch, "Lo sviluppo mercantile," in Cracco and Ortalli, *L'età del Comune*, 131–51, esp. 139.

43. On the problem of control of the major commercial routes, see Rösch, *Venedig und das Reich.* Another highly useful work is Giorgio Cracco, ed., *L'età medievale,* vol. 2 of *Storia di Vicenza* (Vicenza: Neri Pozza, 1988), in particular 86–88. See also Luigi Simeoni, *Il Comune veronese sino ad Ezzelino e il suo primo statuto* (Venice, 1922), reprinted in *Studi su Verona nel Medioevo di Luigi Simeoni,* ed. Vittorio Cavallari, vol. 1, Studi Storici Veronesi, 10 (Verona: Istituto per gli Studi Storici Veronesi, 1959): 27–39; and Gherardo Ortalli and Michael Knapton, eds., *Istituzioni, società e potere nella Marca trevigiana e veronese (secoli XIII–XIV): Sulle tracce di G. B. Verci* (Rome: Istituto Storico Italiano per il Medio Evo, 1988).

44. The rivalry between Venice and Ferrara was ancient: the Venetians had backed Countess Matilda of Canossa.

45. Frederic C. Lane, *Venice, a Maritime Republic* (Baltimore: Johns Hopkins University Press, 1973), 62.

46. Kretschmayr, *Geschichte von Venedig,* 2:568.

47. Giovanni Soranzo, *La guerra fra Venezia e la Santa Sede per il dominio di Ferrara (1308–1313)* (Città di Castello: S. Lapi, 1905).

48. Cessi, *Storia della Repubblica di Venezia,* 282–85.

49. Gerhard Rösch, *I rapporti tra Venezia e Verona per un canale tra Adige e Po nel 1310 nell'ambito della politica del traffico veneziano,* Quaderni, 13 (Venice: Centro Tedesco di Studi Veneziani, 1979).

50. Two studies on this topic are Cracco, *Società e stato nel Medioevo veneziano;* and Marco Pozza, "Podestà e funzionari veneziani a Treviso e nella Marca in età comunale," in Ortalli and Knapton, *Istituzioni società e potere nella Marca trevigiana e veronese,* 291–303.

51. Crouzet-Pavan, *Venise,* 197–205.

52. The term *sedes marinae* comes from Sabellico, *Degli istorici delle cose veneziane i quali hanno scritto per pubblico decreto,* vol. 1, *Istorie veneziane.*

53. Frederic C. Lane and Reinhold C. Mueller, *Coins and Moneys of Account,* vol. 1 of *Money and Banking in Medieval and Renaissance Venice,* 2 vols. (Baltimore: Johns Hopkins University Press, 1997); Reinhold C. Mueller, *The Venetian Money Market: Banks, Panics, and the Public Debt, 1200–1500,* vol. 2 of *Money and Banking in Medieval and Renaissance Venice* (Baltimore: Johns Hopkins University Press, 1997).

54. Gerhard Rösch, "Mercatura e moneta," in Cracco Ruggini et al., *Origini-Età ducale,* 549–73, esp. 551–52.

55. Ibid.

56. Ibid., 569.

57. Rösch, "Lo sviluppo mercantile," 141–42. The agreements with Verona are dated 1175 and 1192; the one with Treviso, 1198; the one with Friuli, 1200. Regarding

the latter, although the doge had held rights over the river port of Pilo since 880, the rest of the system of waters and ports was placed under the jurisdiction of the patriarch of Aquileia. It was perhaps in the twelfth century that the doge obtained from the patriarch protection of merchandise transported on the rivers of Friuli (see Rösch, *Venedig und das Reich*. For the agreements drawn up in the thirteenth century, see Gerhard Rösch, "Il gran guadagno," in Cracco and Ortalli, *L'età del Comune*, 233–62, esp. 250–51).

58. The tower of Le Bebbe, a frontier fortress on the edge of the duchy, served as a customs office. It was the site of a series of conflicts with Padua, which was eager to gain free access to the sea.

59. The fortress of Cavarzere protected the Adige at the border of the duchy.

60. On these waterways, see Rösch, *Venedig und das Reich*.

61. Rösch, "Lo sviluppo mercantile," 144.

62. Wolfgang von Stromer, *Bernardus Teotonicus e i rapporti commerciali tra la Germania meridionale e Venezia prima della istituzione dei Tedeschi*, Quaderni, 8 (Venice: Centro Tedesco di Studi Veneziani, 1978).

63. Philippe Braunstein, "Venezia e la Germania nel Medioevo," in *Venezia e la Germania: Arte, politica, commerci, due civiltà a confronto* (Milan: Electa, 1986), 35–49.

64. The land was purchased by the commune in 1222; the first mention of the *fontecum communis* appears in 1225.

65. Philippe Braunstein, "Relations d'affaires entre Nurembergeois et Vénitiens à la fin du XIVe siècle," *École Française de Rome: Mélanges d'Archéologie et d'Histoire* 76, no. 1 (1964): 227–69.

66. Henry Simonsfeld, *Der Fondaco dei Tedeschi in Venedig und die deutsch-venetianischen Handelsbeziehungen*, 2 vols. (1887; reprint, Aalen: Scientia, 1968).

67. Karl-Ernst Lupprian, *Il fondaco dei Tedeschi e la sua funzione di controllo del commercio tedesco a Venezia*, Quaderni, 6 (Venice: Centro Tedesco di Studi Veneziani, 1978).

68. In 1417 and again in 1418 Emperor Sigismond attempted to turn German merchants away from the port of Venice; in 1426, when Genoa had passed under the domination of the Visconti, the emperor decreed that henceforth that city would be the port of the Empire.

69. Braunstein, "Relations d'affaires," 228.

70. Philippe Braunstein, "Le commerce du fer à Venise au XVe siècle," *Studi Veneziani* 8 (1966): 267–302. For a study of systematic prospecting and mining ventures in the Venetian hinterland after its territorial conquest, see idem, "Les entreprises minières en Vénétie au XVe siècle," *École Française de Rome: Mélanges d'Archéologie et d'Histoire* 77, no. 2 (1965): 529–601; and Annibale Alberti and Roberto Cessi, *La politica mineraria della Repubblica veneta* (Rome: Provveditorio Generale dello Stato, Libreria, 1927).

71. This passage reflects some of what I say in Crouzet-Pavan, *La mort lente de Torcello*, 232–37.

72. A basic reference for all of these problems is Philippe Braunstein, "De la

montagne à Venise: Les réseaux du bois au XVe siècle," *Mélanges de l'École Française de Rome, Moyen Age* 100, no. 2 (1988): 761–99.

73. Some residual concentrations of wooden houses remained, however. On the shift to stone, see Elisabeth Crouzet-Pavan, *"Sopra le acque salse": Espaces, pouvoir et société à Venise à la fin du Moyen Age,* 2 vols., Collection de l'École Française de Rome, 158 (Rome: Istituto Storico Italiano per il Medio Evo, 1992), 1:210–12, 258–59.

74. See Frederic C. Lane, "The Timber Supplies," in Lane, *Venetian Ships and Shipbuilders of the Renaissance* (1934; reprint, Baltimore: Johns Hopkins University Press, 1992), 217–33.

75. Nicolai Rubinstein, "Italian Reactions to Terraferma Expansion in the Fifteenth Century," in *Renaissance Venice,* ed. J. R. Hale (London: Faber; Totowa, N.J.: Rowman & Littlefield, 1973), 197–217.

76. Grubb, *Firstborn of Venice,* 6; Gaetano Cozzi and Michael Knapton, *Storia della Repubblica di Venezia dalla guerra di Chioggia alla riconquista della Terraferma,* vol. 12 of *Storia d'Italia* (Turin: UTET, 1986), 16–17. Both of these texts remark that no one in Italy contested Venice's conquests between 1404 and 1405. The Florentines even saw them as a useful counterweight to the lordship of the Visconti.

77. James Grubb rightly notes that even after Agnadello and the costly reconquest of the Venetian possessions, there was never any question that the Terraferma would obtain equal status with Venice. Venice remained the state, not simply a capital city (see Grubb, *Firstborn of Venice,* x).

78. John Easton Law, "Il Quattrocento a Venezia," in *I secoli del primato italiano: Il Quattrocento,* vol. 8 of *Storia della società italiana,* ed. Giovanni Cherubini et al. (Milan: Teti, 1988), 233–311, esp. 288.

79. Grubb, *Firstborn of Venice,* 16.

80. Benjamin G. Kohl, *Padua under the Carrara, 1318–1405* (Baltimore: Johns Hopkins University Press, 1998), 62–67.

81. For an examination of Venice's very prudent politics in this regard, see Michael Knapton, "Venezia e Treviso nel Trecento: Proposte per una ricerca sul primo dominio veneziano a Treviso," in *Tomaso da Modena e il suo tempo* (Treviso: Comitato Manifestazioni Tomaso da Modena, 1980).

82. Kohl, *Padua under the Carrara.*

83. At the time, Visconti domination extended over Lombardy and parts of Tuscany and Romagna.

84. For a detailed description of all these events, as well as the events that were occurring at the same time in the Levant, see Cozzi and Knapton, *Storia della Repubblica di Venezia,* 3–83.

85. See Law, "Il Quattrocento a Venezia," 300–1; Michael E. Mallett, "L'esercito veneziano in terraferma nel Quattrocento," in *Armi e cultura nel Bresciano, 1420–1870* (Brescia: Ateneo di Brescia, 1981); and Michael E. Mallett and J. R. Hale, *The Military Organisation of a Renaissance State: Venice, c. 1400 to 1617* (Cambridge: Cambridge University Press, 1984).

86. Cozzi and Knapton, *Storia della Repubblica di Venezia,* 212–13.

87. For an analysis of the "black legend" of Venetian domination in its overseas

empire, see Benjamin Arbel, "Entre mythe et histoire: La légende noire de la domina-
tion vénitienne à Chypre," in *Matériaux pour une histoire de Chypre (IVe–XXe siècle),*
Études Balkaniques, Cahiers Pierre Belon, 5 (Paris: Pierre Belon, 1998; distributed by
De Boccard), 83–107.

88. Ventura, *Nobiltà e popolo nella società veneta,* 92–106; Angelo Ventura, "Il
Dominio di Venezia nel Quattrocento," in *Quattrocento,* vol. 1 of *Florence and Venice:
Comparisons and Relations* (Florence: La Nuova Italia, 1979), 168–90. Ventura ad-
justed his interpretation to some extent in response to the debate that it inspired. On
this point, see idem, introduction to *Dentro lo "Stado Italico": Venezia e la Terraferma
fra Quattro e Seicento,* ed. Giorgio Cracco and Michael Knapton (Trent: Gruppo
Culturale Civis, 1984), 165–75.

89. John Easton Law, "Venice and the 'Closing' of the Veronese Constitution in
1405," *Studi Veneziani,* n.s., 1 (1977): 69–103; Gian Maria Varanini, "Note sui consigli
civici veronese (secoli XIV–XV): In margine ad uno studio di J. E. Law," *Archivio
Veneto,* 5th ser., 147 (1979): 5–32, reprinted as "I consigli civici veronesi fra la dominazione viscontea e quella veneziana," in Varanini, *Comuni cittadini e stato regionale:
Ricerche sulla Terraferma veneta nel Quattrocento* (Verona: Libreria Editrice Universitaria, 1992), 185–96 (see esp. 185–86).

90. For an analysis of the same sort of phenomenon in Brescia, see Ferraro,
Family and Public Life in Brescia, 56–57.

91. For an in-depth study of Verona, see Paola Lanaro Sartori, *Un'oligarchia
urbana nel Cinquecento veneto: Istituzioni, economia, società* (Turin: Giappichelli,
1992). For a study of hierarchies within this aristocracy, see idem, "Essere famiglia di
consiglio: Social Closure and Economic Change in the Veronese Patriciate of the
Sixteenth Century," *Renaissance Studies* 8, no. 4 (1994): 428–38.

92. John Easton Law, " 'Super differentiis agitatis Venetiis inter districtuales et
civitatem': Venezia, Verona e il contado nel '400," *Archivio Veneto,* 5th ser., 151 (1981):
5–32.

93. Ceferino Caro Lopez, "Gli Auditori Nuovi e il Dominio di Terraferma," in
Stato, società e giustizia nella Repubblica veneta (sec. XV–XVIII), ed. Gaetano Cozzi, 2
vols. (Rome: Jouvence, 1980), 1:259–316.

94. Cozzi and Knapton, *Storia della Repubblica di Venezia,* 243.

95. Gian Maria Varanini, "La Terraferma al tempo della crisi della lega di Cambrai: Proposte per una rilettura del 'caso' veronese," in Varanini, *Comuni cittadini e
stato regionale,* 397–435; Giuseppe Del Torre, *Venezia e la terraferma dopo la guerra di
Cambrai: Fiscalità e amministrazione (1515–1530)* (Milan: F. Angeli, 1986).

96. These statutes were recast after the conquest, but the task was accomplished
by local jurists. For an analysis of an administrative system that also reflects the more
general problematics of the Venetian system of government in the *dominium,* see
Ivana Pederzani, *Venezia e lo "Stado di Terraferma": Il governo delle comunità nel
territorio bergamasco (sec. XV–XVIII)* (Milan: Vita e Pensiero, 1992).

97. Grubb, *Firstborn of Venice.*

98. James S. Grubb, "Alla ricerca delle prerogative locali: La cittadinanza a Vicenza, 1404–1509," in Cracco and Knapton, *Dentro lo "Stado Italico,"* 177–91.

99. John Easton Law, "A New Frontier: Venice and the Trentino in the Early

Fifteenth Century," *Atti della Accademia Roveretana degli Agiati*, 6th ser., no. 28 (1990): 159–80; Antonio Menniti Ippolito, "La dedizione di Brescia a Milano (1421) e a Venezia (1427): Città suddite e distretto nello stato regionale," in Cozzi, *Stato, società e giustizia nella Repubblica veneziana*, 2:17–58.

100. Michael Knapton, "Il fisco nello stato veneziano di Terraferma tra '300 e '500: La politica delle entrate," in Borelli, Lanaro Sartori, and Vecchiato, *Il sistema fiscale veneto*, 15–58. See also Giuseppe Del Torre, *Il Trevigiano nei secoli XV e XVI: L'assetto amministrativo e il sistema fiscale* (Venice: Cardo, 1990).

101. Rawdon Lubbock Brown, ed., *Itinerario di Marin Sanuto per la terraferma veneziana nell'anno MCCCLXXXIII* (Padua, 1847).

102. Here I am following John Easton Law, "Verona e il Dominio Veneziano: Gli inizi," in *Il primo dominio veneziano a Verona 1405–1509* (Verona: Accademia di Agricoltura Scienze e Lettere di Verona, 1991), 17–33, esp. 27.

103. Gian Maria Varanini, "Mercato subregionale ed economia di distretto nella Terraferma veneta: Il commercio del vino," in Varanini, *Comuni cittadini e stato regionale*, 163–81.

104. Eliyahu Ashtor, "L'exportation des textiles occidentaux dans le Proche-Orient musulman au bas Moyen Age (1370–1517)," in Ashtor, *East-West Trade in the Medieval Mediterranean*, ed. Benjamin Z. Kedar (London: Variorum Reprints, 1986), 303–77.

105. On this point, and for an abundant bibliography, see Crouzet-Pavan, "*Sopra le acque salse*," 1:512–13.

106. On the old equilibrium in the lagoons, see Crouzet-Pavan, *La mort lente de Torcello*, 207–41. For case studies of various rural areas of the Terraferma, see Piergiovanni Mometto, *L'azienda agricola Barbarigo a Carpi: Gestione economica ed evoluzione sociale sulle terre di un villaggio della bassa pianura veronese (1443–1539)* (Venice: Il Cardo, 1992); Anna Bellavitis, *Noale: Struttura sociale e regime fondiario di una podesteria della prima metà del secolo XVI* (Treviso: Canova and Fondazione Benetton, 1994); Giuliano Galletti, *Bocche e biade: Popolazione e famiglie nelle campagne trevigiane dei secoli XV e XVI* (Treviso: Canova, 1994); Mauro Pitteri, *Mestrina: Proprietà, conduzione, colture nella prima metà del secolo XVI* (Treviso: Canova, 1994); Anna Pizzati, *Conegliano: Una "quasi città" e il suo territorio nel secolo XVI* (Treviso: Canova, 1994); and M. Teresa Todesco, *Oderzo e Motta: Paesaggio agrario, proprietà e conduzione di due podesterie nella prima metà del secolo XVI* (Treviso: Canova, 1995).

107. On the spread of sharecropping contracts in Venetian territories beginning in the mid-sixteenth century, when from 10% to 20% of the land was exploited in that manner, see Duilio Gasparini and Mathieu Arnoux, "Le savoir et la pratique: Un bail de métairie en Vénétie au XVIe siècle," *Histoire et Sociétés Rurales* 4 (1995): 232–80.

108. On proprietors in the early modern period, see Giuseppe Gullino, "Quando il mercante costruice la villa: Le proprietà dei Veneziani nella Terraferma," in *Dal Rinascimento al Barocco*, ed. Gaetano Cozzi and Paolo Prodi, vol. 6 of *Storia di Venezia* (Rome: Istituto della Enciclopedia Italiana, 1994), 875–924.

109. The question of land reclaimed for cultivation has elicited a historiographical debate that principally concerns the modern period: see Angelo Ventura, "Con-

siderazioni sull'agricoltura veneta e sull'accumulazione originaria del capitale nei secoli XVI e XVII," *Studi Storici* 3–4 (1968): 647–722; Salvatore Ciriacono, "Investimenti capitalistici e culture irrigue: La congiuntura agricola nella Terraferma veneta (secoli XVI–XVII)," in *Venezia e la Terraferma attraverso le relazioni dei rettori* (Milan: Giuffrè, 1981), 123–58; idem, "Irrigazione e produttività agraria nella Terraferma veneta tra Cinque e Seicento," *Archivio Veneto*, 5th ser., 147 (1979): 73–135; and Giorgio Borelli, "L'agricoltura veronese tra '500 e '600: Una proposta di lettura," in *Uomini e civiltà agraria in territorio veronese*, 2 vols. (Verona: Banca Popolare di Verona, 1982). See also Paola Lanaro Sartori, "Reddito agrario e controllo fiscale nel Cinquecento: La Valpolicella e Verona," in *La Valpolicella nella prima età moderna (1500–c. 1630)*, ed. Gian Maria Varanini (Verona: Centro di Documentazione per la Storia della Valpolicella, 1987), 205–45.

F O U R   *Scenes of Daily Life*

1. Martino da Canale, *Les Estoires de Venise: Cronaca veneziana in lingua francese dalle origini al 1295*, ed. Alberto Limentani (Florence: Olschki, 1972).

2. Ennio Concina, *L'Arsenale della Repubblica di Venezia: Tecniche e istituzioni dal Medioevo all'età moderna* (Milan: Electa, 1984), 9.

3. Frederic C. Lane, *Venetian Ships and Shipbuilders of the Renaissance* (1934; reprint, Baltimore: Johns Hopkins University Press, 1992), 146–75.

4. Concina, *L'Arsenale della Repubblica di Venezia*, 25–26.

5. Ugo Tucci, "La navigazione veneziana nel Duecento e la sua evoluzione tecnica," in *Venezia e il Levante fino al secolo XV*, ed. Agostino Pertusi (Florence: Olschki, 1973), 1, pt. 2: 821–42; Lane, *Venetian Ships and Shipbuilders*, 1–34; Alberto Tenenti and Corrado Vivanti, "Le film d'un grand système de navigation: Les galères marchandes vénitiennes, XIVe–XVIe siècle," *Annales E.S.C.* 16 (1961): 83–86, esp. 84.

6. Egle Renata Trincanato, "Rappresentatività e funzionalità di Piazza San Marco," in *Piazza San Marco: L'architettura, la storia, le funzioni*, by Giuseppe Samonà et al., 3d ed. (Venice: Marsilio, 1982), 83.

7. Elisabeth Crouzet-Pavan, *"Sopra le acque salse": Espaces, pouvoir et société à Venise à la fin du Moyen Age*, 2 vols., Collection de l'École Française de Rome, 158 (Rome: Istituto Storico Italiano per il Medio Evo, 1992), 1:181–84.

8. Ibid., 189–93.

9. Concina, *L'Arsenale della Repubblica di Venezia*, 50–68; Costantino Veludo, *Cenni storici sull'Arsenale di Venezia* (Venice, 1869), 18–19; Mario Nani Mocenigo, *L'Arsenale di Venezia* (Rome: Filippi, 1938), 27.

10. "Est la plus belle chose qui soit en tout le demourant du monde aujourd'huy, et la mieux ordonnée pour ce cas," Philippe de Commynes, *Mémoires*, in *Historiens et chroniquers du Moyen Age*, ed. Albert Pauphilat, Bibliothèque de la Pléiade (Paris: Gallimard, 1952), translated under the title *The Memoirs of Philip de Commines, Lord of Argenton*, ed. Andrew R. Scroble, 2 vols. (London, 1856), 2:171.

11. When passage through the *porto* of San Nicolò grew even more difficult in the latter half of the fifteenth century, the passageway through the outer islands at Malamocco tended to replace it for ship traffic. On this, see the figures given for the

years 1557–50 in Jean-Claude Hocquet, *Le sel et la fortune de Venise*, vol. 2, *Voiliers et commerce en Méditerranée, 1200–1650*, 2d ed. (Lille: Presses Universitaires de Lille, 1982), 167.

12. Crouzet-Pavan, *"Sopra le acque salse,"* 2:866–72.

13. Jules Sottas, *Les messageries maritimes de Venise aux XIVe et XVe siècles* (Paris: Société d'Éditions Géographiques, Maritimes et Coloniales, 1938); Ugo Tucci, "I servizi marittimi veneziani per il pellegrinaggio in Terrasanta nel Medioevo," in *Pellegrini e viaggiatori nell'economia di Roma dal XIV al XVII secolo*, ed. Mario Romani (Milan: Vita e Pensiero, 1958), 43–66; idem, "Mercanti, viaggiatori, pellegrini nel Quattrocento," in *Dal primo Quattrocento al Concilio di Trento*, ed. Girolamo Arnaldi and Manlio Pastore Stocchi, vol. 3 of *Storia della cultura veneta*, pt. 2 (Vicenza: Neri Pozza, 1980), 317–53.

14. Alain Ducellier et al., *Les chemins de l'exil: Bouleversements de l'Est européen et migrations vers l'Ouest à la fin du Moyen Age* (Paris: Colin, 1992), 150–69.

15. Brünehilde Imhaus, *Le minoranze orientali a Venezia, 1305–1510* (Rome: Il Veltro, 1997).

16. Alain Ducellier, "Les Albanais à Venise aux XIVe et XVe siècles," *Centre de Recherches d'Histoire et de Civilisation Byzantines: Travaux et Mémoires* 2 (1967): 405–20; Silvia Moretti, "Gli Albanesi a Venezia tra XV e XVI secolo," in *La città italiana e i luoghi degli stranieri, XIV–XVIII secolo*, ed. Donatella Calabi and Paola Lanaro (Rome: Laterza, 1998), 5–20. Although all of the Dalmatian community was not necessarily concentrated in the immediate vicinity of the *scuola*, for the most part they settled in the eastern part of the *sestiere* of Castello. It should be noted that not all of the *scuole* drew on a sizable, stable nucleus of people of the same origin living in the same neighborhood (see Reinhold C. Mueller, " 'Veneti facti privilegio': Stranieri naturalizzati a Venezia tra XIV e XVI secolo," in ibid., 41–51). Finally, for considerations regarding population movement from Dalmatia, see Reinhold C. Mueller, "Aspects of Venetian Sovereignty in Medieval and Renaissance Dalmatia," in *Quattrocento Adriatico: Fifteenth-Century Art of the Adriatic Rim*, ed. Charles Dempsey (Bologna: Nuova Alfa, 1996; distributed in the United States by Johns Hopkins University Press), 29–56.

17. Giorgio Fedalto, *Ricerche storiche sulla posizione giuridica ed ecclesiastica dei greci a Venezia nei secoli XV e XVI* (Florence: Olschki, 1967), 25–26; idem, "Le minoranze straniere a Venezia tra politica e legislazione," in *Venezia centro di mediazione tra Oriente e Occidente (secoli XV–XVI), Aspetti e problemi*, ed. Hans-Georg Beck, Manoussos Manoussacas, and Agostino Pertusi, 2 vols. (Florence: Olschki, 1977), 1:143–63; idem, "Stranieri a Venezia e a Padova," in Arnaldi and Stocchi, *Dal primo Quattrocento al Concilio di Trento*, pt. 1, 499–535; Dino Geanakopolos, "La colonia greca di Venezia e il suo significato per il Rinascimento," in *Venezia e l'Oriente fra tardo Medioevo e Rinascimento*, ed. Agostino Pertusi (Florence: Sansoni, 1966), 189–91; Heleni Porfyriou, "La presenza greca: Roma e Venezia tra XV e XVI secolo," in Calabi and Lanaro, *La città italiana e i luoghi degli stranieri*, 21–40.

18. Barisa Krekic, *Dubrovnik in the Fourteenth and Fifteenth Centuries: A City between East and West* (Norman: University of Oklahoma Press, 1972); idem, *Dubrovnik, Italy, and the Balkans in the Late Middle Ages* (London: Variorum Reprints,

1980); Susan Mosher Stuard, *A State of Deference: Ragusa/Dubrovnik in the Medieval Centuries* (Philadelphia: University of Pennsylvania Press, 1992).

19. Lane, *Venetian Ships and Shipbuilders*, 231. Jean-Claude Hocquet suggests that the crisis of the latter fifteenth century was not as serious as had been thought, remarking that in Venice the decline affected large-tonnage ships in particular (see Hocquet, *Le sel et la fortune de Venise*, vol. 2, *Voiliers et commerce*, 524–27).

20. Lane, *Venetian Ships and Shipbuilders*, 177–78; Gino Luzzatto, "Per la storia delle costruzioni navali a Venezia nei secoli XV e XVI," in *Scritti storici in onore di Camillo Manfroni nel XL anno di insegnamento* (Padua: A. Draghi, 1925), reprinted in Luzzatto, *Studi di storia economica veneziana* (Padua: CEDAM, 1954), 386–87. For a study of shipwrights as a social group in the early modern age, see Robert C. Davis, *Shipbuilders of the Venetian Arsenal: Workers and Workplace in the Preindustrial City* (Baltimore: Johns Hopkins University Press, 1990); on sailors as a group, see Frederic C. Lane, "Venetian Seamen in the Nautical Revolution of the Middle Ages," in Pertusi *Venezia e il Levante fino al secolo XV*, 1, pt. 1: 403–30, reprinted in Lane, *Studies in Venetian Social and Economic History*, ed. Benjamin G. Kohl and Reinhold C. Mueller (London: Variorum Reprints, 1987), sec. 7. See also Alberto Tenenti, *Naufrages, corsaires et assurances maritimes à Venise, 1592–1609* (Paris: S.E.V.P.E.N., 1959).

21. Egle Renata Trincanato, "Residenze collettive a Venezia," *Urbanistica* 42–43 (1965): 7.

22. Crouzet-Pavan, *"Sopra le acque salse,"* 1:669–75; Robert C. Davis: *The War of the Fists: Popular Culture and Public Violence in Late Renaissance Venice* (New York: Oxford University Press, 1994).

23. Roberto Zago, *I Nicolotti: Storia di una communità di pescatori a Venezia nell'età moderna* (Padua: Francisci, 1982); Elisabeth Crouzet-Pavan, *La mort lente de Torcello: Histoire d'une cité disparue* (Paris: Fayard, 1995), 187–90.

24. Roberto Cessi and Annibale Alberti, *Rialto: L'isola, il ponte, il mercato* (Bologna: Zanichelli, 1934); Donatella Calabi and Paolo Morachiello, *Rialto: Le fabbriche e il ponte* (Turin: Einaudi, 1987); Crouzet-Pavan, *"Sopra le acque salse,"* 1:174–75.

25. Bernard Doumerc, "Il dominio del mare," in *Il Rinascimento: Società ed economia*, ed. Alberto Tenenti and Ugo Tucci, vol. 5 of *Storia di Venezia* (Rome: Istituto della Enciclopedia Italiana, 1996), 113–80, esp. 114–15.

26. Marino Sanuto, *De origine, situ et magistratibus urbis Venetae, ovvero, La Città di Venetia (1493–1530)*, ed. Angela Caracciolo Aricò (Milan: Cisalpino–La Goliardica, 1980), 27–29; Marc'Antonio Sabellico, *De situ urbis Venetae* (ca. 1494), in a modern edition as *Del sito di Venezia città (1502)*, ed. Giancarlo Meneghetti (Venice: Zanetti, 1957).

27. See the descriptions in Cessi and Alberti, *Rialto*, and in Calabi and Morachiello, *Rialto*, 18–37.

28. Calabi and Morachiello, *Rialto*, 33.

29. For an analysis of various texts regarding the founding of Venice and for a bibliography of the question, see Crouzet-Pavan, *La mort lente de Torcello*, 65–69.

30. Sanuto, *De origine*, 25.

31. Sabellico, *Del sito di Venezia*, 18.

32. Richard C. Trexler, "La prostitution florentine au XVe siècle: Patronages et

clientèles," *Annales E.S.C.* 36 (1981): 983–1015; Maria Serena Mazzi, "Il mondo della prostituzione nella Firenze tardomedievale," *Ricerche Storiche* 14 (1984): 337–63; Jacques Rossiaud, "Prostitution, jeunesse et société dans les villes du Sud-Est au XVe siècle," *Annales E.S.C.* 31 (1976): 289–325, reprinted in Rossiaud, *La prostituzione nel Medioevo* (Rome: Laterza, 1984), translated into English by Lydia G. Cochrane under the title *Medieval Prostitution* (Oxford: Basil Blackwell, 1988), 1–52. See also Maria Serena Mazzi, *Prostitute e lenoni nella Firenze del Quattrocento* (Milan: Il Saggiatore, 1991).

33. Elisabeth Pavan, "Police des mœurs, société à Venise à la fin du Moyen Age," *Revue Historique* 4 (1980): 241–88.

34. Elisabeth Crouzet-Pavan, *Venise: Une invention de la ville, XIIe–XVe siècle,* Collection Époques (Seyssel: Champ Vallon, 1997), 161–74. For a general study of theft, see Stefano Piasentini, *"Alla luce della luna": I furti a Venezia (1270–1403)* (Venice: Il Cardo, 1992).

35. Guido Ruggiero, *Violence in Early Renaissance Venice* (New Brunswick, N.J.: Rutgers University Press, 1980).

36. Crouzet-Pavan, *"Sopra le acque salse,"* 2:822–25.

37. Crouzet-Pavan, *Venise,* 291–304. For a study of the socioeconomic conditions leading to the creation of the Venice ghetto, see Benjamin Ravid, "The Religious, Economic, and Social Background and Context of the Establishment of the Ghetti of Venice," in *Gli ebrei e Venezia: Secoli XIV–XVIII,* ed. Gaetano Cozzi (Milan: Comunità, 1987), 211–60; Robert Finlay, "The Foundation of the Ghetto: Venice, the Jews, and the War of the League of Cambrai," *Proceedings of the American Philosophical Society* 126 (1982): 140–54; Brian Pullan, *Rich and Poor in Renaissance Venice: The Social Institutions of a Catholic State, to 1620* (Cambridge: Harvard University Press, 1971); idem, *The Jews of Europe and the Inquisition of Venice: 1550–1670* (Oxford: Basil Blackwell; Totowa N. J.: Barnes & Noble, 1983), 170–75; Donatella Calabi, Ugo Camerino, and Ennio Concina, *La città degli Ebrei: Il ghetto di Venezia, architettura e urbanistica* (Venice: Albrizzi, 1991); Corrado Vivanti, ed., *Dall'alto medioevo all'età dei ghetti,* pt. 1 of *Gli ebrei in Italia,* vol. 11 of *Storia d'Italia, Annali* (Turin: Einaudi, 1996).

38. David Jacoby, "Les juifs de Venise du XIVe siècle au milieu du XVIe siècle," in Beck, Manoussacas, and Pertusi, *Venezia centro di mediazione tra Oriente e Occidente,* 1:163–216; Reinhold C. Mueller, "Les prêteurs juifs de Venise au Moyen Age," *Annales E.S.C.* 30 (1975): 1475–96; Pier Cesare Ioly Zorattini, "Gli ebrei a Venezia, Padova e Verona," in Arnaldi and Stocchi, *Dal primo Quattrocento al concilio di Trento,* 537–76.

39. Philippe Braunstein, "Un étranger dans la ville, Albrecht Dürer," in *Venise 1500: La puissance, la novation et la concorde: Le triomphe du mythe,* ed. Braunstein (Paris: Autrement, 1993), 215–29.

40. Philippe Braunstein, "Remarques sur la population allemande de Venise à la fin du Moyen Age," in Beck, Manoussacas, and Pertusi, *Venezia centro di mediazione tra Oriente e Occidente,* 1:233–43; idem, "Appunti per la storia di una minoranza: La popolazione tedesca di Venezia nel Medioevo," in *Strutture familiari, epidemie, migrazione nell'Italia medievale,* ed. Rinaldo Comba, Gabriella Piccinni, and Giuliano Pinto (Naples: Edizioni Scientifiche Italiane, 1984): 511–27; Giuliano Pinto, "Le città

italiane e i lavoratori della lana nel basso medioevo: Alcune considerazioni," in *Le migrazioni in Europa, secc. XIII–XVIII*, ed. Simonetta Cavaciocchi (Florence: Le Monnier, 1994), 819–24. Also of use is *Forestieri e stranieri nelle città basso-medievali* (Florence: Salimbeni, 1988).

41. Gino Luzzatto, "Vi furono fiere a Venezia?" in Luzzatto, *Studi di storia economica veneziana*, 201–9.

42. Fernand Braudel, *Civilisation matérielle, économie et capitalisme, XVe–XVIIe siècle*, vol. 3, *Le temps du monde* (Paris: Colin, 1979), 112, trans. Siân Reynolds under the title *Civilization and Capitalism, 15th–18th Century*, vol. 3, *The Perspective of the World* (New York: Harper & Row, 1984), 136.

43. Giovanni Monticolo, *I capitolari delle arti veneziane*, 3 vols. (Rome, 1896–1914).

44. Richard Mackenney, *Tradesmen and Traders: The World of the Guilds in Venice and Europe c. 1250–c. 1650* (Totowa, N.J.: Barnes & Noble, 1987). For a comparison with the broader Italian context, see Roberto Greci, *Corporazioni e mondo del lavoro nell'Italia padana medievale* (Bologna: CLUEB, 1988); and Donata Degrassi, *L'economia artigiana nell'Italia medievale* (Rome: La Nuova Italia Scientifica, 1996).

45. See Salvatore Ciriacono, "Industria e artigianato," in Tenenti and Tucci, *Il Rinascimento: Società ed economia*, 523–92, esp. 534.

46. Dennis Romano, *Patricians and Popolani: The Social Foundations of the Venetian Renaissance State* (Baltimore: Johns Hopkins University Press, 1987), chap. 4; Silvia Gramigna and Annalisa Perissa, *Scuole di arti, mestieri e devozione a Venezia* (Venice: Arsenale, 1981).

47. Richard Mackenney, "Corporazioni e politica nel Medioevo a Venezia ca. 1250–1400," in *Venezia tardomedioevale: Istituzioni e società nella storiografia anglo-americana*, Ricerche Venete, 1 (Venice: Canal, 1989), 87–130; idem, "The Guilds of Venice: State and Society in the *Longue Durée*," *Studi Veneziani*, n.s., 34 (1997): 15–44.

48. Women were active in a certain number of trades, the textile industry in particular, but there were no guilds exclusively for women. On the question of women's work, see Simonetta Cavaciocchi, ed., *La donna nell'economia secc. XIII–XVIII* (Florence: Le Monnier, 1990); Maria Giuseppina Muzzarelli, Paola Galetti, and Bruno Andreoli, eds., *Donne e lavoro nell'Italia medievale* (Turin: Rosenberg & Sellier, 1991); Angela Groppi, ed., *Il lavoro delle donne* (Rome: Laterza, 1996).

49. Dennis Romano, *Housecraft and Statecraft: Domestic Service in Renaissance Venice, 1400–1600* (Baltimore: Johns Hopkins University Press, 1996).

50. Crouzet-Pavan, *"Sopra le acque salse,"* 2:751–59.

51. Charles Verlinden, "Venezia e il commercio degli schiavi provenienti dalle coste orientali del Mediterraneo," in Pertusi, *Venezia e il Levante fino al secolo XV*, 1, pt. 2: 911–29.

52. Reinhold Mueller, "Venezia e i primi schiavi neri," *Archivio Veneto*, 5th ser., 148 (1979): 139–42.

53. Iris Origo, "The Domestic Enemy: The Eastern Slaves in Tuscany in the Fourteenth and Fifteenth Centuries," *Speculum* 30 (1955): 321–66.

54. For the sixteenth century, see Isabella Palumbo-Fossati, "L'interno della casa

dell'artigiano e dell'artista nella Venezia del Cinquecento," *Studi Veneziani*, n.s., 8 (1984): 1–45.

55. Philippe Braunstein, "Le commerce du fer à Venise au XVe siècle," ibid. 8 (1966): 267–302.

56. Andrzej Wyrobisz, "L'attività edilizia a Venezia nel XIV e XV secolo," ibid. 7 (1965): 307–43.

57. Nella Fano, "Ricerche sull'arte della lana a Venezia nel XIII e XIV secolo," *Archivio Veneto*, 5th ser., 18 (1936): 73–213.

58. Giovanni Monticolo, "La sede dell'arte della lana a Venezia nei secoli XIII e XIV: Spigolature d'Archivio," *Nuovo Archivio Veneto*, 2d ser., 3 (1892): 351–60; Crouzet-Pavan, *La mort lente de Torcello*, 178–79.

59. Crouzet-Pavan, *"Sopra le acque salse,"* 1:307–8, 2:745–51.

60. Richard Tilden Rapp, *Industry and Economic Decline in Seventeenth-Century Venice* (Cambridge: Harvard University Press, 1976), 6–7; Domenico Sella, "Les mouvements longs de l'industrie lainière à Venise," *Annales E.S.C.* 12 (1957): 29–45; idem, "L'industria della lana a Venezia nei secoli XVI e XVII," in *Storia dell'economia italiana: Saggi di storia economica*, ed. Carlo M. Cipolla (Turin: Edizioni Scientifiche Einaudi, 1959), vol. 1; idem, "The Rise and the Fall of the Venetian Woollen Industry," in *Crisis and Change in the Venetian Economy in the Sixteenth and Seventeenth Centuries*, ed. Brian Pullan (London: Methuen, 1966; distributed in the United States by Barnes & Noble), 106–26.

61. Ciriacono, "Industria e artigianato," 546.

62. Franco Brunello, *Arti e mestieri a Venezia nel Medioevo e nel Rinascimento* (Vicenza: Neri Pozza, 1981); Ciriacono, "Industria e artigianato," 548–49.

63. For the history of the decline of the wool industry in Venice and the Terraferma, see Walter Panciera, *L'arte matrice: I lanifici della Repubblica di Venezia nei secoli XVII e XVIII* (Treviso: Canova, 1996).

64. "Muran, dove si fa veri" is one item on the list drawn up by Marino Sanudo of "cosse notabile si mostrano a' signori in Venexia" (see Sanuto, *De origine*, 62).

65. Crouzet-Pavan, *Venise*, 43–64; Luigi Zecchin, *Vetro e vetrai di Murano: Studi sulla storia del vetro* (Venice: Arsenale, 1986).

66. For a comparison with policies in other cities regarding the protection of industrial secrets, see Giuliano Pinto, "La politica demografica delle città," in Comba, Piccinni, and Pinto, *Strutture familiari, epidemie, migrazioni nell'Italia medievale*, 19–43; idem, "Popolazione e comportamenti demografici in Italia (1250–1348)," in *Europa en los umbrales de la crisis (1250–1350)* (Pamplona: Gobierno de Navarra, Departamento de Educación y Cultura, 1995), 37–62; and Luca Molà and Reinhold Mueller, "Essere straniero a Venezia nel tardo Medioevo: Accoglienza e rifiuto nei privilegi di cittadinanza e nelle sentenze criminali," in Cavaciocchi, *Le migrazioni in Europa*, 839–51. See also the various contributions in *Demografia e società nell'Italia medievale: Secoli IX–XIV*, ed. Rinaldo Comba and Irma Naso (Cuneo: Società per gli Studi Storici della Provincia di Cuneo–Società Italiana di Demografia Storica, 1994).

67. Luigi Zecchin, "Il segreto dei vetrai muranesi del Quattrocento," *Rivista della Stazione Sperimentale del Vetro* 11, no. 4 (1981): 167–72. This Malthusian approach lay

behind the legal procedures against certain non-Venetian master glassworkers in 1481. On these "foreigners," see idem, "Forestieri nell'arte vetraria muranese (1348–1425)," ibid., no. 1 (1981): 17–22.

68. Angelo Santi, *Origine dell'arte vitraria in Venezia e Murano, suo risorgimento e progresso: Cenni storici* (Venice: Scarabellin, 1914), 31.

69. Lise Monnas, "Le luxe industriel," in Braunstein, *Venise 1500*, 157–67.

70. It has been calculated that 672 out of the 4,000 privileges of citizenship granted in the fourteenth and fifteenth centuries went to Tuscans, 281 of whom were Florentines and 259 Lucchesi (see Molà and Mueller, "Essere straniero a Venezia").

71. For an in-depth study of the people involved in the silk industry, entrepreneurs as well as workers, see Luca Molà, *La comunità dei Lucchesi a Venezia: Immigrazione e industria della seta nel tardo medioevo* (Venice: Istituto Veneto di Scienze, Lettere ed Arti, 1994).

72. Ciriacono, "Industria e artigianato," 552–53.

73. Doretta Davanzo Poli, "L'arte e il mestiere della tessitura a Venezia nei secoli XIII–XVIII," in *I mestieri della moda a Venezia dal XIII al XVIII secolo/The Crafts of the Venetian Fashion Industry from the Thirteenth to the Eighteenth Century,* exh. cat. (Venice: Mestieri della Moda a Venezia, 1988; distributed by Edizioni del Cavallo).

74. Roberto Berveglieri, "L'arte dei tintori e il nero di Venezia," in ibid., 55–62.

75. See Romolo Broglio d'Ajano, "L'industria della seta a Venezia," in Cipolla, *Storia dell'economia italiana,* 1:209–62. For technological changes in silk manufacturing, see Carlo Poni, "Archéologie de la fabrique: La diffusion des moulins à soie 'alla bolognese' dans les états vénitiens du XVe au XVIIIe siècle," *Annales E.S.C.* 6 (1972): 1475–96; Alberto Guenzi and Carlo Poni, "Sinergia di due innovazioni: Chiaviche e mulini da seta a Bologna," *Quaderni Storici* 64 (1987): 111–27; Davanzo Poli, "L'arte e il mestiere della tessitura," 39–53; Simonetta Cavaciocchi, ed., *La seta in Europa (secc. XIII–XVIII)* (Florence: Le Monnier, 1993).

76. One text drawn from the records of the silk guild even suggests that in 1560, 30,000 men and women were employed in the various stages of silk manufacturing (see Ciriacono, "Industria e artigianato," 553).

77. For the world of the furriers *(varotarii),* see Romano, *Patricians and Popolani,* chap. 4, especially regarding the wealthy master furriers, such as Bartolomeo Brocha and Bartolomeo Trevisan.

78. Robert Delort, "Un aspect du commerce vénitien au XVe siècle: Andrea Barbarigo et le commerce des fourrures (1430–1440)," *Le Moyen Age* 71 (1965): 29–80, 247–73.

79. Martin Lowry, *The World of Aldus Manutius: Business and Scholarship in Renaissance Venice* (Oxford: Clarendon Press, 1979).

80. Martin Lowry, "L'imprimerie, un nouveau produit culturel," in Braunstein, *Venise 1500,* 53–71.

81. Crouzet-Pavan, *"Sopre le acque salse,"* 2:929–30.

82. Martin Lowry, *Nicholas Jenson and the Rise of Venetian Publishing in Renaissance Europe* (Oxford: Basil Blackwell, 1991).

83. Ennio Concina, *Venezia nell'età moderna: Struttura e funzioni* (Venice: Mar-

silio, 1989); Ugo Tucci, "Venezia nel Cinquecento: Una città industriale?" in *Crisi e rinnovamenti nell'autunno del Rinascimento a Venezia*, ed. Vittore Branca and Carlo Ossola (Florence: Olschki, 1991), 61–83; Salvatore Ciriacono, "Mass Consumption Goods and Luxury Goods: The De-Industrialization of the Republic of Venice from the Sixteenth to the Eighteenth Century," in *The Rise and Decline of Urban Industries in Italy and in the Low Countries (Late Middle Ages–Early Modern Times)*, ed. Harman van der Wee (Louvain, Belgium: Leuven University Press, 1988), 41–61. The phrase "bosom of the Atlantic" is from Sanuto, *De origine*, 9.

84. There may have been as many as three thousand workers in the glass industry in Venice and its environs in the sixteenth century.

F I V E　　*The State in Motion*

1. James S. Grubb, "Memory and Identity: Why Venetians Didn't Keep Ricordanze," *Renaissance Studies* 8, no. 4 (1994): 375–87; Rona Goffen, *Giovanni Bellini* (New Haven: Yale University Press, 1989); Patricia Fortini Brown, *Venetian Narrative Painting in the Age of Carpaccio* (New Haven: Yale University Press, 1988).

2. Gasparo Contarini's *De magistratibus et Republica Venetorum* was published in Venice in 1543 and reprinted in 1544, 1547, 1589, and 1592 in Paris, Basel, and Venice. The success of this treatise is clear from its French and Italian translations and its many subsequent editions (see *Des magistratz et République de Venise composé par Gaspar Contarini*, trans. Jehan Charrier [Paris, 1544]. On Contarini, see Elisabeth G. Gleason, *Gasparo Contarini: Venice, Rome, and Reform* [Berkeley: University of California Press, 1993]).

3. Pierre Mesnard, *L'essor de la philosophie politique au XVIe siècle*, 2d ed. (Paris: J. Vrin, 1951).

4. Jean Bodin, *Les six livres de la République* (Paris, 1577), 751.

5. Renzo Pecchioli, "Il 'mito' di Venezia e la crisi fiorentina intorno al 1500," *Studi Storici* 3, no. 3 (1962): 451–92; Angelo Baiocchi, "Venezia nella storiografia fiorentina del Cinquecento," *Studi Veneziani*, n.s., 3 (1979): 203–81. On Machiavelli and Venice, see Felix Gilbert, "Machiavelli e Venezia," *Lettere Italiane* 21 (1969): 389–98.

6. William J. Bouwsma, *Venice and the Defense of Republican Liberty: Renaissance Values in the Age of the Counter Reformation* (Berkeley: University of California Press, 1968); idem, "Venice and the Political Education of Europe," in *Renaissance Venice*, ed. J. R. Hale (London: Faber, 1973; Totowa, N.J.: Rowman & Littlefield, 1973), 445–66. For an overview, see Gino Benzoni, "Panoramica su Venezia (secc. XVI–XVII)," *Critica Storica* 13 (1976): 128–58.

7. *Dell'historie venetiane del N.H.S. Pietro Giustiniano, di nuovo rivedute et ampliate, nelle quali si contengono tutte le cose notabili occorse dal principio della fondazione della città sino all'anno M.D.LXXV* (Venice, 1670), 2.

8. Apostolo Zeno, ed., *Degli istorici delle cose veneziane i quali hanno scritto per pubblico decreto, tomo settimo che comprende i sei ultimi libri dell'istorie veneziane latinamente scritte dal senatore Andrea Morosini* (Venice, 1720), 6.

9. Giovanni Nicolò Doglioni, *Venetia trionfante e sempre libera* (Venice, 1613), 45.

10. For examples of such theoretical works, see the work of a Florentine, Donato Gianotti, *Dialogus de Republica Venetorum*, in *Thesaurus antiquitatum et historiarum Italiae*, ed. Johannes Georgius Graevius, vol. 1 (Leiden, 1722), cols. 1–124. See also Felix Gilbert, "The Date of the Composition of Contarini's and Gianotti's Books on Venice," *Studies in the Renaissance* 14 (1967): 127–84.

11. One literary example is Angelo, the tyrant of Padua, in Victor Hugo's homonymous *Angelo, tyran de Padoue* (1835) (see Elisabeth Crouzet-Pavan, *Venise: Une invention de la ville, XIIe–XVe siècle*, Collection Époques [Seyssel: Champ Vallon, 1997], 224–25).

12. Girolamo Arnaldi and Lidia Capo, "I cronisti di Venezia e della Marca trevigiana," in *Il Trecento*, ed. Girolamo Arnaldi, vol. 2 of *Storia della cultura veneta* (Vicenza: Neri Pozza, 1976), 272–337.

13. For an analysis of the Venetian chroniclers who argued against such critics, see Franco Gaeta, "Storiografia, coscienza nazionale e politica culturale nella Venezia del Rinascimento," in *Dal primo Quattrocento al Concilio di Trento*, ed. Girolamo Arnaldi and Manlio Pastore Stocchi, vol. 3 of *Storia della cultura veneta*, pt. 2 (Vicenza: Neri Pozza, 1980), pt. 1, 1–91.

14. Pier Paolo Vergerio's *De Republica Veneta* was written about 1412 (see David Robey and John Easton Law, "The Venetian Myth and the 'De Republica Veneta' of Pier Paolo Vergerio," *Rinascimento*, 2d ser., 15 [1975]: 3–59). In his *De gestis, moribus et nobilitatis civitatis venetiarum*, written between 1421 and 1428, Lorenzo de' Monaci developed the themes of Venetian *aequitas* and of a duration founded on the force of laws against attempts at tyrannical subversion (on this topic, see Gaeta, "Storiografia, coscienza nazionale," 17). A few essential dates mark cultural history in the second half of the fifteenth century, when reactions to Venice's Continental policies and its expansion on the Terraferma elicited responses in Venice. Flavio Biondo chose to praise Venetian history and liberty in his *De gestis Venetorum*, written in 1454, and he was rewarded with Venetian citizenship for his pains (see Felix Gilbert, "Biondo, Sabellico, and the Beginnings of Venetian Official Historiography," in *Florilegium Historiale: Essays Presented to Wallace K. Ferguson*, ed. J. G. Rowe and W. H. Stockdale [Toronto: University of Toronto Press, 1971], 275–93; and Gaetano Cozzi, "Cultura, politica e religione nella 'pubblica storiografia' veneziana del Cinquecento," *Bolletino dell'Istituto di Storia della Società e dello Stato Veneziano* 3 [1961]: 215–94). In 1456 Lorenzo Zane suggested to Lorenzo Valla that he write a history of Venice, but nothing came of the project (see Gianni Zippel, "Lorenzo Valla e le origini della storiografia umanistica a Venezia," *Rinascimento* 7 [1956]: 93–133). Lodovico Foscarini dreamed of instituting the post of official historiographer, hoping to have Biondo fill the position, but the project failed. Bernardo Giustiniani wrote his *De origine urbis Venetiarum*, the first cohesive history of the Venetian identity, between 1477 and 1489, during some of the troubled years of the War of Ferrara and the worst moments of the interdict placed on Venice by Sixtus IV (see Patricia H. Labalme, *Bernardo Giustiniani: A Venetian of the Quattrocento*, Uomini e Dottrine, 13 [Rome: Edizioni di Storia e Letteratura, 1969]). Public historiography in Venice truly began with Marc'Antonio Sabellico. Although he never filled the post of official historian,

his *Rerum venetarum,* completed by *De situ urbis Venetae* (ca. 1494) and *De Venetis magistratibus* (1488), provided the model for subsequent histories. Sabellico died in 1506, and in 1515 the Republic decided to provide him with a successor. The following year the Ten conferred that charge on Andrea Navagero. The official historiographer of the Republic would be a patrician. Navagero died without publishing anything, and Pietro Bembo replaced him.

15. Domenico Morosini, *De bene instituta re publica,* ed. Claudio Finzi (Milan: Giuffrè, 1969). For comments on this edition and for an analysis of Morosini's work, see Gaetano Cozzi, "Domenico Morosini e il 'De Bene Instituta Re Publica,'" *Studi Veneziani* 12 (1970): 405–58. For a study of Morosini's program, see Margaret L. King, *Venetian Humanism in an Age of Patrician Dominance* (Princeton: Princeton University Press, 1986), 150. Both King and Cozzi stress Morosini's critical intent.

16. Emulation of the Florentine Republic clearly played a role in this. Hans Baron has scrutinized the origins of a new humanism and its connections with the political and diplomatic situation in a famous work, *The Crisis of the Early Italian Renaissance: Civic Humanism and Republican Liberty in an Age of Classicism and Tyranny,* 2d ed., 2 vols. (Princeton: Princeton University Press, 1983).

17. At the end of the fifteenth century the Florentine crisis provided fodder for a series of analyses comparing Venice and Florence (see Pecchioli, "Il 'mito' di Venezia"; and Baiocchi, "Venezia nella storiografia fiorentina").

18. The best analysis of this problem has been and remains James S. Grubb, "When Myths Lose Power: Four Decades of Venetian Historiography," *Journal of Modern History* 58 (1986): 43–94.

19. Franco Gaeta, "Alcune considerazioni sul mito di Venezia," *Bibliothèque d'Humanisme et Renaissance* 23 (1961): 548–75.

20. One might cite as useful examples of this approach two works by Donald E. Queller: *Two Studies on Venetian Government* (Geneva: Droz, 1977) and *The Venetian Patriciate: Reality versus Myth* (Urbana: University of Illinois Press, 1986).

21. For an example of this recent trend, see John Martin and Dennis Romano, eds., *Venice Reconsidered: The History and Civilization of an Italian City-State* (Baltimore: Johns Hopkins University Press, 2000), papers from a colloquy held at Syracuse University in September 1998 in which the discussion focused on summarizing the problems and surveying research in course. For an example of the criticisms directed at this strongly historiographical (and largely Anglo-Saxon) tendency and for a discussion of the existence of schools, or at least national trends, in current historical production, see the initial pages of Giuseppe Gullino, "Il patriziato," in *Il Rinascimento: Politica e cultura,* ed. Alberto Tenenti and Ugo Tucci, vol. 4 of *Storia di Venezia* (Rome: Istituto della Enciclopedia Italiana, 1996), 379–413.

22. *Degl'istorici delle cose veneziane i quali hanno scritto per pubblico decreto, tomo terzo che comprende gli otto primi libri della prima parte dell'istorie veneziane volgarmente scritte da Paolo Paruta* (Venice, 1718), 121–22.

23. *Degl'istorici delle cose veneziane i quali hanno scritto per pubblico decreto, tomo quarto che comprende i quattro ultimi libri della parte prima e la parte seconda dell'istorie veneziane scritte da Paolo Paruta* (Venice, 1718), 22–23.

24. *Degl'istorici delle cose veneziane i quali hanno scritto per pubblico decreto, tomo sesto che comprende i sei secondi libri dell'istorie latinamente scritte dal senatore Andrea Morosini* (Venice, 1719), 248–49.

25. See, e.g., Giovanni Nicolò Doglioni's version of events in his *Venetia trionfante e sempre libera.*

26. This anecdote is related in Pompeo G. Molmenti, *La storia di Venezia nella vita privata dalle origini alla caduta della Republica,* new ed., 3 vols. (Trieste: Lint, 1978), 2:67. See also Elisabeth Crouzet-Pavan, *"Sopra le acque salse": Espaces, pouvoir et société à Venise à la fin du Moyen Age,* 2 vols., Collection de l'École Française de Rome, 158 (Rome: Istituto Storico Italiano per il Medio Evo, 1992), 2:952–53.

27. Lina Urban, " 'L'andata' dogale a San Vio: Rituali, un quadro, una 'beata,' una chiesa," *Studi Veneziani,* n.s., 28 (1994): 191–202.

28. I might also cite the procession to the church of Santa Giustina to mark the Venetian victory at Lepanto.

29. On such ceremonies and their evolution, see Crouzet-Pavan, *"Sopra le acque salse,"* 2:727–37.

30. Edward Muir, "Idee, riti, simboli del potere," in *L'età del Comune,* ed. Giorgio Cracco and Gherardo Ortalli, vol. 2 of *Storia di Venezia* (Rome: Istituto della Enciclopedia Italiana, 1995), 739–60.

31. On the formation of rituals concerning the doge, see Matteo Casini, *I gesti del principe: La festa politica a Firenze e a Venezia in età rinascimentale* (Venice: Marsilio, 1996); and Alberto Tenenti, "Il potere dogale come rappresentazione," in Tenenti, *Stato: Un'idea, una logica: Dal Comune italiano all'assolutismo francese* (Bologna: Il Mulino, 1987), 193–216.

32. For an analysis of the doge's insignia, see Agostino Pertusi, " 'Quedam regalia insignia': Ricerche sulle insegne del potere ducale a Venezia durante il medioevo," *Studi Veneziani* 7 (1965): 3–123; and Gina Fasoli, "Liturgia e cerimonia ducale," in *Venezia e il Levante fino al secolo XV,* ed. Agostino Pertusi (Florence: Olschki, 1973), 1, pt. 1: 261–95. Some information can be gleaned from older works, such as Bartolomeo Cecchetti, *Il doge di Venezia* (Venice, 1865); and Andrea da Mosto, *I dogi di Venezia nella vita pubblica e privata* (Florence: Giunti Martello, 1983).

33. Edward Muir, *Civic Ritual in Renaissance Venice* (Princeton: Princeton University Press, 1981), 190–92.

34. Philippe de Voisins, *Voyage à Jérusalem de Philippe de Voisins, seigneur de Montaut,* ed. Philippe Tamisey de Laroque (Paris, 1883), 18.

35. Ibid., 251 ff.; Casini, *I gesti del principe.*

36. For bibliography on these questions, see Heinrich Kretschmayr, *Geschichte von Venedig,* 3 vols. (1905–34; reprint, Aalen: Scientia, 1986); and Giuseppe Maranini, *Dalle origini alla serrata del Maggior Consiglio,* vol. 1 of *La costituzione di Venezia,* 2 vols. (1927–31; reprint, Florence: La Nuova Italia, 1974).

37. The *Sapienti* are attested as early as 1141, however (see Gerhard Rösch, *Der venezianische Adel bis zur Schliessung des Grossen Rats: Zur Genese einer Führungsschicht* [Sigmaringen: Thorbecke, 1989]).

38. For the history of the Venetian commune, see Giorgio Cracco, *Società e stato nel Medioevo veneziano (secoli XII–XIV)* (Florence: Olschki, 1967); idem, *Un "altro*

mondo": *Venezia nel Medioevo dal secolo XI al secolo XIV* (Turin: UTET, 1986); and Rösch, *Der venezianische Adel.*

39. Bernhard Schmeidler, *Der Dux und das Comune Venetiarum von 1141–1229: Beiträge zur Verfassungsgeschichte Venedigs vornehmlich im 12. Jahrhundert* (Berlin: Ebering, 1902).

40. Rösch, *Der venezianische Adel;* Andrea Castagnetti, "Il primo comune," in Cracco and Ortalli, *L'età del Comune,* 81–130, esp. 105–6. Both of these authors disagree with the interpretation of Giorgio Cracco, who sees this crisis as a social conflict between landowning families and families engaged in trade.

41. On the composition of this dominant class, see Rösch, *Der venezianische Adel.*

42. Gerhard Rösch rightly insists on the profound community of interests between the families of the first commune, whether ancient or more recently risen to prominence.

43. The *promissio* was thus an oath that defined the prerogatives of the doge. The 1192 text is the first known example. Probably beginning with Domenico Morosini, the oath the doges swore before the commune also included a list of prohibitions (see *Le promissioni del doge di Venezia dalle origini alla fine del Duecento,* ed. Gisella Graziato, Fonti per la Storia di Venezia, sec. 1, Archivi Pubblici [Venice: Comitato Editore, 1986]).

44. At the threshold of the modern age every time the ducal throne fell vacant a commission was called that had the power to institute proceedings, set fines, and evaluate the acts of the "most serene" but late doge. This commission of *inquisitori* was set up in 1501 at the death of Doge Agostino Barbarigo (see Robert Finlay, *Politics in Renaissance Venice* [New Brunswick, N.J.: Rutgers University Press, 1980], 110, 112).

45. As stressed in Rösch, *Der venezianische Adel,* even though the governing families enjoyed a striking revival in the precommunal age, popular power increased at a strongly accelerated pace in the thirteenth century.

46. For a detailed analysis of these elections, see Finlay, *Politics in Renaissance Venice,* 91–96. The twenty-four *case vecchie* were the Badoer, Barozzi, Basegio, Bembo, Bragadin, Contarini, Corner, Dandolo, Dolfin, Falier, Giustiniani, Gradenigo, Memmo, Michiel, Morosini, Polani, Querini, Salamon, Sanudo, Soranzo, Tiepolo, Zane, Zen, and Zorzi families; the sixteen *case nuove* were the Barbarigo, Donà, Foscari, Grimani, Gritti, Lando, Loredan, Malipiero, Marcello, Mocenigo, Moro, Priuli, Trevisan, Tron, Vendramin, and Venier families.

47. Ibid., 115–16.

48. Muir, "Idee, riti, simboli del potere," 745–50.

49. Patricia Fortini Brown, *The Renaissance in Venice: A World Apart* (London: Weidenfeld & Nicolson, 1997), 77–78.

50. Rösch, *Der venezianische Adel.*

51. The city had seventy *contrade* and thirty-five *trentaccie,* although these numbers varied.

52. Castello, San Marco, and Cannaregio to the north; San Polo, Santa Croce, and Dorsoduro to the south.

53. On this topic, see Roberto Cessi, *Storia della Repubblica di Venezia,* new ed. (Florence: Giunti Martello, 1981), 170–73, 203–5.

54. Andrea Padovani, "La politica del diritto," in Cracco and Ortalli, *L'età del Comune*, 303–30, esp. 315 ff.

55. Andrea Padovani, "Curie ed uffici," in ibid., 331–48.

56. Cessi, *Storia della Repubblica di Venezia*, 273–75.

57. Crouzet-Pavan, *"Sopra le acque salse,"* 1:267–86.

58. Enrico Besta, *Il senato veneziano*, Miscellanea di Storia Veneta, 2d ser., 5 (Venice: Reale Diputazione Veneta di Storia Patria, 1899); Gaetano Cozzi and Michael Knapton, *Storia della Repubblica di Venezia dalla guerra di Chioggia alla riconquista della Terraferma*, vol. 12 of *Storia d'Italia* (Turin: UTET, 1986), 108–9.

59. Marino Sanudo, *De origine, situ et magistratibus urbis Venetae, ovvero, La Città di Venetia (1493–1530)*, ed. Angela Caracciolo Aricò (Milan: Cisalpino–La Goliardica, 1980), 93.

60. Not only was the Savi agli Ordini the least prestigious commission but it lost momentum toward the end of the fifteenth century. Its members were not even called together when the Pien Collegio met with the Council of Ten (Cozzi and Knapton, *Storia della Repubblica di Venezia*, 110).

61. Mauro Macchi, *Istoria del Consiglio dei Dieci*, 2 vols. (Turin, 1848–49); Guido Ruggiero, *The Ten: Control of Violence and Social Disorder in Trecento Venice* (Ann Arbor: University Microfilms International, 1980); idem, *Violence in Early Renaissance Venice* (New Brunswick, N.J.: Rutgers University Press, 1980).

62. Renzo Derosas, "Moralità e giustizia a Venezia nel '500–'600: Gli Esecutori contro la bestemmia," in *Stato, società e giustizia nella Repubblica veneta (sec. XV–XVIII)*, ed. Gaetano Cozzi (Rome: Jouvence, 1980), 1:431–528. Unlike the older tribunals, which used ordinary public procedure, this body adopted the procedures of the Ten (see Gaetano Cozzi, "Authority and the Laws in Renaissance Venice," in Hale, *Renaissance Venice*, 293–345; Claudio Povolo, "Aspetti e problemi dell'amministrazione della giustizia penale nella Repubblica di Venezia, secc. XVI–XVII," in Cozzi, *Stato, società e giustizia nella Repubblica veneta*, 1:153–258; and Gaetano Cozzi, *Repubblica di Venezia e stati italiani: Politica e giustizia dal secolo XVI al secolo XVIII* [Turin: Einaudi, 1982], esp. 81–144, "La giustizia e la politica nella Repubblica di Venezia [secoli XV–XVII]").

63. Finlay, *Politics in Renaissance Venice*, 59–81.

64. Cozzi and Knapton, *Storia della Repubblica di Venezia*, 105.

65. The ceiling, or "cielo compartito a quadretti d'oro ripieni di stelli," was made under the dogeship of Michele Steno (see Patricia Fortini Brown, "Committenza e arte di Stato," in *La formazione dello stato patrizio*, ed. Girolamo Arnaldi, Giorgio Cracco, and Alberto Tenenti, vol. 3 of *Storia di Venezia* [Rome: Istituto della Enciclopedia Italiana, 1997], 783–824, esp. 817).

66. Missing from the series is the portrait of Marino Falier, of *damnatio memoriae* (for this episode and the relative texts of the Council of Ten, see ibid., 811).

67. See Finlay, *Politics in Renaissance Venice*, 48. See also Cozzi and Knapton, *Storia della Repubblica di Venezia*, 107–8.

68. Within the framework of this necessarily limited analysis, I have examined only a few principal changes. For a more complete study of institutional adjustments, see Giuseppe Gullino, "L'evoluzione costituzionale," in Tenenti and Tucci, *Il Rinasci-*

mento, 345–78. In particular, the impact of the conquest of the Terraferma requires further investigation.

69. I borrow the phrase "uno stato fermo e terminato" from Niccolò Machiavelli, *Discorsi sopra la prima Deca di Tito Livio.*

70. As Gerhard Rösch notes, the first such definition occurred when the Byzantine nobility of office, the *Amstadel,* became the first nobility of blood, *Geburtsadel* (see Rösch, *Der venezianische Adel*).

71. Stanley Chojnacki, "La grande famille des nobles," in *Venise 1500: La puissance, la novation et la concorde: Le triomphe du mythe,* ed. Philippe Braunstein (Paris: Autrement, 1993), 178–99, esp. 180.

72. See, e.g., Brian Pullan, "Service to the Venetian State: Aspects of Myth and Reality in the Early Seventeenth Century," *Studi Secenteschi* 5 (1964): 95–148.

73. Rösch, *Der venezianische Adel.*

74. This phrase is borrowed from Lane, *Venice, a Maritime Republic* (Baltimore: Johns Hopkins University Press, 1973), 111.

75. Their names also had to be approved by twelve members of the Quarantia.

76. See Kretschmayr, *Geschichte von Venedig;* and for the *Serrata* in particular, Margarete Merores, "Der grosse Rat von Venedig und die sogenannte Serrata von Jahres 1298," *Vierteljahrschrift für Sozial- und Wirtschaftsgeschichte* 21 (1928): 33–113, and Cracco, *Società e stato nel Medioevo veneziano,* 331–50. It should be noted, however, that some writers were quick to remark that the reform of 1297 did little but give official form to criteria that had already been in effect since the mid-thirteenth century, when the dividing line between nobility and "the people" was established by membership in the Great Council (see Merores, "Der grosse Rat," 108).

77. Georgio Cracco's analysis of how the Serrata fortified the power of a small number of families illustrates this viewpoint (see Cracco, *Società e stato nel Medioevo veneziano;* and idem, "Patriziato e oligarchia a Venezia nel Tre-Quattrocento," in *Quattrocento,* vol. 1 of *Florence and Venice: Comparisons and Relations* [Florence: La Nuova Italia, 1979], 71–98).

78. Rösch, *Der venezianische Adel,* chap. 5.

79. Frederic C. Lane, "The Enlargement of the Great Council of Venice," in Rowe and Stockdale, *Florilegium Historiale: Essays Presented to Wallace K. Ferguson,* 236–74, reprinted in Lane, *Studies in Venetian Social and Economic History,* ed. Benjamin G. Kohl and Reinhold C. Mueller (London: Variorum Reprints, 1987), sec. 3. See also Rösch, *Der venezianische Adel,* chap. 6.

80. According to Gerard Rösch (*Der venezianische Adel,* chap. 6), the Tiepolo family belonged to the oligarchy, the inner circle of government. Hence Rösch denies that there could have been a period of lesser tension under Doge Lorenzo Tiepolo, or that the doge pursued a pro-popular policy, as Frederic C. Lane argues.

81. John Easton Law, "Age Qualification and the Venetian Constitution: The Case of the Cappello Family," *Papers of the British School at Rome* 29 (1971): 125–37.

82. Lane, "Enlargement of the Great Council," 245.

83. See Guido Ruggiero, "Modernization and the Mythic State in Early Renaissance Venice: The Serrata Revisited," *Viator* 10 (1979): 245–56, a critique of Stanley Chojnacki, "In Search of the Venetian Patriciate: Families and Factions in the Four-

teenth Century," in Hale, *Renaissance Venice,* 478–90. For views similar to Ruggiero's, see Reinhold C. Mueller, "Espressioni di status sociale a Venezia dopo la 'Serrata' del Maggior Consiglio," in *Studi veneti offerti a Gaetano Cozzi* (Venice: Il Cardo, 1992), 53–61.

84. Chojnacki, "In Search of the Venetian Patriciate"; idem, *The Making of the Venetian Renaissance State: The Achievement of a Noble Political Consensus, 1378–1420* (Ann Arbor: University Microfilms International, 1985).

85. According to Chojnacki in more recent publications.

86. Lane, "Enlargement of the Great Council of Venice," 258–59. For Lane, the Serrata was largely motivated by fear of foreigners and of foreign competition.

87. On the problem of lineage extinction, see Stanley Chojnacki, "La formazione della nobiltà dopo la Serrata," in Arnaldi, Cracco, and Tenenti, *La formazione dello stato patrizio,* 641–725, esp. 651–60.

88. Chojnacki, "In Search of the Venetian Patriciate," 53–54.

89. One of these was Marco Donà (see James C. Davis, *A Venetian Family and Its Fortune: 1500–1900: The Donà and the Conservation of Their Wealth* [Philadelphia: American Philosophical Society, 1975], 33–34). Various members of the Donà family had served in the Great Council during the thirteenth century, but they were excluded because no family member had sat on the Council in the years immediately preceding the Serrata. Marco's role in the repression of the 1310 conspiracy led to the family's introduction into the ranks of the nobility.

90. The *case nuovissime* were admitted after the *case vecchie* and the *case nuove* (see Vittorio Lazzarini, "Le offerte per la guerra di Chioggia e un falsario del Quattrocento," *Nuovo Archivio Veneto,* 3d ser., 4 [1902]: 202–13).

91. Stanley Chojnacki, "Social Identity in Renaissance Venice: The Second Serrata," *Renaissance Studies* 8, no. 4 (1994): 341–58. For a useful synthesis, see idem, "La formazione della nobiltà dopo la Serrata."

92. Chojnacki stresses the presence of individuals and families of a more uncertain status who existed on the fringes of the uncontested nucleus of the nobility in the fourteenth century (see Chojnacki, "La formazione della nobiltà dopo la Serrata," 681 ff.).

93. Chojnacki, "Social Identity in Renaissance Venice," 345 ff.; idem, "La formazione della nobiltà dopo la Serrata." The 1430 law pertained to nobles whose fathers' nobility had not been officially recognized; the laws of 1420 and 1422 concerned noble marriage (see idem, "Marriage Legislation and Patrician Society in Fifteenth-Century Venice," in *Law, Custom, and the Social Fabric in Medieval Europe: Essays in Honor of Bryce Lyon,* ed. Bernard S. Bachrach and David Nicholas, Medieval Institute Publications, Studies in Medieval Civilization, 28 [Kalamazoo: Western Michigan University, 1990], 163–84).

94. Stanley Chojnacki, "Political Adulthood in Fifteenth-Century Venice," *American Historical Review* 91 (1986): 791–810, reprinted as "Political Adulthood," in idem, *Women and Men in Renaissance Venice: Twelve Essays on Patrician Society* (Baltimore: Johns Hopkins University Press, 2000), 227–43.

95. Sanudo, *De origine,* 68.

96. Here I am exploiting the data of the *estimo* of 1379, during the War of

Chioggia (see *Documenti finanziari della Repubblica di Venezia*, Accademia nazionale dei Lincei, 3d ser., vol. 2; and *I prestiti della Repubblica di Venezia*, ed. Gino Luzzatto [Padua: A. Drashi, 1920], 138–95).

97. Dieter Girgensohn, *Kirche, Politik und adelige Regierung in der Republik Venedig zu Beginn des 15. Jahrhunderts*, 2 vols., Veröffentlichungen des Max-Planck-Instituts für Geschichte, 118 (Göttingen: Vendenhoech & Ruprecht, 1996). For a systematic study of Venetians in the service of the papacy in the fifteenth century, see ibid., 1:175–225.

98. This portrait, painted in 1465, is in the Galleria dell'Accademia, Venice.

99. See Grubb, "Memory and Identity." See also Law, "Age Qualification and the Venetian Constitution."

100. Andrea Vendramin was born around 1393; his parents were Bartolomeo Vendramin and Maria Michiel (see Mosto, *I dogi di Venezia*, 135).

101. For an example of collection, see Isabella Palumbo-Fossati, "Il collezionista Sebastiano Erizzo e l'inventario dei suoi beni," *Ateneo Veneto* 22, nos. 1–2 (1984): 201–18.

102. Brown, *Renaissance in Venice*, 124–26.

103. Stanley Chojnacki, "Patrician Women in Early Renaissance Venice," *Studies in the Renaissance* 21 (1974): 176–203, reprinted in Chojnacki, *Women and Men in Renaissance Venice*, 115–31; idem, "Dowries and Kinsmen in Early Renaissance Venice," *Journal of Interdisciplinary History* 5 (1975): 571–600, reprinted as "Dowries and Kinsmen," in Chojnacki, *Women and Men in Renaissance Venice*, 132–52; idem, "The Power of Love: Wives and Husbands in Late Medieval Venice," in *Women and Power in the Middle Ages*, ed. Mary Erler and Maryanne Kowaleski (Athens: University of Georgia Press, 1988), 126–48, reprinted as "The Power of Love: Wives and Husbands," in Chojnacki, *Women and Men in Renaissance Venice*, 153–68.

104. This was the origin of the term *Barnabotti*, given to indigent nobles somewhat later.

105. Chojnacki, "Political Adulthood in Fifteenth-Century Venice"; idem, "Measuring Adulthood: Adolescence and Gender in Renaissance Venice," *Journal of Family History* 17, no. 4 (1992): 371–95, reprinted as "Measuring Adulthood: Adolescence and Gender" in Chojnacki, *Women and Men in Renaissance Venice*, 185–205; idem, "Subaltern Patriarchs: Patrician Bachelors in Renaissance Venice," in *Medieval Masculinities: Regarding Men in the Middle Ages*, ed. Clare A. Lees (Minneapolis: University of Minnesota Press, 1994), 73–90, reprinted as "Subaltern Patriarchs: Patrician Bachelors," in Chojnacki, *Women and Men in Renaissance Venice*, 244–56. See also Elisabeth Crouzet-Pavan, "Un fior del male: I giovani nelle società urbane italiane (secoli XIV–XV)," in *Storia dei giovani*, ed. Jean-Claude Schmitt and Giovanni Levi (Rome: Laterza, 1994), 1:211–77, trans. Camille Nash under the title "A Flower of Evil: Young Men in Medieval Italy," in *A History of Young People in the West*, 2 vols. (Cambridge, Mass.: Belknap Press, 1997), 1:173–221.

106. Marino Sanudo writes, "Zudexi di Proprio, sonno da 40 in suso" and "Signori di Note, da 40 in suso" but also "Zudexi di Examinador tre zoveni soto 40" and "Officiali di Cataveri, sono tre zoveni sopra 40" (Sanudo, *De origine*, 255, 256, 249, 260).

107. Francesco Foscari was born in 1373, became doge in 1423, and died in 1457, the year of his deposition.

108. Crouzet-Pavan, "Un fior del male."

109. Alberto Tenenti, "The Sense of Space and Time in the Venetian World of the Fifteenth and Sixteenth Centuries," in Hale, *Renaissance Venice*, 17–46; Ugo Tucci, "La psicologia del mercante veneziano," in *Mercanti, navi, monete nel Cinquecento veneziano* (Bologna: Il Mulino, 1981), 43–94.

110. Giovanni Orlandini, "Marco Polo e la sua famiglia," *Archivio Veneto Tridentino* 9 (1926); Rodolfo Gallo, "Marco Polo, la sua famiglia e il suo libro," in *Nel VII Centenario della nascita di Marco Polo* (Venice: Istituto Veneto di Scienze, Lettere ed Arti, 1955); Ugo Tucci, "Marco Polo, mercante," in *Venezia e l'Oriente*, ed. Lionello Lanciotti (Florence: Olschki, 1987), 323–37; idem, "Mercanti veneziani in Asia lungo l'itinerario poliano," in ibid., 307–21; idem, "Marco Polo andò veramente in Cina," *Studi Veneziani*, n.s., 33 (1997): 49–60.

111. Michel Vergé-Franceschi, *Henri le Navigateur: Un découvreur au XVe siècle* (Paris: Félin, 1998), 315; Alvise Cà Da Mosto, *Le navigazioni atlantiche del Veneziano Alvise Da Mosto*, ed. Tullia Gasparrini-Leporace, Il Nuovo Ramusio, 5 (Rome: Istituto Poligrafico dello Stato, 1966).

112. Another example would be Giosafat Barbaro (see Ugo Tucci, "I viaggi di Giosafat Barbaro mercante e uomo politico," in *Una famiglia veneziana nella storia: I Barbaro* [Venice: Istituto Veneto di Scienze, Lettere ed Arti, 1996], 117–32).

113. Gino Luzzatto, "L'attività commerciale di un patrizio veneziano del Quattrocento," in *Studi di storia economica veneziana* (Padua: CEDAM, 1954), 167–93.

114. For the history of the Barbarigo wealth, see Frederic C. Lane, *Andrea Barbarigo, Merchant of Venice, 1418–1449* (Baltimore: Johns Hopkins Press, 1944), 17–18, 30, 35, 38.

115. King, *Venetian Humanism in an Age of Patrician Dominance;* Vittore Branca, "Ermolao Barbaro e l'umanesimo veneziano," in *Umanesimo europeo ed umanesimo veneziano,* ed. Vittore Branca, Civiltà Europea e Civiltà Veneziana: Aspetti e problemi, 2 (Florence: Sansoni, 1963), 193–212; idem, "Ermolao Barbaro and Late Quattrocento Venetian Humanism," in Hale, *Renaissance Venice*, 218–43; idem, "L'umanesimo veneziano alla fine del Quattrocento: Ermolao Barbaro e il suo circolo," in Arnaldi and Stocchi, *Dal primo Quattrocento al concilio di Trento*, 123–75.

116. Two studies of libraries before 1480 are Bartolomeo Cecchetti, "Una libreria circolante a Venezia nel secolo XV," *Archivio Veneto* 32, no. 1 (1886): 161–68; and Susan Connell, "Books and Their Owners in Venice, 1345–1480," *Journal of the Warburg and Courtauld Institutes* 35 (1972): 163–86.

117. Bruno Nardi, "Letteratura e cultura veneziana del Quattrocento," in Nardi, *Saggi sulla cultura veneta del Quattro e Cinquecento*, ed. Paolo Mazzantini (Padua: Antenore, 1971); Arnaldo Segarizzi, "Francesco Contarini, politico e letterato veneziano del secolo XV," *Nuovo Archivio Veneto*, 3d ser., 12 (1906): 272–87; Giorgio Castellani, "Giorgio da Trebisonda, maestro di eloquenza a Vicenza e a Venezia," ibid., 2d ser., 11 (1896): 123–42; John Monfasani, *George of Trebizond: A Biography and a Study of His Rhetoric and Logic* (Leiden: Brill, 1976). These works treat neither the

fairly dense network of schools in Venice nor the system of preceptors. On those two themes, see Bartolomeo Cecchetti, "Libri, scuole, maestri, sussidi allo studio in Venezia nei secoli XIV e XV," *Archivio Veneto* 32, no. 2 (1886): 329–63; *Maestri, scuole e scolari in Venezia fino al 1500*, ed. Enrico Bertanza and Giuseppe Dalla Santa, vol. 1 of *Documenti per la storia della cultura in Venezia*, Monumenti Storici Publicati dalla R. Deputazione Veneta di Storia Patria, ser. 1, Documenti, vol. 12 (Venice, 1907); Vittorio Rossi, "Maestri e scuole a Venezia verso la fine del Medioevo," *Rendiconti del Reale Istituto Lombardo di Scienze e Lettere*, 2d ser., 40 (1907): 765–81; Arnaldo Segarizzi, "Cenni sulle scuole pubbliche a Venezia nel secolo XV e sul primo maestro di esse," *Atti del Reale Istituto Veneto di Scienze, Lettere ed Arti* 75 (1915–16): 637–65; J. B. Ross, "Venetian Schools and Teachers, Fourteenth to Early Sixteenth Century: A Survey and a Study of Giovanni Battista Egnazio," *Renaissance Quarterly* 39 (1976): 521–66; and Gherardo Ortalli, *Scuole e maestri tra Medioevo e Rinascimento: Il caso veneziano* (Bologna: Il Mulino, 1996).

118. Bruno Nardi, "La scuola di Rialto e l'umanesimo veneziano," in *Umanesimo europeo ed umanesimo veneziano*, 93–139; Fernando Lepori, "La scuola di Rialto dalla fondazione alla metà del Cinquecento," in Arnaldi and Stocchi, *Dal primo Quattrocento al Concilio di Trento*, pt. 2, 539–605. This school was at first private; it became public in 1441, when the state decided to assume most of its expenses.

119. For interesting remarks on the choice of philosophy and the abandonment of the study of law, see Cozzi and Knapton, *Storia della Repubblica di Venezia*, 159.

120. On Giustiniani (1408–89), see Labalme, *Bernardo Giustiniani*.

121. Vittore Branca distinguishes four periods in the history of Venetian humanism: that of the chancery and the friends of Petrarch; that of the schools; that of the patricians (Francesco Barbaro, Lauro Quirini, etc.); and a last phase of the massive diffusion of humanist themes within the urban patriciate (see Branca, "Ermolao Barbaro e l'umanesimo veneziano"; see also Oliver Logan, *Culture and Society in Venice, 1470–1790: The Renaissance and Its Heritage* [London: Batsford, 1972]).

122. King, *Venetian Humanism in an Age of Patrician Dominance.*

123. The phrase "the second crown of the Republic of Venice" is taken from a treatise by a Venetian citizen, Alessandro Ziliol, *Le due Corone della Nobiltà Viniziana* (on Ziliol, see Anna Bellavitis, *Identité, mariage, mobilité sociale: Citoyennes et citoyens à Venise au XVIe siècle* [Rome: École Française de Rome, 2001]).

124. Giuseppe Trebbi, "La cancelleria veneta nei secoli XVI e XVII," *Annali della Fondazione Luigi Einaudi* 14 (1980): 65–126; Mary Frances Neff, *Chancellery Secretaries in Venetian Politics and Society, 1480–1533* (Ann Arbor: University Microfilms International, 1986); Matteo Casini, "Realtà e simboli del cancellier grande veneziano in età moderna," *Studi Veneziani*, n.s., 22 (1991): 195–251; Andrea Zannini, *Burocrazia e burocrati a Venezia in età moderna: I cittadini originari (sec. XVI–XVIII)* (Venice: Istituto Veneto di Scienze, Lettere ed Arti, 1993).

125. To borrow a definition from Anna Bellavitis, *Identité, mariage, mobilité sociale,* the Venetian citizens were neither a "social class" nor an order: "Empty of all juridical value, the title of Venetian citizen was thus a juridical status linked to birth, residence, and to the fact of having paid taxes that permitted or facilitated the

exercise of certain crafts or professions. Originally connected primarily to commercial activities, it became more and more connected with official posts and the liberal professions."

126. As we have seen, beginning in the thirteenth century many laws were passed that strongly restricted the economic activities of foreign merchants. As a consequence, until the fifteenth century the chief advantage of the privilege of citizenship was to participate in commerce, although at a level much lower than that of the nobles, thanks to the existence of a long list of limitations.

127. Reinhold C. Mueller, "Effetti della guerra di Chioggia (1378–1381) sulla vita economica e sociale di Venezia," *Ateneo Veneto* 19 (1981): 27–42.

128. Bellavitis, *Identité, mariage, mobilité sociale.*

129. Vittorio Lazzarini, "Un maestro di scrittura nella Cancelleria veneziana," in Lazzarini, *Scritti di paleografia e diplomatica*, 2d ed., enl. (Padua: Antenore, 1969), 64–70; Armando Petrucci, "L'écriture dans l'Italie de la Renaissance: Pouvoir de l'écriture, pouvoir sur l'écriture dans la Renaissance Italienne," *Annales E.S.C.* 43 (1988): 823–47, esp. 839; Mary Neff, "A Citizen in the Service of the Patrician State: The Career of Zaccaria de' Freschi," *Studi Veneziani*, n.s., 5 (1981): 33–61 (on Giovanni Antonio Tagliente); Casini, "Realtà e simboli."

130. This measure was probably also intended to eliminate competition from Greeks, who were present in great numbers in Venice at the time (see Bellavitis, *Identité, mariage, mobilité sociale*).

S I X   *The People of the City*

1. James S. Grubb, *Provincial Families of the Renaissance: Private and Public Life in the Veneto* (Baltimore: Johns Hopkins University Press, 1996). For a study that shows some affinities to the methods of microhistory, see Gigi Corazzol, *Cineografo di banditi su sfondo di monti: Feltre, 1634–1642* (Milan: UNICOPLI, 1997).

2. The bibliography on Florentine source materials is immense, and I shall cite only two works as examples. The first is the analysis of the Florentine *catasto* of 1427 in David Herlihy and Christiane Klapisch-Zuber, *Les Toscans et leurs familles: Une étude du catasto florentin de 1427* (Paris: Fondation Nationale des Sciences Politiques/ École des Hautes Études en Sciences Sociales, 1978), published in English, abridged, under the title *Tuscans and Their Families: A Study of the Florentine Catasto of 1427* (New Haven: Yale University Press, 1985). The second is Christiane Klapisch-Zuber, *La maison et le nom: Stratégies et rituels dans l'Italie de la Renaissance* (Paris: École des Hautes Études en Sciences Sociales, 1990).

3. Stanley Chojnacki, "In Search of the Venetian Patriciate: Families and Factions in the Fourteenth Century," in *Renaissance Venice*, ed. J. R. Hale (London: Faber; Totowa, N.J.: Rowman & Littlefield, 1973), 47–90; idem, "Patrician Women in Early Renaissance Venice," *Studies in the Renaissance* 21 (1974): 176–203, reprinted in Chojnacki, *Women and Men in Renaissance Venice: Twelve Essays on Patrician Society* (Baltimore: Johns Hopkins University Press, 2000), 115–31; idem, "Dowries and Kinsmen in Early Renaissance Venice," *Journal of Interdisciplinary History* 5 (1975): 571–600, reprinted as "Dowries and Kinsmen" in Chojnacki, *Women and Men in Renais-*

sance Venice, 132–52; Dennis Romano, *Patricians and Popolani: The Social Foundations of the Venetian Renaissance State* (Baltimore: Johns Hopkins University Press, 1987); Bianca Betto, "Linee di politica matrimoniale nella nobiltà veneziana fino al XV secolo: Alcune note genealogiche e l'esempio della famiglia Mocenigo," *Archivio Storico Italiano* 139 (1981): 3–64; Elisabeth Crouzet-Pavan, *"Sopra le acque salse": Espaces, pouvoir et société à Venise à la fin du Moyen Age*, 2 vols., Collection de l'École Française de Rome, 158 (Rome: Istituto Storico Italiano per il Medio Evo, 1992), 1:374 ff.; idem, *Venise: Une invention de la ville, XIIe–XVe siècle*, Collection Époques (Seyssel: Champ Vallon, 1997), 211–17.

4. To cite only one example, see Margaret L. King, "Personal, Domestic, and Republican Values in the Moral Philosophy of Giovanni Caldiera," *Renaissance Quarterly* 28 (1975): 535–74.

5. Lauro Martines, "A Way of Looking at Women in Renaissance Florence," *Journal of Medieval and Renaissance Studies* 4 (1974): 15–28.

6. Stanley Chojnacki, "Nobility, Women, and the State: Marriage Regulation in Venice, 1420–1535," in *Marriage in Italy, 1300–1620*, ed. Trevor Dean and K. J. P. Lowe (Cambridge and New York: Cambridge University Press, 1998), 128–51, esp. 148–49, reprinted as "Marriage Regulation in Venice, 1420–1535," in Chojnacki, *Women and Men in Renaissance Venice*, 53–75.

7. On the diffusion of the dowry system, see Diane Owen Hughes, "From Brideprice to Dowry in Mediterranean Europe," *Journal of Family History* 3 (1978): 263–96.

8. Crouzet-Pavan, *"Sopra le acque salse,"* 1:448–50; Chojnacki, "Patrician Women"; idem, "Dowries and Kinsmen."

9. In Florence the creation of the *Monte delle doti* aimed at helping farsighted fathers to constitute the indispensable capital (see Julius Kirshner, *Pursuing Honor While Avoiding Sin: The Monte delle doti of Florence* [Milan: Giuffrè, 1978]; and Anthony Molho, *Marriage Alliance in Late Medieval Florence* [Cambridge: Harvard University Press, 1994]).

10. Stanley Chojnacki, "The Power of Love: Wives and Husbands in Late Medieval Venice," in *Women and Power in the Middle Ages*, ed. Mary Erler and Maryanne Kowaleski (Athens: University of Georgia Press, 1988), 126–48, reprinted as "The Power of Love: Wives and Husbands," in Chojnacki, *Women and Men in Renaissance Venice*, 153–68.

11. For an analysis of this sort of rhetoric, see Guido Ruggiero, *The Boundaries of Eros: Sex Crime and Sexuality in Renaissance Venice* (New York: Oxford University Press, 1985), 45 ff.

12. Lauro Martines, "Séduction, espace familial et autorité dans la Renaissance italienne," *Annales, Histoire, Sciences Sociales* 2 (1998): 255–87. For an analysis of a case of the seduction of a young widow, see Gene Brucker, *Giovanni and Lusanna: Love and Marriage in Renaissance Florence* (Berkeley: University of California Press, 1986).

13. Martines, "Séduction, espace familial."

14. I am quoting St. Bernardino of Siena, sermon 48, in *Sancti Bernardini Senensis opera omnia iussu et auctoritate Pacifici M. Perantoni*, Studio et cura PP. Collegii S. Bonaventurae ad fidem codecum edita (Florence: Quaracchi, 1950–), vol. 2.

15. The tale *Ricciarda,* by Giovanni Gherardi da Prato, brilliantly analyzed by Lauro Martines, provides an organ point to my discussion and demonstrates the obsessional importance accorded to female virginity and chastity in these societies (see Lauro Martines, *An Italian Renaissance Sextet: Six Tales in Historical Context,* trans. Murtha Baca [New York: Marsilio, 1994], 19–35).

16. On age at marriage in Tuscany, see Herlihy and Klapisch-Zuber, *Les Toscans et leurs familles,* 394–400. For some indications of the situation in Venice, see Stanley Chojnacki, " 'The Most Serious Duty': Motherhood, Gender, and Patrician Culture in Renaissance Venice," in *Refiguring Women: Perspectives on Gender and the Italian Renaissance,* ed. Marilyn Migiel and Juliana Schiesari (Ithaca: Cornell University Press, 1991), 133–54, reprinted as " 'The Most Serious Duty': Motherhood, Gender, and Patrician Culture," in Chojnacki, *Women and Men in Renaissance Venice,* 169–82.

17. Dennis Romano was among the first to study family structure among the *popolari* (see Romano, *Patricians and Popolani,* chap. 3. See also Crouzet-Pavan, *"Sopra le acque salse,"* 1:417–20; and idem, "Le peuple des quartiers," in *Venise 1500: La puissance, la novation et la concorde: Le triomphe du mythe,* ed. Philippe Braunstein [Paris: Autrement, 1993], 200–14). On the importance of marriage in the milieu of domestic servants, see Dennis Romano, *Housecraft and Statecraft: Domestic Service in Renaissance Venice, 1400–1600* (Baltimore: Johns Hopkins University Press, 1996), 155–67.

18. We of course must distinguish between the milieu of the *popolari grandi* and that of the *popolo minuto.* It is clear that for the wealthier non-noble families behavioral norms tended to reflect those of the patricians, all the more so because intermarriage between the two groups was frequent (see Romano, *Patricians and Popolani,* chap. 3).

19. Crouzet-Pavan, *"Sopra le acque salse,"* vol. 1, chap. 5.

20. Marco Pozza, *I Badoer: Una famiglia veneziana dal X al XIII secolo* (Padua: Francisci, 1982).

21. The term for this process was *tenir parentado* (see Crouzet-Pavan, *Venise,* 211–13).

22. Norbert Huse and Wolfgang Wolters, *The Art of Renaissance Venice: Architecture, Sculpture, and Painting, 1460–1590,* trans. Edmund Jephcott (Chicago: University of Chicago Press, 1990).

23. Frederic C. Lane, "Family Partnerships and Joint Ventures," *Journal of Economic History* 4 (1944): 178–96, reprinted in Lane, *Venice and History: The Collected Papers of Frederic C. Lane* (Baltimore: Johns Hopkins Press, 1966), 36–55; Gino Luzzatto, "Les activités économiques du patriciat vénitien (Xe–XIVe siècle)," *Annales d'Histoire Économique et Sociale* 1 (1937): 25–57, reprinted in Luzzatto, *Studi di storia economica veneziana* (Padua: CEDAM, 1954), 125–65.

24. One example of a successful individual career is that of Andrea Barbarigo, although it should be recalled that relatives established in Crete facilitated the commercial debut of their young kinsman and the Cappello family, kin by alliance, were helpful to him as well: see Frederic C. Lane, *Andrea Barbarigo, Merchant of Venice, 1418–1449* (Baltimore: Johns Hopkins Press, 1944).

25. This was the crux of the problem of intestate successions and of the reimbursement of dowries (see Crouzet-Pavan, *"Sopre le acque salse,"* 1:418–20, 447–58).

26. For a detailed analysis of this process, see ibid., 410–21.

27. The statutes also recognized certain neighbors' rights. On the mechanisms of this circulation of goods within a lineage, see ibid., 421–34.

28. Patricia Fortini Brown, *The Renaissance in Venice: A World Apart* (London: Weidenfeld & Nicolson, 1997), 162–63.

29. Chojnacki, "Patrician Women"; Crouzet-Pavan, *"Sopra le acque salse,"* 1:447–58.

30. Crouzet-Pavan, *"Sopra le acque salse,"* 1:491–92.

31. For a few milestones in this debate, see Richard A. Goldthwaite, *Private Wealth in Renaissance Florence: A Study of Four Families* (Princeton: Princeton University Press, 1968); idem, "The Florentine Palace as Domestic Architecture," *American Historical Review* 77, no. 4 (1972): 977–1012; Jacques Heers, *Le clan familial au Moyen Age: Étude sur les structures politiques et sociales des milieux urbains* (Paris: Presses Universitaires de France, 1993), trans. Barry Herbert under the title *Family Clans in the Middle Ages: A Study of Political and Social Structures in Urban Areas* (Amsterdam: North-Holland, 1977); Francis William Kent, *Household and Lineage in Renaissance Florence: The Family Life of the Capponi, Ginori, and Rucellai* (Princeton: Princeton University Press, 1977); and Klapisch-Zuber, *La maison et le nom*, 13–15.

32. Anna Bellavitis, *Identité, mariage, mobilité sociale: Citoyennes et citoyens à Venise au XVIe siècle* (Rome: École Française de Rome, 2001).

33. Crouzet-Pavan, *"Sopra le acque salse,"* 1:617–68.

34. James S. Grubb, "Memory and Identity: Why Venetians Didn't Keep Ricordanze," *Renaissance Studies* 8, no. 4 (1994): 375–87. For the Freschi family, see Mary Neff, "A Citizen in the Service of the Patrician State: The Career of Zaccaria de' Freschi," *Studi Veneziani*, n.s., 5 (1981): 33–61.

35. Brown, *Renaissance in Venice*, 160–62.

36. Bellavitis, *Identité, mariage, mobilité sociale*.

37. Here I am following the argument in Grubb, "Memory and Identity."

38. The example of Venetian families of the Terraferma who kept such books corroborates this line of analysis (see ibid., 386).

39. On this topic, see the biographical materials presented in Mary Frances Neff, *Chancellery Secretaries in Venetian Politics and Society, 1480–1535* (Ann Arbor: University Microfilms International, 1986).

40. For a fuller treatment of this episode and its connections with the construction of another sanctuary, Santa Maria della Fava, see Crouzet-Pavan, *"Sopra le acque salse,"* 1:617–68.

41. Mario Brunetti, "Venezia durante la peste del 1348," *Ateneo Veneto* 32 ((May–June 1909), nos. 1:289–311, 2:5–42. The catalogue of the exhibition *Venezia e la peste, 1348–1797* (Venice: Marsilio, 1980), contains useful information, in particular for an analysis of demographic change and the effects of epidemics. See also Reinhold C. Mueller, "Aspetti sociali ed economici della peste a Venezia nel medioevo," and "Peste e demografia: Medioevo e Rinascimento," in ibid., 71–76 and 93–96, respectively. For

a population estimate of 65,000 inhabitants about 1363, see Benjamin Z. Kedar, *Merchants in Crisis: Genoese and Venetian Men of Affairs and the Fourteenth-Century Depression* (New Haven: Yale University Press, 1976).

42. Crouzet-Pavan, *"Sopra le acque salse,"* vol. 1, chap. 8.

43. Ibid., vol. 2. For some data concentrating more on the modern period, see *Venezia e la peste*, 77–93, and, in the same volume, Giampaolo Lotter, "L'organizzazione sanitaria a Venezia," 99–102, Richard J. Palmer, "L'azione della Repubblica di Venezia nel controllo della peste: Lo sviluppo della politica governativa," 103–10, and Andreina Zitelli, "L'azione della Repubblica di Venezia nel controllo della peste: Lo sviluppo di alcune norme di igiene pubblica," 111–12. See also Salvatore Carbone, *Provveditori e Sopraprovveditori alla Sanità della Repubblica di Venezia*, Quaderni della Rassegna degli Archivi di Stato, 21 (Rome, 1962); and Angelo Antonio Frari, *Della peste e della pubblica amministrazione sanitaria* (Venice, 1840), vol. 1.

44. These peaks were caused by epidemics in 1307 and 1320. We know of them because in both cases special commissions of *savi* were named to study the cemetery situation.

45. In the absence of comparable data for Venice, see the figures for Florence elaborated on the basis of the 1427 *catasto* in Klapisch-Zuber, *La maison et le nom*, 251: "At the age of forty, 18 percent of Florentine women appear in the census as widows, and at fifty, almost 45 percent."

46. Crouzet-Pavan, *"Sopra le acque salse,"* 1:447 ff.; Richard C. Trexler, "Le célibat à la fin du Moyen Age: Les religieuses de Florence," *Annales E.S.C.* 27 (1972): 1329–50.

47. Ruggiero, *Boundaries of Eros*, 14–15.

48. The clientele of the courtesans was far from being constituted by bachelors alone (see Elisabeth Pavan, "Police des mœurs, société à Venise à la fin du Moyen Age," *Revue Historique* 4 [1980]: 241–88).

49. Richard C. Trexler, "La prostitution florentine au XVe siècle: Patronages et clientèles," *Annales E.S.C.* 36 (1981): 983–1015; Maria Serena Mazzi, *Prostitute e lenoni nella Firenze del Quattrocento* (Milan: Il Saggiatore, 1991), 355–56.

50. Martines, "Séduction, espace familial," 258.

51. Guido Ruggiero, *Violence in Early Renaissance Venice* (New Brunswick, N.J.: Rutgers University Press, 1980). Ruggiero analyses the sentences passed down by the court of the Quarantia and concludes that they were quite moderate.

52. Ruggiero, *Boundaries of Eros*, 128. See also Michael Rocke, *Forbidden Friendships: Homosexuality and Male Culture in Renaissance Florence* (New York: Oxford University Press, 1996).

53. Ruggiero, *Boundaries of Eros*, 137.

54. On the evolution of this repression, the creation of new structures of control instituted in the name of a new public morality, and a general effort to instill purity and fill in gaps that previous communal judiciary instruments had failed to cover completely, see Crouzet-Pavan, *"Sopra le acque salse,"* 2:837 ff.; Mazzi, *Prostitute e lenoni*, 151 ff.; Andrea Zorzi, *L'amministrazione della giustizia penale nella Repubblica fiorentina: Aspetti e problemi* (Florence: Olschki, 1988); and idem, "Giustizia e società a Firenze in età comunale: Spunti per una prima riflessione," *Ricerche Storiche* 18, no. 3 (1988): 449–95. The official discourse of condemnation aside, one might wonder

whether a choice, conscious or unconscious, was made to let things be and to tolerate these reproved practices, even to leave them under the cover of secrecy. The governing elites may have had a presentiment that more strenuous repression would have disturbed the equilibrium of the social groups under their command. Lauro Martines advances the hypothesis that homosexuality among young males and their relations with slave and servant women and with prostitutes ultimately worked to preserve the honor of married women, hence of families (see Martines, *Italian Renaissance Sextet*, 89–90).

55. On symbolic violence, see Elisabeth Crouzet-Pavan, "Violence, société et pouvoir à Venise (XIVe–XVe siècles): Forme et évolution de rituels urbains," *Mélanges de l'École Française de Rome, Moyen Age* 96, no. 2 (1984): 903–936.

56. Elisabeth Crouzet-Pavan, "Un fior del male: I giovani nelle società urbane italiane (secoli XIV–XV)," in *Storia dei giovani*, ed. Jean-Claude Schmitt and Giovanni Levi, 2 vols. (Rome: Laterza, 1994), 1:211–77, trans. Camille Naish under the title "A Flower of Evil: Young Men in Medieval Italy," in *A History of Young People in the West*, 2 vols. (Cambridge, Mass.: Belknap Press, 1997), 1:173–221.

57. Elisabeth Crouzet-Pavan, "Potere politico e spazio sociale: Il controllo della notte a Venezia nei secoli XIII–XV," in *La notte: Ordine, sicurezza e disciplinamento in età moderna*, ed. Mario Sbriccoli (Florence: Ponte alle Grazie, 1991), 30–46, reprinted in Crouzet-Pavan, *Venise*, 160–80; Jacques Rossiaud, "Fraternités de jeunesse et niveaux de culture dans les villes du Sud-Est à la fin du Moyen Age," *Cahiers d'Histoire* 21, nos. 1–2 (1976): 76–102; idem, "Prostitution, jeunesse et société dans les villes du Sud-Est au XVe siècle," *Annales E.S.C.* 31 (1976): 289–325, reprinted in Rossiaud, *La prostituzione nel Medioevo* (Rome: Laterza, 1984), trans. Lydia G. Cochrane under the title *Medieval Prostitution* (Oxford: Basil Blackwell, 1988).

58. See Klapisch-Zuber, *La maison et le nom*, 229 ff. It has been shown that in Italy such rites were aimed especially at the remarriage of widows or widowers.

59. In a similar manner, bands of children were organized to wreak the community's ritual vengeance on what it condemned, reproved, or found impure (see Ottavia Niccoli, "Compagnie di bambini nell'Italia del Rinascimento," *Rivista Storica Italiana* 101, no. 2 [1989]: 346–74, esp. 357, where Niccoli cites various Venetian examples of *guerre di putti*, ritual conflicts involving children. See also Andrea Zorzi, "Rituali e cerimoniali penali nelle città italiane [secc. XIII–XVI]," in *Riti e rituali nelle società medievali*, ed. Jacques Chiffoleau, Lauro Martines, and Agostino Paravicini-Bagliani [Spoleto: Centro di Studi sull'Alto Medioevo, 1994], 141–58).

60. On the *compagnie della calza*, see Lionello Venturi, *Le compagnie della Calza (sec. XV–XVI)* (1909; reprint, Venice: Filippi, 1981); Matteo Casini, *I gesti del principe: La festa politica a Firenze e a Venezia in età rinascimentale* (Venice: Marsilio, 1996); Crouzet-Pavan, "Un fior del male."

61. Through analysis of massive amounts of notarial documentation (receipts and procurations, marriage contracts, wills, and more) we can to some extent reconstitute the networks and the spaces of such relations (see Crouzet-Pavan, "*Sopra le acque salse*," 1:567–611; Romano, *Patricians and Popolani*; Diane Owen Hughes, "Towards Historical Ethnography: Notarial Records and Family History in the Middle Ages," *Historical Methods Newsletter* 7 [1974]: 61–71).

62. Ferry landings were an essential part of local Venetian geography. The wealthier Venetians of course had private craft decorated with their family crest and banner. The number of rowers attached to an aristocratic or bourgeois house can be attested in a variety of ways (see Dennis Romano, "The Gondola as a Marker of Station in Venetian Society," *Renaissance Studies* 8, no. 4 [1994]: 359–74). The common herd paid only pennies to use the *traghetto*. The landing was an unavoidable point of passage, and the altercations and quarrels that broke out there and ended up in the law courts make up one of the surest documentary manifestations of the frequentation of other quarters than one's own and of the uninterrupted traffic of people across the canals.

63. Crouzet-Pavan, *"Sopra le acque salse,"* 1:527–66; Edward Muir, *Civic Ritual in Renaissance Venice* (Princeton: Princeton University Press, 1981), 135–56; Dennis Romano, "Charity and Community in Early Renaissance Venice," *Journal of Urban History* 11, no. 1 (1984): 63–82.

64. Robert C. Davis, *The War of the Fists: Popular Culture and Public Violence in Late Renaissance Venice* (New York: Oxford University Press, 1994).

65. Dennis Romano comes to roughly the same conclusion in *Patricians and Popolani*, chap. 1.

66. I refer the reader to the views of Brian Pullan, with which I totally concur and which are reflected in my argument here (see Brian Pullan, "The *Scuole Grandi* of Venice: Some Further Thoughts," in Pullan, *Poverty and Charity: Europe, Italy, Venice: 1400–1700* [Brookfield, Vt.: Variorum, 1994], sec. 12, p. 288; and Crouzet-Pavan, *"Sopra le acque salse,"* 1:582–97, 619–37).

67. Brian Pullan, "Religious Brotherhoods in Venice," in Pullan, *Poverty and Charity*, sec. 9, p. 1, originally published in Italian as "Natura e carattere delle scuole," in *Le scuole di Venezia*, ed. Terisio Pignatti (Milan: Electa, 1981), 1–40.

68. Richard Mackenney, "Continuity and Change in the Scuole Piccole," *Renaissance Studies* 8, no. 4 (1994): 388–403.

69. In the fifteenth century there were three bakers' confraternities—one for the master bakers, another for workers of Lombard origin, and the third for workers of German origin (see Pullan, "Religious Brotherhoods in Venice," 4).

70. The oldest statutes conserved for a devotional confraternity are those of the Scuola di San Mattio, which date from 1247 (see Mackenney, "Continuity and Change," 389).

71. It was in Venice that the series of prayers that make up the rosary was elaborated as a meditation on the life of the Virgin Mary and that of her Son (see Catherine Vincent, *Les confréries médiévales dans le royaume de France, XIIIe–XVe siècle* [Paris: Albin Michel, 1994], 117–18).

72. For statistics that throw light on this phenomenon, see Mackenney, "Continuity and Change," 394–97.

73. On Florentines in Venice, see Reinhold C. Mueller, "Mercanti e imprenditori fiorentini a Venezia nel tardo medioevo," *Società e Storia* 55 (1992): 29–60; and idem, "Stranieri e culture straniere a Venezia: Aspetti economici e sociali," in *Componenti storico-artistiche e culturali a Venezia nei secoli XIII e XIV*, ed. Michelangelo Muraro (Venice: Ateneo Veneto, 1981), 75–77.

74. The Albanians' brotherhood had 150 members; that of the Greeks may have had as many as 250 members; the Germans' association, dedicated to the Madonna of the Rosary, met in the church of San Bartolomeo and had some 100 members (see Pullan, "Religious Brotherhoods in Venice," 8).

75. "The Scuole Grandi represented a civic religion if by *civic* we mean 'city-wide'" (Pullan, "*Scuole Grandi* of Venice," 287).

76. Pietro Paoletti, *L'architettura e la scultura del Rinascimento in Venezia: Ricerche storico-artistiche,* 2 vols. (Venice, 1893).

77. Patricia Fortini Brown, "Honor and Necessity: The Dynamics of Patronage in the Confraternities of Renaissance Venice," *Studi Veneziani,* n.s., 14 (1987): 179–212; idem, *Venetian Narrative Painting in the Age of Carpaccio* (New Haven: Yale University Press, 1988).

78. Lia Sbriziolo, "Per la storia delle confraternite veneziane: Dalle deliberazioni miste (1310–1476) del Consiglio dei Dieci: Le scuole dei Battuti," in *Miscellanea Gilles Gérard Meersseman* (Padua: Antenore, 1970), 2:715–63; Brian Pullan, *Rich and Poor in Renaissance Venice: The Social Institutions of a Catholic State, to 1620* (Cambridge: Harvard University Press, 1971); idem, *Poverty and Charity.*

79. From its foundation, the Council of Ten passed laws regulating the flagellant confraternities. On the control and the marginal role of the clergy in these institutions, see William B. Wurthmann, "The Council of Ten and the Scuole Grandi in Early Renaissance Venice," *Studi Veneziani,* n.s., 18 (1989): 15–66.

80. Sbriziolo, "Per la storia delle confraternite veneziane."

81. Santa Maria della Misericordia was the first confraternity to establish separate lists of *fratelli da capitolo* and *fratelli alla disciplina* (in 1534).

82. Crouzet-Pavan, *"Sopra la acque salse,"* 2:779–89.

83. Deborah Howard, *Jacopo Sansovino: Architecture and Patronage in Renaissance Venice* (New Haven: Yale University Press, 1975); Manfredo Tafuri, *Venezia e il Rinascimento: Religione, scienza, architettura* (Turin: Einaudi, 1985).

84. David Rosand, *Painting in Cinquecento Venice: Titian, Veronese, Tintoretto* (New Haven: Yale University Press, 1982.

85. In 1581 four of the *scuole grandi* owned 206 houses (Brian Pullan, "Houses in the Service of the Poor in the Venetian Republic," in Pullan, *Poverty and Charity,* sec. 10). In the late sixteenth century the Procuratia di San Marco controlled between three hundred and four hundred houses.

86. The Procurators were divided into two groups, *procuratori de citra* and *procuratori de ultra,* who administered properties situated on one side or the other of the Grand Canal (see Reinhold C. Mueller, *The Procuratori di San Marco and the Venetian Credit Market: A Study of the Development of Credit and Banking in the Trecento* [New York: Arno Press, 1977]).

87. Pullan, *Rich and Poor in Renaissance Venice.*

88. Reinhold C. Mueller, "A Foreigner's View of Poor Relief in Late Quattrocento Venice," in *Pauvres et riches: Société et culture du Moyen Age aux temps modernes: Mélanges offerts à Bronislaw Geremek* (Warsaw: Wydawn Nauk PWN, 1992), 55–63.

89. Santa Maria della Carità operated throughout the area of the Punta di Dorsoduro, which, as we have seen, had been filled in and divided into lots during the

thirteenth century and later became part of the port area. The *albergo* of San Giovanni Evangelista was built in a growing peripheral area in a zone of long-term population expansion. Before it migrated to new quarters near the church of Santi Giovanni e Paolo in the northern part of Venice, the Scuola di San Marco was located in the *sestiere* of Santa Croce, at the western edge of Venice. Santa Maria della Misericordia was in the *sestiere* of Cannaregio, a decidedly peripheral setting and a quarter of developing urbanization with many industrial installations and a high rate of recent in-migration. From the early sixteenth century, the newly founded Scuola di San Rocco invested in recently reclaimed terrains near Sant'Andrea della Zirada and built houses in a charitable aim (on this topic, see Crouzet-Pavan, *"Sopra le acque salse,"* 2:789–96; and Giorgio Gianighian and Paola Pavanini, "Terreni nuovi di Santa Maria Mazor," in *Dietro i palazzi: Tre secoli di architettura minore a Venezia, 1492–1803*, ed. Giorgio Gianighian and Paola Pavanini [Venice: Arsenale, 1984], 45–57). As further proof that the partitioning of space was deliberate, no *scuola* was founded at the edge of the *sestiere* of Castello, where the state assumed direct responsibility for aid and had built hospices for sailors and *arsenalotti* (see Ennio Concina, *Venezia nell'età moderna: Struttura e funzioni* [Venice: Marsilio, 1989]).

90. Mary Margaret Newett, "The Sumptuary Laws of Venice in the Fourteenth and Fifteenth Centuries," in *Historical Essays, First Published in 1902 in Commemoration of the Jubilee of the Owen College, Manchester,* ed. Thomas Frederick Tout and James Tait (Manchester: Manchester University Press, 1907), 245–77, esp. 269–70.

91. In this connection one might cite a letter of Petrarch describing the joyous celebrations that followed a Venetian victory: "One of the highly rare and most admirable things was that despite such a great concourse of people, one failed to see the least disturbance anywhere, the least confusion, even the smallest quarrel, but all were rejoicing in the most perfect union and in the most tender and gracious manner. The square was entirely covered with people of all sexes, all ages, and all conditions. . . . From all the quarters of the city, an immense crowd of citizens, of their own volition, had come running" (quoted in Giustina Renier Michiel, *Origine des fêtes vénitiennes,* 5 vols. [Paris, 1817–27], 2:224–28; originally published as *Origine delle feste veneziane*).

92. See, e.g., André Vauchez, ed., *La religion civique à l'époque médiévale et moderne: Chrétienté et Islam* (Rome: École Française de Rome, 1995).

93. That is, if one excepts the mid-fourteenth-century personification of Venice as a seated female figure bearing the sword of justice in Filippo Calendario's sculpture on the facade of the Ducal Palace (see Wolfgang Wolters, *Storia e politica nei dipinti di Palazzo Ducale: Aspetti dell'autocelebrazione della Repubblica di Venezia nel Cinquecento,* ed. Maddalena Redolfi, trans. Benedetta Heinemann Campana [Venice: Arsenale, 1987], 223–27; originally published as *Der Bilderschmuck des Dogenpalastes: Untersuchungen zur Selbsdarstellung der Republik Venedig im 16. Jahrhundert* [Wiesbaden: Steiner, 1983]).

94. Mary Margaret Newett, *Canon Pietro Casola's Pilgrimage to Jerusalem in the Year 1494* (Manchester: University of Manchester Press, 1907), 137.

95. This altar screen was commissioned from artists in Constantinople by Doge Pietro Orseolo (976–78). It is a thick wooden panel covered with gold and silver leaf

and set with gems, some of them probably stolen during the pillage of the Monastery of the Pantocrator. In its present form it dates from 1345.

96. David Buckton, ed., with the help of Christopher Entwistle and Rowena Prior, *The Treasury of San Marco, Venice* (Milan: Olivetti, 1984).

97. Otto Demus, *The Church of San Marco in Venice: History, Architecture, Sculpture*, Dumbarton Oaks Studies, 6 (Washington, D.C.: Dumbarton Oaks Research Library and Collection, Trustees for Harvard University, 1960); idem, *The Mosaics of San Marco in Venice*, 2 vols. in 4 pts. (Chicago: University of Chicago Press, 1984); idem, "Oriente e Occidente nell'arte del Duecento," in *La civiltà veneziana del secolo di Marco Polo* (Florence: Sansoni, 1979), 109–26, esp. 113–14, 117, reprinted in *Storia della civiltà veneziana,* ed. Vittore Branca (Florence: Sansoni, 1979), 1:399–406; idem, "A Renaissance of Early Christian Art in Thirteenth-Century Venice," in *Late Classical and Mediaeval Studies in Honour of Albert Mathias Friend, Jr.,* ed. Kurt Weitzmann et al. (Princeton: Princeton University Press, 1955).

98. For an analysis of the changes from one representation to the next, see Brown, *Renaissance in Venice,* 24–29.

99. Crouzet-Pavan, *"Sopra le acque salse,"* 2:794–95.

GLOSSARY

acqua alta.
Flooding caused by a combination of a high tide and a wind effect that drives the water into the lagoon.

Arengo.
Assembly in theory comprising all the members of the *populus*. Gradually stripped of powers, it disappeared as a political body.

arsenalotti.
Workers in the Arsenal shipyards.

auditori nuovi.
Auditors for newly acquired Venetian lands on the Terraferma.

ballotte.
Balls used for voting *(ballottar).*

barena.
Lagoon area covered with water only at the highest tides.

cà (casa).
House, either dwelling or family.

calle.
Street.

campo.
Small parish square.

caò.
Edge, tip (of a district).

capicontrada.
Heads of the administrative districts of the *contrada.*

capisestiere.
Heads of the six major administrative divisions of the city.

cittadinus.
Title given to persons holding Venetian citizenship and enjoying the privileges related to that status.

colleganza.
Venetian term for the limited-liability commercial contract of *commenda.*

contado.
Land around a city or under its domination.

contrada (Venice).
Subdivision of the administrative division of the *sestiere.*

Council of Ten.
Council responsible for public order. Instituted after the Tiepolo-Querini conspiracy (1310), it was regularly extended until definitively established in the fifteenth century.

fondaco.
Warehouse.

Fondaco dei Tedeschi.
Lodging and commercial center for German traders.

The Forty.
See Quarantia

fraterna.
A family-based economic association that automatically applied to men to the third degree of consanguinity.

ghetto.
Jewish quarter; the term is taken from the name of the foundries in the *contrada* of San Geremia.

Giustizia Nuova.
Administrative organ for the supervision of taverns and retail wine sales.

Giustizia Vecchia.
Administrative organ for the supervision of the minor guilds and for control of weights and measures.

Great Council.
An outgrowth of the *Consilium Sapientum;* a sovereign organ of the Republic that held legislative power.

lido.
Chain of barrier or littoral islands.

Magistrato alle Acque.
Body governing water use and water ecology.

Marangona.
The name of a bell in the Campanile in Piazza San Marco; its striking defined the workday.

muda.
Convoy of ships of the navigation lines organized by the state.

murazzi.
Defenses of the littoral islands, made up of stone paving, levees, and walls, completed in 1782.

palata.
Palisade; guardpost for the control of lagoon and river routes, hence of communications within the lagoon basin. An essential element in the Venetian customs system.

Pescaria.
Fish market. Venice had two, the first at the market of the Rialto, the second on Piazza San Marco.

Piovego.
Judiciary magistracy composed of three members charged with protection of the public domain.

podestà.

In the Italian communes, the magistrate who assumed the better part of the executive power. The responsibility was given, at the request and by the choice of the government of the commune involved, to an outsider to the community, usually for one year. Chronologically, the institution of the *podestà* came after the first, consular communal phase. In areas under Venetian domination, a Venetian magistrate, who served for one year, elected by the Great Council, was charged with administering the communes of the duchy or certain cities of the Venetian state.

populares veteres.

Older citizen families.

porto.

Passageway through the littoral islands permitting communication between the lagoon and the sea.

Provveditori alla Sanità.

Magistracy instituted in the late fifteenth century, replacing earlier experimental bodies, with responsibility for public health, hence for combating the plague, for quarantine, and for public sanitation.

Provveditori di Comun.

Magistracy responsible for supervision of the wool guild and, in the late fifteenth century, for communication systems in Venice.

Quarantia.

Court of appeals with certain supervisory duties.

Rialto.

From Rivus Altus, the original name of the island. The term became synonymous with the city of Venice. By the late Middle Ages this second usage had become the more common one, except when the word referred to the area of the original island, the bridge, or the market of the Rialto.

rio.

Waterway (the term *canal* was reserved for the two principal waterways of Venice).

rio terrà.
Filled-in waterway.

Savi agli Ordini.
Agency for maritime affairs.

Savi della Guerra.
See Savi di Terra Ferma

Savi di Terra Ferma.
Agency responsible for war, finance, and military affairs on the mainland.

scuola.
Confraternity.

scuola grande.
One of five Venetian flagellant confraternities (six in the modern age).

Senate.
Venetian assembly. Until the late fourteenth century known as the *Consilio dei Pregadi* or *dei Rogati*. Its jurisdiction grew until it became the principal organ of the Republic, inheriting the full powers of the Great Council.

Sensa.
Feast of the Ascension.

Serrata.
Movement instituted in 1297 for reform of the Great Council.

sestiere.
One of six administrative and geographical divisions of Venice.

Signori di Notte.
Judiciary magistracy charged with keeping public order, given wide powers in the thirteenth and fourteenth centuries.

Sposalizio.
Ritual of the marriage of the doge to the sea on Ascension Day.

squero.
Private shipyard.

Terraferma.
Venetian lands or possessions on the mainland.

traghetto.
Ferry, also ferry's place of embarkment.

trentaccia.
Administrative district combining two *contrade.*

tumba.
Raised zone in a swampy stretch.

valli.
Sectors of the lagoon enclosed for fishing.

Venetia.
A province of the Roman Empire; a personification of Venice.

Zecca.
The Mint.

BIBLIOGRAPHY

Acqua Giusti, Antonio dall'. *Il Palazzo Ducale di Venezia*. Venice, 1864.

Agazzi, Michela. *Platea Sancti Marci: I luoghi marciani dall'XI al XII secolo e la formazione della piazza*. Venice: Comune di Venezia, 1991.

Airaldi, Gabriella. *Genova e la Liguria nel Medioevo*. Turin: UTET, 1986.

Alberti, Annibale, and Roberto Cessi. *La politica mineraria della Repubblica veneta*. Rome: Provveditorio Generale dello Stato, Libreria, 1927.

Andenna, Giancarlo. "Il monastero e l'evoluzione urbanistica di Brescia tra XI e XII secolo." In *S. Giulia di Brescia: Archeologia, arte, storia di un monastero regio dai Longobardi al Barbarossa*, edited by Clara Stella and Gerardo Brentagani, 93–118. Brescia: Grafo, 1992.

Arbel, Benjamin. "Colonie d'oltremare." In Tenenti and Tucci, *Il Rinascimento: Società ed economia*, 947–85.

———. "Entre mythe et histoire: La légende noire de la domination vénitienne à Chypre." In *Matériaux pour une histoire de Chypre (IVe–XXe siècle)*, 83–107. Études Balkaniques, Cahiers Pierre Belon, 5. Paris: Pierre Belon, 1998; distributed by De Boccard.

Arnaldi, Girolamo, ed. *Dalle origini al Trecento*. Vol. 1 of *Storia della cultura veneta*. Vicenza: Neri Pozza, 1976.

———. *Il Trecento*. Vol. 2 of *Storia della cultura veneta*. Vicenza: Neri Pozza, 1976.

Arnaldi, Girolamo, and Lidia Capo. "I cronisti di Venezia e della Marca trevigiana." In Arnaldi, *Il Trecento*, 272–337.

Arnaldi, Girolamo, Giorgio Cracco, and Alberto Tenenti, eds. *La formazione dello Stato patrizio*. Vol. 3 of *Storia di Venezia*. Rome: Istituto della Enciclopedia Italiana, 1997.

Arnaldi, Girolamo, and Manlio Pastore Stocchi, eds. *Dal primo Quattrocento al Concilio di Trento*. Vol. 3 of *Storia della cultura veneta*. Vicenza, Neri Pozza, 1980.

Ashtor, Eliyahu. "L'exportation des textiles occidentaux dans le Proche-Orient musulman au bas Moyen Age (1370–1517)." In Ashtor, *East-West Trade in the Medieval Mediterranean*, edited by Benjamin Z. Kedar, 303–77. London: Variorum Reprints, 1986.

———. *Levant Trade in the Later Middle Ages*. Princeton: Princeton University Press, 1983.

———. "Observations on Venetian Trade in the Levant in the XIVth Century." In Ashtor, *East-West Trade in the Medieval Mediterranean*, 533–86.

Averone, Antonio. *Saggio sull'antica idrografia veneta*. Mantua: Aldo Manuzio, 1911.

Azzara, Claudio. "Fra terra e acque: Equilibri territoriali e assetti urbani nella Venezia dai Romani ai Longobardi." In *Venezia: Itinerari per la storia della città*, edited by Stefano Gasparri, Giovanni Levi, and Pierandrea Moro. Bologna: Il Mulino, 1997.

Baiardi, Giorgio Cerboni, Giorgio Chittolini, and Piero Floriani, eds. *Federico di Montefeltro: Lo Stato, le arti, la cultura*. Rome: Bulzoni, 1986.

Baiocchi, Angelo. "Venezia nella storiografia fiorentina del Cinquecento." *Studi Veneziani*, n.s., 3 (1979): 203–81.

Balard, Michel. "La lotta contro Genova." In Arnaldi, Cracco, and Tenenti, *La formazione dello Stato patrizio*, 87–126.

———. *La Romanie génoise: XIIe–début du XVe siècle*. Bibliothèque des Écoles Françaises d'Athènes et de Rome, 235. 2 vols. Rome: École Française de Rome, 1978.

Balestracci, Duccio. "La politica delle acque urbane nell'Italia comunale." *Mélanges de l'École Française de Rome, Moyen Age* 104, no. 2 (1992): 431–79.

———. "Systèmes d'hydraulique urbaine (Italie centrale, fin du Moyen Age)." In *Le contrôle des eaux en Europe occidentale, XIIe–XVIe siècles/Water Control in Western Europe, Twelfth-Sixteenth Centuries*, edited by Elisabeth Crouzet-Pavan and Jean-Claude Maire Vigueur, 115–22. Milan: Bocconi, 1994.

Balestracci, Duccio, and Gabrielle Piccinni. *Siena nel Trecento: Assetto urbano e strutture edilizie*. Florence: Clusf, 1977.

Baron, Hans. *The Crisis of the Early Italian Renaissance: Civic Humanism and Republican Liberty in an Age of Classicism and Tyranny*. 2d ed. 2 vols. Princeton: Princeton University Press, 1983.

Bassi, Elena. "Appunti per la storia del Palazzo ducale di Venezia." *Critica d'Arte* 54 (1962a): 25–38 and (1962b): 45–53.

———. *Palazzi di Venezia: "Admiranda urbis Venetae."* Venice: Stamperia di Venezia, 1976.

Bassi, Elena, and Egle Renata Trincanato. *Il Palazzo Ducale nella storia e nell'arte di Venezia*. Milan: Martello, 1966. Translated under the title *Palace of the Doges in the History and Art of Venice* (Milan: Martello, 1966).

———. "Il Palazzo Ducale nel '400." *Bollettino del Centro Internazionale di Studi di Architettura Andrea Palladio* 6 (1964): 181–87.

Beck, Hans-Georg, Manoussos Manoussacas, and Agostino Pertusi, eds. *Venezia centro di mediazione tra Oriente e Occidente (secoli XV–XVI): Aspetti e problemi*. 2 vols. Florence: Olschki, 1977.

Bellavitis, Anna. *Identité, mariage, mobilité sociale: Citoyennes et citoyens à Venise au XVIe siècle*. Rome École Française de Rome, 2001.

———. *Noale: Struttura sociale e regime fondiario di una podestaria della prima metà del secolo XVI*. Treviso: Canova and Fondazione Benetton, 1994.

Bellavitis, Giorgio, and Giandomenico Romanelli. *Venezia*. Le Città nella Storia d'Italia: Grandi Opere. Rome: Laterza, 1985.

Beloch, Giulio. "La popolazione di Venezia nei secoli XVI e XVII." *Nuovo Archivio Veneto*, 3d ser., 3 (1902): 5–49.

Beltrami, Luca. *La "Cà del Duca" sul Canal Grande ed altre reminiscenze sforzesche in Venezia.* Milan: Allegretti, 1900.

Benevolo, Leonardo. *Storia dell'architettura del Rinascimento.* Bari: Laterza, 1968. Translated by Judith Landry under the title *The Architecture of the Renaissance,* 2 vols. (London: Routledge & Kegan Paul, 1978).

Benzoni, Gino. "Panoramica su Venezia (secc. XVI–XVII)." *Critica Storica* 13 (1976): 128–58.

Berengo, Marino. *La società veneta alla fine del Settecento: Ricerche storiche.* Florence: G. C. Sansoni, 1956.

Berveglieri, Roberto. "L'arte dei tintori e il nero di Venezia." In *I mestieri della moda a Venezia dal XVIII al XVIII secolo/The Crafts of the Venetian Fashion Industry from the Thirteenth to the Eighteenth Century,* 55–62. Exh. cat. Venice: Mestieri della Moda a Venezia, 1988; distributed by Edizioni del Cavallino.

Besta, Enrico. *Il senato veneziano.* Miscellanea di Storia Veneta, 2d ser., 5. Venice: Reale Deputazione Veneta di Storia Patria, 1899.

Betto, Bianca. "Linee di politica matrimoniale nella nobiltà veneziana fino al XV secolo: Alcune note genealogiche e l'esempio della famiglia Mocenigo." *Archivio Storico Italiano* 139 (1981): 3–64.

Beylié, Léon. *L'habitation byzantine: Recherches sur l'architecture civile des Byzantins et son influence en Europe.* Geneva: Falque & E. Perrin; Paris: E. Leroux, 1902.

Bocchi, Francesca. "Suburbi e fasce suburbane nella città dell'Italia medievale." *Storia della Città* 5 (1977): 1–33.

Boldrin, G., and G. Dolcetti. *I pozzi di Venezia, 1015–1906.* Venice, 1910.

Boni, Giacomo. *Il campanile di San Marco riedificato.* Venice, 1912.

Borelli, Giorgio. "L'agricoltura veronese tra '500 e '600: Una proposta di lettura." In *Uomini e civiltà agraria in territorio veronese.* 2 vols. Verona: Banca Popolare di Verona, 1982.

Borelli, Giorgio, Paola Lanaro Sartori, and Francesco Vecchiato, eds. *Il sistema fiscale veneto: Problemi e aspetti, XV–XVIII secolo.* Verona: Libraria Universitaria, 1982.

Borsari, Silvano. "Una famiglia veneziana del Medioevo: Gli Ziani." *Archivio Veneto,* 5th ser., 145 (1978): 27–72.

Bortolami, Sante. "L'agricoltura." In Cracco Ruggini et al., *Origini-Età ducale,* 461–90.

Bouwsma, William J. *Venice and the Defense of Republican Liberty: Renaissance Values in the Age of the Counter Reformation.* Berkeley: University of California Press, 1968.

——. "Venice and the Political Education of Europe." In Hale, *Renaissance Venice,* 445–66.

Branca, Vittore. "Ermolao Barbaro e l'umanesimo veneziano." In *Umanesimo europeo ed umanesimo veneziano,* edited by Vittore Branca, 193–212. Civiltà Europea e Civiltà Veneziana: Aspetti e Problemi, 2. Florence: Sansoni, 1963.

——. "L'umanesimo veneziano alla fine del Quattrocento: Ermolao Barbaro e il suo circolo." In Arnaldi and Stocchi, *Dal primo Quattrocento al Concilio di Trento,* pt. 1, 123–75.

Braudel, Fernand. *Civilisation matérielle, économie et capitalisme, XVe–XVIIIe siècle.* Vol. 3, *Le temps du monde.* Paris: Colin, 1979. Translated by Siân Reynolds under the title *Civilization and Capitalism, 15th–18th Century,* vol. 3, *The Perspective of the World* (New York: Harper & Row, 1984).

Braunstein, Philippe. "Appunti per la storia di una minoranza: La popolazione tedesca di Venezia nel Medioevo." In *Strutture familiari, epidemie, migrazioni nell'Italia medievale,* edited by Rinaldo Comba, Gabriella Piccinni, and Giuliano Pinto, 511–27. Naples: Edizioni Scientifiche Italiane, 1984.

———. "Le commerce du fer à Venise au XVe siècle." *Studi Veneziani* 8 (1966): 267–302.

———. "De la montagne à Venise: Les réseaux du bois au XVe siècle." *Mélanges de l'École Française de Rome, Moyen Age* 100, no. 2 (1988): 761–99.

———. "Les entreprises minières en Vénétie au XVe siècle." *École Française de Rome: Mélanges d'Archéologie et d'Histoire* 77, no. 2 (1965): 529–601.

———. "Un étranger dans la ville: Albrecht Dürer." In Braunstein, *Venise 1500,* 215–29.

———. "Relations d'affaires entre Nurembergeois et Vénitiens à la fin du XIVe siècle." *École Française de Rome: Mélanges d'Archéologie et d'Histoire* 76, no. 1 (1964): 227–69.

———. "Remarques sur la population allemande de Venise à la fin du Moyen Age." In Beck, Manoussacas, and Pertusi, *Venezia centro di mediazione tra Oriente e Occidente,* 1:233–43.

———. "Venezia e la Germania nel Medioevo." In *Venezia e la Germania: Arte, politica, commerci, due civiltà a confronto,* 35–49. Milan: Electa, 1986.

———, ed. *Venise 1500: La puissance, la novation et la concorde: Le triomphe du mythe.* Paris: Autrement, 1993.

Braunstein, Philippe, and Robert Delort. *Venise: Portrait historique d'une cité.* Paris: Seuil, 1971.

Brezzi, Paolo. "La pace di Venezia del 1177 e le relazioni tra la Repubblica e l'Impero." In *Venezia dalla prima crociata alla conquista di Costantinopoli del 1204,* 51–70. Florence: Sansoni, 1965.

Broglio d'Ajano, Romolo. "L'industria della seta a Venezia." In *Storia dell'economia italiana: Saggi di storia economica,* edited by Carlo M. Cipolla, 1:209–62. Turin: Edizioni Scientifiche Einaudi, 1959.

Brown, Patricia Fortini. "Committenza e arte di Stato." In Arnaldi, Cracco, and Tenenti, *La formazione dello stato patrizio,* 783–824.

———. "Honor and Necessity: The Dynamics of Patronage in the Confraternities of Renaissance Venice." *Studi Veneziani,* n.s., 14 (1987): 179–212.

———. *The Renaissance in Venice: A World Apart.* London: Weidenfeld & Nicolson, 1997.

———. *Venetian Narrative Painting in the Age of Carpaccio.* New Haven: Yale University Press, 1988.

———. *Venice and Antiquity: The Venetian Sense of the Past.* New Haven: Yale University Press, 1997.

Brucker, Gene. *Giovanni and Lusanna: Love and Marriage in Renaissance Florence.* Berkeley: University of California Press, 1986.

Brunello, Franco. *Arti e mestieri a Venezia nel Medioevo e nel Rinascimento.* Vicenza: Neri Pozza, 1981.

Brunetti, Mario. "Venezia durante la peste del 1348." *Ateneo Veneto* 32 (May–June 1909), nos. 1:289–311 and 2:5–42.

Brunetti, Mario, Sergio Bettini, Ferdinando Forlati, and Giuseppe Fiocco. *Torcello.* Venice: Libreria Serenissima, 1940.

Buckton, David, ed., with the help of Christopher Entwistle and Rowena Prior. *The Treasury of San Marco, Venice.* Milan: Olivetti, 1984.

Cà Da Mosto, Alvise. *Le navigazioni atlantiche del Veneziano Alvise Da Mosto.* Edited by Tullia Gasparrini-Leporace. Il Nuovo Ramusio, 5. Rome: Istituto Poligrafico dello Stato, 1966.

Calabi, Donatella. "Un nouvel espace public." In Braunstein, *Venise 1500,* 72–93.

Calabi, Donatella, and Paola Lanaro, eds. *La città italiana e i luoghi degli stranieri, XIV–XVIII secolo.* Rome: Laterza, 1998.

Calabi, Donatella, and Paolo Morachiello. *Rialto: Le fabbriche e il ponte.* Turin: Einaudi, 1987.

Calabi, Donatella, Ugo Camerino, and Ennio Concina. *La città degli Ebrei: Il ghetto di Venezia, architettura e urbanistica.* Venice: Albrizzi, 1991.

Cappelletti, Giuseppe. *Storia della Repubblica di Venezia dal suo principio sino al giorno d'oggi.* 13 vols. Venice, 1848–55.

Carbone, Salvatore. *Provveditori e Sopraprovveditori alla Sanità della Repubblica di Venezia.* Quaderni della Rassegna degli Archivi di Stato, 21. Rome, 1962.

Carile, Antonio. "Le origini di Venezia nella tradizione storiografica." In Arnaldi, *Dalle origini al Trecento,* 135–66.

Carile, Antonio, and Giorgio Fedalto. *Le origini di Venezia.* Bologna: Pàtron, 1978.

Carli, Enzo. *Pienza: La città di Pio II.* 2d ed. Rome: Editalia, 1967.

Casini, Matteo. *I gesti del principe: La festa politica a Firenze e a Venezia in età rinascimentale.* Venice: Marsilio, 1996.

———. "Realtà e simboli del cancellier grande veneziano in età moderna." *Studi Veneziani,* n.s., 22 (1991): 195–251.

Cassini, Giocondo. *Piante e vedute prospettiche di Venezia (1479–1855).* Venice: Stamperia di Venezia, 1971.

Castagnetti, Andrea. "Il primo comune." In Cracco and Ortalli, *L'età del Comune,* 81–130.

Castellani, Giorgio. "Giorgio da Trebisonda, maestro di eloquenza a Vicenza e a Venezia." *Nuovo Archivio Veneto,* 2d ser., 11 (1896): 123–42.

Cavaciocchi, Simonetta, ed. *La donna nell'economia secc. XIII–XVII.* Florence: Le Monnier, 1990.

———. *La seta in Europa (secc. XIII–XVIII).* Florence: Le Monnier, 1993.

Cecchetti, Bartolomeo. *Il doge di Venezia.* Venice, 1865.

———. "La facciata della Cà d'Oro dello scalpello di Giovanni e Bartolomeo Buono." *Archivio Veneto* 31, no. 1 (1886): 201–4.

———. "Una libreria circolante a Venezia nel secolo XV." *Archivio Veneto* 32, no. 1 (1886): 161–68.

——. "Libri, scuole, maestri, sussidi allo studio in Venezia nei secoli XIV e XV." *Archivio Veneto* 32, no. 2 (1886): 329–63.

——. "La vita dei Veneziani nel 1300. Parte 1. La città, la laguna." *Archivio Veneto* 27 (1884): 5–54, 321–37; 28 (1884): 5–29, 267–96; 29 (1885): 9–48. Reprinted as *La vita dei Veneziani nel 1300* (1885–86; reprint, Bologna: Forni, 1980).

Cessi, Roberto. *Documenti relativi alla storia di Venezia anteriori al mille.* Vol. 1, *Secoli V–IX.* New ed. Padua: Gregoriana, 1942.

——. "Evoluzione storica del problema lagunare." In *Atti del Convegno per la conservazione e difesa della laguna e città di Venezia*, 23–64. Venice: Ferrari, 1960.

——. "L'iscrizione torcellana del secolo VII." In *Le origini del ducato veneziano.* Naples: Morano, 1951.

——. "Il problema della Brenta dal secolo XII al secolo XV." In *La laguna di Venezia*, edited by Gustavo Brunelli et al., vol. 1, pt. 4, t. 7, fasc. 1, pp. 1–77. Venice: Ferrari, 1943.

——. *Storia della Repubblica di Venezia.* New ed. Florence: Giunti Martello, 1981.

——. "Lo sviluppo dell'interramento nella laguna settentrionale e il problema della Piave e del Sile fino al secolo XV." In *La laguna di Venezia*, edited by Gustavo Brunelli et al., vol. 1, pt. 4, t. 7, fasc. 1, pp. 79–108. Venice: Ferrari, 1943.

——. *Venezia ducale.* Vol. 1, *Duca e popolo.* Venice: Deputazione di Storia Patria per le Venezie, 1963.

Cessi, Roberto, and Annibale Alberti. *Rialto: L'isola, il ponte, Il mercato.* Bologna: Zanichelli, 1934.

Cherubini, Giovanni, and Giovanni Fanelli, eds. *Il palazzo Medici Riccardi di Firenze.* Florence: Giunti, 1990.

Chittolini, Giorgio, and Elena Fasano Guarini. "Gli stati dell'Italia centro-settentrionale tra Quattro e Cinquecento: Continuità e trasformazioni." *Società e Storia* 21 (1983): 617–40.

Chojnacki, Stanley. "Dowries and Kinsmen in Early Renaissance Venice." *Journal of Interdisciplinary History* 5 (1975): 571–600. Reprinted as "Dowries and Kinsmen" in Chojnacki, *Women and Men in Renaissance Venice*, 132–52.

——. "La formazione della nobiltà dopo la Serrata." In Arnaldi, Cracco, and Tenenti, *La formazione dello stato patrizio*, 641–725.

——. "La grande famille des nobles." In Braunstein, *Venise 1500*, 178–99.

——. "In Search of the Venetian Patriciate: Families and Factions in the Fourteenth Century." In Hale, *Renaissance Venice*, 47–90.

——. *The Making of the Venetian Renaissance State: The Achievement of a Noble Political Consensus, 1378–1420.* Ann Arbor: University Microfilms International, 1985.

——. "Marriage Legislation and Patrician Society in Fifteenth-Century Venice." In *Law, Custom, and the Social Fabric in Medieval Europe: Essays in Honor of Bryce Lyon*, edited by Bernard S. Bachrach and David Nicholas, 163–84. Medieval Institute Publications, Studies in Medieval Civilization, 28. Kalamazoo: Western Michigan University, 1900.

——. "Measuring Adulthood: Adolescence and Gender in Renaissance Venice." *Journal of Family History* 17, no. 4 (1992): 371–95. Reprinted as "Measuring Adulthood: Adolescence and Gender" in Chojnacki, *Women and Men in Renaissance Venice*, 185–205.

——. " 'The Most Serious Duty': Motherhood, Gender, and Patrician Culture in Renaissance Venice." In *Refiguring Women: Perspective on Gender and the Italian Renaissance*, edited by Marilyn Migiel and Juliana Schiesari, 133–54. Ithaca: Cornell University Press, 1991. Reprinted as " 'The Most Serious Duty': Motherhood, Gender, and Patrician Culture" in Chojnacki, *Women and Men in Renaissance Venice*, 169–82.

——. "Nobility, Women, and the State: Marriage Regulation in Venice, 1420–1535." In *Marriage in Italy: 1300–1650*, edited by Trevor Dean and K. J. P. Lowe, 128–51. Cambridge: Cambridge University Press, 1998. Reprinted as "Marriage Regulation in Venice, 1420–1535," in Chojnacki, *Women and Men in Renaissance Venice*, 53–75.

——. "Patrician Women in Early Renaissance Venice." *Studies in the Renaissance* 21 (1974): 176–203. Reprinted in Chojnacki, *Women and Men in Renaissance Venice*, 115–31.

——. "Political Adulthood in Fifteenth-Century Venice." *American Historical Review* 91 (1986): 791–810. Reprinted as "Political Adulthood" in Chojnacki, *Women and Men in Renaissance Venice*, 227–43.

——. "The Power of Love: Wives and Husbands in Late Medieval Venice." In *Women and Power in the Middle Ages*, edited by Mary Erler and Maryanne Kowaleski, 126–48. Athens: University of Georgia Press, 1988. Reprinted as "The Power of Love: Wives and Husbands" in Chojnacki, *Women and Men in Renaissance Venice*, 153–68.

——. "Social Identity in Renaissance Venice: The Second Serrata." *Renaissance Studies* 8, no. 4 (1994): 341–58.

——. "Subaltern Patriarchs: Patrician Bachelors in Renaissance Venice." In *Medieval Masculinities: Regarding Men in the Middle Ages*, edited by Clare A. Lees, 73–90. Minneapolis: University of Minnesota Press, 1994. Reprinted as "Subaltern Patriarchs: Patrician Bachelors" in Chojnacki, *Women and Men in Renaissance Venice*, 244–56.

——. *Women and Men in Renaissance Venice: Twelve Essays on Patrician Society.* Baltimore: Johns Hopkins University Press, 2000.

Cicognara, Leopoldo, Antonio Diedo, and Giannantonio Selva. *Le fabbriche più cospicue di Venezia misurate, illustrate e intagliate dai membri della veneta reale Accademia di belle arti.* 2 vols. Venice, 1840.

Ciriacono, Salvatore. *Acque e agricoltura: Venezia, l'Olanda e la bonifica europea in età moderna.* Milan: F. Angeli, 1994.

——. "Industria e artigianato." In Tenenti and Tucci, *Il Rinascimento: Società ed economia*, 523–92.

——. "Investimenti capitalistici e culture irrigue: La congiuntura agricola nella Terraferma veneta (secoli XVI–XVII)." In *Venezia e la Terraferma attraverso le relazioni dei rettori*, 123–58. Milan: Giuffrè, 1981.

——."Irrigazione e produttività agraria nella Terraferma veneta tra Cinque e Seicento." *Archivio Veneto*, 5th ser., 147 (1979): 73–135.

——. "Mass Consumption Goods and Luxury Goods: The De-Industrialization of the Republic of Venice from the Sixteenth to the Eighteenth Century." In *The Rise and Decline of Urban Industries in Italy and in the Low Countries (Late Middle Ages–Early Modern Times)*, edited by Herman van der Wee, 41–61. Leuven, Belgium: Leuven University Press, 1988.

——. "Scrittori d'idraulica e politica delle acque." In Arnaldi and Stocchi, *Dal primo Quattrocento al Concilio di Trento*, pt. 2, 491–512.

Comba, Rinaldo, and Irma Naso, eds. *Demografia e società nell'Italia medievale: Secoli IX–XIV*. Cuneo: Società per gli Studi Storici della Provincia di Cuneo-Società Italiana di Demografia Storica, 1994.

Concina, Ennio. *L'Arsenale della Repubblica di Venezia: Tecniche e istituzioni dal Medioevo all'età moderna*. Milan: Electa, 1984.

——. *Dell'arabico: A Venezia tra Rinascimento e Oriente*. Venice: Marsilio, 1994.

——. "Le plus grand chantier de l'Occident: L'Arsenal." In Braunstein, *Venise 1500*, 39–52.

——. *Structure urbaine et fonctions des bâtiments du XVIe au XIXe siècle: Une recherche à Venise*. Venice: UNESCO and Save Venice, 1982.

——. *Venezia nell'età moderna: Struttura e funzioni*. Venice: Marsilio, 1989.

Concina, Ennio, ed. *Arsenali e città dell'Occidente europeo*. Rome: La Nuova Italia Scientifica, 1987.

Connell, Susan. "Books and Their Owners in Venice, 1345–1480." *Journal of the Warburg and Courtauld Institutes* 35 (1972): 163–86.

Contento, Aldo. "Il censimento della popolazione sotto la Repubblica veneta." *Nuovo Archivio Veneto*, 2d ser., 19 (1900): 5–42, 179–240.

Corazzol, Gigi. *Cineografo di banditi su sfondi di monti: Feltre, 1634–1642*. Milan: UNICOPLI, 1997.

Cornaro, Flaminio. *Ecclesiae Torcellanae antiquis monumentis nunc etiam primum editis illustratae, pars prima*. Venice, 1749.

——. *Ecclesiae venetae, antiquis monumentis nunc etiam primum editis illustratae ac in decades distributae*. 13 vols. Venice, 1749.

La coscienza cittadina nei comuni italiani del Duecento. Centro di Studi sulla Spiritualità Medievale, 11. Todi: Accademia Tudertina, 1973.

Cozzi, Gaetano. "Authority and the Law in Renaissance Venice." In Hale, *Renaissance Venice*, 293–345.

——. "Cultura, politica e religione nella 'pubblica storiografia' veneziana del Cinquecento." *Bolletino dell'Istituto di Storia della Società e dello Stato Veneziano* 3 (1961): 215–94.

——. "Domenico Morosini e il 'De Bene Instituta Re Publica.' " *Studi Veneziani* 12 (1970): 405–58.

——. *Repubblica di Venezia e stati italiani: Politica e giustizia dal secolo XVI al secolo XVIII*. Turin: Einaudi, 1982.

——, ed. *Stato, società e giustizia nella Repubblica veneta (sec. XV–XVIII)*. 2 vols. Rome: Jouvence, 1980.

Cozzi, Gaetano, and Michael Knapton. *Storia della Repubblica di Venezia dalla guerra di Chioggia alla riconquista della Terraferma*. Vol. 12 of *Storia d'Italia*. Turin: UTET, 1986.

Cracco, Giorgio. *Un "altro mondo": Venezia nel Medioevo dal secolo XI al secolo XIV*. Turin: UTET, 1986.

———. "Mercanti in crisi: Realtà economiche e riflessi emotivi nella Venezia del tardo Duecento." In *Studi sul medioevo veneziano*, edited by Giorgio Cracco, Andrea Castagnetti, and Silvana Collodo. Turin: Giappichelli, 1981.

———. "Patriziato e oligarchia a Venezia nel Tre-Quattrocento." In *Quattrocento*, vol. 1 of *Florence and Venice: Comparisons and Relations*, 71–98. Florence: La Nuova Italia, 1979.

———. *Società e stato nel Medioevo veneziano (secoli XII–XIV)*. Florence: Olschki, 1967.

———, ed. *L'età medievale*. Vol. 2 of *Storia di Vicenza*. Vicenza: Neri Pozza, 1988.

Cracco, Giorgio, and Michael Knapton, eds. *Dentro lo "Stado Italico": Venezia e la Terraferma fra Quattro e Seicento*. Trent: Gruppo Culturale Civis, 1984.

Cracco, Giorgio, and Gherardo Ortalli, eds. *L'età del Comune*. Vol. 2 of *Storia di Venezia*. Rome: Istituto della Enciclopedia Italiana, 1995.

Cracco Ruggini, Lellia, Massimiliano Pavan, Giorgio Cracco, and Gherardo Ortalli, eds. *Origini-Età ducale*. Vol. 1 of *Storia di Venezia*. Rome: Istituto della Enciclopedia Italiana, 1992.

Crouzet-Pavan, Elisabeth. "Entre collaboration et affrontement: Le public et le privé dans les grands travaux urbains." In *Tecnologia y sociedad: Las grandes obras públicas en la Europa medieval*, 363–80. Pamplona: Gobierno de Navarra, 1995.

———. "Un fior del male: I giovani nelle società urbane italiane (secoli XIV–XV)." In *Storia dei giovani*, edited by Jean-Claude Schmitt and Giovanni Levi, 1:211–77. 2 vols. Rome: Laterza, 1994. Translated by Camille Naish under the title "A Flower of Evil: Young Men in Medieval Italy," in *A History of Young People in the West*, 2 vols. (Cambridge, Mass.: Belknap Press, 1997), 1:173–221.

———. *La mort lente de Torcello: Histoire d'une cité disparue*. Paris: Fayard, 1995.

———. "Le peuple des quartiers." In Braunstein, *Venise 1500*, 200–14.

———. "Politique urbaine et stratégie de pouvoir dans l'Italie communale." In *Enjeux et expressions de la politique municipale: XIIe–XVe siècle*, edited by Denis Menjot and Jean-Luc Pinol, 7–20. Paris: L'Harmattan, 1997.

———. "Potere politico e spazio sociale: Il controllo della notte a Venezia nei secoli XIII–XV." In *La Notte: Ordine, sicurezza e disciplinamento in età moderna*, edited by Mario Sbriccoli, 30–46. Florence: Ponte alle Grazie, 1991. Reprinted in Crouzet-Pavan, *Venise: Une invention de la ville*.

———. "*Sopra le acque salse*": *Espaces, pouvoir et société à Venise à la fin du Moyen Age*. 2 vols. Collection de l'École Française de Rome, 158. Rome: Istituto Storico Italiano per il Medio Evo, 1992.

———. *Venise: Une invention de la ville, XIIe–XVe siècle*. Collection Époques. Seyssel: Champ Vallon, 1997.

———. "Violence, société et pouvoir à Venise (XIVe–XVe siècles): Forme et évolution de rituels urbains." *Mélanges de l'École Française de Rome, Moyen Age* 96, no. 2 (1984): 903–36.

Davanzo Poli, Doretta. "L'arte e il mestiere della tessitura a Venezia nei secoli XIII–XVIII." In *I mestieri della moda a Venezia dal XIII al XVIII secolo/The Crafts of the Venetian Fashion Industry from the Thirteenth to the Eighteenth Century.* Exh. cat. Venice: Mestieri della Moda a Venezia, 1988; distributed by Edizioni del Cavallo.

Davis, James C. *A Venetian Family and Its Fortune, 1500–1900: The Donà and the Conservation of Their Wealth.* Philadelphia: American Philosophical Society, 1975.

Davis, Robert C. *Shipbuilders of the Venetian Arsenal: Workers and Workplace in the Preindustrial City.* Baltimore: Johns Hopkins University Press, 1990.

———. *The War of the Fists: Popular Culture and Public Violence in Late Renaissance Venice.* New York: Oxford University Press, 1994.

Day, John. "Les instruments de gestion du monde." In Braunstein, *Venise 1500,* 142–56.

Degrassi, Donata. *L'economia artigiana nell'Italia medievale.* Rome: La Nuova Italia Scientifica, 1996.

Delogu, Paolo, André Guillou, and Gherardo Ortalli. *Longobardi e Bizantini.* Storia d'Italia, edited by Giuseppe Galasso, 1. Turin: UTET, 1980.

Delort, Robert. "Un aspect du commerce vénitien au XVe siècle: Andrea Barbarigo et le commerce des fourrures (1430–1440)." *Le Moyen Age* 71 (1965): 29–80, 247–73.

Del Torre, Giuseppe. *Il Trevigiano nei secoli XV e XVI: L'assetto amministrativo e il sistema fiscale.* Venice: Il Cardo, 1990.

———. *Venezia e la terraferma dopo la guerra di Cambrai: Fiscalità e amministrazione (1515–1530).* Milan: F. Angeli, 1986.

Demus, Otto. *The Church of San Marco in Venice: History, Architecture, Sculpture.* Dumbarton Oaks Studies, 6. Washington, D.C.: Dumbarton Oaks Research Library and Collection, Trustees for Harvard University, 1960.

———. *The Mosaics of San Marco in Venice.* 2 vols. in 4 pts. Chicago: University of Chicago Press, 1984.

———. "Oriente e occidente nell'arte veneta del Duecento." In *La civiltà veneziana del secolo di Marco Polo,* 109–26. Florence: Sansoni, 1955. Reprinted in *Storia della civiltà veneziana,* edited by Vittore Branca (Florence: Sansoni, 1979), 1:399–406.

———. "A Renaissance of Early Christian Art in Thirteenth-Century Venice." In *Late Classical and Mediaeval Studies in Honour of Albert Mathias Friend Jr.,* edited by Kurt Weitzmann et al. Princeton: Princeton University Press, 1955.

Derosas, Renzo. "Moralità e giustizia a Venezia nel '500–'600: Gli Esecutori contro la bestemmia." In *Stato, società e giustizia nella Repubblica veneta (sec. XV–XVIII),* edited by Gaetano Cozzi, 1:431–528. Rome: Jouvence, 1980.

Dorigo, Wladimiro. *Venezia origini: Fondamenti, ipotesi, metodi.* 3 vols. Milan: Electa, 1983.

Doumerc, Bernard. "Gli armamenti marittimi." In Arnaldi, Cracco, and Tenenti, *La formazione dello stato patrizio*, 617–40.

———. "La crise structurelle de la marine vénitienne au XVe siècle: Le problème du retard des 'mude.'" *Annales E.S.C.* 40 (1985): 605–23.

———. "La difesa dell'impero." In Arnaldi, Cracco, and Tenenti, *La formazione dello stato patrizio*, 237–50.

———. "Il dominio del mare." In Tenenti and Tucci, *Il Rinascimento: Società ed economia*, 113–80.

———. "Le rôle ambigu de la *muda* vénitienne: Convoi marchand ou unité de combat." In *Histoire maritime: Thalassocraties et période révolutionnaire*, 139–54. Paris: CTHS, 1991.

Ducellier, Alain. "Les Albanais à Venise aux XIVe et XVe siècles." *Centre de Recherches d'Histoire et de Civilisation Byzantines: Travaux et Mémoires* 2 (1967): 405–20.

Ducellier, Alain, Bernard Doumerc, Brünehilde Imhaus, and Jean de Miceli. *Les chemins de l'exil: Bouleversements de l'Est européen et migrations vers l'Ouest à la fin du Moyen Age*. Paris: Colin, 1992.

Fano, Nella. "Ricerche sull'arte della lana a Venezia nel XIII e XIV secolo." *Archivio Veneto*, 5th ser., 18 (1936): 73–213.

Fanti, Mario. "Le lottizzazioni monastiche e lo sviluppo urbano di Bologna nel Duecento." *Atti e Memorie della Deputazione di Storia Patria per la Romagna*, n.s., 27 (1976): 121–43.

Fasoli, Gina. "Liturgia e cerimonia ducale." In Pertusi, *Venezia e il Levante fino al secolo XV*, 1, pt. 1, 261–95.

———. "Nascita di un mito." In *Studi storici in onore di Gioacchino Volpe per il suo 80° compleanno*, 1:445–79. Florence: Sansoni, 1958.

Favaro, Antonio. "Notizie storiche sul magistrato veneto alle acque." *Nuovo Archivio Veneto*, 3d ser., 9 (1905): 179–99.

Fedalto, Giorgio. "Le minoranze straniere a Venezia tra politica e legislazione." In Beck, Manoussacas, and Pertusi, *Venezia centro di mediazione tra Oriente e Occidente*, 1:143–63.

———. *Ricerche storiche sulla posizione giuridica ed ecclesiastica dei greci a Venezia nei secoli XV e XVI*. Florence: Olschki, 1967.

———. "Stranieri a Venezia e Padova." In Arnaldi and Stocchi, *Dal primo Quattrocento al Concilio di Trento*, pt. 1, 499–535.

Fees, Irmgard. *Reichtum und Macht im mittelalterlichen Venedig: Die Familie Ziani*. Tübingen: M. Niemeyer, 1988.

Ferraro, Joanne M. *Family and Public Life in Brescia, 1580–1650: The Foundations of Power in the Venetian State*. Cambridge: Cambridge University Press, 1993.

Filiasi, Giacomo. *Memorie storiche de' Veneti primi e secondi*. 9 vols. Venice, 1796–98.

———. *Ricerche storico-critiche sull'opportunità della laguna veneta pel commercio sull'arti e sulla marina di questo stato*. Venice, 1803.

Finlay, Robert. "Crisis and Crusade in the Mediterranean: Venice, Portugal, and the Cape Route to India (1498–1509)." *Studi Veneziani*, n.s., 28 (1994): 45–90.

———. "The Foundation of the Ghetto: Venice, the Jews, and the War of the League of

Cambrai." *Proceedings of the American Philosophical Society* 126 (1982): 140–54.

———. *Politics in Renaissance Venice.* New Brunswick, N.J.: Rutgers University Press, 1980.

Fiocco, Giuseppe. *La casa veneziana antica.* Rome, 1949.

Franchetti Pardo, Vittorio. *Storia dell'urbanistica dal Trecento al Quattrocento.* Bari: Laterza, 1982.

Franzoi, Umberto. "Le trasformazioni edilizie e la definizione storico-architettonica di Piazza San Marco." In *Piazza San Marco: L'architettura, la storia, le funzioni,* by Giuseppe Samonà et al., 43–77. 3d ed. Venice: Marsilio, 1982.

Franzoi, Umberto, Teresio Pignatti, and Wolfgang Wolters. *Il Palazzo Ducale di Venezia.* Treviso: Canova, 1990.

Frari, Angelo Antonio. *Della peste e della pubblica amministrazione sanitaria.* Venice, 1840.

Gaeta, Franco. "Alcune considerazioni sul mito di Venezia." *Bibliothèque d'Humanisme et Renaissance* 23 (1961): 548–75.

———. "Storiografia, coscienza nazionale e politica culturale nella Venezia del Rinascimento." In Arnaldi and Stocchi, *Dal primo Quattrocento al Concilio di Trento,* pt. 1, 1–91.

Galletti, Giuliano. *Bocche e biade: Popolazione e famiglie nelle campagne trevigiane dei secoli XV e XVI.* Treviso: Canova, 1994.

Gallina, Mario. *Una società coloniale del Trecento: Creta tra Venezia e Bisanzio.* Venice: Deputazione Editrice, 1989.

Gallo, Rodolfo. "Marco Polo, la sua famiglia e il suo libro." In *Nel VII Centenario della nascita di Marco Polo.* Venice: Istituto Veneto di Scienze, Lettere ed Arti, 1955.

Gasparini, Duilio, and Mathieu Arnoux. "Le savoir et la pratique: Un bail de métairie en Vénétie au XVIe siècle." *Histoire et Sociétés Rurales* 4 (1995): 232–80.

Gattinoni, Gregorio. *Il campanile di San Marco.* Venice: Fabbris, 1910.

Geanakoplos, Dino. "La colonia greca di Venezia e il suo significato per il Rinascimento." In *Venezia e l'Oriente fra tardo Medioevo e Rinascimento,* edited by Agostino Pertusi, 189–91. Florence: Sansoni, 1966.

Geary, Patrick J. *Furta Sacra: Thefts of Relics in the Central Middle Ages.* Princeton: Princeton University Press, 1978.

Gianighian, Giorgio, and Paola Pavanini, eds. *Dietro i palazzi: Tre secoli di architettura minore a Venezia, 1492–1803.* Venice: Arsenale, 1984.

Gilbert, Felix. "Biondo, Sabellico, and the Beginnings of Venetian Official Historiography." In *Florilegium Historiale: Essays Presented to Wallace K. Ferguson,* edited by J. G. Rowe and W. H. Stockdale, 275–93. Toronto: University of Toronto Press, 1971.

———. "Machiavelli e Venezia." *Lettere Italiane* 21 (1969): 389–98.

———. "Venice and the Crisis of the League of Cambrai." In Hale, *Renaissance Venice,* 274–92.

Ginatempo, Maria, and Lucia Sandri. *L'Italia delle città: Il popolamento urbano tra Medioevo e Rinascimento (secoli XIII–XVI).* Florence: Le Lettere, 1990.

Girgensohn, Dieter. *Kirche, Politik und adelige Regierung in der Republik Venedig zu Beginn des 15. Jahrhunderts.* Veröffentlichungen des Max-Planck-Instituts für Geschichte, 118. 2 vols. Göttingen: Vandenhoeck & Ruprecht, 1996.

Gleason, Elisabeth G. *Gasparo Contarini: Venice, Rome, and Reform.* Berkeley: University of California Press, 1993.

Goffen, Rona. *Giovanni Bellini.* New Haven: Yale University Press, 1989.

———. *Piety and Patronage in Renaissance Venice: Bellini, Titian, and the Franciscans.* New Haven: Yale University Press, 1986.

Goldthwaite, Richard A. "The Florentine Palace as Domestic Architecture." *American Historical Review* 77, no. 4 (1972): 977–1012.

———. *Private Wealth in Renaissance Florence: A Study of Four Families.* Princeton: Princeton University Press, 1968.

Goy, Richard J. "Architectural Taste and Style in Early Quattrocento Venice: The Facade of the Cà d'Oro and Its Legacy." In *War, Culture, and Society in Renaissance Venice: Essays in Honour of John Hale,* edited by David S. Chambers, Cecil H. Clough, and Michael E. Mallett. London: Hambledon Press, 1993.

———. *The House of Gold: Building a Palace in Medieval Venice.* Cambridge: Cambridge University Press, 1992.

Gramigna, Silvia, and Annalisa Perissa. *Scuole di arti, mestieri e devozione a Venezia.* Venice: Arsenale, 1981.

Greci, Roberto. *Corporazioni e mondo del lavoro nell'Italia padana medievale.* Bologna: CLUEB, 1988.

Groppi, Angela, ed. *Il lavoro delle donne.* Rome: Laterza, 1996.

Grubb, James S. "Alla ricerca delle prerogative locali: La cittadinanza a Vicenza, 1404–1509." In Cracco and Knapton, *Dentro lo "Stado Italico,"* 177–91.

———. *Firstborn of Venice: Vicenza in the Early Renaissance State.* Baltimore: Johns Hopkins University Press, 1988.

———. "Memory and Identity: Why Venetians Didn't Keep Ricordanze." *Renaissance Studies* 8, no. 4 (1994): 375–87.

———. *Provincial Families in the Renaissance: Private and Public Life in the Veneto.* Baltimore: Johns Hopkins University Press, 1996.

———. "When Myths Lose Power: Four Decades of Venetian Historiography." *Journal of Modern History* 58 (1986): 43–94.

Guenzi, Alberto, and Carlo Poni. "Sinergia di due innovazioni: Chiaviche e mulini da seta a Bologna." *Quaderni Storici* 64, no. 1 (1987): 111–27.

Guidoni, Enrico. "Un monumento della tecnica urbanistica duecentesca: L'espansione di Brescia del 1237." In *La Lombardia: Il territorio, l'ambiente, il paesaggio,* edited by Carlo Pirovano, 1:127–36. 5 vols. Milan: Electa, 1981.

Gullino, Giuseppe. "Il patriziato." In *Il Rinascimento: Politica e cultura,* edited by Alberto Tenenti and Ugo Tucci, vol. 4 of *Storia di Venezia,* 379–413. Rome: Istituto della Enciclopedia Italiana, 1996.

———. "Quando il mercante costruisce la villa: Le proprietà dei Veneziani nella Terraferma." In *Dal Rinascimento al Barocco,* edited by Gaetano Cozzi and Paolo

Prodi, vol. 6 of *Storia di Venezia*, 875–924. Rome: Istituto della Enciclopedia Italiana, 1994.

Hale, J. R., ed. *Renaissance Venice*. London: Faber; Totowa, N.J.: Rowman & Littlefield, 1973.

Heers, Jacques. *Le clan familial au Moyen Age: Étude sur les structures politiques et sociales des milieux urbains*. New edition. Paris: Presses Universitaires de France, 1993. Translated by Barry Herbert under the title *Family Clans in the Middle Ages: A Study of Political and Social Structures in Urban Areas* (Amsterdam: North-Holland, 1977).

———. "Les villes d'Italie centrale et l'urbanisme: Origines et affirmation d'une politique (environ 1200–1350)." *Mélanges de l'École Française de Rome, Moyen Age* 101, no. 1 (1989): 67–93.

Herlihy, David, and Christiane Klapisch-Zuber. *Les Toscans et leurs familles: Une étude du catasto florentin de 1427*. Paris: Fondation Nationale des Sciences Politiques/École des Hautes Études en Sciences Sociales, 1978. Published in English, abridged, under the title *Tuscans and Their Families: A Study of the Florentine Catasto of 1427*. New Haven: Yale University Press, 1985.

Hocquet, Jean-Claude. "Expansion, crises et déclin des salines dans la lagune de Venise au Moyen Age." In *Mostra storica della laguna veneta*. Exh. cat. Venice: Stamperia di Venezia, 1970. Reprinted in Hocquet, *Chioggia, capitale del sale nel Medioevo*, translated by Carla Neri. Padua: Libraria Editrice, 1991.

———. "Le saline." In Cracco Ruggini et al., *Origini-Età ducale*, 515–48.

———. *Le sel et la fortune de Venise*. Vol. 1, *Production et monopole;* vol. 2, *Voiliers et commerce in Méditerranée, 1200–1650*. 2d ed. 2 vols. Lille: Presses Universitaires de Lille, 1982.

———. "Le sel supporte les épices." In Braunstein, *Venise 1500.*

Howard, Deborah. *The Architectural History of Venice*. London: B. T. Batsford, 1980.

———. *Jacopo Sansovino: Architecture and Patronage in Renaissance Venice*. New Haven: Yale University Press, 1975.

———. "Venice as a Dolphin: Further investigations into Jacopo de' Barbari's View." *Artibus et Historiae* 35 (1997): 101–12.

Hubert, Étienne. *Espace urbain et habitat à Rome du Xe siècle à la fin du XIIIe siècle*. Rome: École Française de Rome, 1990.

Huse, Norbert, and Wolfgang Wolters. *The Art of Renaissance Venice: Architecture, Sculpture, and Painting, 1460–1590*. Translated by Edmund Jephcott. Chicago: University of Chicago Press, 1990.

Imhaus, Brünehilde. *Le minoranze orientali a Venezia, 1305–1510*. Rome: Il Veltro, 1997.

Ioly Zorattini, Pier Cesare. "Gli ebrei a Venezia, Padova e Verona." In Arnaldi and Stocchi, *Dal primo Quattrocento al Concilio di Trento*, pt. 1, 537–76.

Ivanoff, Nicola. "I cicli allegorici della Libreria e del Palazzo ducale di Venezia." In *Rinascimento europeo e veneziano*, edited by Vittore Branca, 281–99. Civiltà Europea e Civiltà Veneziana, 3. Florence: Sansoni, 1967.

Jacoby, David. "La colonisation militaire vénitien de la Crète au XIIIe siècle: Une nouvelle approche." In *Le partage du monde: Échanges et colonisation dans la Méditerranée médiévale*, edited by Michel Balard and Alain Ducellier, 297–314. Paris: Publications de la Sorbonne, 1998.

———. "L'expansion occidentale dans le Levant: Les Vénitiens à Acre dans la seconde moitié du XIIIe siècle." In Jacoby, *Recherches sur la Méditerranée orientale du XIIe au XVe siècle: Peuples, sociétés, économies*, 225–64. London: Variorum Reprints, 1979.

———. "Les juifs de Venise du XIVe siècle au milieu du XVIe siècle." In Beck, Manoussacas, and Pertusi, *Venezia centro di mediazione tra Oriente e Occidente*, 1:163–216.

Karpov, Sergei Pavlovic. *L'impero di Trebisonda: Venezia, Genova e Roma (1204–1461): Rapporti politici, diplomatici e commerciali*. Translated by Eleonora Zambelli. Edited by Virginia Cappelletti and Franco Tagliarini. Rome: Il Veltro, 1986.

Kedar, Benjamin Z. *Merchants in Crisis: Genoese and Venetian Men of Affairs and the Fourteenth-Century Depression*. New Haven: Yale University Press, 1976.

Kent, Francis William. *Household and Lineage in Renaissance Florence: The Family Life of the Capponi, Ginori, and Rucellai*. Princeton: Princeton University Press, 1977.

Kindleberger, Charles P. *The World Economic Primacy, 1500 to 1990*. New York: Oxford University Press, 1996.

King, Margaret L. "Personal, Domestic, and Republican Values in the Moral Philosophy of Giovanni Caldiera." *Renaissance Quarterly* 28 (1975): 535–74.

———. *Venetian Humanism in an Age of Patrician Dominance*. Princeton: Princeton University Press, 1986.

Kirshner, Julius. *Pursuing Honor While Avoiding Sin: The Monte delle doti of Florence*. Milan: Giuffrè, 1978.

Klapisch-Zuber, Christiane. *La maison et le nom: Stratégies et rituels dans l'Italie de la Renaissance*. Paris: École des Hautes Études en Sciences Sociales, 1990.

Knapton, Michael. "Il fisco nello stato veneziano di Terraferma tra '300 e '500: La politica delle entrate." In Borelli, Lanaro Sartori, and Vecchiato, *Il sistema fiscale veneto*, 15–58.

———. "Venezia e Treviso nel Trecento: Proposte per una ricerca sul primo dominio veneziano a Treviso." In *Tomaso da Modena e il suo tempo*. Treviso: Comitato Manifestazione Tomaso da Modena, 1980.

Kohl, Benjamin G. *Padua under the Carrara, 1318–1405*. Baltimore: Johns Hopkins University Press, 1998.

Krekic, Barisa. *Dubrovnik in the Fourteenth and Fifteenth Centuries: A City between East and West*. Norman: University of Oklahoma Press, 1972.

———. *Dubrovnik, Italy, and the Balkans in the Late Middle Ages*. London: Variorum Reprints, 1980.

———. "Venezia e l'Adriatico." In Arnaldi, Cracco, and Tenenti, *La formazione dello stato patrizio*, 51–85.

Kretschmayr, Heinrich. *Geschichte von Venedig*. 3 vols. 1905–34. Reprint, Aalen: Scientia, 1986, vol. 1.

Labalme, Patricia H. *Bernardo Giustiniani: A Venetian of the Quattrocento.* Uomini e
 Dottrine, 13. Rome: Storia e Letteratura, 1969.
Laguna, fiumi, lidi: Cinque secoli di gestione delle acque nelle Venezie. Venezia: La
 Press, 1983.
Lanaro Sartori, Paola. "Essere famiglia di consiglio: Social Closure and Economic
 Change in the Veronese Patriciate of the Sixteenth Century." *Renaissance
 Studies* 8, no. 4 (1994): 428–38.
———. *Un'oligarchia urbana nel Cinquecento veneto: Istituzioni, economia, società.*
 Turin: Giappichelli, 1992.
———. "Reddito agrario e controllo fiscale nel Cinquecento: La Valpolicella e Verona."
 In *La Valpolicella nella prima età moderna (1500–c. 1630)*, edited by Gian
 Maria Varanini, 205–45. Verona: Centro di Documentazione per la Storia
 della Valpolicella, 1987.
Lane, Frederic C. *Andrea Barbarigo, Merchant of Venice, 1418–1449.* Baltimore: Johns
 Hopkins Press, 1944.
———. "The Crossbow in the Nautical Revolution of the Middle Ages." In *Economy,
 Society, and Government in Medieval Italy: Essays in Memory of Robert L.
 Reynolds,* edited by David Herlihy, Robert S. Lopez, and V. Slessarev, 161–
 71. Explorations in Economic History, 7. Kent, Ohio: Kent State University
 Press, 1969. Reprinted in Lane, *Studies in Venetian Social and Economic
 History,* edited by Benjamin G. Kohl and Reinhold C. Mueller (London:
 Variorum Reprints, 1987), sec. 6.
———. "The Enlargement of the Great Council of Venice." In *Florilegium Historiale:
 Essays Presented to Wallace K. Ferguson,* edited by J. G. Rowe and W. H.
 Stockdale, 236–74. Toronto: University of Toronto Press, 1971. Reprinted in
 Lane, *Studies in Venetian Social and Economic History,* edited by Benjamin
 G. Kohl and Reinhold C. Mueller (London: Variorum Reprints, 1987), sec.
 3.
———. "Family Partnerships and Joint Ventures." *Journal of Economic History* 4
 (1944): 178–96. Reprinted in Lane, *Venice and History,* 36–55.
———. "The Mediterranean Spice Trade: Its Revival in the Sixteenth Century." *Ameri-
 can Historical Review* 45 (1940): 581–90. Reprinted in Lane, *Venice and
 History,* 25–34.
———. "Merchant Galleys, 1300–34: Private and Communal Operations." *Speculum*
 38 (1963): 179–205. Reprinted in Lane, *Venice and History,* 193–226.
———. "Ritmo e rapidità di giro d'affari nel commercio veneziano del Quattrocento."
 In *Studi in onore di Gino Luzzatto,* 1:254–73. 4 vols. Milan: Giuffrè, 1949.
 Reprinted as "Rhythm and Rapidity of Turnover in Venetian Trade of the
 Fifteenth Century" in Lane, *Venice and History,* 109–27.
———. "Tonnages, Medieval and Modern." *Economic History Review,* 2d ser., 17
 (1964): 213–33. Reprinted in Lane, *Venice and History,* 345–70.
———. "Venetian Seamen in the Nautical Revolution of the Middle Ages." In Pertusi,
 Venezia e il Levante fino al secolo XV, 1, pt. 1, 403–30.
———. *Venetian Ships and Shipbuilders of the Renaissance.* 1934. Reprint. Baltimore:
 Johns Hopkins University Press, 1992.

——. *Venice, a Maritime Republic*. Baltimore: Johns Hopkins University Press, 1973.

——. *Venice and History: The Collected Papers of Frederic C. Lane*. Baltimore: Johns Hopkins Press, 1966.

Lane, Frederic C., and Reinhold C. Mueller. *Coins and Moneys of Account*. Vol. 1 of *Money and Banking in Medieval and Renaissance Venice*. Baltimore: Johns Hopkins University Press, 1985.

Lanfranchi, Bianca, and Luigi Lanfranchi. "La laguna dal secolo VI al XIV." In *Mostra storica della laguna veneta*, 74–84. Venice: Stamperia di Venezia, 1970.

Lanfranchi, Luigi. "I documenti sui più antichi insediamenti monastici nella laguna veneziana." In *Le origini della chiesa di Venezia*, edited by Franco Tonon, 143–50. Contributi alla Storia della Chiesa di Venezia, 1. Venice: Studium Cattolico Veneziano, 1987.

Lanfranchi, Luigi, and Gian Giacomo Zille. "Il territorio del ducato veneziano dall'VIII al XII secolo." In *Dalle origini del Ducato alla IV Crociata*, vol. 2 of *Storia di Venezia*, 3–65. Venice: Centro Internazionale delle Arti e del Costume, 1958.

Law, John Easton. "Age Qualification and the Venetian Constitution: The Case of the Cappello Family." *Papers of the British School at Rome* 29 (1971): 125–37.

——. "A New Frontier: Venice and the Trentino in the Early Fifteenth Century." *Atti della Accademia Roveretana degli Agiati*, 6th ser., no. 28 (1990): 159–80.

——. "Il Quattrocento a Venezia." In *I secoli del primato italiano: Il Quattrocento*, vol. 8 of *Storia della società italiana*, edited by. Giovanni Cherubini et al., 233–322. Milan: Teti, 1988.

——. " 'Super differentiis agitatis Venetiis inter districtuales et civitatem': Venezia, Verona e il contado nel '400." *Archivio Veneto*, 5th ser., 151 (1981): 5–32.

——. "The Venetian Mainland State in the Fifteenth Century." *Transactions of the Royal Historical Society*, 6th ser., 2 (1992): 153–74.

——. "Venice and the 'Closing' of the Veronese Constitution in 1405." *Studi Veneziani*, n.s., 1 (1977): 69–103.

Lazzarini, Vittorio. "Filippo Calendario: L'architetto della tradizione del palazzo ducale." *Nuovo Archivio Veneto*, 2d ser., 7 (1894): 429–46.

——. "Una iscrizione torcellana del secolo VII." *Atti del R. Istituto Veneto di Scienze, Lettere ed Arti* 73 (1913–14): 387–97. Reprinted in Lazzarini, *Scritti di paleografia e diplomatica*.

——. "Un maestro di scrittura nella Cancelleria veneziana." In Lazzarini, *Scritti di paleografia e diplomatica*, 64–70.

——. "Le offerte per la guerra di Chioggia e un falsario del Quattrocento." *Nuovo Archivio Veneto*, 3d ser., 4 (1902): 202–13.

——. *Scritti di paleografia e diplomatica*. 2d ed., enl. Padua: Antenore, 1969.

Lebe, Reinhard. *Quando San Marco approdò a Venezia: Il culto dell'Evangelista e il miracolo politico della Repubblica di Venezia*. Translated by Luciano Tosti, revised by Virginia Cappelletti and Franco Tagliarini. Rome: Il Veltro, 1969.

Leciejewicz, Lech. "Alcuni problemi dell'origine di Venezia alla luce degli scavi a Torcello." In *Le origini di Venezia: Problemi esperienze proposte*, 55–64. Venice: Marsilio, 1981.

Leciejewicz, Lech, Eleonora Tabaczynska, and Stanislaw Tabaczynsky. *Torcello: Scavi 1961–62*. Rome: Istituto Nazionale di Archeologia e Storia dell'Arte, 1977.

Lepori, Fernando. "La scuola di Rialto dalla fondazione alla metà del Cinquecento." In Arnaldi and Stocchi, *Dal primo Quattrocento al Concilio di Trento*, pt. 2, 539–605.

Lieberman, Ralph. *Renaissance Architecture in Venice, 1450–1540*. New York: Abbeville, 1982.

Logan, Oliver. *Culture and Society in Venice, 1470–1790: The Renaissance and Its Heritage*. London: Batsford, 1972.

Lopez, Ceferino Caro. "Gli Auditori Nuovi e il Dominio di Terraferma." In Cozzi, *Stato, società e giustizia nella Repubblica veneta*, 1:259–316.

Lopez, Roberto Sabatino. *Storia delle colonie genovesi nel Mediterraneo*. 2d ed. Genoa: Marietti, 1996.

Lorenzi, Giambattista. *Monumenti per servire alla storia del Palazzo Ducale di Venezia*. Venice, 1869.

Lotter, Giampaolo. "L'organizzazione sanitaria a Venezia." In *Venezia e la peste*, 99–102.

Lowry, Martin. "L'imprimerie, un nouveau produit culturel." In Braunstein, *Venise 1500*, 53–71.

———. *Nicholas Jenson and the Rise of Venetian Publishing in Renaissance Europe*. Oxford: Basil Blackwell, 1991.

———. *The World of Aldus Manutius: Business and Scholarship in Renaissance Venice*. Oxford: Clarendon Press, 1979.

Ludovico il Moro: La sua città e la sua corte, 1480–1499. Milan: Archivio di Stato di Milano, 1983.

Lupprian, Karl-Ernst. *Il fondaco dei Tedeschi e la sua funzione di controllo del commercio tedesco a Venezia*. Quaderni, 6. Venice: Centro Tedesco di Studi Veneziani, 1978.

Luzzatto, Gino. "Les activités économiques du patriciat vénitien (Xe–XIVe siècles)." *Annales d'Histoire Économique et Sociale* 1 (1937): 25–57. Reprinted in Luzzatto, *Studi di storia economica veneziana*, 125–65.

———. "L'attività commerciale di un patrizio veneziano del Quattrocento." In Luzzatto, *Studi di storia economica veneziana*, 167–93.

———. "Capitale e lavoro nel commercio veneziano dei secoli XI e XII." In Luzzatto, *Studi di storia economica veneziana*, 89–116.

———. "La commenda nella vita economica dei secoli XIII e XIV con particolare riguardo a Venezia." In *Atti del convegno di studi storici del diritto marittimo medievale*. Naples: Meridionali, 1934.

———. "Per la storia delle costruzioni navali a Venezia nei secoli XV e XVI." In Luzzatto, *Studi di storia economica veneziana*, 386–87.

———. *Storia economica di Venezia dal XI al XVI secolo*. Venice: Centro Internazionale delle Arti e del Costume, 1961.

———. *Studi di storia economica veneziana*. Padua: CEDAM, 1954.

———. "Tasso d'interesse e usura a Venezia nei secoli XIII–XV." In *Miscellanea in onore di Roberto Cessi*, 1:191–202. 3 vols. Rome: Storia e Letteratura, 1958.

———. "Vi furono fiere a Venezia?" In Luzzatto, *Studi di storia economica veneziana,* 201–9.

Macchi, Mauro. *Istoria del Consiglio dei Dieci*. 2 vols. Turin, 1848–49.

Mackenney, Richard. "Continuity and Change in the Scuole Piccole." *Renaissance Studies* 8, no. 4 (1994): 388–403.

———. "Corporazioni e politica nel Medioevo a Venezia ca. 1250–1400." In *Venezia tardomedioevale: Istituzioni e società nella storiografia angloamericana*, 87–130. Ricerche Venete, 1. Venice: Canal, 1989.

———. "The Guilds of Venice: State and Society in the *Longue Durée*." *Studi Veneziani*, n.s., 34 (1997): 15–44.

———. *Tradesmen and Traders: The World of the Guilds in Venice and Europe, c. 1250–c. 1650*. Totowa, N.J.: Barnes & Noble, 1987.

Maire Vigueur, Jean-Claude. "L'essor urbain dans l'Italie médiévale: Aspects et modalités de la croissance." In *Europa en los umbrales de la crisis (1250–1350)*, 171–204. Pamplona: Gobierno de Navarra, Departamento de Educación y Cultura, 1995.

Mallett, Michael E. "L'esercito veneziano in terraferma nel Quattrocento." In *Armi e cultura nel Bresciano, 1420–1870*. Brescia: Ateneo di Brescia, 1981.

Mallett, Michael E., and J. R. Hale. *The Military Organisation of a Renaissance State: Venice, c. 1400 to 1617*. Cambridge: Cambridge University Press, 1984.

Mantova e i Gonzaga nella civiltà del Rinascimento. Mantua: Arnaldo Mondadori, 1977.

Maranini, Giuseppe. *Dalle origini alla serrata del Maggior Consiglio*. Vol. 1 of *La costituzione di Venezia*. 2 vols. 1927–31. Reprint, Florence: La Nuova Italia, 1974.

Maretto, Paolo. *La casa veneziana nella storia della città dall'origine all'Ottocento*. Venice: Marsilio, 1986.

———. *L'edilizia gotica veneziana*. Rome: Istituto Poligrafico della Stato, 1960.

Mariacher, Giovanni. *Il Palazzo Ducale di Venezia*. Florence: Del Turco, 1950.

Martines, Lauro. *An Italian Renaissance Sextet: Six Tales in Historical Context*. Translated by Murtha Baca. New York: Marsilio, 1994.

———. "Séduction, espace familial et autorité dans la Renaissance italienne." *Annales, Histoire, Sciences Sociales* 2 (1998): 255–87.

———. "A Way of Looking at Women in Renaissance Florence." *Journal of Medieval and Renaissance Studies* 4 (1974): 15–28.

Marzemin, Giuseppe. *Le origini romane di Venezia*. Venice: Fantoni, 1936.

Mazzaoui, Maureen Fennell. *The Italian Cotton Industry in the Later Middle Ages, 1100–1600*. Cambridge: Cambridge University Press, 1981.

Mazzarino, Santo. "Il concetto storico-geografico dell'unità veneta." In Arnaldi, *Dalle origini al Trecento*, 1–28.

Mazzariol, Giuseppe. *I palazzi del Canal Grande*. Novara: Istituto Geografico De Agostini, 1981.

Mazzariol, Giuseppe, and Terisio Pignatti. *La pianta prospettica di Venezia del 1500 disegnata da Jacopo de Barbari.* Venice: Cassa di Risparmio di Venezia, 1962.

Mazzi, Giuliana. "Note per una definizione della funzione viaria a Venezia." *Archivio Veneto,* 5th ser., 134 (1973): 6–29.

Mazzi, Maria Serena. "Il mondo della prostituzione nella Firenze tardomedievale." *Ricerche Storiche* 14 (1984): 337–63.

———. *Prostitute e lenoni nella Firenze del Quattrocento.* Milan: Il Saggiatore, 1991.

Mazzucco, Gabriele. *Monasteri benedettini della laguna veneziana.* Venice: Biblioteca Nazionale Marciana and Arsenale, 1983.

McAndrew, John. *Venetian Architecture of the Early Renaissance.* Cambridge, Mass.: MIT Press, 1980.

McCleary, Nelson. "Note storiche ed archeologiche sul testo della 'Translatio sancti Marci.'" *Memorie Storiche Forogiuliesi* 27–29, nos. 10–12 (1931–33): 223–64.

McKee, Sally. "Women under Venetian Colonial Rule in the Early Renaissance: Observations on Their Economic Activities." *Renaissance Quarterly* 51, no. 1 (1998): 34–67.

Medin, Antonio. *La storia della Repubblica di Venezia nella poesia.* Milan: Hoepli, 1904.

Menniti Ippolito, Antonio. "La dedizione di Brescia a Milano (1421) e a Venezia (1427): Città suddite e distretto nello stato regionale." In Cozzi, *Stato, società e giustizia nella Repubblica veneziana,* 2:17–58.

Merores, Margarete. "Der grosse Rat von Venedig und die sogenannte Serrata von Jahres 1298." *Vierteljahrschrift für Sozial- und Wirtschaftsgeschichte* 21 (1928): 33–113.

Mesnard, Pierre. *L'essor de la philosophie politique au XVIe siècle.* 2d ed. Paris: J. Vrin, 1951.

Michiel, Giustina Renier. *Origine des fêtes vénitiennes,* 5 vols. Paris, 1817–27. Originally published as *Origine delle feste veneziane.*

Molà, Luca. *La comunità dei Lucchesi a Venezia: Immigrazione e industria della seta nel tardo medioevo.* Venice: Istituto Veneto di Scienze, Lettere ed Arti, 1994.

Molà, Luca, and Reinhold C. Mueller. "Essere straniero a Venezia nel tardo Medioevo: Accoglienza e rifiuto nei privilegi di cittadinanza e nelle sentenze criminali." In *Le migrazioni in Europa, secc. XIII–XVIII,* edited by Simonetta Cavaciocchi, 839–51. Florence: Le Monnier, 1994.

Molho, Anthony. *Marriage Alliance in Late Medieval Florence.* Cambridge: Harvard University Press, 1994.

Mollat, Michel, Philippe Braunstein, and Jean-Claude Hocquet. "Réflexions sur l'expansion vénitienne en Méditerranée." In Pertusi, *Venezia e il Levante fino al secolo XV,* 1, pt. 2, 515–39.

Molmenti, Pompeo. *La storia di Venezia nella vita privata dalle origini alla caduta della Repubblica.* New ed. 3 vols. Trieste: Lint, 1978.

Mometto, Piergiovanni. *L'azienda agricola Barbarigo a Carpi: Gestione economica ed evoluzione sociale sulle terre di un villaggio della bassa pianura veronese (1443–1539).* Venice: Il Cardo, 1992.

Monfasani, John. *George of Trebizond: A Biography and a Study of His Rhetoric and Logic.* Leiden: Brill, 1976.

Monnas, Lise. "Le luxe industriel." In Braunstein, *Venise 1500,* 157–67.

Monticolo, Giovanni. "La sede dell'arte della lana a Venezia nei secoli XIII e XIV: Spigolature d'Archivio." *Nuovo Archivio Veneto,* 2d ser., 3 (1892): 351–60.

Moretti, Silvia. "Gli Albanesi a Venezia tra XV e XVI secolo." In Calabi and Lanaro, *La città italiana e i luoghi degli stranieri,* 5–20.

Moro, Pierandrea. "Venezia e l'Occidente nell'alto medioevo: Dal confine longobardo al pactum lotariano." In *Venezia: Itinerari per la storia della città,* edited by Stefano Gasparri, Giovanni Levi, and Pierandrea Moro. Bologna: Il Mulino, 1997.

Mosto, Andrea, conte da. *I dogi di Venezia nella vita pubblica e privata.* Florence: Giunti Martello, 1983.

Mueller, Reinhold C. "Aspects of Venetian Sovereignty in Medieval and Renaissance Dalmatia." In *Quattrocento Adriatico: Fifteenth-Century Art of the Adriatic Rim,* edited by Charles Dempsey, 29–56. Bologna: Nuova Alfa, 1996; distributed in U.S. by Johns Hopkins University Press.

———. "Aspetti sociali ed economici della peste a Venezia nel medioevo." In *Venezia e la peste,* 71–76.

———. "I banchi locali a Venezia nel tardo Medioevo." *Studi Storici* 1 (1987): 145–55.

———. "'Chome d'ucciello di passagio': La demande saisonnière des espèces et le marché des changes à Venise au Moyen Age." In *Études d'histoire monétaire, XIIe–XIXe siècles,* edited by John Day, 195–219. Lille: Presses Universitaires de Lille, 1984.

———. "Effetti della guerra di Chioggia (1378–1381) sulla vita economica e sociale di Venezia." *Ateneo Veneto* 19 (1981): 27–42.

———. "Espressioni di status sociale a Venezia dopo la 'Serrata' del Maggior Consiglio." In *Studi veneti offerti a Gaetano Cozzi,* 53–61. Venice: Il Cardo, 1992.

———. "A Foreigner's View of Poor Relief in Late Quattrocento Venice." In *Pauvres et riches: Société et culture du Moyen Age aux temps modernes: Mélanges offerts à Bronislaw Geremek,* 55–63. Warsaw: Wydawn Nauk PWN, 1992.

———. "Mercanti e imprenditori fiorentini a Venezia nel tardo medioevo." *Società e Storia* 55 (1992) 29–60.

———. "Peste e demografia: Medioevo e Rinascimento." In *Venezia e la peste,* 93–96.

———. "Les prêteurs juifs de Venise au Moyen Age." *Annales E.S.C.* 30 (1975): 1475–96.

———. *The Procuratori di San Marco and the Venetian Credit Market: A Study of the Development of Credit and Banking in the Trecento.* New York: Arno Press, 1977.

———. "The Role of Bank Money in Venice, 1300–1500." *Studi Veneziani,* n.s., 3 (1979): 47–96.

———. "Venezia e i primi schiavi neri." *Archivio Veneto,* 5th ser., 148 (1979): 139–42.

———. *The Venetian Money Market: Banks, Panics, and the Public Debt, 1200–1500.* Vol. 2 of *Money and Banking in Medieval and Renaissance Venice.* Baltimore: Johns Hopkins University Press, 1997.

———. "'Veneti facti privilegio': Stranieri naturalizzati a Venezia tra XIV e XVI secolo." In Calabi and Lanaro, *La città italiana e i luoghi degli stranieri*, 41–51.

Muir, Edward. *Civic Ritual in Renaissance Venice*. Princeton: Princeton University Press, 1981.

———. "Idee, riti, simboli del potere." In Cracco and Ortalli, *L'età del Comune*, 739–60.

Muratori, Saverio. *Studi per una operante storia urbana di Venezia*. Rome: Istituto Poligrafico dello Stato, 1959.

Mutinelli, Fabio. *Annali urbani di Venezia dall'anno 810 al 12 maggio 1797*. Venice, 1841.

Muzzarelli, Maria Giuseppina, Paola Galetti, and Bruno Andreoli, eds. *Donne e lavoro nell'Italia medievale*. Turin: Rosenberg & Sellier, 1991.

Nani Mocenigo, Mario. *L'Arsenale di Venezia*. Rome: Filippi, 1938.

Nardi, Bruno. "Letteratura e cultura veneziana del Quattrocento." In Nardi, *Saggi sulla cultura veneta del Quattro e Cinquecento*, edited by Paolo Mazzantini. Padua: Antenore, 1971.

———. "La scuola di Rialto e l'umanesimo veneziano." In *Umanesimo europeo ed umanesimo veneziano*, edited by Vittore Branca, 93–139. Civiltà Europea e Civiltà Veneziana, Aspetti e Problemi, 2. Florence: Sansoni, 1963.

Neff, Mary Frances. *Chancellery Secretaries in Venetian Politics and Society, 1480–1533*. Ann Arbor: University Microfilms International, 1986.

———. "A Citizen in the Service of the Patrician State: The Career of Zaccaria de' Freschi." *Studi Veneziani*, n.s., 5 (1981): 33–61.

Nehlsen–von Stryk, Karin. *Die Venezianische Seeversicherung im 15. Jahrhundert*. Ebelsbach: Gremer, 1986.

Newett, Mary Margaret. "The Sumptuary Laws of Venice in the Fourteenth and Fifteenth Centuries." In *Historical Essays, First Published in 1902 in Commemoration of the Jubilee of the Owens College, Manchester*, edited by Thomas Frederick Tout and James Tait, 245–77. Manchester: Manchester University Press, 1907.

Niccoli, Ottavia. "Compagnie di bambini nell'Italia del Rinascimento." *Rivista Storica Italiana* 101, no. 2 (1989): 346–74.

Nichol, Donald M. *Byzantium and Venice: A Study in Diplomatic and Cultural Relations*. Cambridge: Cambridge University Press, 1988.

———. "La Quarta Crociata." In Cracco and Ortalli, *L'età del Comune*, 151–81.

Niero, Antonio. "I santi patroni." In *Il culto dei santi a Venezia*, edited by Silvio Tramontin, 75–98. Biblioteca Agiografica Veneziana, 2. Venice: Studium Cattolico Veneziano, 1965.

Ongaro, Max. *Il Palazzo Ducale di Venezia: Guida storico artistica*. Venice: Borin & Dal Poz, 1927.

Origo, Iris. "The Domestic Enemy: The Eastern Slaves in Tuscany in the Fourteenth and Fifteenth Centuries." *Speculum* 30 (1955): 321–66.

Orlandini, Giovanni. "Marco Polo e la sua famiglia." *Archivio Veneto Tridentino* 9 (1926).

Ortalli, Gherardo. *Scuole e maestri tra Medioevo e Rinascimento: Il caso veneziano*. Bologna: Il Mulino, 1996.

———. "Venezia dalle origini a Pietro II Orseolo." In Delogu, Guillou, and Ortalli, *Longobardi e Bizantini*, 339–438.

Ortalli, Gherardo, and Michael Knapton, eds. *Istituzioni, società e potere nella Marca Trevigiana e Veronese (secoli XIII–XIV): Sulle tracce di G. B. Verci.* Rome: Istituto Storico Italiano per il Medio Evo, 1988.

Owen Hughes, Diane. "From Brideprice to Dowry in Mediterranean Europe." *Journal of Family History* 3 (1978): 263–96.

———. "Towards Historical Ethnography: Notarial Records and Family History in the Middle Ages." *Historical Methods Newsletter* 7 (1974): 61–71.

Padovani, Andrea. "Curie ed uffici." In Cracco and Ortalli, *L'età del Comune*, 331–48.

———. "La politica del diritto." In Cracco and Ortalli, *L'età del Comune*, 303–30.

Palmer, Richard J. "L'azione della Repubblica di Venezia nel controllo della peste: Lo sviluppo della politica governativa." In *Venezia e la peste*, 103–10.

Palumbo-Fossati, Isabella. "Il collezionista Sebastiano Erizzo e l'inventario dei suoi beni." *Ateneo Veneto* 22, nos. 1–2 (1984): 201–18.

———. "L'interno della casa dell'artigiano e dell'artista nella Venezia del Cinquecento." *Studi Veneziani*, n.s., 8 (1984): 1–45.

Panciera, Walter. *L'arte matrice: I lanifici della Repubblica di Venezia nei secoli XVII e XVIII.* Treviso: Canova, 1996.

Paoletti, Pietro. *L'architettura e la scultura del Rinascimento in Venezia: Ricerche storico-artistiche.* 2 vols. Venice, 1893.

Pavan, Elisabeth. "Police des mœurs, société à Venise à la fin du Moyen Age." *Revue Historique* 4 (1980): 241–88.

Pavanello, Giuseppe. "Della caduta dell'Impero romano alla costituzione di nuovi centri politici e della laguna veneta propriamente detta." In *La laguna di Venezia*, edited by Gustavo Brunelli et al., pt. 3, *La storia della laguna fino al 1140*, chap. 28, 53–73. Venice: Ferrari, 1935.

———. "Di un'antica laguna scomparsa (La laguna eracliana)." *Archivio Veneto Tridentino* 3 (1923): 263–307.

———. *La laguna di Venezia (Note illustrative e breve sommario storico).* Rome: Provveditore Generale dello Stato, 1931.

Pecchioli, Renzo. "Il 'mito' di Venezia e la crisi fiorentina intorno al 1500." *Studi Storici* 3, no. 3 (1962): 451–92.

Pederzani, Ivana. *Venezia e lo "Stado di Terraferma": Il governo delle comunità nel territorio bergamasco (sec. XV–XVIII).* Milan: Vita e Pensiero, 1992.

Pertusi, Agostino. "Ai confini tra religione e politica: La contesa per le reliquie di S. Nicola tra Bari, Venezia e Genova." In *Saggi veneto-bizantini*, edited by Giovanni Battista Parenti, 139–86. Florence: Olschki, 1990.

———. "L'iscrizione torcellana dei tempi di Eraclio." *Studi Veneziani* 4 (1962): 9–39.

———. "Le profezie sulla presa di Costantinopoli (1204) nel cronista veneziano Marco (c. 1295) e le loro fonti bizantine (Pseudo Costantino Magno, Pseudo Daniele, Pseudo Leone il Saggio)." *Studi Veneziani*, n.s., 3 (1979): 13–46.

———. "'Quedam regalia insignia': Ricerche sulle insegne del potere ducale a Venezia durante il medioevo." *Studi Veneziani* 7 (1965): 3–123.

———, ed. *Venezia e il Levante fino al secolo XV.* Florence: Olschki, 1973.

Petrucci, Armando. "L'écriture dans l'Italie de la Renaissance: Pouvoir de l'écriture, pouvoir sur l'écriture dans la Renaissance italienne." *Annales E.S.C.* 43 (1988): 823–47.

Petti Balbi, Giovanna. *Una città e il suo mare: Genova nel Medioevo.* Bologna: CLUEB, 1991.

Peyer, Hans Conrad. *Stadt und Stadtpatron im mittelalterlichen Italien.* Zurich: Europa, 1955.

Piasentini, Stefano. *"Alla luce della luna": I furti a Venezia (1270–1403).* Venice: Il Cardo, 1992.

Pignatti, Teresio. *Palazzo Ducale.* Novara: Istituto Geografico De Agostini, 1964.

———. "La pianta di Venezia di Jacopo de Barbari." *Bolletino dei Musei Civici Veneziani* 1–2 (1964): 9–49.

Pincus, Debra. "Christian Relics and the Body Politic: A Thirteenth-Century Relief Plaque in the Church of San Marco." In *Interpretazioni veneziane: Studi di storia in onore di Michelangelo Muraro,* edited by David Rosand, 39–57. Venice: Arsenale, 1984.

Pinto, Giuliano. "Le città italiane e i lavoratori della lana nel basso medioevo: Alcune considerazioni." In *Le migrazioni in Europa, secc. XIII–XVIII,* edited by Simonetta Cavaciocchi, 819–24. Florence: Le Monnier, 1994.

———. "La politica demografica delle città." In *Strutture familiari, epidemie, migrazioni nell'Italia medievale,* edited by Rinaldo Comba, Gabriella Piccinni, and Giuliano Pinto, 19–43. Naples: Edizioni Scientifiche Italiane, 1984.

———. "Popolazione e comportamenti demografici in Italia (1250–1348)." In *Europa en los umbrales de la crisis (1250–1350),* 37–62. Pamplona: Gobierno de Navarra, Departamento de Educación y Cultura, 1995.

Pistarino, Geo. *Genovesi d'Oriente.* Genoa: Civico Istituto Colombiano, 1990.

———. *I Signori del Mare.* Genoa: Civico Istituto Colombiano, 1992.

Pitteri, Mauro. *Mestrina: Proprietà, conduzione, colture nella prima metà del secolo XVI.* Treviso: Canova, 1994.

Pizzati, Anna. *Conegliano: Una "quasi città" e il suo territorio nel secolo XVI.* Treviso: Canova, 1994.

Poni, Carlo. "Archéologie de la fabrique: La diffusion des moulins à soie 'alla bolognese' dans les états vénitiens du XVe au XVIIIe siècle." *Annales E.S.C.* 27 (1972): 1475–96.

Porfyriou, Heleni. "La presenza greca: Roma e Venezia tra XV e XVI secolo." In Calabi and Lanaro, *La città italiana e i luoghi degli stranieri,* 21–38.

Povolo, Claudio. "Aspetti e problemi dell'amministrazione della giustizia penale nella Repubblica di Venezia, secoli XVI–XVII." In Cozzi, *Stato, società e giustizia nella Repubblica veneta,* 1:153–258.

Pozza. Marco. *I Badoer: Una famiglia veneziana dal X al XIII secolo.* Padua: Francisci, 1982.

———. "Penetrazione fondiaria e relazioni commerciali con Venezia." In *Il Medioevo,* edited by Daniela Rando and Gian Maria Varanini, vol. 2 of *Sto-*

ria di Treviso, edited by Ernesto Brunetta, 299–321. Venice: Marsilio, 1991.

———. "Podestà e funzionari veneziani a Treviso e nella Marca in età comunale." In Ortalli and Knapton, *Istituzioni, società e potere nella Marca Trevigiana e Veronese,* 291–303.

———. "I proprietari fondiari in Terraferma." In Cracco and Ortalli, *L'età del Comune,* 661–80.

Pullan, Brian. *The Jews of Europe and the Inquisition of Venice: 1550–1670.* Oxford: Basil Blackwell; Totowa, N.J.: Barnes & Noble, 1983.

———. "Natura e carattere delle scuole." In *Le scuole di Venezia,* edited by Terisio Pignatti. Milan: Electa, 1981.

———. *Poverty and Charity: Europe, Italy, Venice: 1400–1700.* Brookfield, Vt.: Variorum, 1994.

———. *Rich and Poor in Renaissance Venice: The Social Institutions of a Catholic State, to 1620.* Cambridge: Harvard University Press, 1971.

———. "Service to the Venetian State: Aspects of Myth and Reality in the Early Seventeenth Century." *Studi Secenteschi* 5 (1964): 95–148.

Quadri, Antonio. *La piazza di San Marco considerata come monumento d'arte e di storia.* Venice, 1831.

Quadri, Antonio, and Dionisio Moretti. *Il Canal Grande di Venezia.* Venice, 1828.

Queller, Donald E. *Two Studies on Venetian Government.* Geneva: Droz, 1977.

———. *The Venetian Patriciate: Reality versus Myth.* Urbana: University of Illinois Press, 1986.

Racine, Pierre. "Poteri medievali e percorsi fluviali nell'Italia padana." *Quaderni Storici,* n.s., 61 (1986): 9–32.

Rapp, Richard Tilden. *Industry and Economic Decline in Seventeenth-Century Venice.* Cambridge: Harvard University Press, 1976.

Ravalli Modoni, G. A. "Scrittori tecnici di problemi lagunari." In *Mostra storica della laguna veneta,* 169–73. Venice: Stamperia di Venezia, 1970.

Ravegnani, Giorgio. "La Romania veneziana." In Cracco and Ortalli, *L'età del Comune,* 183–233.

Ravid, Benjamin. "The Religious, Economic, and Social Background and Context of the Establishment of the Ghetti of Venice." In *Gli ebrei e Venezia: Secoli XIV–XVIII,* edited by Gaetano Cozzi, 211–60. Milan: Comunità, 1987.

Reeves, Marjorie. *The Influence of Prophecy in the Late Middle Ages: A Study in Joachimism.* Oxford: Clarendon Press, 1969.

Renouard, Yves. *Les hommes d'affaires italiens du Moyen Age.* Paris: Colin, 1949.

Richard, Jean. "Chypre du protectorat à la domination vénitienne." In Pertusi, *Venezia e il Levante fino al secolo XV,* 1, pt. 2, 657–77.

Rippe, Gérard. *Padoue et son territoire, Xe–XIIIe siècle: Société et pouvoir.* Bibliothèque des Écoles Françaises d'Athènes et de Rome. Rome: École Française de Rome, forthcoming.

Robey, David, and John E. Law. "The Venetian Myth and the 'De Republica Veneta' of Pier Paolo Vergerio." *Rinascimento,* 2d ser., 15 (1975): 3–59.

Rocke, Michael. *Forbidden Friendships: Homosexuality and Male Culture in Renaissance Florence.* New York: Oxford University Press, 1996.

Rollet-Andriane, Louis-Jacques, and Michel Conil Lacoste. *Sauver Venise.* Paris: Robert Laffont, 1971.

Romanelli, Giandomenico. "Venezia tra l'oscurità degli'inchiostri: Cinque secoli di cartografia." Introduction to *Venezia, piante e vedute: Catalogo del fondo cartografico a stampa, Museo Correr,* edited by Susanna Biadene. Venice: Stamperia di Venezia, 1982.

———, ed. *Palazzo Ziani: Storia, architettura, decorazioni.* Venice: Albrizzi, 1994.

Romano, Dennis. "Charity and Community in Early Renaissance Venice." *Journal of Urban History* 11, no. 1 (1984): 63–82.

———. "The Gondola as a Marker of Station in Venetian Society." *Renaissance Studies* 8, no. 4 (1994): 359–74.

———. *Housecraft and Statecraft: Domestic Service in Renaissance Venice, 1400–1600.* Baltimore: Johns Hopkins University Press, 1996.

———. *Patricians and Popolani: The Social Foundations of the Venetian Renaissance State.* Baltimore: Johns Hopkins University Press, 1987.

Rompiasio, Giulio. *Metodo in pratica di sommario, o sia Compilazione delle leggi, terminazioni ed ordini appartenenti agli Ill. ed Ecc. Collegio e Magistrato alle Acque.* Strumenti per la Ricerca Archivista, Sezione 1, Repertori Antichi, 1. 1733. Facsimile reprint edited by Giovanni Caniato. Venice: Ministero per i Beni Culturali e Ambientali, 1988.

Rosand, David. *Painting in Cinquecento Venice: Titian, Veronese, Tintoretto.* New Haven: Yale University Press, 1982.

———. " 'Venezia figurata': The Iconography of a Myth." In *Interpretazioni veneziane: Studi di storia dell'arte in onore di Michelangelo Muraro,* edited by David Rosand, 177–96. Venice: Arsenale, 1984.

Rösch, Gerhard. "Il gran guadagno." In Cracco and Ortalli, *L'età del Comune,* 233–62.

———. *I rapporti tra Venezia e Verona per un canale tra Adige e Po nel 1310 nell'ambito della politica del traffico veneziano.* Quaderni, 13. Venice: Centro Tedesco di Studi Veneziani, 1979.

———. "Lo sviluppo mercantile." In Cracco and Ortalli, *L'età del Comune,* 131–51.

———. *Venedig und das Reich: Handels- und verkehrspolitische Beziehungen in der deutschen Kaiserzeit.* Tübingen: Niemeyer, 1982.

———. *Der venezianische Adel bis zur Schliessung des Grossen Rats: Zur Genese einer Führungsschicht.* Sigmaringen: Thorbecke, 1989.

Ross, J. B. "Venetian Schools and Teachers, Fourteenth to Early Sixteenth Century: A Survey and a Study of Giovanni Battista Egnazio." *Renaissance Quarterly* 39 (1976): 521–66.

Rossi, Vittorio. "Maestri e scuole a Venezia verso la fine del Medioevo." *Rendiconti del Reale Istituto Lombardo di Scienze e Lettere,* 2d ser., 40 (1907): 765–81.

Rossiaud, Jacques. "Fraternités de jeunesse et niveaux de culture dans les villes du Sud-Est à la fin du Moyen Age." *Cahiers d'Histoire,* 21, nos. 1–2 (1976): 76–102.

———. "Prostitution, jeunesse et société dans les villes du Sud-Est au XVe siècle."

Annales E.S.C. 31 (1976): 289–325. Reprinted in Rossiaud, *La prostituzione nel Medioevo* (Rome: Laterza, 1984). Translated by Lydia G. Cochrane under the title *Medieval Prostitution* (Oxford: Basil Blackwell, 1988).

Rubinstein, Nicolai. "Italian Reactions to Terraferma Expansion in the Fifteenth Century." In Hale, *Renaissance Venice,* 197–217.

Ruggiero, Guido. *The Boundaries of Eros: Sex Crime and Sexuality in Renaissance Venice.* New York: Oxford University Press, 1985.

——. "Modernization and the Mythic State in Early Renaissance Venice: The Serrata Revisited." *Viator* 10 (1979): 245–56.

——. *The Ten: Control of Violence and Social Disorder in Trecento Venice.* Ann Arbor: University Microfilms International, 1980.

——. *Violence in Early Renaissance Venice.* New Brunswick, N.J.: Rutgers University Press, 1980.

Sacerdoti, Adolfo. "Le colleganze nella pratica degli affari e nella legislazione veneta." *Atti dell'Istituto Veneto di Scienze, Lettere ed Arti* 59 (1899–1900): 1–45.

Sagredo, Agostino, and Federico Berchet. *Il Fondaco dei Turchi in Venezia: Studi storici ed artistici.* Milan, 1860.

Santi, Angelo. *Origine dell'arte vitraria in Venezia e Murano, suo risorgimento e progresso: Cenni storici.* Venice: Scarabellin, 1914.

Sardella, Pierre. *Nouvelles et spéculations à Venise au début du XVIe siècle.* Cahier des Annales, 1. Paris: Colin, 1948.

Sbriziolo, Lia. "Per la storia delle confraternite veneziane: Dalle deliberazioni miste (1310–1476) del Consiglio dei Dieci: Le scuole dei Battuti." In *Miscellanea Gilles Gérard Meersseman,* 2:715–63. 2 vols. Padua: Antenore, 1970.

Scattolin, Giorgia. *Contributo allo studio dell'architettura civile veneziana dal IX al XIII secolo: Le case-fondaco sul Canal Grande.* Venice: Nuova Editoriale, 1961.

Schmeidler, Bernhard. *Der Dux und das Comune Venetiarum von 1141–1229: Beiträge zur Verfassungsgeschichte Venedigs vornehmlich im 12. Jahrhundert.* Berlin: Ebering, 1902.

Schulz, Juergen. "The Houses of the Dandolo: A Family Compound in Medieval Venice." *Journal of the Society of Architectural Historians* 52 (1993): 391–415.

——. "Jacopo de Barbari's View of Venice: Map Making, City Views, and Moralized Geography before the Year 1500." *Art Bulletin* 60, no. 3 (1978): 425–74.

——. "Maps as Metaphors: Mural Map Cycles in the Italian Renaissance." In *Art and Cartography: Six Historical Essays,* edited by David Woodward, 97–122, 223–29. Chicago: University of Chicago Press, 1987.

——. "La piazza medioevale di San Marco." *Annali di Architettura* 4–5 (1992–93): 134–56.

——. "The Printed Plans and Panoramic Views of Venice." *Saggi e Memorie di Storia dell'Arte* 7 (1970): 13–37.

——. "Urbanism in Medieval Venice." In *City-States in Classical Antiquity and Medieval Italy: Athens and Rome, Florence and Venice,* edited by Anthony Molho, Kurt Raaflaub, and Julia Emlen, 419–45. Stuttgart: Steiner, 1991.

Schwarzenberg, Claudio. *Ricerche sull'assicurazione marittima a Venezia dal dogado di Pasquale Cicogna al dogado di Paolo Renier.* Milan: Giuffrè, 1969.

Segarizzi, Arnaldo. "Cenni sulle scuole pubbliche a Venezia nel secolo XV e sul primo maestro di esse." *Atti del Reale Istituto Veneto di Scienze, Lettere ed Arti* 75 (1915–16): 637–65.

———. "Francesco Contarini, politico e letterato veneziano del secolo XV." *Nuovo Archivio Veneto*, 3d ser., 12 (1906): 272–87.

Seguso, Lorenzo, and Angelo Seguso. *Delle sponde marmoree, overe dei pozzi e degli antichi edifizii della Venezia marittima.* Venice, 1859.

Sella, Domenico. "L'industria della lana a Venezia nei secoli XVI e XVII." In *Storia dell'economia italiana: Saggi di storia economica*, edited by Carlo M. Cipolla. Vol. 1. Turin: Edizioni Scientifiche Einaudi, 1959.

———. "Les mouvements longs de l'industrie lainière à Venise." *Annales E.S.C.* 12 (1957): 29–45.

———. "The Rise and the Fall of the Venetian Woollen Industry." In *Crisis and Change in the Venetian Economy in the Sixteenth and Seventeenth Centuries*, edited by Brian Pullan, 106–26. London: Methuen, 1966; distributed in U.S. by Barnes & Noble.

Selmi, Paolo. "Politica lagunare della Veneta Repubblica dal secolo XIV al secolo XVIII." In *Mostra storica della laguna veneta*, 105–15. Venice: Stamperia di Venezia, 1970.

Simeoni, Luigi. *Il Comune veronese sino ad Ezzelino e il suo primo statuto.* Venice, 1922. Reprinted in Simeoni, *Studi su Verona nel Medioevo di Luigi Simeoni*, edited by Vittorio Cavallari, vol. 1, Studi Storici Veronesi, 10 (Verona: Istituto per gli Studi Storici Veronesi, 1959).

Simoncini, Giorgio. *Città e società nel Rinascimento.* 2 vols. Turin: Einaudi, 1974.

Simonsfeld, Henry. *Der Fondaco dei Tedeschi in Venedig und die deutsch-venetianischen Handelsbeziehungen.* 2 vols. 1887. Reprint, Aalen: Scientia, 1968.

Soranzo, Giovanni. *La guerra fra Venezia e la Santa Sede per il dominio di Ferrara (1308–1313).* Città di Castello: S. Lapi, 1905.

Sottas, Jules. *Les messageries maritimes de Venise aux XIVe et XVe siècles.* Paris: Société d'Études Géographiques, Maritimes et Coloniales, 1938.

Spinelli, Giovanni. "I primi insediamenti monastici lagunari nel contesto della teoria politica e religiosa veneziana." In *Le origini della chiesa di Venezia*, edited by Franco Tonon, 151–66. Contributi alla Storia della Chiesa di Venezia, 1. Venice: Studium Cattolico Veneziano, 1987.

Stefani, Giuseppe. *L'assicurazione a Venezia dalle origini alla fine della Serenissima.* 2 vols. Trieste: Assocurazioni Generali di Trieste e Venezia, 1956. Translated by Arturo Dawson Amoruso under the title *Insurance in Venice from the Origins to the End of the Serenissima* (Trieste: Assocurazioni Generali di Trieste e Venezia, 1958).

Stöckly, Doris. *Le système de l'incanto des galées du marché à Venise (fin XIIIe–milieu XVe siècle).* Leiden: Brill, 1995.

Stromer, Wolfgang von. *Bernardus Teotonicus e i rapporti commerciali tra la Germania meridionale e Venezia prima della istituzione dei Tedeschi.* Quaderni, 8. Venice: Centro Tedesco di Studi Veneziani, 1978.

Stuard, Susan Mosher. *A State of Deference: Ragusa/Dubrovnik in the Medieval Centuries.* Philadelphia: University of Pennsylvania Press, 1992.

Sznura, Franek. *L'espansione urbana di Firenze nel Dugento.* Florence: La Nuova Italia, 1975.

Tafuri, Manfredo. *Jacopo Sansovino e l'architettura del '500 a Venezia.* Padua: Marsilio, 1972.

———. *Venezia e il Rinascimento: Religione, scienza, architettura.* Turin: Einaudi, 1985.

———, ed. *"Renovatio urbis": Venezia nell'età di Andrea Gritti, 1523–1538.* Rome: Officina, 1984.

Tassini, Giuseppe. *Alcuni palazzi ed antichi edifici di Venezia storicamente illustrati.* Venice, 1879.

———. "Palazzo del doge Marino Falier." *Nuovo Archivio Veneto,* 2d ser., 6 (1893): 269–70.

———. "Quattro palazzi di Venezia." *Archivio Veneto* 3 (1872): 120–25.

———. "Tre celebri vere di pozzo in Venezia." *Archivio Veneto* 2 (1871): 442–47.

Tchentsova, Vera. "Le commerce vénitien en Grèce du XIIIe à la première moitié du XVe siècle d'après les données prosopographiques." In *Le partage du monde: Échanges et colonisation dans la Méditerranée médiévale,* edited by Michel Balard and Alain Ducellier. Paris: Publications de la Sorbonne, 1998.

Tenenti, Alberto. *Cristoforo da Canal: La marine vénitienne avant Lépante.* Paris: S.E.V.P.E.N., 1962.

———. *Naufrages, corsaires et assurances maritimes à Venise, 1592–1609.* Paris: S.E.V.P.E.N., 1959.

———. "Il potere dogale come rappresentazione." In *Stato: Un'idea, una logica: Dal Comune italiano all'assolutismo francese,* 193–216. Bologna: Il Mulino, 1987.

———. "The Sense of Space and Time in the Venetian World of the Fifteenth and Sixteenth Centuries." In Hale, *Renaissance Venice,* 17–46.

———. "Il senso del mare." In *Il mare,* edited by Alberto Tenenti and Ugo Tucci, vol. 12 of *Storia di Venezia,* 7–76. Rome: Istituto della Enciclopedia Italiana, 1990.

———. "Venezia e la pirateria nel Levante: 1300–c. 1460." In Pertusi, *Venezia e il Levante fino al secolo XV,* 1, pt. 2, 705–71.

Tenenti, Alberto, and Ugo Tucci, eds. *Il Rinascimento: Società ed economia.* Vol. 5 of *Storia di Venezia.* Rome: Istituto della Enciclopedia Italiana, 1996.

Tenenti, Alberto, and Corrado Vivanti. "Le film d'un grand système de navigation: Les galères marchandes vénitiennes, XIVe–XVIe siècle." *Annales E.S.C.* 16 (1961): 83–86.

Tentori, Cristoforo. *Della legislazione veneziana sulla preservazione della laguna: Dissertazione storico-filosofico-critica.* Venice, 1792.

Thiriet, Freddy. *Histoire de Venise.* Que sais-je? 522. Paris: Presses Universitaires de France, 1969.

———. "Les itinéraires des vaisseaux vénitiens et le rôle des agents consulaires en Romanie gréco-vénitienne aux XIVe–XVe siècles." In *Venezia e le grandi linee dell'espansione commerciale,* 188–215. Venice, 1956.

———. *La Romanie vénitienne au Moyen Age: Le développement et l'exploitation du domaine colonial vénitien, XIIe–XVe siècles.* 2d ed. Paris: Boccard, 1975.

Tiepolo, Maria Francesca. "Difesa a mare." In *Mostra storica della laguna veneta*, 133–38. Venice: Stamperia di Venezia, 1970.

Todesco, M. Teresa. *Oderzo e Motta: Paesaggio agrario, proprietà e conduzione di due podesterie nella prima metà del secolo XVI.* Treviso: Canova, 1995.

Torres, Duilio. *La casa veneta.* Venice, 1933.

Tramontin, Silvio. "Realtà e leggende nei racconti marciani veneti." *Studi Veneziani* 12 (1970): 35–58.

———. "San Marco." In *Il culto dei santi a Venezia*, edited by Silvio Tramontin, 41–73. Biblioteca Agiografica Veneziana, 2. Venice: Studium Cattolico Veneziano, 1965.

Trebbi, Giuseppe. "La cancelleria veneta nei secoli XVI e XVII." *Annali della Fondazione Luigi Einaudi* 14 (1980): 65–126.

Trexler, Richard C. "Le célibat à la fin du Moyen Age: Les religieuses de Florence." *Annales E.S.C.* 27 (1972): 1329–50.

———. "La prostitution florentine au XVe siècle: Patronages et clientèles." *Annales E.S.C.* 36 (1981): 983–1015.

Trincanato, Egle Renata. *Appunti per una conoscenza urbanistica di Venezia.* Venice: Filippi, 1954.

———. "Rappresentatività e funzionalità di Piazza San Marco." In *Piazza San Marco: L'architettura, la storia, le funzioni*, by Giuseppe Samonà et al. 3d ed. Venice: Marsilio, 1982.

———. "Residenze collettive a Venezia." *Urbanistica* 42–43 (1965).

Tucci, Ugo. "Alle origini dello spirito capitalistico a Venezia: La previsione economica." In *Studi in onore di Amintore Fanfani*, 3:545–57. 6 vols. Milan: Giuffrè, 1962.

———. "Le commerce vénitien du vin de Crète." In *Maritime Food Transport*, edited by Klaus Friedland, 199–211. Cologne: Böhlau, 1994.

———. "Marco Polo, mercante." In *Venezia e l'Oriente*, edited by Lionello Lanciotti, 323–37. Florence: Olschki, 1987.

———. "Marco Polo andò veramente in Cina." *Studi Veneziani*, n.s., 33 (1997): 49–60.

———. "Mercanti, viaggiatori, pellegrini nel Quattrocento." In Arnaldi and Stocchi, *Dal primo Quattrocento al Concilio di Trento*, pt. 2, 317–53.

———. "Monete e banche nel secolo del ducato d'oro." In Tenenti and Tucci, *Il Rinascimento: Società ed economia*, 753–806.

———. "La navigazione veneziana nel Duecento e la sua evoluzione tecnica." In Pertusi, *Venezia e il Levante fino al secolo XV*, 1, pt. 2, 821–41.

———. "La psicologia del mercante veneziano." In *Mercanti, navi, monete nel Cinquecento veneziano*, 43–94. Bologna: Il Mulino, 1981.

———. "I servizi marittimi veneziani per il pellegrinaggio in Terrasanta nel Medioevo." In *Pellegrini e viaggiatori nell'economia di Roma dal XIV al XVII secolo*, edited by Mario Romani, 43–66. Milan: Vita e Pensiero, 1958.

———. "Venezia nel Cinquecento: Una città industriale?" In *Crisi e rinnovamenti nell'autunno del Rinascimento a Venezia,* edited by Vittore Branca and Carlo Ossola, 61–83. Florence: Olschki, 1991.

——. "I viaggi di Giosafat Barbaro mercante e uomo politico." In *Una famiglia veneziana nella storia: I Barbaro,* 117–32. Venice: Istituto Veneto di Scienze, Lettere ed Arti, 1996.

Urban, Lina. "'L'andata' dogale a San Vio: Rituali, un quadro, una 'beata,' una chiesa." *Studi Veneziani,* n.s., 28 (1994): 191–202.

Urban Padoan, Lina. "La festa della Sensa nelle arti e nell'iconografia." *Studi Veneziani* 10 (1968): 291–353.

Vacani, Camillo, barone di Forteolivolo. *Della laguna di Venezia e dei fiumi nelle attigue provincie: Memorie.* Florence, 1867.

Valcanover, Franco, and Wolfgang Wolters, eds. *L'architettura gotica veneziana.* Venice: Istituto Veneto di Scienze, Lettere ed Arti, 2000.

Varanini, Gian Maria. "L'espansione urbana di Verona in età comunale: Dati e problemi." In *Spazio, società, potere dell'Italia dei Comuni,* edited by Gabriella Rossetti, 1–26. Naples: Liguori, 1986.

——. "Mercato subregionale ed economia di distretto nella Terraferma veneta: Il commercio del vino." In Varanini, *Comuni cittadini e stato regionale: Ricerche sulla Terraferma veneta nel Quattrocento,* 163–81. Verona: Libreria Editrice Universitaria, 1992.

——. "Note sui consigli civici veronesi (secoli XIV–XV): In margine ad uno studio di J. E. Law." *Archivio Veneto,* 5th ser., 147 (1979): 5–32. Reprinted as "I consigli civici veronesi fra la dominazione viscontea e quella veneziana" in Varanini, *Comuni cittadini e stato regionale: Ricerche sulla Terraferma veneta nel Quattrocento* (Verona: Libreria Editrice Universitaria, 1992), 185–96.

——. "La Terraferma al tempo della crisi della lega di Cambrai: Proposte per una rilettura del 'caso' veronese." In Varanini, *Comuni cittadini e stato regionale: Ricerche sulla Terraferma veneta nel Quattrocento,* 397–435. Verona: Libreria Editrice Universitaria, 1992.

Vauchez, André. *Ordini mendicanti e società italiana, XIII–XV secolo.* Translated by Michele Sampaolo. Milan: Il Saggiatore, 1990.

——, ed. *L'antichità e il Medioevo.* Vol. 1 of *Storia dell'Italia religiosa,* edited by Gabriele De Rosa, Tullio Gregory, and André Vauchez. Rome: Laterza, 1993.

Veludo, Costantino. *Cenni storici sull'Arsenale di Venezia.* Venice, 1869.

Venezia e la peste, 1348–1797. Exh. cat. Venice: Marsilio, 1980.

Ventura, Angelo. "Considerazioni sull'agricoltura veneta e sull'accumulazione originaria del capitale nei secoli XVI e XVII." *Studi Storici* 3–4 (1968): 647–722.

——. "Il Dominio di Venezia nel Quattrocento." In *Quattrocento,* vol. 1 of *Florence and Venice: Comparisons and Relations,* 168–90. Florence: La Nuova Italia, 1979.

——. *Nobiltà e popolo nella società veneta del Quattrocento e Cinquecento.* 2d ed. Milan: UNICOPLI, 1993.

Venturi, Lionello. *Le compagnie della Calza (sec. XV–XVI)*. 1909. Reprint, Venice: Filippi, 1981.

Vergé-Franceschi, Michel. *Henri le Navigateur: Un découvreur au XVe siècle*. Paris: Félin, 1998.

Verlinden, Charles. "Venezia e il commercio degli schiavi provenienti dalle coste orientali del Mediterraneo." In Pertusi, *Venezia e il Levante fino al secolo XV*, 1, pt. 2: 911–29.

Vincent, Catherine. *Les confréries médiévales dans le royaume de France, XIIIe–XVe siècle*. Paris: Albin Michel, 1994.

Vivanti, Corrado, ed. *Dall'alto medioevo all'età dei ghetti*. Pt. 1 of *Gli ebrei in Italia*, vol. 11 of *Storia d'Italia, Annali*. Turin: Einaudi, 1996.

Wartburg, Marie-Louise von. "Production du sucre de canne à Chypre: Un chapitre de technologie médiévale." In *Coloniser au Moyen Age*, edited by Michel Balard and Alain Ducellier, 126–31. Paris: Colin, 1995.

Wolters, Wolfgang. *Der Bilderschmuck des Dogenpalastes: Untersuchungen zur Selbsdarstellung der Republik Venedig im 16. Jahrhundert*. Wiesbaden: Steiner, 1983.

———. "Les miroirs du palais ducal." In Braunstein, *Venise 1500*, 19–38.

Wurthmann, William B. "The Council of Ten and the Scuole Grandi in Early Renaissance Venice." *Studi Veneziani*, n.s., 18 (1989): 15–66.

Wyrobisz, Andrzej. "L'attività edilizia a Venezia nel XIV e XV secolo." *Studi Veneziani* 7 (1965): 307–43.

Zago, Roberto. *I Nicolotti: Storia di una comunità di pescatori a Venezia nell'età moderna*. Padua: Francisci, 1982.

Zannini, Andrea. *Burocrazia e burocrati a Venezia in età moderna: I cittadini originari (sec. XVI–XVIII)*. Venice: Istituto Veneto di Scienze, Lettere ed Arti, 1993.

Zanotto, Francesco. *Il Palazzo Ducale di Venezia*. 4 vols. Venice, 1853.

Zecchin, Luigi. "Forestieri nell'arte vetraria muranese (1348–1425)." *Rivista della Stazione Sperimentale del Vetro* 11, no. 1 (1981): 17–22.

———. "Il segreto dei vetrai muranesi del Quattrocento." *Rivista della Stazione Sperimentale del Vetro* 11, no. 4 (1981): 167–72.

———. *Vetro e vetrai di Murano: Studi sulla storia del vetro*. Venice: Arsenale, 1986.

Zendrini, Bernardino. *Memorie storiche dello stato antico e moderno delle lagune di Venezia e di quei fiumi che restarono divertiti per la conservazione delle medesime*. 1811. Reprint, Sala Bolognese: Forni, 1988. Vol. 1.

Zevi, Bruno. *Biagio Rossetti, architetto ferrarese, il primo urbanista moderno europeo*. Turin: Einaudi, 1960.

Zippel, Gianni. "Lorenzo Valla e le origini della storiografia umanistica a Venezia." *Rinascimento* 7 (1956): 93–133.

Zitelli, Andreina. "L'azione della Repubblica di Venezia nel controllo della peste: Lo sviluppo di alcune norme di igiene pubblica." In *Venezia e la peste*, 111–12.

Zorzi, Andrea. *L'amministrazione della giustizia penale nella Repubblica fiorentina: Aspetti e problemi*. Florence: Olschki, 1988.

———. "Giustizia e società a Firenze in età comunale: Spunti per una prima riflessione." *Ricerche Storiche* 18, no. 3 (1988): 449–95.

———. "Rituali e cerimoniali penali nelle città italiane (secc. XIII–XVI)." In *Riti e rituali nelle società medievali,* edited by Jacques Chiffoleau, Lauro Martines, and Agostino Paravicini-Bagliani, 141–58. Spoleto: Centro di Studi sull'Alto Medioevo, 1994.

Zug Tucci, Hannelore. "Pesca e caccia in laguna." In Cracco Ruggini et al., *Origini-Età ducale,* 490–514.

INDEX

Acre, xviii, 62, 64, 65, 70, 71

Adda River, 129

Adige River, 57, 58, 114, 116; as route, 112, 118; and trade, 103, 117, 118, 125, 297n. 18

Adria, 109, 114

Adriatic Sea, 37, 48, 64, 65, 73, 87, 94, 193; Venetian control of, 59–60, 63, 70, 74, 77, 84, 93, 113

Aegean Sea, 62, 65, 71, 72, 73, 77, 81, 87

Agnadello, Battle of, xx, 94, 128, 132

Aigues-Mortes, 93, 155

Alaric, king of the Visigoths, 5

Albania, 77, 81, 88, 146; Albanians in Venice, 147, 169, 170

Alboin, chief of the Lombards, 5

Aleppo, 83

Alexander III, pope, 47, 48

Alexandria, 61, 63, 64, 71, 75, 77, 83, 87, 93, 95, 170, 219; St. Mark and, xvii, 53–54

Alexius I Comnenus, Byzantine emperor, 61

Alghero, 73

Alps, 103, 123, 125, 297n. 22; routes and passes through, 119, 120, 121, 123, 155

Altino, 4, 6, 7, 106, 108, 296n. 6

Amadi family, 178, 242, 243

Amalfi, 56, 61, 117

Ammiana, 41, 57, 107

Ancona, 63, 65, 176

Antonio Veneziano, 287n. 7

Antwerp, 83, 90

Apennines, 103

Apulia, 63, 88, 131, 146

Aquileia, 5, 6, 52, 53, 57, 123; patriarch of, 4, 52, 111, 120

Aragon, 72, 123

Arbel, Benjamin, 89

architecture: church, 33–35; domestic, 30, 31; public, 141, 143, 146

Arengo, 194, 197, 198, 201, 203, 210

Argos, 77

aristocracy, 199, 214, 216–17, 219, 227; of the Terraferma, 134–35

Aristotle, 181

army, 88, 132, 146

Arsenal, 74, 82, 86, 95, 96, 122, 125, 143–44, 148, 181, 190; administration of, 140, 194, 204, 207; Arsenale Nuovissimo, 143, 181; Arsenale Nuovo, 141; growth of, xviii, 24, 139–41, 143, 166; neighborhood of, 147, 148–49, 252

Ascalon, xvii, 65

Ascension, Feast of the, 48–49, 164–65, 193

Asia, 70, 154, 177, 222

Asia Minor, 61, 70, 71, 73

Attila, king of the Huns, 6, 98

auditori nuovi, xix, 134, 136

Augsburg, 120, 154

Augustine, St., 160

Augustinian Order, 12

Avogaria di Comun, *avogadori di comun*, 195, 208, 214, 217, 243

Badoer, Marco, doge, 108, 109

Badoer family, 12, 108–9, 197, 236

Bagnolo, Peace of, xx, 131

Baldwin II, king of Jerusalem, 62

Balkans, 77, 80, 146, 147, 169

Balla d'Oro, 216, 221

banks, banking, xx, xxi, 89, 91–92, 159

Carpaccio, Vittore, 124, 170, 287n. 7, 296n. 3

Carrara, Francesco da, lord of Padua, 74

Carrara, Francesco Novello II da, 128

Carrara, Francesco Novello III da, 129

Carrara family, 15, 128, 134

Cassiodorus, 4–5, 56–57, 100, 103

Castelletto (public brothel), 159–60, 161, 247

Castello, *sestiere* of, 19, 23, 58, 140, 149, 169, 305n. 16, 330n. 89

Castello Tebaldo, 114

Castro, 73

Catalonia, xix, 73, 79

Cattaneo family, 76

Cavarzere, 7, 112, 300n. 59

Celsi, Lorenzo, doge, 206

Cephalonia, 81, 88

Cerigo, 88

Cervia, 81, 94, 114, 297n. 22

Cessi, Roberto, 112

Ceuta, 70

Champagne, 119

chancellery, ducal, xx, 195, 204, 225, 227

charity, 148, 220, 234, 257, 262, 263–64

Chioggia, 99, 103–4, 105, 112, 128, 214; *porto* at, 36; War of, xix, 74, 76, 79, 100, 207, 226

Chios, 72, 75, 76

Chojnacki, Stanley, 216, 220

chronicles, 1, 6, 7, 79, 98, 99, 188, 200, 211–12, 219, 221, 268; family, 218, 242, 243

Church, the, 218; careers in, 216, 218

churches and parishes, 9–10, 33–35, 255, 257–58, 269. *See also individual names*

Cilicia, 61

citizens, xx, 199, 226–28; families of, 199, 212, 214, 215, 226

Cittanova, 6

Cividale, 6

Clement V, pope, 114

Coducci, Mauro, 24, 31, 35, 258

coins, coinage, 89–90, 91, 116–17, 120, 179

Collegio, Pien Collegio, 207

Colleoni, Bartolomeo, 131, 132, 192

Cologne, 154

Comacchio, 57, 58, 60, 128, 297n. 18

commune, xvii, 133, 151, 183, 188, 197, 198, 201, 204–5, 206, 212; in Italy, 21

Commynes, Philippe de, 1, 242, 284n. 77

Concordia, 5, 6

confraternities, 243, 255, 256, 258, 259–61; of immigrant groups, 147, 208, 260

Confraternity of the Rosary, 260

Conrad II, Holy Roman emperor, 117

Constantine VII, Porphyrogenitus, Eastern Roman emperor, 57, 58

Constantinople, xvii, xviii, xx, 23, 59, 60–61, 62–63, 64, 66, 67, 71, 81, 143, 269; trade with, 63, 70, 80, 87, 93, 123, 170, 174, 177; Venetians in, xvii, xviii, 61, 64–65, 69, 71, 81, 199

Consuls of the Merchants (Consoli sulla Mercanzia), 157, 172–73

Contarini, Domenico, doge, 22

Contarini, Gasparo, 127–28, 184–85, 193, 228

Contarini family, 30, 108, 197, 199, 217, 236

Corfu, 61, 63, 67, 77, 87, 88

Corinth, 61, 63

Corner, Antonio, 225

Corner, Caterina, xx, 81

Corner, Marco, 39–40, 41, 224

Corner family, 31

Coron, 67, 81, 87

Corte de Parangon, 178

Costanziaca, 41

Council of Forty, xviii, xix, 195, 204, 207

Council of Ten, xviii, 186, 195, 207–8, 209, 213, 225, 226, 248, 250, 261, 262, 326n. 51

Council of the Rogati (Pregadi), 204

Council of the Sapienti (Consilium Sapientum), xvii, 197, 201, 203

Cracco, Giorgio, 110, 166

crafts and trades, 19, 157, 165, 166, 167, 171, 310n. 77

Crema, 131, 132

Cremona, 5, 123, 131

Crete, xviii, 61, 64, 67, 73, 86, 87, 88, 170, 199, 212

Pepin, king of Italy, 100

Pera, 71

Pergola, Paolo della, 225

Persia, 73, 98

Perugia, xviii, 21, 261

Perugino, Pietro, 287n. 7

Pescatore, Enrico, count of Malta, 70

Petrarch (Francesco Petrarca), xix, 156, 180, 321n. 121, 330n. 91

Phocaea, 71

Piave River, 4, 117, 120, 125, 297n. 18

Piazza San Marco, 19–21, 24, 50, 146, 164, 166, 191–95, 265, 266, 267, 268, 270; Bocha di Marzaria, 164; Campanile, 160, 268; clock tower, 24, 164, 192, 268; fairs in, 164–65; Libreria, 180; Loggetta, xxi, 24; Ospizio Orseolo, 22; Piazzetta, 32, 141, 145–46, 156; processions and ceremonies in, 192–95, 267–68; reconstruction of, 22–23, 141–42, 180, 183

Pienza, 25

Piovego, xviii, 19, 21, 104–5, 204

piracy, 60, 65, 73, 85, 170

Piran, 94, 297n. 22

Pisa, 72, 73, 84, 93, 131; trade rivalry with, 62, 64, 65, 70

Pisanello (Antonio Pisano), 287n. 7

Pisani, Vettor, 74, 76, 292n. 85

Pius II, pope, 81

plague, xix, xxi, 13, 17, 73, 74, 144–45, 165, 169, 244–45, 263

Pliny (the Elder), 276n. 7

Pola, 74, 87

Poland, 186

Polani, Pietro, doge, xvii, 197

Polesine, 131

police, 19, 161, 162, 186, 203, 204, 208, 245, 250

political power, 31, 97, 183–91, 211, 213, 214, 224, 238

Polo, Marco, 177, 222

Ponte, Antonio da, 25

Ponte dei Pugni, 149

Ponte della Paglia, 145

Ponte Lungo, 172

Pontus, 71, 75

population, size of, 11, 12–13, 19, 73, 74, 169, 171, 244

Pordenone (Giovanni Antonio Sacchiense), 48

Po River, 57, 94, 103, 108, 112, 116, 118, 132, 297n. 18; control of, 58, 113–14

port, 24, 39, 40, 58, 93, 122, 139, 140, 141, 144, 162, 166

porti, 36, 38, 45, 74, 99, 145. See also individual names

Portogruaro, 124, 150, 173

Porto Lungo, Battle of, 73

Portugal, 82–83, 100–101, 170, 222–23

Prague, 120

Preveza, Battle of, 82

printing, xx, 179–81

prisons, 25, 159

Priuli, Girolamo, 82, 99

processions, 22, 192–93, 194–95, 261–63, 267–68, 270

Procuratie, 22, 23, 192

Procuratie Nuove, 24–25

Procuratie Vecchie, xx, 24

Procurators of San Marco, 146, 164, 193, 195, 203, 204, 205, 209, 226, 263

prostitution, 159–60, 248, 266

Provence, xix, 79

Provveditori alla Sanità, 144, 165, 245

Provveditori di Comun, 167

Pullen, Brian, 259

Punta della Dogana, 94, 145

Punta della Trinità, 145

Punta Salvore, battle of, 287n. 4

Quarantia. See Council of Forty

Querini, Guglielmo, 223

Querini, Marco, xviii, 109. See also Tiepolo-Querini conspiracy

Querini family, 109, 156, 237

Quirini, Lauro, 321n. 121

Ragusa, 87, 147

Ravenna, 5, 57, 62, 114, 132, 196

Redentore, Church of the, 35

San Michele in Isola: church of, 281n. 62; monastery of, 180
San Nicolò dei Mendicoli, church of, 33, 149
San Nicolò del Lido, Porto di, 11, 36, 40, 48, 140, 144
San Pietro, 148, 269
San Polo, *sestiere* of, 33, 162, 266
San Provolo, church of, 146
San Rocco, Scuola Grande of, xx, 258, 261, 263, 330n. 89
San Salvatore, church of, 163
San Severo, church of, 147
San Silvestro, church of, 162, 260
San Simeone Profeta, church of, 173
San Teodoro: church of, 22, 122; Scuola Grande of, 261
San Tomà, church of, 12
San Vio, church of, 192
San Zaccaria, monastery of, 22, 35, 108, 150
Sansovino, Jacopo, xxi, 24, 31, 32, 180, 192
Sant'Alvise, church of, 174
Sant'Andrea della Zirada, church of, 23, 330n. 89
Sant'Antonin, church of, 146
Sant'Antonio, 23, 244, 149; Punta di, 145
Sant'Erasmo, island of, 37, 107
Santa Croce, *sestiere* of, 330n. 89
Santa Eufemia, church of, 33
Santa Giustina, church of, 172, 314n. 28
Santa Maria dei Miracoli, church of, xx, 35, 242, 243, 281n. 62
Santa Maria della Carità, Scuola Grande of, 261, 329n. 89
Santa Maria della Misericordia, Scuola Grande of, 261, 264, 329n. 81, 330n. 89
Santa Maria di Nazaret, island of, 144
Santa Maria Gloriosa dei Frari, church of, 35, 258, 260
Santa Maria Nuova, church of, 163, 178
Santa Maria Zobenigo, church of, 112
Santa Marina, church of, 178, 193
Santa Marta: island of, 99; Punta di, 39
Santa Sofia, church of, 33
Santa Ternità, church of, 148
Santi Apostoli, church of, 163, 178

Santi Giovanni e Paolo, Campo, 258; church of, 12, 172, 258, 262, 330n. 89
Santissimo Sacramento, *scuola* of, 260
Santo Spirito, church of, 147
Santorini, 69
Sanudo, Marco, 69
Sanudo, Marino, 55, 87, 92, 96, 136, 150, 155, 157–58, 181, 187, 200, 206, 207, 209, 211, 217, 225, 260, 267, 270
Sanudo, Marino, called Torsello, 82
Sanudo family, 218
Sarpi, Paolo, 287n. 5
Savi agli Ordini, 205, 206
Savi del Consiglio (Savi Grandi), 206
Savi di Terra Ferma (della Guerra), xix, 207, 209
Savonorola, Girolamo, 185
Scaliger War, 115. *See also* della Scala family
Scamozzi, Vicente, 25
Scarpagnino (Antonio Abbondi), 24, 26, 32
schools, xx, 180, 225, 227
sculpture, 172, 184, 330n. 93
scuole grandi, 258, 261–64
scuole piccole, 260, 261, 328n. 70
Scutari, xix, 77, 81
sea routes, 82–83, 89, 100–101
Segretario alle Voci, 219
Senate, 26, 89, 94, 98, 102, 143, 153, 176, 180, 193, 206, 208, 209; composition of, 186, 204, 206–7
Sensa, 48–49, 164–65, 193
Serbia, xix, 77, 80
Sercambi, Giovanni, 234
Sermini, Gentile, 234
Serrata, xviii, 183–84, 203, 211, 213, 214, 215, 216, 218. *See also* Great Council
sestiere, 21, 203, 205; *capisestiere*, 21, 205
Sforza, Galeazzo Maria, duke of Milan, 131
Sforza family, 131
shipping, 93–94, 95, 147; lanes, 87, 95–96. *See also* sea routes
shipping lines (*mude*), 63, 79, 80, 94–95, 141; contracts for, 95; schedule for, 63, 141, 154–55

64, 88, 121, 123, 126, 155; pepper, 65, 95, 97, 101, 156; precious metals, 58, 120, 123, 159, 179; silver, 120, 121, 154; stone, 88; sugar, 63, 88, 97, 154, 172; textiles, 72, 93, 121, 137, 154, 157, 171; wax, 88, 154; wheat, 57, 63, 88, 117, 122, 142; wine, 57, 88, 95, 122, 123, 126, 155. *See also* fishing; leather; salt; silk trade; slaves; spices; wood, timber; wool, woolens

Tradonico, Piero, doge, xvii, 116, 197

Trapani, 71

Traù, 62

Trebizond, 73, 87, 170

Trent, Trentino, 118, 120, 136

Trevisan, Bartolomeo, 310n. 77

Trevisan chronicle, 213

Treviso, 6, 62, 106–7, 108, 117, 118, 122, 125, 128, 135, 136, 150, 173, 176, 225, 291n. 65; district of, 102, 109, 118; March of, 108, 109, 110, 112–13, 128, 133

Tribuno, Piero, doge, 27, 58

Trieste, 131

Tripoli, 61

Tron, Nicolò, doge, 223

Tunis, 70, 79, 155

Turin, Peace of, xix, 65, 74, 128

Turks, xix, xx, xxi, 72, 75, 77, 79, 80–82, 85–86, 89, 133, 146, 165

Tuscany, 89, 103, 115, 189, 242, 244; Grand Duchy of, 101

Twelve Marys, Feast of the, 254, 268

Tyre, xvii, 62, 70

Tyrol, 118

Ulm, 120, 154

Urbino, 25

Valla, Giorgio, 225

Valla, Lorenzo, 312n. 14

Varna, xix, 80

Vatican, Galleria delle Carte Geografiche, xiii, xv

Vendramin, Andrea, 239

Vendramin, Andrea, doge, 219, 223, 239

Vendramin, Bartolomeo, 319n. 100

Vendramin, Gabriele, 239

Vendramin, Luca, 219

Vendramin family, 219, 239

Venerabile, del, *scuola,* 260

Venetia, 49; Roman province of, 3–4, 6, 111, 128, 138

Venetian Republic, xxi, 101, 127, 185–86, 188, 206

Venice: administrative divisions of, 203; Duchy of, xvii, 10, 53, 102, 111, 183, 277n. 18; origins of, 3, 4, 7, 158; Peace of, xviii, 47, 48, 113; representations of, xiii, 18, 55, 231; representatives of, 115, 199, 204; urban development in, 10–13, 23, 291; use of space in, 252–54, 265

Venier, Antonio, doge, 199

Venier family, 237

Ventura, Angelo, 134

Vergerio, Pier Paolo, 312n. 14

Verme, Jacopo del, 132

Verona, xix, 5, 114, 123, 129, 132, 134, 137, 225; war with, xviii, 115, 118, 128

Veronese, Guarino, 225

Veronese, Paolo, 47, 48

Verrochio, Andrea del, 192

Viaro family, 109

Vicenza, xix, 5, 101, 115, 129, 135, 137, 150, 176, 225

Vienna, 154

Vigevano, 25

Vigna Murata, La, island of, 144

Villach, 123

Visconti, Filippo Maria, 129

Visconti, Gian Galeazzo, 128, 129

Visconti family, 128, 129, 134, 300n. 68

Visigoths, 5

Vivarini, Alvise, 287n. 7

Voisins, Philippe de, 196

voyages of discovery, 101, 222–23

Waldrada, 111

Wallerstein, Immanuel, 55

warehouses, 155, 162; flour, 155; grain, 141–42; oil, 155; salt, 140, 142, 143; ship's biscuit, 147; textiles, 173